Earlene Reaves

ART IN EVERYDAY LIFE

HARRIET GOLDSTEIN

VETTA GOLDSTEIN

ART in Everyday Life

FOURTH EDITION

THE MACMILLAN COMPANY · NEW YORK

To Mildred Weigley Wood

Preface to the Fourth Edition

In this edition, many substitutions have been made in the illustrations, and a new chapter has been added. The new illustrations in the area of house design reflect some of the changes in the modern way of living. Trends toward simplified, more informal living, a lessening of regional differences, and houses that are easy to maintain are seen in both contemporary and traditional designs.

The new chapter, entitled "The House as a Unit," considers some of the important values in planning a home, along with the art that is involved. Expressed through the analysis of two houses, the chapter approximates a guide toward a philosophy of home planning and furnishing which a reader might use as his basis for the selection of a suitable home for himself and his family. Such a study as this can help a person learn how a house may affect family living and can aid him in recognizing a flexible plan that can be adapted to the changing stages in a family's needs.

H. and V. G.

Preface to the Third Edition

For this third edition, the book has been revised throughout. New illustrations and topics have been added, and some which seemed less important for present needs have been dropped. New material has been included—particularly in the areas of store display, industrial design, and table appointments; there is a new section on suggestions for choosing men's clothes; and because of the interest in photography as a creative art activity, some specific suggestions on composition have been made for the amateur photographer. The subject of the modern spirit in painting, sculpture, house design, and furnishing has been amplified; the chapters on picture selection and flower arrangement are greatly expanded; and additions have been made to the topic "Character or Decorative Quality in Design." New illustrations of costumes, exteriors, and interiors have replaced most of those used in the earlier editions, and text as well as pictures have been added. The number of photographs of rooms furnished by boys and girls with small and average budgets has been increased with the idea of stimulating young people to make their rooms attractive and pleasant according to their own likes. Photographs made in color have been used to give suggestions for planning color schemes.

With all of its changes, the book remains basically what it was when it was first written—a study of the application of the fundamental principles of design and color. Fashions come and go, popular standards change, but "style" and beauty are lasting. It is a concern for an appreciation of these more permanent qualities and the wish to apply them in our surroundings that impels us to seek an understanding of their fundamentals.

H. and V. G.

Preface to the First Edition

THE OBJECT of this book is to show the principles of art as they are seen in familiar works of art, and as they are related to every day problems, such as house design and decoration, store decoration, costume design, advertising, and city planning. In each of these fields one works with sizes, shapes, colors, and textures, which must be selected and arranged in accordance with principles of beauty. These principles are fully explained, and they are applied in so many various fields that even the person without native ability can learn to apply them to any problem.

A significant feature of the book is the profusion of illustrations —both photographs and drawings—which clearly demonstrate the main points of the text. These are so fully described in the legends that it is possible quickly to review the facts contained in the book by studying the illustrations.

The first part of the book is devoted to an explanation of the principles of art. The illustrations in these chapters are from the fields of fine arts, from exterior and interior design, costume design, and from business. They should help one to solve the simplest as well as the most complicated problems.

The chapters on color explain, simply and clearly, the two most commonly used color systems,—the Prang and the Munsell. Color knowledge is applied to the solution of problems in the fields of homemaking and business, and the reader is given sound reasons for making color selections and arrangements.

A chapter called *How to Make a Design* explains and illustrates a very simple method of working out designs for different purposes.

In another chapter, a typical art problem has been analyzed, in order to point out the factors which the reader should consider in making designs, or making purchases which he hopes to enjoy over a long period.

Under *Dress Design*, suggestions are given for planning costumes, which in color and design will be economical, beautiful, and becoming to different types of people. Historic, rather than modern costumes have been chosen to illustrate the principles of art in clothing design, because of the danger of confusing fashion with beauty in the styles that are seen every day. A simple method of drawing a lay figure is explained, and fully diagramed. Four figures are reproduced, which are large enough to trace for use in designing costumes. These are drawn according to the proportions of the average woman's figure, the fashion figure, and the average high school girl.

The material on *Interior Design*, which includes chapters on *Flower Arrangement* and *Picture Selection and Arrangement*, deals with the meaning of design and with the selection and arrangement of house furnishings. These chapters show the difference between the expressions of formality and informality; between the social and the domestic spirit in art; and the difference between masculine, feminine, and impersonal qualities in design. An important part of this section is *Making the Best of One's Possessions*, where attention is given to problems of rearrangement and elimination. The photographs of interiors show a variation of materials ranging from the simplest to the more costly, and emphasize the fact that the individuality and charm of a room do not depend upon the cost of one's belongings, but upon the beauty of their form, color, and texture, and the way in which they are arranged.

It is highly desirable that the reader should think of the illustrations merely as groups containing sizes, shapes, and colors, arranged to show a principle or an idea, and to translate the objects themselves into his own belongings. In this way, the store decorator, for example, will find suggestions in the material which applies directly to homemaking, while the general reader may gain ideas from all the fields.

The very close interrelation of the æsthetic and the practical in this work should serve to increase the reader's enjoyment of art, and at the same time enable him to bring beauty into his surroundings. The book is planned to serve as a text-book for students of art, of home economics, and of salesmanship, and it is hoped that it may be a helpful reference book for salesmen, store decorators, advertisers, and homemakers.

Acknowledgment is made to many authors and teachers whose work has unconsciously molded the thoughts and the experiences of the writers: to Finch, Van Slyck, and McConville, who, through their advertising manager, Mr. C. E. Lawrence, gave permission to reprint material and illustrations from *Art Principles in Selling* (prepared by Harriet Goldstein for the advertising service of "The Finch Merchant's Advertiser's Club"); to those who generously permitted the photographing of their homes and their possessions, as well as to those who have allowed the reproduction of photographs, and advertisements; to the students and the homemakers whose discussions of the photographs helped us to select the pictures which would be most helpful to others. The authors wish especially to express their appreciation to the friends who read the manuscript during its preparation, and gave much valuable criticism.

H. and V. G.

Table of Contents

Chapter I

Chapter II

Chapter III

Chapter IV

Greek oblong; how to divide a space.—Lines which apparently alter proportions: application to exterior design, to interior design and to dress.—Scale or consistent sizes: application to exterior design, to house furnishing and to dress.

Chapter V

Chapter VI

Chapter VII

Chapter VIII

cool hues; advancing and receding hues; hues and the seasons; effect of different hues; hue summarized.—Value: definition; value of normal colors; how to change values; tints and shades; effect of different values; value summarized.—Intensity or chroma: how to determine complementary colors; how to change intensity (complementary colors); complementary colors in the Prang system; how to make colors appear more or less intense; texture as it influences intensity; intensity as an indication of taste; summary of intensity.—Prang color notation.—Making a color chart.—The Munsell color system: the color sphere; hue; value; chroma; Munsell color notation; complementary hues in the Munsell system.—Color in vision (psychology): colors and the emotions; receding and advancing colors; the effect of colors upon each other.—Color in physics: colors in light; the effect of pigment mixtures; the effect of mixtures of colored lights; the effect of colored lights upon colored materials.

Chapter IX

How to develop judgment in regard to color combinations.—Balance in color: the law of areas; balancing bright and dull colors, balancing light and dark colors, balancing warm and cool colors; complementary colors; "crossing" or repetition.—Proportion in color.—Rhythm in color.—Emphasis in color.—Harmony in color: background colors; beauty in color schemes; keyed color; keying through neutralizing, through mixing, through glazing, through veiling, through topping, through tying, through texture.—Sources for color harmonies.—Standard color harmonies.—Related color harmonies: one hue; analogous.—Contrasting color harmonies: complementary; double complementary; split complementary; triads; how to use contrasting colors.

Chapter X

The steps in solving an art problem: application to the selection of a rug; to the selection of a table cover.

Chapter XI

The designing process as a form of organization.—Factors involved in the making of a design.—The analysis of the making of a design.—Steps in designing a woven runner and an embroidered runner.—The interpretation of ideas.—Applications to textile design; to embroidery design; to dishes; to decorating and garnishing food; to decorative animals; to photography.—Steps in designing a room.—Steps in designing a costume.—How to mount a picture: the Law of Margins; the Law of Optics.—How to letter.

Chapter XII

Chapter XIII

Chapter XIV

Chapter XV

Contents

Chapter XVI

Chapter XVII

Chapter XVIII

line, feminine and intermediate furnishings.—Domestic, social
and impersonal qualities.

Chapter XIX

The hall.—The living room: grouping furnishings for comfort
and convenience; order in furniture arrangement; the importance
of books and accessories; color for walls; pattern for walls; ceilings; woodwork; floors and floor coverings; color, texture and design in curtains; the hanging of curtains; planning a color
scheme; lighting; lamps; furniture.—The dining room.—The
kitchen.—The bedroom.—A special room in the house.

Chapter XX

Elimination.—Rearrangement.—Concealment.—Some   do's
and don't's for decorative arrangements.

Chapter XXI

The appeal of a picture.—Styles in painting.—The influence
of primitive art.—The modern dance as an art form.—The composition of a picture.—Pattern, line and color in pictures.—
The suitability of the picture to the room.—Pictures in relation
to the background of a room.—How to frame a picture.—How
to hang pictures.—How to judge picture arrangements.—Substitutes for pictures.

Chapter XXII

Beauty of line and color in flower arrangements.—Color combinations.—Selection of vases.—Placing the bouquet.—The arrangement of flowers.—The importance of leaves.—Flowers and

their substitutes for the dining room table.—Floating arrangements.—Weeds.—Winter bouquets.—Japanese flower arrangement.

Chapter XXIII

Some requirements for a good house plan.—A house planned
for an unusual lot.—Unity in the various rooms of the house.—
A plan for a small, expandable house.—Modern furnishing in a
small modern house.—Creating a livable home.

Chapter XXIV

List of Illustrations

ART IN EVERYDAY LIFE

Chapter One

THE IMPORTANCE OF GOOD TASTE

THE TITLE of this book, *Art in Everyday Life,* has a particular significance. It implies the belief that art may be so much a part of our
daily living that it will help us to do more beautifully the simple,
homely things of life as well as the more unusual. As we surround
ourselves with beauty, art actually becomes a part of our life and
personality—not to be set apart for occasional enjoyment, but rather
to be sought and enjoyed in everything we do and in everything we
select.

We are all of us consumers. Every time we make a purchase, however humble, we are consciously or unconsciously using our power to
choose. Since art is involved in most of the objects seen and used
every day, one of the great needs of the consumer is a knowledge of
the principles fundamental to good taste. *Good taste, in the field of
art, is the application of the principles of design to the problems in
life where appearance as well as utility is a consideration.* With the
development of our appreciation of these principles, the meaning of
the term "principles of design" broadens and deepens. These principles are never static. They should be regarded as flexible guides to
be used in producing a desired result. It has been said that good taste
is doing unconsciously the right thing, at the right time, in the right
way. In *Joseph Vance,* Dr. Thorpe says, "I keep on hoping for the
development, in Joey, of the faculty of Good Taste. . . . It's a
quality of the inner soul, that gives a bias to the intellect." Few people are born with this rare gift, but, fortunately for us, good taste in
art can be acquired by applying the principles of beauty deliberately
until the time is reached when the right thing is done unconsciously.

*Good taste
and the
consumer*

Good taste, then, includes the selection and arrangement of all our belongings—our communal as well as our personal possessions. For the sake of economy as well as beauty, it is important that every individual should understand and apply these principles of art. Since the appearance of the things we acquire causes us to enjoy some of them permanently, while others please for only a little while, it is an advantage to be able to judge discriminately. Beauty is determined not by the cost but by the quality of the objects chosen. (See figures 1 and 2.) Most people who enjoy the effect of richness would like to know how to appreciate the restraint which marks the difference between the rich and the gaudy, while others who like simple things wish to recognize the point where plainness ceases to be beautiful and becomes monotonous and unimaginative. Training will show where merely a variation of proportions or the addition of some simple note of contrast will result in a quality and beauty that might otherwise be lacking.

The idea is all too prevalent that art is decoration and that an object must be ornamented if it is to have "art quality." This idea must be abandoned before anyone can have a true appreciation of art. The person who has this appreciation gains perfect satisfaction from an undecorated object if it is beautiful in shape, color, and texture and is suited to its purpose. When decoration is used it should be simple. Over-decoration is one of the worst faults.

Taste is molded, to a very large extent, by the things which surround us, and family taste is trained by the objects selected by the home-maker. It is, therefore, a very great privilege for children to live in a home in which there is a high standard of beauty. We like to think of standards for beauty as broad and adaptable, and to regard them as goals that are never fixed. They shift and change, and each of us hopes that his own standards will keep moving forward. Although our standards can scarcely be too high, we are obliged frequently to recognize and accept the fact that it is not always possible to reach them. Nearly always there are limitations in our way, and so our choices may have to represent a compromise due to such factors as: what happens to be available at the particular time and place of the purchase; the amount of money to be spent; and the likes and

Figure 1. (Craig Ellwood, Designer. Photograph by George Szanik.) Good taste is shown in the colors as well as in the background and furnishings in this room. Because the living room serves also as the bedroom in this small house, a quiet color was used in the matching walls and carpet to give the greatest effect of size. The notes of contrasting color and the quality of the decorative objects are important here.

Figure 2. (Decorator, Paul T. Frankl, A.I.D.) This room illustrates the quality of good taste. Here, expressed through the personality of a particular family, we see the principles of design applied in terms of use and beauty. The good books, comfortable furniture, flowers, and beautiful accessories make this an enjoyable room in which to live. Objects and motifs from earlier cultures, combined with contemporary forms, have given the room a timeless appearance.

Figure 3. (Designer, Henry Dreyfus. Photograph by Julius Shulman.) Simple lines, suitable textures, and interest in color and design distinguish this furniture. The pieces are suited to their purposes and are consistent in combination.

Figure 4. Detail from an Otomi Ayate or carrying cloth, Mexico. This old Mexican Indian embroidery illustrates "character" or "style" in design, for its inventive, simplified forms and unusual colors combine to give the work the property of design commonly known as "decorative quality."

dislikes of the people who are going to live with the article purchased. After all, it is important that people enjoy their possessions, and we study art mainly for the happiness it will bring into our lives. There are some who believe that people should have what they like even though it is in bad taste. That is a matter for each of us to decide, but, at least, it is important to know when and why our choice is bad so that our decision may be deliberate. Accordingly, we should like to emphasize this well-known bit of advice: Never be forced to make a poor choice through a lack of the information which would have helped in making a good one.

Too often it is thought that art is synonymous with drawing and painting and sculpture, and the fact that pictures and statues are but two of many kinds of art expression is often overlooked. More and more it is coming to be realized that ability is involved not only in the creation of works of art, but in appreciation as well. When a person is appreciating a beautiful object, he is engaged in a creative experience, for the active enjoyment of art is a form of participation in it. Furthermore, the interpretation of that impression to another so that he, too, may learn to appreciate beauty is another of the aspects of this many-sided experience we call art. How many times have we heard, "I'm no artist. I can't even draw a straight line." As a matter of fact the man who can draw the straightest line may not have a particle of artistic ability, and the one who cannot draw may be an artist in one of the best senses of the word. The woman who selects beautiful furnishings for her home or the salesperson who chooses the right suit and hat for a customer has done a piece of work that calls for much the same kind of knowledge as that possessed by a designer or painter. These are all questions of art or design, and the only real difference is in the materials used. This is easily recognized when the meaning of design is clearly defined.

Design is the selecting and arranging of materials, with two aims —order and beauty. One man uses an ordinary piece of canvas and some paints, and people cross continents to see his picture; another man, using the same materials, produces a worthless daub. What is the difference? It is just the variation in the qualities of order and beauty—order that denotes organization or structure, and beauty

[margin note: Appreciation a creative experience]

[margin note: Design]

that shows character through the interpretation of an idea by an individual.

This interest in order and beauty is not confined to the painter. The person who says that he is not really concerned with art because he never intends to paint a picture or make a hat, a dress, or a table, is sure, at some time or other, to select such things and perhaps help someone else select them; and, what is more, after he has purchased them, he must relate them to objects already in his possession. Solving these problems of purchasing and arranging requires the same knowledge of the principles of art as goes into the creation of objects. The original idea and the actual process of making are all that the purchaser does not have to supply.

Think of how much it would mean to everyone who selects articles of clothing and home furnishings to want to live with these things until they are actually worn out! Homemakers who are planning to furnish their homes or to rearrange those already furnished are anxious to have an art basis for the decisions they must make. Men and women wish to know what colors and lines are becoming and unbecoming; salespeople would like to be able to tell customers, with reasons, that certain patterns and colors in wall papers, draperies, or rugs are good, where these colors and patterns are good, and how they should be combined. All such problems call for good taste and can be solved by the application of fundamental art principles to the selection of objects and to their use in a particular place. These principles, which, broadly speaking, may be thought of as measuring sticks against which to judge taste, will be discussed under the chapter headings: (1) *harmony*, (2) *proportion*, (3) *balance*, (4) *rhythm*, and (5) *emphasis*.

Chapter Two

STRUCTURAL AND DECORATIVE DESIGN

DESIGN IS defined as any arrangement of lines, forms, colors, and textures. It involves the problem of choosing these forms and colors, and then of arranging them. A good design shows an orderly arrangement of the materials used and, in addition, creates beauty in the finished product.

There are two kinds of design—*structural and decorative. Structural design is the design made by the size, form, color, and texture of an object, whether it be the object itself, in space, or a drawing of that object worked out on paper. Decorative design is the surface enrichment of a structural design. Any lines, colors, or materials that have been applied to a structural design for the purpose of adding a richer quality to it constitute its decorative design.* Structural design is far more important than decorative design because it is essential to every object, while decoration is the "luxury" of design. Definition of structural and decorative design

REQUIREMENTS OF A GOOD STRUCTURAL DESIGN

The most significant phrase in the art world today is "form follows function." Through the teaching and the practice of Louis Sullivan and Frank Lloyd Wright, that expression has influenced the modern art of Europe and America. Form follows function. But Mr. Wright is concerned about the too frequent misinterpretations of that statement. He would make it clear that the real meaning is "form and function are one." His own term—*"organic work"*—is the essence of that principle on which the best of the new architecture and decoration and the industrial arts is based. The principle

5

Figure 5. Bowls by Glen Lukens, Los Angeles, California (group of third-prize-winning bowls, Seventh National Ceramic Exhibition, Syracuse Museum of Fine Arts). The structural designs of these bowls show beauty of form and interesting textures, and all of the bowls are notably suitable for use. (Courtesy of Syracuse Museum of Fine Arts.)

Figure 6. The structural design of this vase is poor because of its bad proportions. In spite of its fine color and texture it is not a good vase because it is so wide at the top that it is unbalanced and unstable and is therefore not suited to its purpose, which is to hold flowers.

6

is as old as the work of primitive man, but every once in a while it emerges with the light of a new meaning. There is no better principle to keep before us as a standard for design. Seasonal fashions bring us toward and away from that ideal, but it still remains a standard by which to measure true beauty.

If an object is intended for use, the requirements of its structural design are fourfold:

1. *That, in addition to being beautiful, it be suited to its purpose*
2. *That it be simple*
3. *That it be well proportioned*
4. *That it be suited to the material of which it is made and to the processes which will be followed in making it.*

Only when the designer has fulfilled all of these requirements may he ask if the form, the color, and the texture have given enough interest to the object, or if there is a sense of bareness which needs to be relieved. The bowls in figure 5 are examples of structural designs in which the forms, colors, and textures of the pottery are so beautiful that one does not feel the need for decoration. The crackle, which is an inherent part of the structural design, gives an added interest to the three bowls at the left. Figure 6 shows a poor structural design. This vase is poor in spite of its good texture and color because it is not suited to its purpose. Its proportions are poor and it is so unbalanced that it would be an unstable flower container. A comparison of these two illustrations emphasizes good structure as the first requirement of any object if it is to give lasting satisfaction.

Figures 7 and 8 center the attention upon the fact that a good design is suited to the material of which it is made and to the processes followed in making it. Obviously the lamp, made to imitate a candle, does not tell the truth. We know that the candle and the "flame" are not real, in spite of the dripping paint which imitates wax. A close scrutiny would show that the metal was shaped by spinning it on a lathe, and the occasional hammer marks on its surface do not convince us that it was shaped with a hammer. The handle is a good size and shape for carrying the lamp, but the cord shows

Figure 7. This is a good, consistent design for a lamp. The base is sturdy and the shade protects the eyes from the glare of the bulb. The appearance of the smooth metal indicates the manner in which it was shaped, and the subtle curves are attractive. (Courtesy of Nessen Studio, Inc.)

that the lamp was not meant to be carried. If every one of us could remember to stop for a moment before making a purchase, and ask ourselves these questions, "What is it for?" and "How was it made?" there would be very little such material in our attics for white elephant sales. By way of contrast figure 7 illustrates the use of metal honestly treated. It shows the intrinsic character of the metal, and it does not pretend to be anything other than it is—a metal lamp with a bent arm to adjust the position of the light.

Figure 8. This is a poor structural design for an electric lamp. It seeks to imitate another form of lighting the candle—even to the false dripping on the vertical support, and the flame-like type of bulb. The regularly spaced hammer marks, added after the shade was shaped, are obviously trying to imitate hand work. This lamp illustrates what is meant by "insincerity" in design.

Figure 9. From Miller Vocational High School, Minneapolis. *An object that is to be used may serve its purpose and, at the same time, show imagination. This pewter tea strainer shows an honest use of metal and an individual design.*

Figures 9 and 10 show a similar comparison. The pewter tea strainer and the china lemon juicer and strainer have something in common in that their uses are similar. Both were meant to be individual and amusing, but the difference between them is the difference between something clever and something absurd. The pewter strainer is obviously suited to its intended purpose, and the young designer merely suggests a spirit of play in the scallops and the design of the handle.

Repeatedly in recent years, we have heard it said that art is entering the modern home through the kitchen. Those who make this statement do not have in mind such objects as embroidered dish towels and pot holders or fly swatters decorated with wool flowers

Figure 10. *A lemon juicer and strainer in the form of a swan with roses painted on it is so incongruous that it has no excuse for being.*

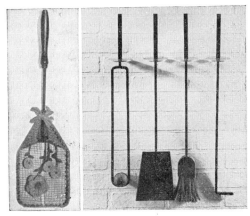

Figure 11. Since the decoration of an object should be
consistent with its use, a fly
swatter decorated with wool
flowers is manifestly absurd.

Figure 12. (Designer, Mel
Bogart.   Photograph   by
George Szanik.) Each fireplace   accessory   shows   a
straightforward   handling   of
metal to serve the designer's
purpose, and each is an excellent illustration of "form
that follows function." (Courtesy of Felmore Associates.)

as seen in figure 11. This kind of decoration is the height of incon-
gruity. Those who have an appreciation of "fitness to purpose" recognize that decoration such as simple bands of color would be
suitable to objects planned for humble use.

The fireplace accessories shown in Figure 12 illustrate what is
meant by "functional design." Each of the tools is not only suited
to the particular purpose for which it was designed, but it looks
right for its use. The severity of the lines of black metal is softened
by a few subtle curves and the brass disks. Nothing has been added
to these designs for the sake of their appearance, yet it is evident
that they measure up to the requirements of a good structural design. They have character and beauty because of their fitness to their
purpose, their frank simplicity of form, their good proportions, and
the suitability of their materials to their use and to the process of
their manufacture.

REQUIREMENTS OF A GOOD DECORATIVE DESIGN

Having decided that the object will be enhanced by decoration,
and that its structural design is simple and beautiful as well as functional, the designer plans his decoration. No matter what his problem may be—whether it be the decoration of a vase, a costume, a

room, or a chair, his design should fulfill all of the following considerations:

1. The decoration should be used in moderation.
2. The decoration should be placed at structural points, and it should strengthen the shape of the object.
3. There should be enough background space to give an effect of simplicity and dignity to the design.
4. Surface patterns should cover the surface quietly.
5. The background shapes should be as carefully studied and as beautiful as the patterns placed against them.

Figure 13. The potters of Persia almost more than those of any other land had a keen appreciation of the clay and glazes with which they worked. They often left the bases of bowls unglazed so that the actual fabric could be seen and touched. Their structures are usually well proportioned. Their decoration was never imitative of natural forms, but was beautifully conventionalized.

6. The decoration should be suitable for the material and for the service it must give.

Examples of good decorative designs on good structures are seen in the vases in figure 14. Each of these vases illustrates all of the points considered in the list of requirements. It is interesting to notice in the vase at the center that the three lines forming the decoration are so closely related to the structure that they may be considered either as structural or decorative design.

Figure 14. Bowls designed by Edgar Littlefield. Group of prize-winning bowls—third prize in the National Ceramic Exhibition, Syracuse Museum of Fine Arts. In these vases decorative design has been used to supplement and enhance the structures. In each case the decoration is simple, and is subordinated to the shape, actually adding strength to the structural form instead of calling the interest away from it. (Courtesy of Syracuse Museum of Fine Arts.)

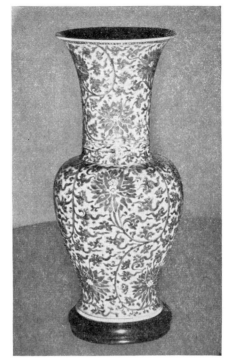

Figure 15. The good effect of this structural design has been spoiled by the addition of the decoration, which is too naturalistic and too elaborate.

Figure 16. Chinese Porcelain. While this Chinese vase is beautiful in its structural and decorative design, it is too emphatic to be used as a flower container. It would make a rich note of emphasis in a decorative scheme. (Courtesy of the Walker Art Galleries.)

The designer whose work shows fine quality adapts and conventionalizes, or stylizes, his design to suit the material he is using. He does not attempt to deceive by imitating real objects, such as flowers and fruit done in wood, clay, or threads, but having decided to take a flower or leaf idea as the theme of his decoration, he alters it to suit:

Conventionalization

1. The shape of the object
2. The purpose for which the object will be used
3. The limitations of his material
4. The tools and processes he must use.

The Persian bowl, figure 13, is a good example through which to study conventionalization. It is clear, even from a photograph, that this is a bowl made from ordinary clay. The flowers and leaf forms are reminiscent of nature, but the artist obviously did not think of imitating real flowers. He was interested only in producing a beautiful bowl. There is no attempt to conceal the fact that the design was painted on with a brush, and it was done with vitality and directness.

The person who makes an intelligent selection of any object needs to have as good a judgment of structural and decorative design as the designer. A comparison of the vases in figures 14 and 15 will make this point clear. All are intended to hold flowers. All have good structural designs. But there the similarity ends. The man who designed the vases in figure 14 appreciated the fact that they were to be a background for flowers, and for that reason must be less conspicuous than the flowers placed in them. Next, he studied the shapes of the vases to see where the decoration might be placed in order to enhance them. He believed that decoration should be a part of structure and should grow out of it. With suitable tools he worked out good patterns. As long as the proportions and shapes in the design were pleasing and the background shapes agreeable, he was satisfied. He was not at all concerned about our ability to identify his original motif, whether it be a flower, a bud, or a leaf; it is adapted to its use, or in other words, conventionalized, and the result is good. The man who designed figure 15 has produced an ugly vase because he was interested only in imitation and display. The leaves have not been conventionalized or adapted to the decoration of a flat surface, but have been modeled to imitate a cluster of real leaves and then painted in natural colors to complete the deception. The designer ignored the structural design of his vase and draped his decoration over it, letting it fall where it would. His decoration is too emphatic to make a background for flowers, and, besides being unsuitable for use, the vase lacks beauty, and therefore has no excuse for being.

Some objects are created for the sake of beauty only and are not connected in the designer's mind with practical use. A painting illustrates this kind of creation, and if it is beautiful it may be hung in a gallery and enjoyed as an object of quality. However, if the same picture were considered for a home, it should, in addition, be in harmony with the spirit of the room. We might analyze the vase in figure 16 in a similar way. It is rich in design, full of color, and has beauty in itself. We recognize that it will add interest in a room if it is given the right setting. In selecting an object of this kind, let us appreciate its beauty as well as its limitations, for we must know that this is not the sort of vase that one would use for flowers. Since it is good in its structural design and beautiful in color and decoration, it fulfills the requirements of a good design and does not need to serve a practical use. When objects are chosen for their appearance alone, they should be judged critically, because our taste must grow up toward beauty and must learn to shrink from choices that are inferior.

If a design is to give the maximum amount of satisfaction it cannot stop at being merely correct. It must have character (sometimes called style) and individuality. When a design possesses a positive or dramatic appearance, it is said to be "decorative" or to have "decorative quality." The terms "decorative" and "decorative quality," used in this sense to denote character in a design, should be distinguished from "decorative design," which means any decoration added to structural design. "Decorative quality" is never found in a design that is "pretty" or sentimental, and it does not appear in imitative designs. Simplicity is an attribute of "decorative quality," while fussy elaboration is never associated with it. *Character of "decorative quality" in design*

This attribute of style or character in design is seen very clearly in the sculptured panel on the Bayon (figure 17). This temple built by the Khmers in the jungles of Cambodia has sculptured panels of such vigor and of so high a standard in decorative quality that it may serve as an illustrated definition of what is meant by character in design. The Khmer used the forms he knew—the trees and birds and animals—to tell the story of his life. With sensitive taste he flattened these forms so that they were related to the architecture and created patterns revealing a discipline and a stylization of unusually high order.

Figure 17. Bayon. Angkor-Thom, Cambodia. Ninth Century A.D.
When the Khmers carved this panel on their temple, they were telling a story in stone. Their instinct for fitness led them to flatten the forms into a two-dimensional pattern, and their aesthetic sense made them shape each detail beautifully and relate it to the whole. Their designs have unusual character.

A theme similar to that of the sculpture on the Bayon is found in the embroidered bands of the old Mexican "ayate" or carrying cloth which was used by the Indians for altar cloths and for carrying candles on their religious pilgrimages (figure 4). Besides illustrating character in design, a comparison of the two examples shows clearly what is meant by adapting a design to the materials, the tools, and the processes to be used in its execution. Birds and trees, people and animals are found in both themes, and they have been adapted to suit the technique and materials of sculptured decoration on the one hand, and on the other, of wool embroidery or weaving. The fanciful shapes and stylized colors in the Mexican work show that they

Figure 18. This house is an example of good structural design and of decoration that strengthens structure. The simple roof and consistently proportioned windows and wall spaces form a background for the decorative color of the door and window frames.

Figure 19. The features that make this house poor in design are due to a lack of under-standing of the essentials of good structural and decorative design.

have a native sense of design strongly marked by "decorative quality." Additional illustrations and a more detailed discussion of character or "decorative quality" will be found in Chapter XI under the topic of "Making and Judging Designs."

The Greeks knew the principle of making structural design more important than decoration, and they applied it to everything they did. The Parthenon is a typical example of their dignity and restraint in decoration. (See figure 62, p. 64.) Note that when one looks at the Parthenon his first impression is of a beautiful structure, and after that the decoration comes to his attention. This decoration is not put on with a lavish hand, but with a great deal of reserve; and it has been placed only on those spaces which have grown out of the construction of the building, as is seen in the frieze. Appreciation of the design of the Parthenon should lead one to enjoy fine structural design and reserve in any building. It is clear that the house in figure 18 is a good design. It is simple and well proportioned, and the shapes of all of the parts grow so easily and naturally out of the principal mass of the building that the first impression is one of unity. A thoughtful scrutiny will show that the lines and textures are so pleasantly related to the land and to the trees behind it that the house seems a natural part of its setting. The simple structural design is marked by the continuity of the roof line. The window openings are arranged in an orderly fashion, and their shapes are consistent and well related to the wall spaces. The treatment of the walls and the wood shingles of the roof give an impression of unaffected sincerity. The planting is unstudied and informal, and its lines echo the structural lines of the house. Decorative accents in the architectural design have been limited to a use of contrasting color on the door and window frames.

Compare the serenity of the house in figure 18 with the restlessness of figure 19, where the poor design has resulted from a desire for novelty along with a mistaken sense of beauty. The house is placed in a beautiful setting of trees, and the textures of the walls and the wood shingle roof are good, but the roof lines are so broken that it looks fussy. The windows, too, contribute to the lack of unity because there are too many shapes, sizes, and treatments. The spotted colored brick of the foundation wall is another disturbing element. In the attempt to create an informal house, such unfortunate features have been used as the birdhouse on the garage, the little shuttered window on the garage door, and the octagonal window on the front of the house. As a result, the house has become a confusing collection of shapes, sizes, and ideas. It is easy to recognize this as a striking illustration of poor structural and decorative design.

Figure 20. (Burton Schutt, Architect. Photograph by Maynard Parker.) A contemporary house which is distinguished by the emphasis upon good structural design. The house and its site are strikingly integrated.

In no other architecture has there been more emphasis upon structural design than in the type that is commonly called "organic" or "functional." (See figures 235, page 358, and 237, page 359.) Although the work varies according to the interpretation of different architects, the essential character remains the same. In some examples there is almost an exaggeration of simplicity. Decorative design is infrequently used, and when it is, it shows unmistakable reserve. It cannot be assumed that simplicity alone will make a design good. Indeed, some of the modern work is meaningless and dull. The less-skilled architects have mistaken some of the superficial qualities for

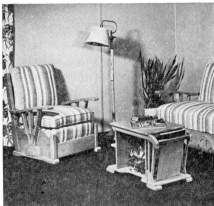

Figures 21 (left) and 22 (above).
Whether one prefers the traditional or
the modern style in furniture, the basis for judging it will be the same.
Comparing the furniture in figures 21
and 22, it is clear that the chair in figure 21 is good in structural design. It
is comfortable, well-proportioned, and
simple in line. In the traditional furniture in figure 22, the over-elaborate
decoration calls attention to the meaningless lines and clumsy proportions of
the structural designs. (Figure 21 is a
chair of Danish beech designed by
E. Kindt-Larsen, Copenhagen, for
John Stuart, Inc., New York City.)

the essential character of the work, and as a result there are too
many instances of poorly proportioned, boxlike houses that are very
commonplace in appearance. It is interesting to see that Americans
are coming more and more to understand and enjoy the honesty and
simplicity of the functional house; and even when it is not adopted
completely as a design inspiration for new houses, its influence is
very apparent in the simplification of many of the houses that are
being built in traditional styles. In the house illustrated in figure 20,
there is a strong feeling for design, but it is design formulated by
these considerations: a concern for the climate and the site; a desire

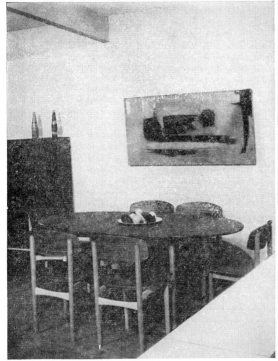

Figures 23 (left) and 24. Figure 24 is a distorted interpretation of a type of design that is well done in figure 23. Because the three-legged chairs are not beautiful in line and are easily unbalanced, they compare very unfavorably with the excellent design of the chairs in figure 23. (Figure 23 designed by Mogensen. Courtesy of Baldwin Kingrey. Photograph by Harry Weese.)

for a consistent use of the materials from which the building is constructed; and most important, the wish to provide a gracious and fitting setting for a family's living pattern. Notice that the design emphasis has been placed upon the skillful proportions in the mass of the house and in the relationship of the separate parts. Necessary elements have become handsome through the sheer quality of the spacing. There is a sound message for all in the integrity and simplification of this type of house design.

There is a steady trend towards better quality in furniture design. It is becoming generally recognized that furniture must pass the tests of good structural and decorative design. Furniture, therefore, must be useful and comfortable and soundly constructed if it is to serve its purpose well; and it should depend for its beauty more upon good structural design than upon decoration. Furniture should

Design in furniture

be so fine in its proportions and in its lines that it needs very little, if any, decoration. The modern furniture shown in figure 3 illustrates these points, and demonstrates the dignity and satisfaction inherent in those simple, good designs which give a distinct impression of belonging together.

The contrast is startling between the good and bad designs of the chairs in the traditional and modern styles in figures 21, 22, 23, and 24. In figure 21, the well-proportioned modern chair with its subtle curves, which not only enhance the structure but make it feel more pleasant to the touch, contrasts sharply with the restless designs in figure 22. In the latter we see poor structural lines and over-decoration unrelated to the structure. Obviously, one must be fortified with good standards when he goes out to shop because even as supposedly simple a style as the one called "functional" is often misinterpreted, as the three-legged chair in figure 24 shows so clearly. Whereas the mistakes in the designs of the furniture in figure 22 are seen in the decorative as well as the structural designs, the worst fault in the chair in figure 24 lies in its structural design. It lacks stability, and its curves are exaggerated. Such a design would soon become disappointing, while the lack of pretense and the good design of the truly functional chair in figure 23 would still be enjoyed even if it were no longer "in the mode."

Structural and decorative design in dress

The subject of structural and decorative design in dress will be fully discussed under the topic of "Shape Harmony" on page 40 and illustrated by figures 43 to 48. Another illustration of design in the field of dress is shown in figure 25. These handkerchiefs are typical of "what to do" and "what not to do" in applied design. Since the lines of the decoration should conform to the shape of the object or depart from it only to a moderate degree, it is readily seen that the left handkerchief is well designed, and that the right one is not. The appliquéd leaf motifs give a spotty effect, unrelated to the shape of the handkerchief, while the heavy flower form seems to cut awkwardly across the corner. Compare the impression of this design with the orderly aspect of the handkerchief at the left. This, too, is a commercial design in which the leaf theme was used, but here each shape grows easily out of another, and the arrangement is re-

Figure 25. The requirements of good structural and decorative design have been fulfilled in A. B is a poor design because the appliquéd forms are at variance with the shape of the handkerchief so that instead of the pleasing effect produced by A, the result appears disorderly and scattered.

lated to the framework of the handkerchief. Figure 26, a dress of the Empire period, has the characteristically good structural design of a period when dress was based upon the simplicity of Greek dress. The lines of the dress and the decoration on it and in the hair are so well related to the lines of the human figure that the costume is an outstanding illustration of good structural and decorative design.

The relation of utility to beauty has been emphasized throughout this discussion of structural and decorative design, for the permanent enjoyment of the objects one purchases depends upon this relationship. A moment's thought will serve to call to mind many familiar cases of the oversight of this factor in design. There is the handsome but uncomfortable chair; its curves are graceful, and its decoration is pleasing to the eye, but the structure is so designed that it does not form a good support for the back, and a line of decoration, which comes just across the shoulders, causes much discomfort. Unlike a vase, a chair may not exist as a purely decorative object, and so it is obvious that there is no place for an

Utility in structural and decorative design

Figure 26. This dress of the Empire period shows structural and decorative designs which have stood the test of time. It is reminiscent of the costume of the Greeks, and has come into popularity at intervals since the early nineteenth century. It is simple, comfortable, and attractive—all essentials of good taste.

elaborately carved chair back. Among other objects besides uncomfortable furniture, one recalls more than a few pitchers and teapots that look well on the shelf, but have uncomfortable handles and are so designed that they drip when liquid is poured from them.

From these examples, it is seen that utility is a factor involved in design in general, for *the shape of an object should first of all conform to its purpose, and the decoration should not interfere with its function.*

If we wish to discover what makes a design so good that it outlasts the swing of fashion, we may turn to the art museums or to their bulletins to see what we can learn from those designs which have stood the test of time. Two advantages to ourselves may be gained by recognizing what is good in design: first, a growth in an understanding of what makes for beauty, and second—a very practical gain, for it is greatly in the direction of economy—the ability to make our own choices so that they would have a lasting quality.

As we go on to the study of each of the principles of design it is important always to remember that beauty is the goal toward which we are striving. The art principles are aids to be stored in our knowledge through our experience. They should be ready to be drawn upon as needed for the making of discriminating choices.

Chapter Three

HARMONY

Definition of
harmony

HARMONY IS the fundamental requirement in any piece of work in which appearance, as well as use, has to be considered. It is the most important of all the principles of design. *Harmony is the art principle which produces an impression of unity through the selection and arrangement of consistent objects and ideas.* When all the objects in a group seem to have a strong "family resemblance," that group illustrates the principle of *harmonious selection;* and when these "friendly" articles are so arranged that the leading lines follow the shape of the object on which they are placed, harmony has been secured in both *selection* and *arrangement.* How much likeness should be sought and how much variety or contrast is appropriate are the questions to be decided in any situation. One enjoys a certain amount of variation for the sake of interest, but for the sake of harmony this variation must always stop just short of absolute contradiction in any important matter. Similarly, there should be something in common among all the large things which are to be put together, but the smaller objects used for accent and variety may contrast. The smaller the amount of this contrasting note, the stronger the difference between the contrasting objects may be.

In both the fine and applied arts, it is usual to think of the principle of harmony as having five aspects. These are harmony of: (1) line and shape, (2) size, (3) texture, (4) idea, and (5) color.

Harmony in
composition

Gauguin's landscape serves excellently as an illustration of harmony (figure 27). The picture is a horizontal oblong in which the horizontal lines of the composition give a feeling of repose and the vertical lines give an impression of dignity. Transitional, or modi-

Figure 27. "Te raau rahi," by Paul Gauguin, 1848–1903.
   The principle of harmony is clearly shown in this painting. The horizontal
lines of the hut repeat and emphasize the shape of the picture. The vertical
lines of the dark tree trunk and the figure of the girl at the right give strength
to the composition. The curved lines of the trees and the slanting line of the
roof create transition which softens the opposing horizontal and vertical lines
and gives unity to the design. (Courtesy of Paul Reinhardt Galleries.)

fying lines have been used in the contour of the roof and in the
forms of the branches so that the contrast of the horizontal and
vertical lines is not too marked. It is through the study of such
examples from the field of the fine arts that designers have come to
understand some of the general principles of art and to see that
they may be applied to their own arrangements.

   It is possible to reduce the types of line in a composition to *Repetition,*
three main groups: lines which follow or repeat one another; lines *contrast, and*
which contrast with one another; and transitional lines, which *transition*
soften or modify the others.

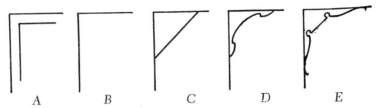

Figure 28. The main types of line. A, repetition. B and C, contrast.
D and E, transition.

When a set of lines is drawn within a corner, following the lines of the corner, repetition occurs. This is the simplest kind of harmony (figure 28A). When a horizontal and a vertical line come together as in a right angle or a corner, these lines are in *opposition* to each other and form a *contrast* (figure 28B). Strictly speaking, any line that cuts across a corner from one opposition line to another is a transitional line; but a straight line drawn across a corner, as in figure 28C, is so sudden and sharp a contrast that it cuts off the corner harshly. That type of line is called *contradiction*. *Transitional* line in its best sense is an easy, graceful line which leads from one line or shape to another, giving harmony instead of contradiction. If a curved line were drawn across a corner, as in figure 28D, the sharpness of the opposition of the horizontal and vertical lines would be modified, and that effect is transition. Throughout this book the term "transition" is used to express a softening, modifying line that harmonizes opposing lines. It will be found that curved lines make an easy transition from one straight line to another and that when straight lines are used they are made less severe if combined with a suggestion of curved line. (See figure 28E.)

HARMONIOUS LINES AND SHAPES

A combination of lines results in shapes. Applying the three types of line—repetition, contrast, and transition—to shapes that are seen in combination with one another, it will be seen that shapes corresponding to one another are in perfect harmony (figure 29A). The most harmonious shape that can be put into a rectangle is another rectangle of the same shape, and a circle makes the closest

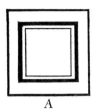
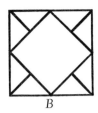
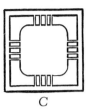

A   B   C

Figure 29. A, lines that repeat one another create shapes which show per-fect harmony through uniformity. B, lines that contradict one another create shapes which form sharp contrasts. C, transitional, or modifying, lines create shapes which have pleasing variety with unity.

harmony within another circle. Lines that oppose or contradict each other form contrasts in shapes and are the opposite of harmony (figure 29B). Some examples of these contradicting shapes are triangles and diamond shapes within squares, oblongs, and circles. Such combinations should be used only where extreme contrasts are desired. Transitional lines have a graceful, softening effect, and have the power to bring together shapes which might in themselves be inharmonious (figure 29C).

Figure 30. "Diagonal Composition," by Piet Mondrian.

This composition is the work of one of the greatest masters of abstract art. It is a study in extreme simplification. Here, contrast—the most forceful of all the types of line or shape—is seen at its best. This is not just a square placed at right angles to the framework of another square. A study of the lines and the shapes created by the lines reveals subtle variety and interest. (Courtesy of the artist.)

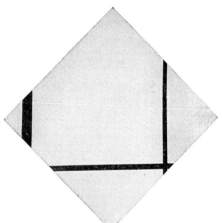

In the abstract painting by Mondrian (figure 30), we see a com-position built within the most difficult of all forms—the diamond. This is an example of extreme contrast in line interpreted in the mind of a master. Mondrian has studied simplification in design until his work has reached an abstract beauty such as that to be found in the field of mathematics. The sensitive adjustment between the lines and spaces in this composition would quickly be apparent to anyone who would experiment by varying either the width or the position of any of the lines.

Figures 31, 32, and 33. Varied types of line were employed to create the designs of these three pieces of bark-cloth. The tapa from Fiji seen in figure 31 shows a strongly contrasting diamond shape tied into the square by the cross lines and pattern in the center and corners, as well as by the strength of the border design.

In this Samoan tapa, the regular repetition of the triangles alternating with the bands of diagonal lines creates a surface design that is striking.

The design of figure 33 is made up largely of transitional lines, and the effect is rather quiet. Here, the contrast of the diamond shapes has been modified through their continuous repetition, their small size, and the proximity of the transitional lines.

Contrasting lines and shapes have made a strong appeal to primitive artists, and in the pieces of old tapa from Fiji (figure 31) and Samoa (figure 32) are seen examples of extreme contrasts in lines that have been arranged with a vigor that is elemental. The tapa designer of figure 33 has made use of transitional lines to connect his series of diamond shapes, and here the force has been greatly modified.

Figure 34. Pole Martin Temple, Old Chichen-Itza, Yucatan.
The richly carved borders on this Mayan temple are made up largely of contrasting diagonal lines and triangular shapes that have been repeated so regularly that they have become related to the shapes within which they are placed. The diagonals in the borders have been given a feeling of stability by the addition of still stronger vertical and horizontal lines.

Early work, but not so primitive in feeling, is the decoration on the Mayan temple in figure 34. Notice how the contrasting diagonals in the sculptured borders on the building have been stabilized by the introduction of stronger vertical and horizontal lines. While there is beauty in the diamond shape as it is repeated to form a surface pattern in the border of the Mayan temple, it becomes a harsh note when used as an isolated spot in the door or walls of a house.

The amateur photographer who is interested in composition can often make commonplace negatives yield interesting patterns if he understands the effective use of lines. The composition in figure 35B was found by cutting two "L" shaped pieces of paper to make an adjustable frame or finder, and moving them about over the direct print from the negative, figure 35A. Notice that the photographer made his picture dramatic through the use of a contrasting line for the prow of the ship instead of the too-apparent repetition of the vertical and horizontal lines in the original print. Retention of the nearly horizontal line of the chain served to relate the lines of the new arrangement with the rectangular form of the com-

Figure 35. Photographs by Wilbur M. Nelson, A.R.P.S.

A (below). The vertical line of the ship and the horizontal line of the chain oppose each other so strongly that the effect is harsh and would become trite.

B (right). Compare this enlargement with the direct print in A. Here, the horizontal line of the chain was retained to harmonize with the shape of the picture, but the line of the prow was placed slightly at an angle, thus creating a transitional line, and giving a sense of action to the composition.

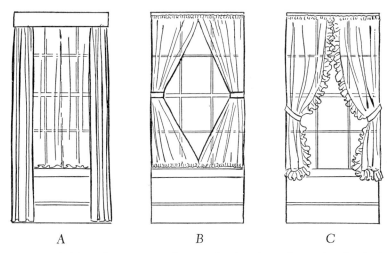

A	B	C

Figure 36. Shape harmony applied to the hanging of curtains. In A there is perfect harmony and the effect is natural and restful. In B there is contradiction, and the shapes created are inharmonious. In C the softness of the ruffle and the transitional lines of the curve modify the unrelated shape seen against the architectural background of the window.

position. The variations that were made in the proportions of all the spaces have also helped to change this photograph from a quite ordinary snapshot to a composition that has distinction.

In figure 36 the three types of shape are shown in the way the curtains have been hung. In A there is shape harmony, and the lines strengthen the shape of the window. This effect is the most desirable because the lines harmonize with the lines of the house, and all the shapes are consistent. B shows lack of shape harmony, and the queer, unrelated shape that is left after the curtain has been pulled back in this fashion has nothing in common with anything in a room and is not beautiful enough in itself to merit such undue attention. When it is desired to have the curtains tied back, it is much better to keep the lines transitional, suggesting as much as possible the rectangular shape of the window. When glass curtains are as sheer as these suggested in the drawing C, the contrast between them and the uncurtained portion of the window will be less conspicuous than if the curtain material is heavy.

Figure 37. (Architect, Edwin H. Lundie.) This doorway shows the use of the three types of line: lines that repeat the structure of the house; those that form the sharp variation of the pediment; and the curved lines of the transom and arch which give a transitional effect. Notice how the lines of the shrubs strengthen the corner of the house and lead the eye up toward the doorway. The low planting between unifies the two groups.

In the doorway shown in figure 37, the three types of shape have been successfully combined. Horizontal and vertical lines repeat the main lines of the house, and the contrasting lines of the angle over the doorway are gracefully tempered by the use of the transitional curve of the arch. This design is restrained and is varied enough in line to hold the interest.

Transitional lines in planting

In planting about the house, flowers and shrubs may be used to give a transitional line between the vertical lines of the house and the horizontal line of the ground. To see the use of transitional lines in the entire planting scheme of one house and lot, figures 37, 38, and 225 on page 351 may be studied. Figure 225 shows the corner planting as well as the front and side of the house. The planting in this yard is informal, and it relates the house and the garage to the grounds. The line of planting at the foundation is sufficiently varied for beauty and it is low at intervals so that the house gains an appearance of stability. This plan of landscaping avoids two undesirable extremes—the starkness that results from no planting, and the loss of an apparent relationship between the house and ground which is felt when tall shrubbery is planted in an unbroken mass. Planting at the edges has made it possible to have large spaces for flowers without sacrificing the fine open space of the lawn (figure 38). Tall shrubs and trees have been placed where they provide screens to shut off undesired views and to gain privacy for the living-porch at the back of the house. The vines on the garage and the house help to soften the opposing vertical lines of the buildings and the horizontal line of the ground. The variation in the lines of the planting has supplied the same type of interest that one usually associates with rolling land.

Figure 38. The planting of this sixty-foot lot is informal and interesting. Transition is introduced in the varied curves of the border and in the placement of the lowest flowers in the front, leading gradually to the higher plants and trees in the background and to those placed at the sides of the yard for privacy. The hollyhocks and the vines serve to unify the vertical lines of the garage and the horizontal line of the ground.

In any arrangement where a number of shapes are used, there should always be an effect of organization, or, in other words, of orderly arrangement. If a sense of order is to result, shape harmony must be present. Large objects or masses should be placed to follow the boundary lines of the enclosing shape, and only the smaller objects should vary from the general directions. To give variety, some of the small objects may be placed at slightly varied angles. Too many angles that sharply contradict the leading lines result in confusion instead of interesting variety. The two illustrations, figures 39 and 40, show both the application and the violation of shape harmony in the furnishing of a room.

In figure 40 there is a feeling of harmony throughout the room. The large sofa has been placed parallel to the lines of the room; the chairs, which are small, movable objects, could naturally form transitional lines in the room and so they are placed in such positions here that people could talk easily to one another. The coffee table gives another transitional line in the room. The fabrics that have been used on the furniture and for the curtains are in complete harmony with the wood-paneled wall and the exposed beamed ceiling, which establish the mood of this informal, domestic room. The curtains harmonize with the tone of the wall and are hung simply—to be pulled open or closed when desired. The simple wrought iron and plain pottery lamps, with practical and attractively tailored shades, are suited to their use. The rectangular picture makes a pleasant shape against the fireplace wall and it is grouped with the furniture below it. Compare this room with the one in figure 39 and note the differences in taste and understanding of design. In figure 39 the sofa and the table are placed to harmonize with the lines of the room but the chairs by the fireplace should be turned more to face into the room. In this position they would give a sociable grouping and supply a transitional line between the corner fireplace and the other walls of the room. The large picture is a good size and shape for the fireplace wall and it is well hung, but the other pictures should be changed. Those on each side of the hanging shelf should be taken down because, like most strong diamond shapes, they do not harmonize with the lines around them. On the opposite

Figure 39. The curtains on the door and the choice and arrangement of some pictures violate the principle of shape harmony. A comparison of these furnishings with those in figure 40 reveals the poor design of lamps and furniture.

Figure 40. (Photograph by Robert C. Cleveland.) Harmony is an important factor in making this an attractive, homelike living room: the placement of the large sofa and the hanging of the curtains harmonize with the shape of the room, and the arrangement of the chairs creates transitional lines that unify the room; the sturdy fabrics are consistent with the wood paneling and beamed ceiling; the lamps are simple and well designed. The harmonious lines and plain surfaces in this room have given it an impression of serenity.

wall, the two horizontal pictures are hung in steps that make another line at variance with the architectural lines of the room. If these were hung above each other they would form an orderly rectangle on the wall. Tieing the center curtain panel in this fashion has created a shape that contradicts the lines of the door. This is accentuated even more by the lines of the dark fabric that is used as trimming. Carrying the four dark bands across the curtains of the side windows has made additional lines of conflict. There are places where a divided curtain can be used to advantage to gain privacy at the lower half of the window or to cut out some of the strong light that comes into a room from the upper half. (See figure 224.) In general, however, it would be better to have two divided curtains rather than four and to avoid strongly contrasting bands that call so much attention to the separate divisions. The carpeting, the conventional design of the chintz covered sofa, and the fabrics on the chairs harmonize with maple furniture. However, the meaningless curves in the end table and on the stretcher of the coffee table become even more noticeable when contrasted with the good lines of the furniture in the room in figure 40. The lamps are bad in design: the shades are fussy, the glass chimney on an electric lamp is inconsistent, and the lamp bases violate harmony of ideas. Teakettles should be used as teakettles, not as lamp bases, and they are as inappropriate for this purpose as are sculptured animals or human figures.

Figure 41 shows how transitional lines can bring grace into a flower arrangement and be used to harmonize the strong contrast between the vertical lines of tall flowers and a low horizontal bowl. In this arrangement the effect of transition is due to the varied heights of the three flowers and the curved lines of the leaves.

Shape harmony in table setting

Figure 42 is an example of shape harmony as expressed in the setting of the table for a simple meal. The same principle would be followed for the most elaborate dinner. Note how the rectangular place mats harmonize with the shape of the table. Notice, also, how the lower line of napkin and silver, placed an inch from the edge, creates a line parallel to that of the table; how the napkin has been folded into a rectangular shape rather than the triangular shape which is so frequently seen; how the placing of the salt and pepper

Figure 41. In this arrangement the sharply opposing lines of the tall flowers have been related to the low, horizontal bowl by means of the transitional lines of the leaves and by cutting the three flowers to different heights.

39

Figure 42. So that order and harmony may be secured among the many objects used in setting the table, the bottom line of the silver, napkins, and plates should be parallel to the edge of the table; and the other appointments placed to harmonize with either the length or width of the table.

shakers, the water glass, the relish and jelly bowls, and each piece of silver harmonizes with one of the dimensions of the table. When placing the serving dishes, the oblong ones should be placed so that their lines follow those of the table.

When the table is set it should appear balanced as well as harmonious. Colors and masses should balance from one end of the table to the other, and from side to side. A brightly colored dish of jelly or relish might be placed at one end of the table to balance a larger amount of duller color at the other end. Sparkle and interest are gained by balancing colors in this manner.

Two design elements should be considered in a dress:

Shape harmony in dress design

1. *The structural design, which includes the silhouette and the lines within the dress*
2. *The decorative design.*

Since a dress design in itself is not considered as a complete unit, but as something to be worn on a human figure, its lines should suggest some relationship to the lines of the figure. This means that

Figure 43. Figures 43 to 46 illustrate types of structural and decorative designs in dress. In figure 43 the silhouette of the peasant costume from Latvia is in harmony with the figure, and the lines of the decoration are in perfect accord with the structural lines of the dress. This illustration shows what is meant by "conservative dress."

Figure 44. Costume of 1910. The dress follows the figure too closely for freedom in walking. The diamond-shaped medallions show absolute lack of shape harmony in relation to the dress, and are placed without reference to the lines of the structure.

its outline will follow the form closely enough to have something in common with it, yet not so closely as to appear uncomfortable. In order that it may suggest the beauty of the figure, it should not bulge at unexpected places. Historic costumes show that silhouettes fall into three main groups: first, the natural silhouette, as seen in figure 43, which is good because it harmonizes with the figure; second, the extreme silhouette, either following the figure too

Figure 45. The late Renaissance silhouette distorted rather than en-hanced the lines of the human figure.

closely, as in figure 44, or opposing it too greatly, as seen in figure 45; and third, a silhouette that is just between these two extremes showing a variation in the outline but not enough of a change from the line of the figure to lack harmony (figure 46).

Those interested in dressing economically should pay attention to shape harmony when buying clothes. In looking over old fashion magazines, one will see that it is not the details of the old dress that look queer now, but the general outline or silhouette in relation to the figure. This leads one to the conclusion that where the lines of the dress are simple, harmonizing with the lines of the figure and neither contradicting nor following them too closely, the dress can be worn several seasons without becoming conspicuous (figure 43).

The lines within the dress, such as the lines created by yokes, vests, collars, panels, tucks, and trimming are influenced very little by fashion. These lines may always be so chosen that they will be becoming to the person who is to wear the dress, and they should create shapes that are beautiful and in harmony with the lines of the figure, the silhouette of the dress, and all the other shapes appearing together. In figure 43 the lines within the dress show perfect har-

Figure 46. The silhouette and the lines in this dress of the early Renaissance show the effect of transitional lines which neither oppose the figure nor follow it too closely.

mony. In figure 44 there is lack of harmony. Figure 46 shows the use of the transitional line within the dress and in the silhouette.

The use of any of the three types of line—repetition, contrast, or transition—has a definite effect upon the appearance of the shape against which the lines are placed. This may be seen by looking at figure 29. The lines in A, which repeat the enclosing shape, have the effect of calling attention to its squareness positively. The contradicting lines of B have emphasized the squareness harshly by the extreme contrast of the shapes. C has been made to appear less severely square because of the use of the transitional line. One may take advantage of these effects to secure apparent changes in the appearance of things where an actual alteration is impossible.

The use of line to alter the appearance of shapes

In order to apply the artist's methods of using harmonizing, contrasting, and transitional lines to the selection of neck openings for faces of different shapes, one must remember that:

1. *If the shape of the neckline repeats the shape of the face, it emphasizes it.*

Figure 47. The faces in all of these illustrations are alike. Their apparent difference in shape is due to the effect of the lines of the head-dress and neck opening. A (1540). Curved lines are seen to make the face appear rounder. B (Louis XIV). A high head-dress or hat, or a long pointed neckline will give unusual length and slenderness to the face. C (1560). Horizontal lines worn near the face make it appear broader, shorten the neck, and widen the shoulders. D (Tyrolean peasant). Transitional lines, which follow none of the extremes, are softening and flattering to the features.

2. If the shape of the neckline contradicts the shape of the face, it also emphasizes it.

3. If the neckline takes a transitional line—that is, a shape between the last two which neither repeats nor contradicts it —it modifies and softens the lines.

For faces which are too square or too round, the best results come from using transitional shapes, such as long ovals and long rectangles. A knowledge of the effect of various lines apparently to change proportions is useful here and will lead one to see that square and round faces need a long line, obtained by fitting the collar closely against the neck and carrying down to an oval. This oval may be slightly inclined toward a point as it gets farther away from the face when the power to contrast becomes less strong (see figure 47).

A woman who has a drooping mouth or a receding chin should not buy a hat with drooping lines (figure 48). Similarly, a straight

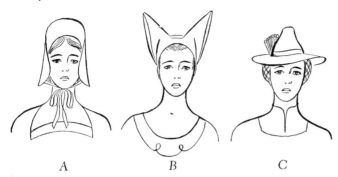

Figure 48. To show that facial expression may be modified by the choice of line in hat and dress. A (1840–1850). Drooping lines exaggerate a drooping mouth through the repetition of directions. B (1650). Contradicting lines call attention by contrast. C (Tyrolean peasant). Transitional lines, neither repeating nor contrasting, seem to modify the curve of the mouth.

severe brim is poor for a square face. If the face is round, one should not emphasize it by a round crown or a closely fitted turban, but rather bring a transitional or a broken line into the brim or trimming and attempt to secure the softening influence of a shadow.

Having considered shape harmony in relation to the structural design of a dress, the next step is to determine where the decorative design, if any, should be placed. Since good decorative design always harmonizes with structure, the placing of the decoration will be conditioned by the structural lines that have been chosen. Figure 43 is an example of well-placed decoration, while figure 44 is poor. The diamond-shape motifs in the latter are out of harmony with the structure of the dress, and they have been put at places which have no relation to it. One likes to feel that the decoration has grown out of the design of the dress and has not been dropped on, as it appears to have been on this one. Diamond shapes are exceedingly difficult to use in design, because they are related to very few structures. In addition to their use as designs on clothing, one frequently sees them very badly used as windows in the doors and walls of a house and as monograms on household linens. Diamond

Shape harmony in the decoration of a dress

Figure 49. Marble Head of Aphrodite. Greek, IV Century B.C.
A beautiful example of shape harmony is seen in the way the hair of the Aphrodite has been arranged. *(Courtesy of the Minneapolis Institute of Arts.)*

shapes may be used successfully if they are connected by lines strong enough to carry the eye along the structure on which they are placed, or arranged so closely together that they form a band, as shown on the belt of the dress in figure 44.

Shape harmony applied to hairdressing
Looking over the pages of historic costume, one smiles and marvels at the various ways in which woman has dressed her hair —there have been periods in which all resemblance to the human head has been ignored or contradicted; there have been others where the arrangement has been perfectly rational and very beautiful. The simple hairdress of the Greek head of Aphrodite may well be taken as a standard by which to judge all these other modes (figure 49). Her hair is dressed so that the resulting silhouette is in perfect harmony with the shape of her head, and interest has been gained through the slight variation at the sides. Only when one's

head is beautifully shaped and the features are regular, can one afford to call attention to the outline by wearing the hair drawn
severely away from the face, with a knot in the back. For most
women, a style that has a broken outline is more becoming and permits them apparently to shorten a high forehead, or to give a broken
line around a face that is too square or too round. Too large a hairdress or one made up of queer puffs out of harmony with the head
should be avoided.

In advertisements and showcards, all of the big shapes should *Shape har-*
take the general shape of the enclosing form. In layouts for ad- *mony in ad-*
vertisements and posters it is often necessary to group several small *vertising*
horizontal oblongs to give the effect of a vertical movement to
harmonize with a vertical oblong. If circles, triangles, or diamond
shapes are used, they must be recognized as striking contrasts and
be used only where an unusual emphasis is desired. Figure 50 shows

*Figure 50. A strik-
ing advertisement in
which the dramatic
diagonal lines are
held in by the transi-
tional lines of the
wide borders. (Cour-
tesy of The Mil-
waukee Road.)*

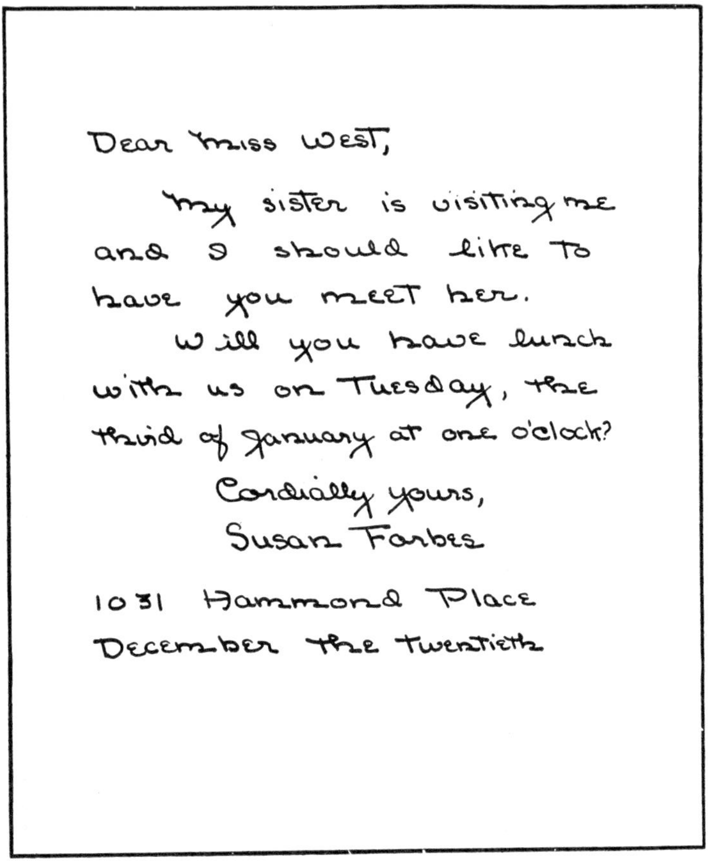

Dear Miss West,

  My sister is visiting me
and I should like to
have you meet her.
  Will you have lunch
with us on Tuesday, the
third of January at one o'clock?
      Cordially yours,
      Susan Forbes

1031 Hammond Place
December the Twentieth

Figure 51. Whether a letter is typed or written, it will appear most attractive if the mass of the writing harmonizes with the shape of the paper and if enough plain space is left at the bottom of the sheet to give a pleasant effect of balance.

how strong diagonal lines may be related to an oblong by means of transitional lines. Although an advertisement should have a dramatic quality in order to catch the attention, there is danger of going too far in the attempt to do something unusual, with chaos as a result. If the designer remembers that there should always be a feeling of shape harmony in every layout, he will use erratic shapes and lines sparingly, in order that a dramatic rather than a distracting effect may be gained.

In store arrangements, if an appearance of unity and of dignity is desired, the counters, tables, and display racks should be placed parallel with the walls. Large objects displayed on tables, ledges, etc., should also follow the lines of the building; and, to give variety, some of the smaller objects may be placed at slightly different angles. If some of the smaller articles are placed so that they create contradicting lines, these lines may be agreeably softened by the use of transitional lines secured through objects which in themselves have this kind of line. All that has been said about shape harmony in the house carries over directly into the problem of arranging a store or a window display. *Shape harmony in store arrangements*

The daily process of writing a letter and addressing an envelope presents a similar art problem. Three art principles are called into use: shape harmony, proportion, and balance. Proportion, that the writing will not be too large for the space it is to occupy; balance, that the block of writing be placed high enough so that it does not appear to be falling off the paper; and shape harmony, which may be secured by creating a block of writing similar in shape to that of the paper, beginning each line directly under the line above, and attempting to space the words so that the ends of the lines at the right are as nearly in the same vertical line as possible. (See figure 51.) *Writing a letter and addressing an envelope*

HARMONIOUS OR CONSISTENT SIZES

In the chapter on "Proportion," it will be seen that when sizes which are too different are used together they are inconsistent. The aspect of proportion called "scale" is allied to harmony in the sense of "harmonious or consistent sizes," and it is pointed out in the next chapter that the desire for harmony should lead small women to avoid wearing very large hats or furs, and should prevent the placing of large vases or lamps on small tables. Since the understanding and the application of the principle of proportion will assure harmony of sizes, we may go directly to the consideration of harmonious or consistent textures.

HARMONY OF TEXTURES

The homemaker, the window designer, and salespeople will be interested in cultivating a feeling for harmony in texture. More and more, people are saying not only, "How does it look?" but also, "How does it feel?" But although texture may be explained as the way a material feels when the finger tips are run lightly along its surface, the sensation of texture is suggested also through the eye. This interest in texture has become an important consideration to the manufacturer of objects made from the new plastics as well as from the traditional materials.

Perhaps no people have developed aesthetic appreciation through the sense of touch more than the people of old China. There the art of "feeling jade" for the beauty of its texture was considered to be so fine that the finger tips were carefully trained so as to be "worthy to touch jade." In our own environment we, too, can give as well as gain much pleasure through discriminating combinations of texture.

Many schemes just miss being successful because the person who planned them did not recognize that very coarse textures have nothing in common with very fine ones. There is, however, a group of textures which occupies a middle ground and may be used with either the coarser or the finer textures. For example, the coarse texture of oak suggests sturdiness, and one may use flax rugs, denim, monk's cloth, homespun, crash, or similar coarse textures with oak furniture; or, working up to the middle group there are the finer textured fabrics, cretonnes, printed linen, and some chintzes. On the other hand, the thin, fine silks, lustrous rayons, velvets, satins, taffetas, and highly glazed chintzes, especially those with delicate designs, are textures which are out of harmony with oak but go well with walnut, mahogany, and enameled furniture, because of the fine, satinlike grain of these woods and their smooth surface. These fine textures have no relationship to the coarse group but they have enough in common with the middle group to be introduced when it is desirable to take away from the thinness or the "overdressed" effect which may come

with too much fine texture. An example of poor texture combination sometimes seen in the shops is cane furniture upholstered in
lustrous rayon. These textures are entirely unsuited to each other
and are ridiculous to the person thinking in terms of consistent combinations. A group of well-related textures is seen in the brick fireplace and its accessories in figure 54, page 53. Here the textures of
the pottery and brass appear to have something in common with
the texture of the brick, which seems to be related to brass, to iron,
and to sturdy pottery, but not to delicate glass or to other similar
fine textures. When changing fashions in dress bring unexpected
texture combinations, a sense of harmony will permit a person to
follow the new fashion with taste, and the result may be stimulating
in its newness. But an exaggeration of the new idea might appear
merely incongruous. This is sometimes seen in the excellent effect
of sequins, rhinestones, or pearls combined with fine fabrics, and
the impression of inconsistency when they are badly used.

HARMONY OF IDEAS

It is not enough that sizes, shapes, colors, and textures should *Harmony of*
have something in common, but there must be harmony in the ideas *ideas in ex-*
presented together. We see this in comparing figures 52 and 53. In *terior design*
figure 53 all the elements seem to be in accord and they are all
suited to the idea of a modest, unpretentious home. The columns
on the porch of the house in figure 52 do not harmonize with the
house. There is something imposing about the classic orders, and
the grace and beauty of an Ionic column suggests a temple, an art
museum, or a stately home. It is not in keeping with a small cottage.
Note the use of the well-proportioned, simple posts in figure 53.
There is little danger of erring on the side of too great simplicity.
While an Ionic column requires a formal setting, a support such as
that in figure 53 is appropriate for either the simplest or the finest
dwelling.

Just as all the elements in the exterior of the house must agree, so *Harmony of*
must there be harmony and sincerity in the ideas suggested by the *ideas in house*
furnishings of the house. Things that might appear well in a mansion *furnishing*

Figure 52. There is a lack of harmony in the idea of a classic column on the porch of this modest cottage. Compare with this the simple, well-proportioned posts used in figure 53.

would be distinctly out of place in a cottage. Rich period furniture needs a formal setting, and it is incongruous to try to introduce the Italian or French Renaissance into a small, informal house. The

Figure 53. All of the architectural details used here are in harmony with the idea of a small, modest home.

Figure 54. The well-related furnishings in the room above are instrumental in creating an atmosphere of harmony and sincerity.

Figure 55. There is lack of consistency between the two chairs shown here. The brocaded chair is too ornate for the other chair as well as for the spirit of the room.

chair in figure 55, with its brocade and fringe, though by no means so pretentious as much furniture one sees, is a misfit in the quiet domestic scene indicated by the kettle on the hearth and the cottage chair. Compare this room with figure 54. Here there are no discordant notes; background, furniture, accessories, and fireplace belong together and to the spirit of the informal home. If an effect of greater richness than this is desired in a room, one would need to have all of the details correspondingly fine. This may be observed in the living room in figure 56. The furniture is rather light in scale, and the upholstery fabrics are smooth, yet there is an impression of reserve in the appearance of the surfaces because they do not have too high a luster.

If table appointments are to look well together and to appear to belong with the house and its owners, it is important for young people to consider this aspect of harmony when they choose their

Figure 56. This gracious room shows rich textures used with restraint to harmonize with the furniture, which is equally fine in type.

first pieces of silver or china to start their collection. In order to illustrate harmony of ideas in the furnishings for the table, some typical designs and textures in silver, glass, and china have been assembled into harmonious groups. Those in A, figure 57, are sturdy, domestic, and informal in spirit or feeling. B is the intermediate group. C includes those which are fine or formal and social in feeling, and in D there is a collection of modern and impersonal designs. It should be observed that the idea of cost has not influenced these characteristics, or the combinations in the illustrations, for plated silver and inexpensive glass and china are to be found in the most formal and elaborate patterns, while some of the most costly examples are seen in the most unpretentious patterns. It is readily observed that all of the designs in the informal group may easily be combined with those in the intermediate group, and all those of the formal group could be used with any of the examples in the intermediate group. However, there is so much difference in the qualities of the rugged Mexican glass and plate and the first two silver patterns in A and the formal, elaborate spoon, glass, and plate at the right in C that they would never be combined on the same table. The examples in D show the amount of variation to be found in the designs that are suited to the type of house called functional, but they are not limited to the modern house. Each of these silver patterns may be classified as going toward the intermediate, with the first spoon having more of the characteristics of the fine group, and the third spoon suggesting the first, or sturdy, group of textures and ideas. Similarly, the engraved glass and the plate with the conventionalized wreath could take their places among the finer textures although they would also combine well with the intermediate group. A glance at the monogram on the second spoon in this modern group shows that when the type of engraving selected for silver is suggested by the character of the pattern, it becomes a part of the design. Of course, it is apparent that the linens to be used with these combinations of table appointments should have the same feeling of simplicity or richness in texture and design as the dishes and glass and silver.

The homemaker who does her own housework likes to have a

Figure 57A, B, C, and D. Many examples chosen from among a host of good designs in china, glass, and silver are pictured in A, B, and C. Each of these patterns would be attractive in the home for which it is appropriate. They are grouped to show designs and textures that range from the most rugged through the intermediate, to the finest and richest types. It is obvious that the Mexican plate and glass and the first silver pattern at the

B

left, in A, could not be combined with the last plate in C, which has grouped with it elaborately cut glass and the richly ornamented silver pattern. B illustrates the so-called intermediate type of design and texture, and the examples in this group could be combined successfully with those in either A or C. D illustrates some modern designs, any combination of which would be consistent together.

D

Figure 58. (Designer, Greta Magnusson Grossman. Photograph by Julius Shulman.) This drop-leaf table makes an attractive place to eat in the kitchen. A sliding panel shuts off the view of the kitchen from the living area when desired. The informal dishes are harmonious here.

pleasant place to eat in her kitchen. Figure 58 shows a drop-leaf table used for this purpose. Breakfasts or snacks are easy to serve here and placed as it is, it affords a view into the living-dining room. Colorful, simple dishes and smart, practical linens may be chosen for this purpose, and if they are stored conveniently can save many steps in the day's work.

A window display of men's shirts and bolts of broadcloth has unity of idea because one may easily lead one's imagination to follow the stages from broadcloth to garments. An equally well-arranged window displaying men's shirts, kitchen ranges, and picture frames would be a poor display. A striking example of inconsistent ideas is a window display of overalls combined with bouquets of roses tied with tulle bows.

Harmony of ideas for window designs

Another very important application of harmony of ideas appears in the treatment of the decoration for clothing and for many objects used in the home. A beautiful bouquet of roses makes a definite appeal when it is seen at the florists, but the imitation of it, done with all the accuracy of the skilled craftsman, is inappropriate when embroidered on a dress, or painted on a plate to be used for meals, when it stares out realistically and restlessly from a wall paper with hundreds of companions, or when it appears on a sofa cushion which we might turn upside down to rest against. Harmony of ideas will direct one to conventionalize roses or any other theme borrowed from nature before employing it as a feature in weaving, embroidery, or the decoration of china, or in any other practical purpose. Designs should not imitate the fruit store or the florist, but involve a group of beautiful and well-arranged masses, not inconsistent with the use to which the object is to be put.

Harmony in the treatment of a decorative motif

In the group of plates, figures 59 A, B, C, we have illustrations of the right and the wrong use of the floral idea. In A the decoration is merely a picture of a bouquet in no way connected, either in placing or treatment, with the plate which it is meant to adorn. B shows another example of the floral idea, but the shapes have

Figures 59A, B, and C. A. This design is too naturalistic to be used on china. B and C. The motifs on these plates have been so stylized that, although the forms resemble ideas from nature, there is no attempt at imitation. Observe the degrees of conventionalization from B to C, where the nature form is merely suggested. In both plates the design has character and is suitable for use.

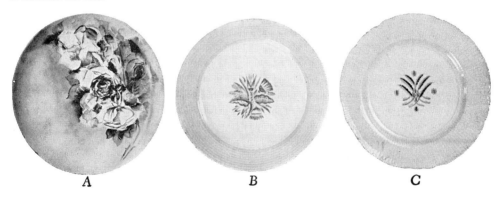

A   B   C

Figure 60. Imitations of natural flowers, fruits, birds, and animals are not suitable on wearing apparel or on objects for household use. The naturalistic daisies are quite out of place on the dress at the right. Compare with this the consistent decoration used for the peasant dress.

been changed to fit the use of the plate. This motif is good in size, and the treatment of the flower idea reveals invention in form and in color. It has a theme similar to the one in A, but here the designer has adapted rather than imitated flower forms. The other plate, C, illustrates the conventionalization of a flower in which the design is even more abstract.

Figure 60B shows naturalistic daisies spotted over a child's dress. This is poor because the main lines of the decoration should accord with the main lines of the dress, and, furthermore, the decoration should be conventionalized. Comparing this dress with the peasant dress in A, we see that the same daisy idea is the inspiration of the embroidery, but the peasant treatment is much more beautiful.

It should be understood that it is not necessary to have an association of ideas in order to have harmony. In fact, it is possible to carry association of ideas so far that it becomes ridiculous, as when cheese dishes are decorated with cheese and mice, honey jars are shaped like bee-hives (with a bee for the handle), and kitchen towels have cups and saucers embroidered on them. Designs which avoid the suggestion of an obvious relationship are all the better on articles intended for use.

HARMONY OF COLOR

Color harmony, the fifth aspect of the subject of harmony, is considered in the chapter on "How to Use Color."

One becomes so accustomed to the things done and seen constantly that it is much easier to enjoy and evaluate other people's work than one's own. For this reason, it is suggested that the reader at first analyze, constructively, the things all about him; then, with a better understanding, and with definite convictions, he will be able to pass sound judgment on his own selections and arrangements.

Chapter Four

PROPORTION

Aspects of
proportion THE *principle of proportion is sometimes called the "law of relationships."* There are three practical problems in proportion which con-
front us in everyday tasks. These are:

1. *How to achieve arrangements which will hold the interest*
2. *How to make the best of given sizes and shapes*
3. *How to judge what sizes may successfully be grouped together.*

There are definite means by which to solve these problems:

1. *In order to achieve arrangements that will hold the interest
   one must know how to create beautiful space relationships.*
2. *In order to make the best of given sizes and shapes one must
   be able to produce a semblance of change in appearance, if it
   is desirable.*
3. *In order to judge what sizes may be grouped together successfully, it is necessary to grasp the underlying significance of
   scale.*

INTEREST THROUGH SPACE RELATIONSHIPS

How long will a row of pickets in a fence or the ticking of a
clock hold the interest? Obviously, only an instant. But introduce
an element a little bit out of the ordinary, such as an unusual gate
or the striking of a clock, and interest is immediately stimulated.
If an arrangement is built on the plan of three squares, the mind
will record those squares without a pause as it did the pickets on the
fence, and the eye will not be arrested. But suppose two squares

62

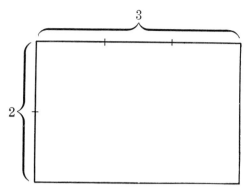

Figure 61. The Greek oblong, which is a standard of good proportion. The
sides are in the relation of two parts to three.

were used with an oblong, or two oblongs with a square, one
would have to look an instant longer before that picture was re-
corded; and in that instant he would actually perceive that group
more clearly than the one composed of three squares. Here, then,
one is on the heels of an answer to the question of how to arouse
the interest.

Every time two or more things are put together proportions are
established, whether good or bad. Some people have an instinct
for good proportion, and whatever combinations they plan are sure
to please the eye, but most people have to acquire this trait. Fortunately it is one that can be acquired. The best method is to adopt
a standard, and then, by comparing the results of experiments with
that standard, one will soon arrive at the point of having a true
"feeling" for fine space relationships.

The ancient Greeks, after centuries of striving for beauty, ar- Greek oblong
rived at the point where nearly everything they made exhibited
good spacing. The oblong which they used as the basis of their space
divisions is sometimes called "the golden oblong" and is a recognized standard for space relationships. This Greek oblong measured approximately two units on the short side and three on the
long (figure 61). Most people find this more beautiful than a
square, because the equal sides make a square more obvious. The
Greek oblong has more beauty than a very long, narrow oblong, in

Figure 62. The Parthenon, Athens.
In the Parthenon all the proportions are based upon the principle that the
relationship of about two parts to three (a relationship which is not too
apparent), is beautiful, and that equal or mechanical sizes are uninteresting.
(Courtesy of the University Prints.)

which the breadth and the length vary so greatly that they do not
seem to be related. A study of the Parthenon, which is the most perfectly proportioned building in the world, illustrates the highest
achievement of the Greeks in planning space relationships (figure
62). Compare the oblong formed by the front of the building with
that formed by the side, and note the height of the front in reference
to its width. The same beautiful ratio is carried out in the smallest
detail of the building. While the ratio of about 2:3 or 3:5 is the
relationship used by the Greeks for their flat surfaces, their standard
for solids is a ratio of about 5:7:11. The designer of today who goes
to the Greeks for his inspiration is likely to gain beauty if he interprets their proportions in terms of his own problem, whereas, if he
is intent only on copying their details, his building is likely to be
merely a collection of historic fragments. The most modest house
can have the essential character of Greek art without having a single

Figure 63. The excellent design of this house is due largely to its good proportions. Its mass or silhouette is based upon the proportions of the Greek oblong. The details of the house—dormers, eaves, chimneys, door, windows, and columns—are well scaled to the size of the house. (Courtesy of The Architect's Small House Service Bureau.) (Russell F. Whitehead, Architect.)

so-called "classical detail," if it is based on Greek ideals of simplicity, fitness, and fine proportions. A comparison of the small houses in figures 63 and 64 strengthens the conviction that as a rectangle ap-

Figure 64. A comparison of this house with the one in figure 63 shows that although the styles are similar in origin, this house is inferior in design. Its mass is based upon the square instead of the oblong. Its dormer is too large for the size of the house, and the chimney is too small. The sizes of all the parts are less beautiful than those of the other house.

proaches a square it becomes less pleasing, and that the best results depend on being able to approximate Greek proportions. The use of the Greek oblong and of Greek space divisions in the design of the fireplace in figure 224, page 350 has added beauty to a simple room. Because of its delightful spacing this fireplace will never cease to give pleasure to its owners.

Figure 65. Somewhere near A would be the most interesting point within this space to place an important object or to divide the space.

How to divide a space into two interesting parts

Perhaps no art problem occurs so often (even where one does not realize that a question of art is involved) as the one in which a space has to be divided into two or more parts: when a name is written on a card; when the division of a wall space or the parts of a garment are planned; or when a group of objects is arranged; or in countless other situations where the same principle is called into play. If the particular division is to be into two parts, the most satisfying result is achieved when the dividing line or object is placed at a point a little more than one-half and a little less than two-thirds the distance from one end or the other (figure 65). However, this point should not be located mechanically, and these proportions are only approximate. Any position within the limits is potentially pleasing, and there is no necessity for a stereotyped choice.

Dividing a space into more than two interesting parts

Dividing a space into more than two parts by means of lines or objects presents three possibilities:

1. *All the spaces may differ. For example, in the diagram, figure 66A, and in the Danish plate illustrated in figure 67, all the stripes and the spaces between them are different. This gives the greatest variety obtainable. This type of spacing is excellent for relatively small areas or for a few spaces, but there is a possibility that the effect may appear confused and inharmonious if a great many of these divisions must be seen and compared at one time.*

2. *All the spaces may be alike. In figure 66B and in the black and white material in figure 68, every stripe is the same width, and*

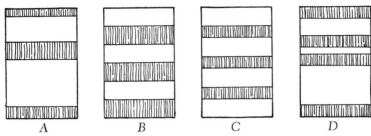

Figure 66. Interesting variety or monotony is gained through spacing. A shows variety throughout. There is no repetition in its lines or in the spaces between them. B shows monotony in its repetition because all the lines and spaces are alike. In C the spaces differ from the lines, while in D the spaces are different from the lines and from each other.

the spaces between them are the same width as the stripes. If carried too far, this kind of repetition makes for monotony. If such a plan is used, it would be well to introduce sufficient variation in the color or texture to supply the interest that is lacking in the spacing.

3. There may be a variation in some of the spaces and repetition in others. In figure 66C and in figure 66D, a stripe is repeated at intervals alternating with a space from which it differs in width. In figure 69, and in the collar, figure 70, the tucks, which are the mark of division in this example, are alike in width, and the spaces between them vary. The converse of this arrangement would be seen if tucks of varying width were interspersed with identical spaces. C and D achieve harmony through the repetition of the same unit, but without sacrificing the agreeable element of variation.

Additional examples of these types of space division are pictured in figures 71 to 73. In houses where two building materials are used, their distribution is important. One material should appear to predominate. For example, when brick and clapboarding are used in equal amounts, the impression of unity is destroyed (figure 71). This distracting effect can be relieved by painting the brick the color of the clapboarding. Brick and wood have been attractively combined in the house in figure 72, for they are used in varied propor-

Figure 67. The spacings used in the bands of this plate have given it distinction. The plan is similar to figure 66A, where neither the bands nor the spaces between them are of the same width.

Figure 68. As in the repeated lines and spaces illustrated in the diagram in figure 66B, the spacing in this design is lacking in interest and would become monotonous if it were over-used.

68

Figure 69. The raffia box represents a design in which a stripe is repeated at intervals with varied spaces between. There is an ingenious amount of variety in the spacings, yet the design is held together by the lines which are repeated. In plan this is similar to figure 66C.

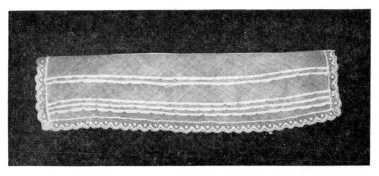

Figure 70. Here the repetition of the tucks gives unity, while the difference in the spaces between lends variety. This is a typical application of the kind of spacing in figure 66D.

tions and painted the same color. Just as a house that is divided into two equal parts will lack interest, so will a garment similarly divided. The variety in the divisions of the dress in figure 73C contributes interest to the costume, while the equal proportions in the second dress, figure 73B, make it appear dull and unflattering to the figure. In the Parthenon, the columns will be found narrower than the spaces between them, producing a subtle effect of far greater beauty than if they were equal. Figure 73A recalls the columns of the

Parthenon in the arrangement of stripes and spaces, and the dress in figure 73C owes its interest to a similar use of repetition and variety.

Figures 71 and 72. When two kinds of building material are used in nearly equal proportions, they tend to cut a house into two parts. This is especially true when the materials are as different as the dark brick and white paint in figure 71. There is an impression of unity in figure 72 because the brick in the lower part of the house is painted like the clapboarding and is used in a varied amount, and the roof is plain.

Figure 73A, B, and C. Costumes of,
A, Second Empire; B, 1929; C, Four-
teenth Century. A and C show the charm
that can be given to a costume when the
designer is aware of the inherent interest
in subtle space divisions. (B) A garment
that is divided into two equal parts appears commonplace.

Figure 74A. This arrangement is monotonous because the proportions are poor. The objects are so placed that they divide the background into equal spaces and the heights are too much alike.

When arranging objects on a shelf one should attempt to secure interest in their heights and in the spaces between them. For instance, figure 74A is commonplace because of the equal spaces between the ends of the cabinet and the objects and between the units themselves. Moreover, all three are too nearly the same height. Substituting the larger basket and moving the objects has introduced variety both in the heights and the spaces (figure 74B).

Frequently one has to arrange groups of objects within a larger group. Perhaps it is desired to assemble several pictures so that they will harmonize with a particular wall space. One may wish to group rows of braid or tucks within a given space; to place buttons on a dress; or it may be that an embroiderer wishes to repeat an interesting unit at unequal intervals on a band or a collar. Whatever the nature of the problem, it is generally true that if single units or

Figure 74B. *This is more interesting than A because the heights of the objects and the spaces between them show more varied proportions.*

objects in a group are to be viewed as units, they may be separated by spaces wider than the unit measure; but if objects are to be seen as a group, the spaces between them should be smaller than the size of the objects. If this group is to be related to another near it, the space between the two should be smaller than the space occupied by either. This plan, shown in figure 75, has been followed in arranging the objects on the dressing table in figure 104, on page 103, and in grouping the pictures above the table in figure 241, on page 366.

Odd numbers are more interesting than even numbers, and three objects grouped with three, or two objects with three, are likely to make a more satisfying arrangement than two and two, or two and four, or any combination involving even numbers. The arrangement of the tucks in the collar in figure 70 follows this plan of two units used with a group of three, and a study of this example will show how easy it is to augment interest through this method of grouping.

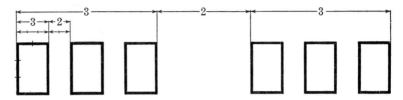

Figure 75. This shows a plan which may be followed in arranging objects so that they will group well. Think of each one of these blocks as a picture, a button, or a bolt of fabric—in fact, anything you wish to arrange in a group. Each group is seen as a unit because there is less space between the objects than the width of the object. The two groups are easily seen together because there is less space between them than the area of each group. Note that all spaces follow Greek proportions. See an application in the arrangement of pictures in figure 241 on page 366.

PRODUCING A CHANGE OF APPEARANCE

Lines which apparently alter proportions

Figure 76 shows two rectangles of exactly the same size. In one a horizontal line has been drawn, and in the other a vertical line. Where the eye is carried across the rectangle it looks shorter and wider, and where it is carried up and down the effect is that of apparently increasing the height and decreasing the width. It is often said that horizontal lines add width and vertical lines add height. While this is true, a second effect may be produced which must also be taken into account. Vertical lines can be so arranged that they will carry the eye from one line to the next, and while they still add height to an object they will also add width. Let us however confine ourselves to the statement that a *vertical movement* makes an object look taller and more slender, and a *horizontal movement* has the opposite effect. An illustration of this principle is seen in the buildings in figures 77A and B. Although the proportions of the Palais de Justice and the Palazzo Isolani are practically the same, the Palais de Justice appears to be the higher building. This is because all the lines draw the eye upward, while the lines and the repetition of arches in the other building carry the eye horizontally.

Thus it is seen that if, for the sake of economy, one plans a house that approaches a square, it is possible in a measure to overcome the

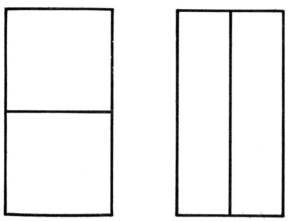

Figure 76. *Two oblongs of the same size showing that when the eye is carried up and down the height seems increased and the width decreased, while carrying the eye across tends to add width and decrease height.*

disadvantages of this plan by the shape and the arrangement of the openings. (See figures 78 and 79.) In figure 79, where the windows and porch are themselves nearly squares, monotony results from the emphasis laid upon this aspect of the house. Compare with this figure 78 where a more interesting effect has been obtained by the use of shutters on the windows, and variety achieved through the treatment of the doorway. Although a one-story house is less likely to appear as square as a house with two stories, both types should be studied carefully so as to relate them to the landscape. The house in figure 81 shows the application of some architectural devices that will make a small one-story house appear horizontal in effect. The unbroken roof line, the wide overhang that casts a shadow line, and windows designed in bands all carry the eye horizontally. The use of one material for the front of the house, the garage, and the fence also creates a horizontal movement and ties the house to the lot. The house in figure 80 is on a small lot, yet it could have been made to appear larger than it is and more beautifully proportioned. The wide light stucco band separates the house from the ground and breaks the continuity of a horizontal movement. Painting the ventilator a contrasting color emphasizes the break in the roof line. The

Figure 77A. The Palais de Justice, Rouen.

Figure 77B. The Palazzo Isolani, Bologna. These two buildings have approximately the same proportions in their silhouette, but the lines of A carry the eye upward and make the building appear higher than B, where the leading lines carry the eye across.

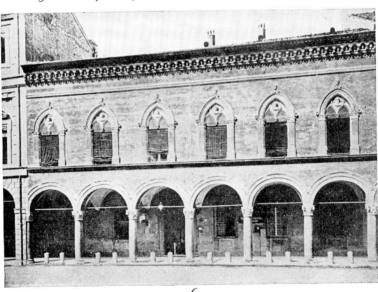

Figure 78. This house, based somewhat upon the plan of the square, is made to appear less square because the foundation and roof are low, and the windows and doors are interesting in proportion and are so spaced as to create a horizontal effect.

unrelated window shapes call attention to each as a separate unit and do not carry the eye smoothly across the front of the house. This lack of unity in the windows is made more conspicuous by the use of the strongly contrasting color trim. A better plan for the design of the windows and the color scheme would have improved greatly the appearance of this house.

Figure 79. A house which appears to be made up of several squares is uninteresting.

Figure 80. The appearance of this house would have been improved if the sizes and shapes of the windows were related to the wall spaces, and a less contrasting color had been used at the base of the house and on the ventilator on the roof.

Figure 81. This house is well proportioned and its lines are related to the lot. It appears larger than it is because a horizontal effect has been given to the design through an unbroken roof line; the windows, which are good in shape and size, carry the eye across the house, and there is a unified color relationship between the side wall and the wood used for the front of the house, the garage, and the fence. (Kenbo Corporation.)

When it is understood that the correct use of lines may thus ap- *The effect of lines upon the appearance of a room* parently alter proportions, countless puzzling problems will be solved. The room that is too low may have a ceiling lighter than the walls or a suggestion of vertical stripe in the paper. Rooms in which a part of the ceiling is slanting are made to appear lower when the ceiling color is brought down to the wall, but seem higher when the color of the wall is used on the slanting surface and a lighter color on the ceiling. Windows that are too short may have long, narrow draperies and no valance, and the chair that is too low may have a vertically striped cover (but remember not to choose stripes that will carry the eye across rather than up and down.) The placing of pictures and accessories may be used to emphasize height or width in a room. For example, a vertical hanging will produce an impression of height. A high room can be made to seem lower by carrying the color of the ceiling down to the tops of the windows, or having the ceiling darker than the walls; by the use of low bookcases and furniture; and by the suggestion of a horizontal movement in the design of the fireplace and the arrangement of all the furnishings in the room (figure 102). A room that is unusually long can seem shortened by placing important groups of furniture at the central axis. The use of more than one rug also appears to decrease the size of the room. To increase the apparent width of a room a valance or cornice board may be used across a group of windows, and rugs may be so placed that their lines will carry the eye across the room.

No one wants to appear too different from the fashionable figure *The effect of lines upon the appearance of the individual* of the time. In some countries of the world a woman's beauty is measured in terms of bulk, and people there naturally dress to give the illusion of weight. Here, where slenderness is the standard of beauty, the opposite illusion is sought. If a person understands how to use lines effectively, she can make herself approach more nearly whatever standards she has set. In figure 82 the women's figures are the same height, but the vertical direction of the lines of the dress in B makes that woman look taller and more slender, while the horizontal movement in A decreases the apparent height and adds width. It is amazing to see the transformations that can be brought

Figure 82A and B. Costume of, A, 1830; B, Thirteenth Century. A, Horizontal effects are charming on a slender, well-proportioned person but would make a large woman look very broad and short. B, striking emphasis down the center front of a costume adds immeasurably to the effect of height and slenderness. This is an excellent device for a stout woman, but should be shunned by one who is too tall and thin. Notice that these figures are the same height, and the difference in their appearance is due to the direction of the movement of the lines.

about through illusions created by an intelligent use of lines. In Chapter XV there is a table of suggestions that summarizes the best lines for various types of face and figure. In order to associate the basic principle with these recommendations, we shall list some typical suggestions concerning the use of lines that apparently alter proportions. A tall thin person should choose dominant lines that carry the eye across the figure, because horizontal and curved lines add width. From among the offerings in current fashion, the tall, thin man should choose the nearest approach to broad padded shoulders; wide lapels; coats with deep yokes and fullness belted at the waistline; the wider and fuller trousers; light coat with dark trousers; and the broader hat brims with the lower crowns. Women who wish to look shorter should select such lines as may be gained from suits with contrasting jackets; dresses with contrasting blouses or bodice tops; shorter, wider skirts; peplums and flared tunics; broad belts; broadened shoulders; bloused bodices; and the lower hats with brims. All of these lines that look so well on the too-tall, too-slender person should be avoided by those who are short or stout. This group should avoid a horizontal movement in the lines of hats and garments, and should seek to direct the eye up and down the center of the figure, rather than across it.

A person, any of whose proportions vary from the normal, may select clothing with lines designed to direct the eye away from the unusual feature. For example, a woman who has too large a bust should not compress the waist for then attention would be called to the unusual size. Rather, she should build out the waist slightly, and, if she is short, she could also employ lines that carry the eye up and down the center of the figure. If the hips are conspicuous, an accented line might be used down the center of the skirt. If the shoulders are too square, it is unwise to accentuate them with yokes or square collars. In making such adjustments, the entire figure should be studied so that the whole effect may not suffer for the sake of a detail.

SCALE

The third aspect of the principle of proportion is called "scale." *Definition of scale* An intelligent critic may say, "This building is excellent. All its parts are in scale." Or, "How well scaled this table is." Scale, in this sense, means (1) that the sizes of all the elements making up the structure have a consistent, pleasing relationship to the structure and to each other; and (2) that the size of the structure is in good proportion to the different objects combined with it. A very small

Figure 83. All of the architectural details in this small house are well scaled to each other and to the size of the house.

Figure 84. The dormers are strikingly out of scale with this small house. Other changes that would have improved the house are: a lower foundation, a plainer roof, the elimination of the dark bricks in the chimney, and the use of two instead of three windows at the right of the entrance.

object never looks so small as when it is placed near a very large one. That is because the two sizes are not consistent. They accentuate each other by contrast, and would be said to be "out of scale." By following a consistent scale, it is possible to create illusions that cause astonishment when the actual sizes of objects are realized. An illustration was experienced in witnessing a well-staged puppet play. The puppeteer, whose stage properties were in perfect scale

Figures 85 and 86. The bulky chair and sofa in figure 85 are out of scale with the room. Compare them with the well-designed furniture in figure 86 which is intermediate in scale and suited to a room of average size. (Figure 86, courtesy of MGM Studios.)

with the puppets, gave his audience the ever-increasing impression of watching normal people and objects. He gave a dramatic illustration of the way scale will deceive the eye when, at the end of the performance, he stood near the stage, and looked like a giant.

It is very largely because all parts of the house in figure 83 are in scale that it is so successful. Compare it with figure 84, and it will be seen that when the scale is bad a house is not a unit but a jumble of parts. Whenever a dormer, a window, or a porch is too large or too small it will attract undue attention and destroy the

Scale in exteriors

effect of unity in the house. In this case the dormers are out of scale with the size of the house, and the group of three windows at the right is too large for the wall space. In figure 83 the dormers are small enough to take their proper place in the whole design and, because they are shingled like the roof, an appearance of unity is attained. All of the other architectural details—the chimney, windows, doorway, and the overhang of the roof—are in scale with the size of the house. Two other examples of good and poor scale in exterior design are compared in figures 63 and 64.

Scale in house furnishing The person who would select and arrange things to look well together must develop a feeling for scale. He must know, for example, that bulky-looking furniture will seem to crowd a room of average size, which would hold a number of smaller pieces quite satisfactorily (figure 85). If large pieces must be used in a small room, there should be as few as possible, upholstered in an inconspicuous color and pattern. On the other hand, if the furniture seems too small for the room, it should be arranged in groups, so that the size of the group, and not the size of each piece, may become the unit for comparison. The maximum appearance of size may be given to a room through the use of furnishings comparatively small in scale.

Scale is judged not only by the size of the whole mass of an object, but also by the relationship of each part to every other part, and to the whole mass. Two chairs of the same outside dimensions will appear different in scale if the arms and legs of one are very heavy, and of the other very light.

There is a mistaken idea that furniture, to be comfortable, must be huge. This is unfortunate, because it has led many people who live in average-sized rooms to crowd them with bulky pieces. If they knew that comfort is more a matter of the design and construction of the piece than of its size, and that equal comfort can be obtained with smaller pieces, our small houses and apartments would show much better scale and would be more attractive. The chair, sofa, and table in figure 85 illustrate this common mistake. Unusually large pieces of furniture call more attention to themselves than to the room as a whole. It should be noted that the heavy curves of the sofa and the angular effect of the chair have little in common. Now study figure 86. Here the furnishings are intermediate in scale—neither very fine nor unusually heavy. The two chairs and sofa are large enough for comfort, but not so large as to dominate the room. With the floor space gained, it is possible to use additional pieces of furniture to make a room more enjoyable. The furniture in this room makes an interesting comparison with that in figure 85. Here, there is a sense of grace in the slender lines of the chairs and sofa which does not in any way interfere with the feeling of strength. Although the chairs are large enough to be comfortable, they have the advantage of being light enough to be moved about easily to form any other grouping that is desired in the room. A glance back at figure 56 shows a more social type of room in which furniture and textures of a finer, lighter scale are used well. Fabrics, too, have scale. Under the topic of "Harmony in Textures" fabrics were grouped in three classes: coarse materials, which suggest large scale; fine textures, which suggest small scale; and third, an intermediate group, which may be used with either of the first two groups as well as with objects of an intermediate scale. Fabrics show scale in pattern as well as texture. Large figures are suitable for large pieces of furniture to be used in large rooms, and small patterns are consistent with small pieces of furniture for use in small or average rooms.

Scale in dress can be used to make one look larger or smaller as *Scale in dress* well as to give the impression of a delightful consistency between a costume and its wearer. Violation of scale in dress results in unrelated effects and often culminates in the ridiculous. For example, who has not seen the tall, stout woman who makes herself look larger by wearing a very small hat with a dainty flower or tiny feather for its trimming note; or whose dresses are trimmed with a few very small buttons or narrow lines of contrasting color, and who invariably carries a diminutive handbag? Of course there is danger that, on being shown her error, this woman might select patterns and accessories that are too large and thus increase her appearance of size by the opposite extreme. Similarly, the small woman should avoid large designs because they would be "out of scale" with her size and would make her look smaller.

Chapter Five

BALANCE

"Everybody who comes in here wants to re-arrange the furniture," was the complaint of an irritated attendant in a demonstration room. The reason was only too apparent. With too many of the heavy pieces of furniture at one end of the room, the room seemed to tip, and the visitors had an unconscious impulse to correct the fault. Balance in design is so natural that one is not even aware of it when it is present, but when it is violated there is a sense of discomfort or annoyance.

Stated briefly, *Balance is rest or repose.* This restful effect is obtained by grouping shapes and colors around a center in such a way that there are equal attractions on each side of that center.

The youngest schoolboy can balance objects if he is told that balance works on the same principle as the seesaw. Equal weights will balance when they are the same distance from the center. If unequal, the heavier weight must be moved toward the center and the lighter weight away from it before balance is obtained. (See figures 87A, B, and C.) Balance in art can be explained quite as simply as balance in weights. The only difference is that it is not so much a question of how much the object weighs as of how much attention it attracts. If one boy wore a brown sweater and another wore red, in balancing them against a background one would follow the same principle as for balancing unequal weights, and would place the boy in red nearer the center of the wall, while the less conspicuous boy would be moved farther away. The brighter the red sweater the nearer it would have to come toward the center line, and the duller the brown sweater the farther off it should go.

FORMAL AND INFORMAL BALANCE

It has been seen that the center of the space under consideration is the point around which all attractions must be adjusted. If objects are alike or are equally forceful in appearance, they will attract the same amount of attention, and therefore should be equidistant

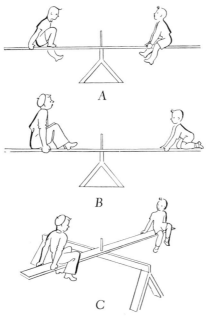

Figure 87A, B, and C. The principle of the seesaw applied to balance in art.

A, identical weights or equal attractions balance each other at the same distance from the center. This kind of balance in art is called formal balance and may be bisymmetrical or obvious in type. B, unequal weights or attractions balance each other at different distances from the center. The greater attraction must be placed toward the center and the weaker one farther away. If one object is half as big or half as attractive as the other it will be placed twice as far from the center. This is called informal, asymmetric, or occult balance. C. Another method of balancing large objects with smaller objects, besides the one shown in B, where both are placed upon the same horizontal line, is illustrated in C. Here the large object comes toward the foreground, and is balanced by placing the smaller one in the background. In other words, it gives the effect of being seen in perspective. This method of balancing is used especially in pictorial composition, in designing store windows, and in arranging stage settings.

Figure 88. Formal balance. "Music" by Pinturicchio.
When a painter desires a stately, dignified effect in his picture he is apt to use formal balance, or the principle of figure 87A, where equal attractions appear on each side of the center. (Courtesy of Anderson, Rome.)

from the center. (See figures 103 and 104.) This kind of balance is known as *formal balance*. Formal balance is called *bisymmetrical balance* when the objects on each side of the center are identical, and *obvious balance* when the objects are not alike but are equal in their power of attraction. Formal balance is quiet, dignified, and gives a sense of precision.

Figure 89. Informal balance. "Southern France," by Derain, 1880–
Here is a subtle balance of large and small masses which are unequal in
their power to attract the attention. The larger tree and vertical dark trees
behind it at the right, were placed close to the center of the composition and
balanced by the smaller light tree much farther from the center as in figure
87B. Notice how the eye is satisfied and the sense of balance is completed
by the introduction of the church steeple in the distance, placed as the small
boy is in figure 87C. (Courtesy of the Phillips Memorial Gallery)

If, however, objects do not attract the same amount of attention,
they must be placed at different distances from the center (figure
105). This second type of balance is called *informal*, or *occult*, or
asymmetric balance. Informal balance is more subtle than formal
balance and affords greater opportunity for variety in arrangements.
Its success depends upon training the eye to recognize a restful
composition.

Pinturicchio's "Music" (figure 88) is an illustration of a formal
arrangement in which the figures on either side of the center line

Balance in pic-
torial com-
position

Figure 90. This bisymmetric design adapted by the Persians from the pomegranate is dignified and formal.

Figure 91. (Stencil by Maxine Downie Nelson.) In contrast to the design above, this bisymmetrically designed hanging for a child's room expresses a spirit of play.

are so nearly alike that they attract the same amount of attention. The lights and darks are in practically the same relative positions, and the figures have been balanced so skillfully that, even though both sides are not identical, one has the impression of symmetry.

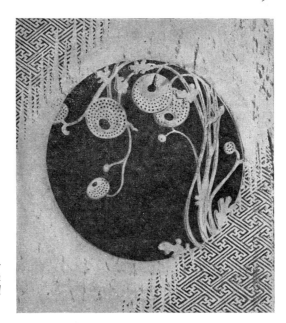

Figure 92. An old Jap-
anese stencil, showing a
delightful use of informal
or occult balance.

In Derain's landscape "Southern France" (figure 89), there is a
delicate adjustment of forces that differ greatly. Through the sensitive placement of each form we receive a distinct impression of
balance of the informal type. If we care to analyze the manner in
which the picture is composed, we see that the larger light tree at
the right, with the group of dark trees behind it, is balanced comfortably by the small tree placed farther from the center line. The
steeple of the church off in the distance takes its place in the balancing of the picture just as the small boy takes his position for balance
out on the long end of the board in figure 87C.

Many of the early periods produced formal expressions in their
art, and numerous examples of bisymmetric balance are found in
their designs. The pomegranate design which is shown in figure 90
is attributed to the Persians, and this motif has been adapted to
formal design in many periods. Because of its stateliness it was often
used in the rich fabrics that upholstered the chairs of the Renaissance. Much of the impressiveness of this design is due to symmetry.
However, bisymmetrically balanced designs are not always stately.

*Formal and in-
formal balance
in decorative
design*

The gaily colored stencil in figure 91 was made for a hanging in a child's room and shows a playful mood.

The characteristic designs of the classical period are formal, whereas the art of Japan is informal. Japanese artists understood the art of occult balance, and they acquired such expertness that their painting, prints, and stencils are remarkable for their subtlety and spontaneity. One of their typical designs is seen in the stencil pattern in figure 92. Here is a perfect adjustment of unequal spots on either side of the center line. The exquisite grace of the lines combined with the subtle balance of forms stimulate the imagination of anyone who looks at it. The embroidery in figure 93 shows a ship, bird, and flower design that is characteristic of the islands of Greece. The distribution of the motifs gives this design a mobile quality which is typical of occult balance.

Figure 93. An informally balanced design seems especially suited to this entertaining embroidery from one of the islands of Greece. Here the birds are longer than the width of a sail and flower stalks are as tall as masts.

Figure 94. Palazzo Sagredo, Venice.
A suggestion of the romantic character of the life of the Venetians is expressed in the informally balanced design of this Gothic palace. The openings in this building have been placed with such a sensitive feeling for equilibrium that one has the impression that nothing could be removed from the design without disturbing its balance.

Just as the painter arranges his composition on canvas, so the *Balance in* architect has to balance doors and windows, porches and dormers *exterior design* around the central axis of a building. Whether he uses formal or informal balance depends largely upon the following conditions:

1. *The spirit of the age in which he lives*
2. *The use to which the building is to be put*
3. *The type of people for whom the building is planned*
4. *His own personality.*

In glancing back over history, one sees that in the periods that were filled with a spirit of romance, everything done was expressive of that spirit. In the golden days of Venice, the bright fantasy of

Figure 95. Palazzo Bartolini, Florence.
  Bisymmetric balance seems particularly appropriate as a setting for the social and political life of the Florentines during the Renaissance period. (Courtesy of University Prints.)

the times was echoed in the graceful, occult designs of many of the
Venetian palaces (figure 94). In Florence, art found a very different

Figure 96. (Reinhard M. Bischoff, Architect. Photograph by Gustav Anderson.) The use of bisymmetric balance has established a keynote of reserve. The design has gained distinction through its simplicity and its beautiful proportions. (Courtesy of House Beautiful.)

expression; the seriousness of the Florentines in the early Renaissance period, so vividly reflected in the work of Michelangelo, is seen in their stately, unadorned, bisymmetric palaces—the natural outcome of their lives and thoughts (figure 95). In the same way the spirit of Puritanism led to restrained, formal designs in the buildings erected in the American Colonial times; in their large public buildings and in their small dwellings as well, the Colonists put their own personalities into their work.

Two houses are shown here to illustrate how formal and informal balance appear in a building. In comparing them, notice their

Figure 97. *This house is balanced informally. The dark doorway is placed near the center, and the light gables grouped with it form a mass which is balanced at the left by the windows, the dormer, and the light chimney, each placed at varied distances from the center.*

difference in spirit as well as the means by which the effect was secured. If a line were drawn through the center of the house in figure 96, it would be found that everything on one side is repeated on the other side, and so this house is bisymmetrical, or formally balanced. The house in figure 97 is informally balanced, and the architect obtained a feeling of restfulness by carrying out the principle illustrated by the large and small boys on the seesaw. In figure 97 the dark doorway is near the center of the house, and the mass formed by the dark door and the light gables is balanced by adjusting the windows, the dormer, and the light chimney at different distances from the center.

Balance in advertising
       In the advertisements in papers and magazines, the principle of equal and unequal weights as related to balance is all-important. Except that here one is working with cuts or drawings, blocks of type, and white margins, the procedure does not differ much from any other art problem involving balance. Figure 98 shows the method employed in making layouts for advertisements. The weight

Figure 98. An artist's layout for an advertisement. The sketch shows the manner in which the objects to be illustrated and the copy are studied as masses to be balanced around a center.

of the illustrations and the weight of the type are carefully adjusted, and the amount of margin left is an additional factor to be considered in the balancing of the whole layout. Whether formal or informal balance is used may depend upon the mood suggested by the material being advertised, or if specific cuts are to be included rather than drawings which can be any size or weight, the cuts may determine the manner of their placement. When a layout is balanced, it will give the impression that it would remain in a horizontal position if it were suspended from the center by an imaginary string.

In the two sketches for cards in figures 99A and B, the severity of formal balance has been chosen for the school supply advertise-

LOMBARD

DETROIT ∘∘° MICHIGAN

PERFUMES

Figure 99A and B. In advertising materials that are distinctly practical, the exactness of formal balance seems appropriate, while the freedom of occult balance is well suited to objects that suggest delicacy.

Figure 100. Formal balance. A window that impels and holds your interest. The small articles are grouped into identical patterns at each end of the composition and placed bisymmetrically. The circles of soap and the bubbles in the center panel are less rigidly arranged, following the obvious type of formal balance. (Bloomingdale's. Photograph by Worsinger.)

Figure 101. Informal balance. Placing the masks and large card near the center draws attention to the accessories grouped with them and gives the accented motif for this window display. The larger group is balanced by the smaller articles placed farther out. (J. and J. Slater. Photograph by Virginia Roehl, Inc.)

ment, while the grace and subtlety inherent in informal balance seemed better suited to the idea of perfumes.

The attention value of a display is one of its major considerations from the point of view of the store, and skillful balance is one of the vital elements in those windows which hold the eye. The problem of the display man differs from that of the advertiser in that the third dimension—depth—is an important factor. A window resembles a stage much more than it does a poster or an advertisement. Two diagrams are shown in the chapter on Emphasis that suggest a very easy way to secure a balanced window when objects or groups of objects of unequal sizes or attractions are to be used (figures 155 and 156 on pages 167 and 168). This method would be useful whether one is arranging floor plans or elevations. The in-

Balance in store display

formally balanced window in figure 101 resembles the diagram in figure 155, for the rectangular floor plan of the window contains a display that creates a similar triangular floor plan within the rectangle. In making informally balanced arrangements, one would place the principal feature of the display near the center of the window and would then balance smaller objects around the main center in much the same manner as seen in the diagram or described in Derain's landscape in figure 89. Informally balanced groups often seem more varied than formally balanced arrangements, and they may hold the interest a little longer because they are not quite so quickly grasped and passed over by the mind.

In the window in figure 100, the two kinds of formal balance are clearly seen. Bisymmetric balance is carried throughout the window except in the central panel of the background where obvious balance is employed, for the large circle is on the center line and the other forms are distributed so that equal weights are placed on each side of the line. In balancing objects one will make some interesting discoveries. For example, it will be found that an empty space is often more emphatic than a full one, just as a sudden silence in the midst of a long loud piece of music seems even more striking than the music. A large space left around an object will lend it so much more emphasis that it will be as important an attraction as a much larger one. By moving the articles forward and back, and to the right and left, one will soon discover just how much empty space a small unit needs between it and a larger one in order to secure balance. An object that is very striking or peculiar in shape or color will have the same power of attraction as a larger one that is simple and inconspicuous; two such objects then would balance each other at equal distances from the center, even though there is a great difference in their appearance. Until a worker has trained his eye so that balance becomes instinctive, he should remember always to judge the whole display rather than to concentrate his attention on any of its parts.

Balance in interior design

In placing the furnishings of a room, the architectural openings must be taken into consideration. Very often balance is secured by having a large piece of furniture on one wall of a room as a balance to an opening on an opposite wall. The large pieces of furniture should be placed first, with regard to balancing centers of interest in the room. The smaller movable objects would then be arranged so that they will make convenient groups as well as balanced units. After the furniture has been arranged the attention is turned to the balance within each group. A well-balanced wall will have the same amount of attraction on both sides of its center line. A well-balanced room will have approximately the same amount of attraction on opposite walls and, although the two side walls may be somewhat heavier than the end walls, there should be the feeling that the attractions are about equally distributed around the room.

Figure 102 illustrates a balanced arrangement of furnishings in a living room. From any position the eye rests upon a balanced composition, yet the adjustment of the forms and the light and

Figure 102. (Richard J. Neutra, Architect.) There is a sense of repose in this room. While the effect seems unstudied, actually the furnishings have been placed with a careful regard to balance.

Figure 103. (Photograph by Mattie Edwards Hewitt.) The quaint details in the decorative objects suggested the precision of a formal grouping. (Courtesy of the Architect's Small House Service Bureau.)

dark masses seems so natural that the method used in balancing the room is not at once apparent.

Anyone interested in the meaning of designs will find that the kind of balance used in the arrangement of furniture and decorative objects helps to give an individual quality to a group. It also influences the character of the room. Bisymmetrical arrangements convey a feeling of formality, but it can be formality with the simplicity and charm of colonial days, as in figure 103. However, if formal balance is carried to an extreme it may result in effects that are cold or stereotyped.

An arrangement which illustrates the second type of formal

Figure 104. Obvious balance. A symmetrical arrangement which illustrates the second type of formal balance. The two mirrors were placed at the same distance from the center as the grouped lamp, boxes, and figure, because they attract the eye with equal force. This type of balance combines something of the regularity of bisymmetric balance with the variety of the occult.

balance—obvious balance—is shown in figure 104. This is a symmetrical arrangement in which the balancing masses are not alike, yet they have the same amount of force. The large mirror and small hand mirror attracted the same amount of attention as the two small boxes and Chinese figure grouped with the lamp, and so the masses were placed at equal distances from the center. This type of balance gives to a room an effect halfway between the precision of bisymmetrical balance and the variety of the occult.

There is more intimacy in informal arrangements than in formal, and a sort of chatty, conversational quality is likely to characterize a room where informal balance prevails. If one compares the informal arrangements of figure 105 with the bisymmetrical one in figure 103, he will notice that the effects are essentially different. There are freedom and variation in the uneven groupings, and while the other arrangement is quaint, it is more reserved.

It is not necessary that all the parts of a room should agree in

Figure 105. When objects as different from each other as these are to be
used in a group, they naturally call for the informal type of balance.

being either formal or informal in arrangement. For example, one
might use a formal arrangement on the desk, an informal grouping
on the bookcase, and a combination of formal and informal balance
on the fireplace, as is seen in figure 106. This type of balance makes
an impression which lies between the formal and the informal.
There is more variety than if the same objects were repeated

throughout, yet a certain dignity comes from the repetition of some of the objects.

In working for a balanced room, one should continually test both halves to see that one half does not present much greater attraction to the eye than the other. In arranging the room the four walls, with everything seen against them, must balance. If one

Figure 106. A combination of formal and informal balance gives to an arrangement a feeling of stability with variety.

side seems too heavy, it is necessary to add a brighter color, a more striking shape, or simply more material to the weaker side, and to keep adjusting the attractions until the whole room looks restful.

Objects seen in an upright position have a tendency to appear to be dropping in space. It is therefore agreeable to the eye to have the center of attraction come slightly above the mechanical center of the object. Thus it will be seen that a figure appears to be balanced even though the weight is somewhat greater in the upper half of the body. When this effect is exaggerated, however, the figure appears unstable. There are times when one must look carefully in order to avoid violation of balance in an ensemble. The fashions of some seasons make a woman look as if she would topple over from the sheer weight of her hat and furs. The woman of taste avoids exaggeration in dress, and so she finds herself choosing the more conservative fashions which will not make her look gro-

Balance in dress

Figure 107. Costume of the French Revolution. A distinctive design based on formal balance gives a smartly tailored appearance to an ensemble.

tesque. In her choice of hats she should consider not only the balance in the hat itself (in order to select one that will look as if it would stay firmly on her head) but also the balance of the hat with her height, the width of her hips and shoulders, and the length and width of her skirt. Many women try on hats when seated and are able only to judge the effect on the face and shoulders; as a result they are frequently surprised when they see the entire figure reflected in a mirror.

Whether the dress and hat shall show formal or informal balance is a matter of personal preference, for they may be equally attractive. Formal balance is likely to suggest a trim and tailored effect especially suited to clothes for business, street, and school wear. When introduced into an afternoon or evening dress, it gives an air of reserve (figure 107). The informal balance may show more subtlety and variety; it suggests grace, and is particularly suited to soft ma-

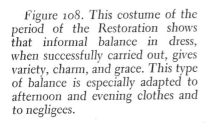

Figure 108. This costume of the period of the Restoration shows that informal balance in dress, when successfully carried out, gives variety, charm, and grace. This type of balance is especially adapted to afternoon and evening clothes and to negligees.

terials (figure 108). If a striking band or other decorative note is to be used only on one side of a dress, it should not be placed too far from the center line. If it is placed far out at the boundary of the figure, the dress will appear unbalanced, unless something is placed on the other side to balance it.

(Note. Balance in color is discussed in the chapter on Color, pages 197 to 199).

Chapter Six

RHYTHM

Ask any group of persons what rhythm means to them and classify their answers. It will be interesting to see how much agreement will be found in the fundamental idea expressed, even though the individuals will have widely differing definitions. To one, the first thought of rhythm may suggest something that is graceful or sinuous. To another, the first reaction would lead toward a feeling of something that is spontaneous, energetic, or primitive. The action of a dance, the whorl of a shell, the recurring patterns on the water where a pebble has been dropped, a sonorous poem, a lilting song, the beat of martial music, a primitive negro mask—all of these varied patterns have in common the quality of movement organized in the direction of beauty.

Definition of rhythm

While rhythm may be defined as a form of movement, it must be recognized that not all movement in design is rhythmic. Sometimes movement is distracting. In art, rhythm means an easy, connected path along which the eye may travel in any arrangement of lines, forms, or colors. *Rhythm, then, is related movement.* In a perfectly plain space there is no movement; there is simply a resting place, and the eye remains quiet at any point where it happens to fall. The moment that pattern is placed upon that plain space, or an object is placed against it, the eye will begin to travel along lines suggested by the object or the pattern, and at that moment movement is created. This movement may be organized and easy, and thus rhythmic; or it may be very restless, distracting, and lacking in rhythm.

Figure 109. The shell of a paper-nautilus. The pattern of this shell makes one aware of the rhythms found in nature.

There are three outstanding methods of obtaining rhythmic movement:

How to gain rhythm

1. Through the repetition of shapes
2. Through a progression of sizes
3. Through an easily connected, or a continuous line movement.

RHYTHM THROUGH REPETITION

The principle of rhythm as it is gained through *repetition* is recognized when one is conscious of the swing of the beautifully spaced, regularly repeated columns of the Parthenon, which may in a way be likened to the strokes of a perfectly trained crew of oarsmen. When a shape is regularly repeated at proper intervals, a movement is created which carries the eye from one unit to the next in such a way that one is not conscious of separate units, but of a rhythmic advancement making it easy for the eye to pass along the entire length of the space. The greatest enjoyment of rhythmic

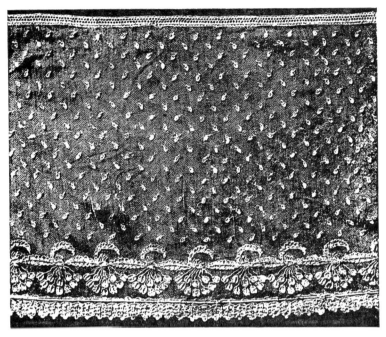

Figure 110. The lace designs in figures 110, 111, and 114 show the various ways in which rhythm may be gained. This is an example of rhythm achieved through the repetition of the motifs in the border.

sequence is to be found in nature forms. The shell of the paper-nautilus pictured in figure 109 shows the beauty that can be gained when repetition is carried along in such rhythmic measures. Our enjoyment of this shell is spontaneous, and at first it does not occur to us to analyze it; but if we do, we find that it is the subtle variation in the spacing which causes us to welcome the repetition of the shapes. In addition, the sequences in the contour of the shell give its form a progressive movement that delights the eye. In the lace design in figure 110, there is a rhythm which seems almost to have melody. The regularity in the repetition of the leaves forming the edge of the lace sets off the more varied repetition of the upper units. In securing rhythm through repetition, one must be careful to avoid monotony in spacing, for good proportion is a necessary accompaniment to repetition if beauty is to result. Moreover, when intervals are too far apart the movement will lack rhythm.

There are any number of practical applications of this principle of rhythmic repetition. Combined with good spacing it makes for pleasing effects when one is, for example, stitching rows of braid or tucks on a dress; placing groups of buttons; repeating dots, squares, or any shape of spot in embroidery; or putting out rows of objects in a store display. It is interesting to remember that repeating a shape a number of times gives an effect of repose; and sometimes a shape which, alone, is difficult to use as a single unit in design, will be successful when it is repeated at close intervals. This was illustrated in Chapter III when triangles and diamond shapes, which are unrelated to most forms, were used successfully in borders where they were placed close together. A rhythmic effect is achieved in a costume when a suggestion of the tucks or braid on the skirt is repeated in the waist or a note of color is carried from one part of an ensemble to another.

RHYTHM THROUGH A PROGRESSION OF SIZES

The second way of obtaining rhythm is through a progression of sizes. The lace pattern in figure 111 shows how the eye is carried along an easy route by this method. While a regular progression of sizes may be satisfying enough for scallops on lace and embroidery,

Figure 111. The design in this lace illustrates rhythm gained through a progression of sizes.

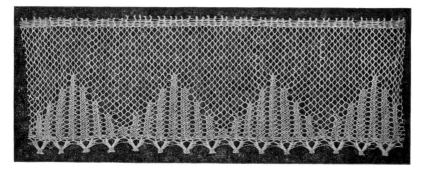

Figure 112. Japanese Print, by Toyokuni, 1769–1825.
A masterly use of rhythmic arrangements in line and color and light and
dark masses is found in some of the old Japanese prints. Observe how the
eye can enter this picture at any point and travel with ease over the entire
composition.

one enjoys a more varied progression when large objects are involved. Progressing sizes create a rapid movement of the eye, and
they are often badly used. An example of this misuse is seen in the
arrangement of pictures or other objects against a wall in a series
of steps that carry the eye up toward the ceiling, and hence away
from the part of the room around which one would like to have
the interest centered. While a series of steps is undesirable because

Figure 113. (Photograph by Wilbur M. Nelson, A.R.P.S.) In the world of nature there are many small objects which we pass over with never an appreciative glance at the beauty contained within them. A striking example of this is found in the rhythmic sequences revealed in this enlargement of the whorl of a shell.

it leads the eye to the wrong place in the room, a group of objects in which there is no variation in height may be monotonous. In order to avoid both extremes, one should use a series of varied heights such as are shown in the objects on the mantel in figure 123. If a low box had been substituted for the picture as the central object in this group, the progression would have been too abrupt.

RHYTHM THROUGH A CONTINUOUS LINE MOVEMENT

Compositions that show rhythm through continued line are likely to be made up very largely of curves. While all of the forms of rhythmic movement were seen in the natural pattern of the shell of the paper-nautilus, the rhythm to be found in the continued

Figure 114. The eye is led easily along this design by the continuous line movement.

Figure 115. The lines of this pattern go in such discordant directions that the design lacks rhythm, and the eye becomes fatigued in the attempt to follow them.

Figure 116. The three types of rhythmic movement are seen here. There is rhythm through the continuous line in the center of the bottom border, and repetition in the row of dots above this line, while the wavelike lines in the open space above show rhythm through progression.

movement of a line is plainly shown in figure 113. This enlargement of the spiral of a shell brings out the beauty in the sequence of its line movement and in the rhythmical gradations of its spaces. One finds many fine examples of this type of rhythm in Greek sculpture and in Japanese prints. Just such an impression of continuous line is illustrated in the print in figure 112. There is a swinging movement throughout the entire picture, and no matter where the eye enters, it is carried along by the suggestion of an easy, flowing arrangement of the lines, lights and darks, and colors, so that the gaze travels over the whole picture without the least sensation of hindrance. The rhythm in this composition is so striking that it produces much the same sensation as does a graceful dance.

The same type of rhythm seen in the Japanese print characterizes the pattern of the lace in figure 114. Here the free swing of the wide, undulating line is echoed and reëchoed in the other parts of the design. Compare the rhythm of this pattern with the lace shown in figure 115. In this case every line seems to be defying every other line, resulting in just as marked a lack of rhythm as there would be if two dancers were out of step with each other, and out of time with the music. If lines similar to these were repeated over a large area, as on a wall, they would create a very restless atmosphere in the entire room.

Frequently one finds an arrangement in which all three kinds of rhythmic movement are used. This is very apt to be the case in large schemes, such as room arrangements, but designs for lace and embroidery and other handicrafts sometimes show this combination. Figure 116 is an illustration of the variety to be secured through using the simplest elements—the dot and the line—and combining them in these three ways. Upon looking at the band at the lower edge we find that the rise and fall of the line through the center creates rhythm by means of the continuous line; above that the dot is repeated rhythmically. Note that the spaces between the dots have an interesting proportion when compared with size of the dots. There is rhythm through progression of sizes in the wave-like line running through the wider open band of the lace, and it is interesting to see how this swift motion has been related to the

Figure 117. A rhythmic effect in this gable-root style of architecture is achieved when the pitch of the roof lines of the body of the house, the gables, and the dormers are based upon angles of about the same degree.

borders and given more of the appearance of a band by the repetition of the small flowerlike unit in each open space.

Rhythm in exterior design   The principle of rhythmic line movement comes into frequent use in the design of a house. Perhaps it can be recognized more easily if one starts from a point where there is no apparent movement. In the outline of a square house the horizontal and vertical lines are of equal force, and so they balance each other. Compare with a square house a house made up of ells and gables. It is easily seen that there is a great deal of movement in the lines of this type of house, and if it is to be pleasing to the eye, the movement should be rhythmic. This irregular, rhythmic type of house design was very popular in England during the Tudor period, and many of our Colonial houses show a similar form of rhythm in the gabled roofs and the angles of the dormers. In figure 117, one is aware of rhythm in the lines of this modern adaptation of an English house. When many gables are used, the architect is careful to have the angles of these gables, their placing, and the variation of their sizes similar

Figure 118. Compare this orderly rhythmic arrangement of the doors and windows on the side of this house with the unrelated movement seen in figure 119.

Figure 119. Note the un-rhythmic placing of the windows on the side of this house.

enough so that the eye will feel an easy relationship as it is led from one to the other.

Perhaps the one place in house design where lack of rhythm is most frequently seen is in the arrangement of door and windows on the side of the house. In working out a house plan, one usually begins with the arrangement of the rooms and then places the doors and windows in order to secure the best light and air and wall space for the furniture. Unfortunately these openings do not always look well in relation to each other after the house is built. A glance at figure 119 will show the result of not having thought through the problem of door and window arrangement to the point of foreseeing how they would look in the finished house. It is not difficult to balance doors and windows symmetrically as in the typical Colonial house. In this style the stairway usually comes in the center of the house, the windows of each floor come on the same straight line, and no unusual line movement is created. But the problem becomes more complicated when there is a side stairway which needs light, a basement door on the level of the street, and windows to be placed in the first, second, and even the third floors. In figure 118 these openings have been so adjusted that there is a sense of order in the arrangement, while in figure 119 one recognizes that they have been considered only from the point of view of the interior plan. The result in the latter is the formation of an unrhythmical diagonal line which is unrelated to the lines of the house.

Rhythm in   Passing from the exterior of the house to the interior, one must
interior design determine how much movement will be enjoyed in the design of a house over a long period of time, and where rhythmic patterns and arrangements will be most pleasing.

It should be remembered that movement involves degree as well as kind, and in order to attain rhythm without producing uneasy, wasteful movement it is desirable at times to have complete absence of movement, such as is found in plain surfaces in wall paper and carpets. It is very easy to imagine a wall paper or rug pattern with a bold, swinging, rhythmic line which may be very agreeable when seen in a small piece, but, repeated over so large an area as the whole wall or floor, it will show too much action and will detract from the objects in the room. In other words, the coverings of walls, and floors as well, should either be plain or have a very quiet design in order to create the effect of their being backgrounds for the many furnishings which will be placed against them. One can enjoy more emphatic rhythmic movement in small areas, such as curtain materials, or in pictures, than in wall papers and rugs.

Wall coverings   The ideal background against which pictures and other objects are to be placed is one that has a suggestion of texture, but not too

A

Figure 120A. Diagonal lines in wall paper have nothing in common with the lines of a room, and when they are as conspicuous as these, they create too much distracting movement to make a good background.

Figure 120B. The movement in a diagonal pattern becomes less noticeable as the contrast between the lights and darks decreases. This paper would take its proper place as a background.

Figure 120C. The type of diagonal line design that makes the quietest background is one in which the repeat is small and the pattern shows very little contrast in its light and dark values.

B

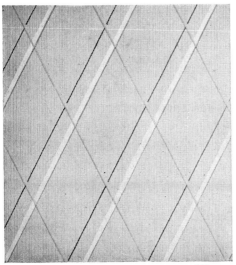

C

119

definite line movement. For this reason, stippling and sand-finished plaster make excellent walls. Next to these in desirability is paper with a pattern that shows just a vibration of light and dark and pattern, but not too noticeable a movement.

Such conspicuous diagonal lines as are seen in figure 120A make the poorest kind of background, because they create very rapid action in opposite directions. When there is as little contrast between the lights and darks of the pattern and the background as there is in the paper shown in figure 120B, the diagonal movement is very much less noticeable. Such a paper would make a background against which one could enjoy the people and the objects in the room. The third paper, figure 120C, has a very conservative diagonal pattern. Here the cream-colored lines are so nearly like the yellow background, and the diamond shapes are so small that the pattern becomes very unobtrusive. This type of paper makes an attractive wall in a room where one wishes to have merely a suggestion of pattern. In striped paper the lines are closely related to the structural lines of the room, and if the lights and darks of the stripes show an easy transition from one to the other there will be an agreeable amount of movement not inconsistent for a background. As the contrast between the lights and darks in the stripes increases, it will be found that the movement will quicken correspondingly, and the paper will become less desirable for use as a background.

Floor coverings   If one wishes to have the floors form a quiet base for the room, the same good judgment should be used in the selection of the designs for the floor coverings as for the walls. A comparison of the two rugs in figures 121A and B will demonstrate that the eye travels along lines suggested by a design. Where these lines are conspicuously diagonal, contradicting the structural lines of the room and contrasting with the background in their light and dark values, they become very annoying (figure 121B). On the other hand, where the lines of the design are more transitional and the values are similar, the resulting movement is agreeable (figure 121A). As with the wall covering, the most useful carpet designs are those which show merely a vibration of pattern and color.

When the amount of desirable movement for walls and carpets

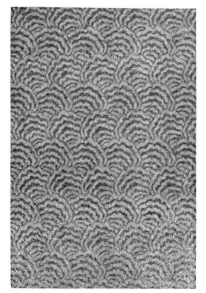

Figure 121A. This is a good type of figured rug because the design is flat in effect, it covers the surface compactly, and there is little contrast in light and dark.

Figure 121B. When crossing diagonal lines are repeated over a large surface the pattern is apt to become very distracting. These designs are especially confusing for wall and floor coverings if there is a strong contrast of light and dark.

has been decided, one is ready to think of the design of the furnishings. The first requirement of a good design is that it be suitable for its purpose, and this must be considered before the type of design is selected. In a room with quiet walls the figured pattern of a drapery material may display a greater degree of movement than would be pleasant for walls and rugs. Here the area is comparatively small, and the material hangs in folds, breaking up the definiteness of the movement of the design.

When a person selects furniture he prefers to have it suggest stability rather than movement, and so he chooses either straight lines or restrained curves. Too much straight line will result in monotony, and this becomes more noticeable if many straight line pieces are used together. The period of Mission furniture showed how tire-

Furniture design

Figure 122. This eighteenth-century chair, designed by Thomas Chippendale, illustrates beautiful rhythmic lines and spaces. (Courtesy of the Metropolitan Museum of Art.)

some the straight line may become when it is unrelieved by curves. Curved lines give movement, but if they are exaggerated, or are used in too many pieces of furniture, the room will look restless. The ideal design for furniture is one in which there is enough of the straight line to give dignity and stability, and enough of the rhythmic curve to relieve the severity of the design. (See figure 2, following page 2.)

The chair in figure 122, designed by Thomas Chippendale, is a beautiful example of rhythm gained through repetition as seen in the ladder back, and of the rhythm attained through the rhythmic progression in the sizes of the carved motifs in the cross pieces. This

Figure 123. The fireplace in this room has been made more important by the way in which the furniture has been arranged. Note that the lines of the furniture lead the eye easily to this center of interest. There is an agreeable variety in the progression of the sizes of the objects on the mantel and a pleasant proportion in the spaces between the objects.

chair has refinement and grace of line, combined with beauty of proportions.

When one has learned to recognize rhythm, he will discover that its use in arranging the furnishings in a room goes far toward conveying an impression of livableness. On the other hand, there is a scattered, unsociable effect in a room where the furnishings are placed without regard to line movement. One of the fundamental principles in the arrangement of furniture is that it be grouped according to its use. A knowledge of shape harmony will lead one to place the main lines of each group so that they will conform to the lines of the room, but one needs to know how to control the movement of the eye if the effect is to be perfectly successful. The furniture and decorative objects should be so arranged in the room as to carry the eye toward the centers of interest where it should remain at rest for a while. Any point in the room that is considered interesting or important may easily be emphasized by the arrangement of

Furniture arrangement

Figure 124A. The movement of the lines in the portraits keeps the eye within the group and unifies the arrangement.

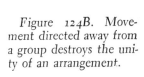

Figure 124B. Movement directed away from a group destroys the unity of an arrangement.

the furnishings. If there is a fireplace, the strongest movement made
by the lines of the furnishings may direct the eye to it. This is illustrated in the living room in figure 123, where the comfortable furniture has been grouped around the fireplace for the sake of sociability,
and the lines of each piece carry the gaze directly to the point the
family regarded as of greatest interest. If a view from a group of windows is enjoyed, the eye may be led there. Or if a bookcase is the
most attractive spot in the room, the leading lines may be so placed
that the eye will go there first of all. In a well-balanced room there
will be a center of interest on each wall. If these are cleverly planned,
there will be some line or color in each unit to lead the eye from
that wall to the next, connecting them and unifying the room.

It is not enough to use the rhythmic movement gained through
grouping the large pieces of furniture; each separate object in the
room should be examined for its line movement before it is placed.
It would be interesting and profitable for decorators and advertisers
to watch the audiences attending a series of talks in a certain lecture
room. In this room two portraits hang just above the speaker's desk.
A profile portrait of Washington at the left faces out to the left, and
a profile portrait of Lincoln at the right faces toward the right. This
creates a movement on both sides of the desk which carries the gaze
away from the speaker. Even the ablest lecturer is handicapped in
that room, and an average speaker finds it very difficult to hold the
attention of his audience because the unrhythmic movement caused
by the placing of the pictures carries the eye away from the speaker
so forcefully as soon to become a positive annoyance to anyone sensitive to line. Reversing the positions of the portraits would actually
help a speaker to retain the attention of his audience. A glance at
figures 124A and B emphasizes this point. The window is the focal
point on this wall, and it is clear that the arrangement of the pictures
in A is correct because their lines carry the eye toward, rather than
away from, the center of interest. Since most objects as well as pictures direct the eye in some definite direction, it is well to know how
to make the best use of this movement.

Rhythmic line movement does much to make a woman's costume
beautiful. Curved lines have more relationship to the human figure

Arrangement of pictures to gain rhythm

Rhythmic movement in dress

Figure 125A and B. In the Victorian costume (A) the exaggerated design is erratic. The angular lines at the neck, the point on the tunic, and the horizontal direction of the band below it create directions that make the costume tiresome and confusing. In the costume of the Empire period (B) the movement is entirely consistent and related.

than angles, and for that reason a series of subtle curves is more pleasing than a series of angles in dress (figure 125B). Knowledge of the effect of line movement in giving the appearance of altering proportions will make the designer select either a dominant horizontal or a vertical movement for the person who is to wear the costume. If the curved line has been chosen for the waist, as in a yoke or jacket, the lines of the skirt will be simple—either a slight suggestion of curve, or a straight line. When the neckline shows angles, the tunic is pointed, and the skirt has a horizontal band, there is bound to be lack of rhythm (figure 125A). Periodically the course of the mode brings such fashions as the erratic one seen in this Victorian dress. But it must be noted that even in a fashion which produced so many overloaded costumes, there were some that had a certain quaintness and charm. At such times an appreciation of the elements of beauty makes it possible for a woman to enjoy the stimulation of the new mode and yet express it in the most attractive way to be found in the current fashion.

Just as furniture may be arranged to lead toward the important centers in a room, so may a dress be planned to make the most of the wearer's good points. It is possible for a costume to have lines that will carry the eye directly toward any feature the designer may wish to emphasize, and away from anything to which it is not desired to call attention. Lines leading rhythmically to the face may be secured by the use of bands of trimming near the face or by the outline of collars and necklaces. All these seem to form a frame that holds the eye near the face and centers the attention there.

Figure 126. In the window below, the central group attracts the eye, and attention is kept within the display by the use of rhythmic patterns of dark and light forms throughout the arrangement.

A   B

Figure 127. A, the position of the component parts of the advertisement at the left carries the attention gradually but steadily toward the company's name. B, somebody else is getting the benefit of the stationery advertisement because the line of the envelopes leads the eye to the advertisement below.

Rhythm in store displays and advertising

Of all the people who are working out arrangements, the window designer and the advertiser have the greatest responsibility for knowing how to control the movements of the eyes. A designer whose display carries the eye away from something important is actually wasting his firm's money. In every display there are major and minor attractions as well as rather unimportant objects used merely to fill in. In some displays there is such lack of organization that the eye is not led to any particular point and utter confusion results. If the designer had known how to handle line, these objects could have been so placed as to lead the attention to the major attractions, and yet every separate entity could have been seen more easily.

It has been shown that when a group of lines or objects is placed against a background, the gaze has a tendency to move along them. If the eye finds an easy and connected path to travel, the arrangement is said to be rhythmic, and this is the most effective as well as the most economical kind of movement (figure 126). On the other hand, if a group suggests a jerky, restless, or disconnected movement, it lacks rhythm, and such arrangements do not hold the attention.

The application of this principle of rhythm to advertising is very obvious. A glance at figure 127A will show the efficiency that results from the ability to control line movement as compared with the unsuccessful use of line in figure 127B, where the position of the envelopes directs the attention to the advertisement below. These examples show that lines and colors should be so arranged that the eye will go more or less rapidly to the point where attention should be focussed. They also show that it is possible to use rapid movement very effectively if it is understood and controlled.

RADIATION

A brief discussion of radiation is included in this chapter since it, as well as rhythm, is a method of obtaining organized movement. Radiation is the type of movement that grows out of a central point or axis. It may be observed in the diverging lines which form the pattern of snow crystals and some leaves. Radiation is used very commonly in designs for store displays and by the person who makes designs for embroidery, since it is the plan for many geometric patterns. Three illustrations of radiation are given in figures 128, 129, and 109. In the rose window the straight lines lead abruptly toward and away from the center; therefore the designer found it necessary to restrain this rapid action by means of a heavy band around the outside of these radiating lines. In the brass dish, the curved lines of the motif in the center lead the eye around its circumference as well as toward

Figure 128. S. Chiara, Assisi.
Radiation is apparent in the plan of this rose window. Here the straight radiating lines are held in, and the effect of the circle is strengthened by the decorated borders and the band around the edge.

Figure 129. Brass dish, Italian, XV Century. The embossed design in the center of this dish shows the kind of movement known as "radiation." Note that the curves of these radiating lines help to unify the design. (Courtesy of the Minneapolis Institute of Arts.)

the center, and this movement helps to suggest the circle. Because the structure of the circle is inferred by the design itself, these lines do not have to be held in so securely at the outside boundary as when the radiating lines are straight. The lines of the shell of the paper-nautilus in figure 109 show both rhythm and radiation. Here the radiating lines bear a close resemblance to the lines of the brass dish in figure 129. The design in the center of the dish is an example of radiation and repetition, whereas the shell has lines and spaces of varied measures and so combines radiation and rhythmic progression or sequence. A fourth illustration of radiation is seen in the lines of the muntins in the fanlight transom over the door in figure 37.

Chapter Seven

EMPHASIS

THOUGH AN arrangement may be well balanced, its proportions good, and its contents in perfect harmony, it may still be dull and uninteresting. In spite of its merits, the eye will pass over it because there is no particular point to arrest the attention. In other words, the arrangement lacks emphasis, and lacking it, fails to attract—fails to give any active sense of enjoyment.

Emphasis is the art principle by which the eye is carried first to the most important thing in any arrangement, and from that point to every other detail in the order of its importance. Whenever any object is selected or arranged with reference to its appearance, this principle of emphasis is used, and the success of the result depends upon a knowledge of:

1. What *to emphasize*
2. How *to emphasize*
3. How much *to emphasize*
4. Where to place *emphasis.*

Simplicity the most important factor in emphasis

Although it may seem paradoxical, the answer to the question of "How much emphasis shall I use?" is "Keep it simple." Next to appropriateness for its purpose, the best quality of any object is simplicity. Without exception, the standards for judging utilitarian objects are:

1. *Suitability to purpose,*
2. *Simplicity, and*
3. *Beauty.*

When one turns to historic art for standards of beauty and simplicity, two periods in the history of art are foremost. These two are the best periods of Greek and of Japanese art. Simplicity is really the keynote of these two great schools, and if only one can capture that spirit of reserve—of simplicity—he will possess the most important single factor in art. (See figures 62, 112, and 136.) The way to achieve simplicity is to understand emphasis and subordination; in other words, to know how to subordinate the less important details in an arrangement so that they may become supplementary or supporting accents rather than competing centers of interest. In many rooms and any number of costumes, this quality of reserve has been successfully accomplished, but, unfortunately, we see too many practical art problems worked out with distracting results. There is the woman who wears patterned shoes, a plaid skirt, a figured blouse, and a much-trimmed hat; and everyone has seen the room with figured wall paper freely hung with pictures, carpeted with conspicuously patterned rugs, and still further confused with figured furniture covers, crowded shelves, and bric-a-brac. Why are these combinations bad? Because people have not been content to choose an outstanding feature or features in the room or the costume and subordinate the others, but have put equal emphasis upon all, with resulting chaos.

WHAT TO EMPHASIZE

In order that there may be an impression of clarity in any arrangement, whether it is in a room, a house design, a picture, or a costume, the designer would find it helpful to form a rather definite plan. In making the plan, he would classify his material and arrange it according to what he considered the most important and what the least. In each field of decoration the most important features may vary, but the one that should have the least emphasis is likely to be the same: it is the background against which objects are to be seen. From this observation we may draw one of the most important concepts in art: Backgrounds should be less conspicuous than the objects to be seen against them.

Subordination and standards for backgrounds

HOW TO EMPHASIZE

There are several means by which one may create emphasis, or attract attention, and the most important of these are:

1. *By the placing or grouping of objects*
2. *By the use of contrasts of color*
3. *By using decoration*
4. *By having sufficient plain background space around objects*
5. *By contrasting or unusual lines, shapes, or sizes.*

Sometimes all five of these methods may be combined in one single design, as in a design for a building, a room, or a very large store window. Usually, however, one, two, or three of these means will give all the force needed.

Grouping or placing of objects

Grant Wood's "Midnight Ride of Paul Revere" (figure 130) illustrates emphasis gained through grouping. The feeling of the dramatic moment in the little Colonial town has been captured by the artist and interpreted in a manner that suggests the designs of primitive Italian paintings. In this composition the ideas have, in a way, been summarized in order to convey the impression the painter wished to give. The principal group is unmistakable—the church, the clustered houses, and the rider; then the subordinate centers, each with its own little group—the people and the house at the right; the closely packed trees in the background—all take their place so as to make the picture seem a unit. It is interesting to see how, in spite of the many details, there is no sense of confusion. It is because these details are relevant and are put into their proper place in an organized design that the painting has gained its unity.

Amateur photographers can find unexpected beauty in some of their pictures if they know how to make use of emphasis (figures 131A and B). The discriminating eye of the photographer who made the quick snapshot of a passing train saw possibilities in his negative that an unthinking person might not recognize. To the casual glance, A is just an ordinary photograph divided into two parts. Your eye is carried rather uncomfortably from the light posts at the right to the water on the left, and then back again to the posts. It is plain to see the beauty resulting from the removal of the conflicting center of interest. An illustration of a well-planned center of interest in another field occurs in the living room in figure 123.

Since the eye is quickly attracted by strong contrasts of light and dark, or by contrasting color, one of the most striking means of calling attention to any object is to place it against a background with which it contrasts. Rembrandt obtained a dramatic quality in his "Presentation in the Temple" by the way in which he distinguished his main center of interest with strong lights and subdued the rest

Emphasis through contrasts of color

Figure 130. Midnight Ride of Paul Revere, by Grant Wood.
The inventive organization of the details into a decorative pattern has given this painting unusual interest. A large number of units can be used successfully in one arrangement if they are grouped so as to form clearly defined centers of interest with adequate space around each group. (Courtesy of the artist.)

Figure 131A and B. (Photograph by Harland P. Nasvik.) Composing a photograph is much like painting a picture. B, an unstudied snapshot of a passing train, has two centers of equal importance and so the composition seems divided. That it contained so fine a picture as A should interest the amateur photographer, for it shows what a knowledge of design can mean to the person who wishes to make good pictures.

Figure 131B.

Figure 132. Presentation in the Temple, by Rembrandt, 1607–1669.
A picture in which the attention is directed to the main center of interest and
held there because of the strong contrast of light and dark.

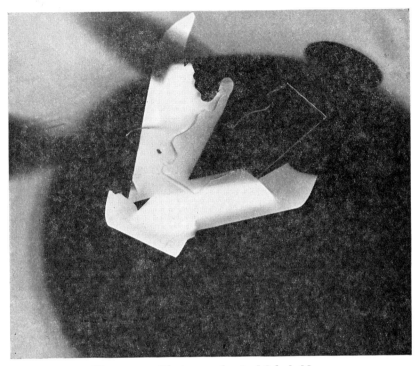

Figure 133. Photogram by L. Moholy-Nagy.

An abstract photograph made without a camera by placing the objects on
sensitized paper and exposing it to light. This study in contrasts of form and
texture in gradations of white, gray, and black illustrates the possibilities for
creative work in the new field of "painting with light," in which this artist
was a master.

of the picture by suffusing it with gradually deepening shadows
(figure 132). It is interesting to note how this master of the use of
lights and darks prevented the harshness likely to occur with extreme
value contrasts by balancing the large areas of strong light with small
notes of light placed in other parts of the picture. The modern artist
L. Moholy-Nagy was a master of the abstract art of "painting with
light" (figure 133). This abstract photograph does not depend
upon any recognizable subject matter for its interest and beauty. It
is to be enjoyed for the drama of its gradations from white toward

black, for the element of the unusual in its form, and for the manipulation of light and shadow to produce beautiful and subtle pattern. The bits of glass, with their edges picking up and holding back the light, introduce a sensitive study in transparencies. A valuable lesson may be gained by a careful study of these pictures; if striking contrasts of light and dark are to be used in any decorative scheme of a considerable size, they should be tied together. This can be done by combining with them a large amount of intermediate values somewhere between these two extremes. The arrangement that shows equal amounts of light and dark would be as confusing as two equal centers of interest in a picture. The final effect of a good composition should be that of a dark scheme accented with lights, or of a light scheme made interesting through its dark notes.

Nothing could be more desirable than to have all decoration as *Emphasis* well used as that found on the Parthenon. This building sets a *gained through* remarkably high standard in the use of decoration as a means of *the use of* gaining emphasis. Besides showing how the eye is attracted to pattern, it goes further and proves how complete satisfaction may arise from an economical use of the right kind of emphasis. The chapter on Structural and Decorative Design outlined the need for a fine form or structure in any object before decoration is even considered. When a satisfactory form is obtained, the worker may decorate it in such a way that the beauty of the structure will be enhanced. There is perhaps no better example of the subordination of decoration to structure than in the carvings on the frieze of the Parthenon. Here the structure suggested the place for the sculpture, and, although the beauty of the building is not dependent upon the carvings, interest is added by their introduction.

Occasionally one finds a highly decorated object made for no other purpose than to please the eye. If it is truly beautiful, it has reason to exist, and one frequently brings an object of this sort into decorative arrangements in order to lend a certain note of emphasis, either through its color or its pattern. Jewelry is an illustration of this type of emphasis in dress. A pendant, for example, may be rich in jewels and intricate in pattern. The choice of the proper gown on which to wear the pendant then becomes the art problem, for the pendant will be thought of as the center of interest on the dress, and will bear the same relationship to the dress that the carvings on the frieze bear to the Parthenon. The Chinese vase shown in figure 16 is an example of a similar note of emphasis in a room. It is to be enjoyed for its own beauty and not to be used as a container for flowers.

Decoration in surface patterns

In order to judge a good surface pattern, one must first consider the way it is to be used. A surface pattern that is good for a background has two main characteristics. First, the design covers the surface rather closely, and second, there is very little contrast between the lights and darks. One is constantly confronted with table linens, dress fabrics, wall papers, rugs, and upholstery materials that have surface pattern. Unless choices are made with a complete understanding of how much emphasis may be secured through pattern, one is apt to make unwise selections and discover that the material that seemed attractive in the shop looks too conspicuous made into a dress or seen in the room. The two things, then, of greatest importance in selecting surface patterns for backgrounds are value contrast and the amount of plain space around each figure. The two previous topics showed, first, that if objects are packed together closely, they attract less attention than when widely separated; and second, if there is a strong contrast between lights and darks, an object is much more conspicuous than when the values are very similar. If these two considerations are kept in mind, one will not go far wrong in choosing a surface pattern to serve as a background; if the design is flat, covers the surface well, and is close in value, it will be quiet in effect. (See figures 121A, 196, and 224.)

Emphasis through plain space around objects

As one learns the value of using plain spaces, there comes a corresponding change in the choice and arrangement of objects. Certain schemes begin to produce a peace of mind when one sees them—a most welcome contrast to the feeling of confusion and unrest caused by crowded arrangements. Psychological experiments show that an individual has the capacity to enjoy only a limited number of things at one time, and that when this amount has been exceeded he actually sees less rather than more. Botticelli's beautiful "Allegory" (figure 134) may be made to illustrate two important things about the principle of emphasis. First, an object gains importance when it is

Figure 134. Giovanna Tornabuoni with Venus and the Graces, by Botticelli, 1446–1510
Botticelli has called particular attention to the lovely Giovanna Tornabuoni by the large amount of plain space which he has left around her. This use of plain background is the most effective way to call attention to the fine quali- ties an object possesses. (Courtesy of the University Prints, Boston.)

separated from the things around it and is given enough plain space for a background. (See also figure 299, page 446.) Second, when ob- jects are placed close together they are seen as a group and not as in- dividual units. (See also figure 265, page 403.)

There is no question as to what Botticelli intended for the main center of interest in this picture, for the figure of the Florentine lady, darker than the background and set off by plain space, attracts the attention immediately, while Venus and the three Graces have been grouped to form a secondary center of interest. This use of plain spaces is one of the most important considerations in emphasis, because plain backgrounds bring out the quality of every object seen against them. (See figure 251, page 387.)

Emphasis
gained by
means of con-
trasts or un-
usual lines and
colors

"The Rice Granary" by the Mexican painter Miguel Covarrubias
is an illustration of the use of an unusual line to focus the attention
(figure 135). The introduction of the arch of the rice granary creates
a contrasting form among these vertical figures and trees, and the
eye is held by the unexpectedness of the shapes which thus arise.

In order to discover how much force there is in anything unusual,
glance quickly at a shop window or a table full of new books in their
paper jackets and see what first attracts the attention. After noting
the order in which these things catch the eye, look again to see what
features the objects possessed to make them outstanding. This may
be illustrated by a description of a table on which there were about
twenty books in paper jackets. The table was not large, and the
whole group could be seen at a single glance. In the assortment, the
jackets varied from light to dark, from gay to dull, and each had a
different design. The first book to attract the attention had a check-
erboard pattern of dark blue and white, with each check about five-
eighths of an inch square. The second book to be noticed was a
brilliant orange, and the third had an unusual head against a plain
background. The other covers were much more nearly equal in their
appeal, though some of them were so quiet in their effect, with their
orderly arrangement of printed matter and conservative color, that
they seemed willing to wait for the consideration due them. What
made the three books stand out beyond their neighbors? The first
had a very striking and unusual contrast of light and dark, the second
a conspicuous color, and the third an unusual pattern set off by plain
space. Thus one realizes that anything unusual in line, shape, color,
or size becomes emphatic.

This type of emphasis is applied in underlining words in a letter
or capitalizing them in print. Newspaper headlines show the power
of emphasis through unexpected sizes. In any design, this force may
be gained through a change in size or shape, or by an unusual line or
color. Unless the designer is constantly aware of the power of the
unusual, the attention of his audience may wander or actually be
directed to some purely irrelevant detail, and thus the significance
of the design as a whole may be lost completely.

Figure 135. Rice Granary by Miguel Covarrubias.

Covarrubias centered the emphasis on the two Balinese girls
by the use of the arched roof, which brought an unusual direction into a composition made up so largely of vertical lines.
(Courtesy of The Art Digest.)

Figure 136. Door of the North porch, Erechtheum, Athens. The doorway of the Erechtheum shows perfection in its emphasis. This doorway has not been excelled for the beauty of its spacing and the quality of its decoration. (Courtesy of the University Prints.)

HOW MUCH TO EMPHASIZE

In order that one may get a general as well as a comparative idea of how much emphasis is desirable in the different fields of applied design, various problems will be discussed in each of these fields. Because the suitable amount of emphasis varies with every problem, emphasis may be regarded as a graded scale, and the greatest amount of force that can be used with good taste for each of these types will come at a different point on this imaginary scale. Surfaces to be considered as backgrounds against which other objects must be seen should register emphasis at a point near zero in the scale. The person who seeks distinction in his work will usually stop short of the full amount of possible emphasis and try to create instead an impression of having held something in reserve. The two doorways seen in fig-

Figure 137. (Reinhard and Hofmeister, Architects. Samuel H. Gottscho, Photographer.) Greater restraint and more forceful emphasis would be difficult to achieve. (Courtesy of The Architectural Forum.)

ures 136 and 137 have been chosen to illustrate this impression of restraint. The design of the Erechtheum is one of the most perfect examples of emphasis known. In this doorway there are no irrelevant details, and only enough emphasis is used in the design to befit the dignity of the entrance to a temple. Observe that the greatest amount of carving is placed upon the head of the doorway, and the beautifully spaced rosettes carry the emphasis down, making the frame of the door subordinate to the head. With all its simplicity and reserve of decoration there is no suggestion of barrenness in the design, for its beautiful proportions, the rhythmic repetition of all its parts, and the subtle variety in the light and shadow created by the moldings are characteristics of a masterpiece. The doorway in figure 137 illustrates purely functional design. Here there is no decoration as the term is commonly understood, but merely a monogrammatic device—the identification of the building. This doorway is decorative and impressive because of the beautiful restraint. We repeat that the best general answer to the question "How much emphasis will it be well to use?" is "Keep it simple."

The materials of which a house is built should influence the amount of emphasis used in its design. If more than one kind of material is to be used, care should be taken to keep one of these dominant. One should see at a glance that a house is brick with some stone, or stucco with brick or wood. In the chapter on Proportion, figures 71 and 72 show that equal amounts of two or three materials divide the interest and make a house appear disorganized. If one material prevails and the other is used merely for emphasis, unity results. The different types of building material supply varying amounts of emphasis, and, just as the interior designer plans where to use plain surfaces and where to employ pattern, the architect considers the possibilities of stucco, wood, and brick and finds that some materials supply all the emphasis needed in an exterior, while some are so plain that color and pattern may be introduced for emphasis. When stones or bricks are joined by lines of mortar a pattern is formed, more or less emphatic depending upon the contrast between the building material and the mortar. The most successful houses are those in which there is no striking difference between the color of the mortar and the brick or stone, and in which the architectural design is kept simple, in order that the texture and the color of the walls may supply the emphasis. Walls of shingles or clapboards have less pattern than most masonry walls and, if they are stained or painted white or a quiet color, make pleasing wall surfaces. If stucco is used to finish the walls of a house, its color and texture should be carefully selected. The most desirable texture for the average house is one that is neither so rough that it will appear too emphatic for the size of the house, nor so smooth that it will be glaring. Since walls are backgrounds they should be simple, and all exaggerated treatments, such as conspicuous marks of the trowel, or the spattering of a contrasting color, detract from the appearance of a house. A moderate amount of vibration of color and of light and shadow resulting from some slight irregularities in the texture of natural materials can give a pleasing surface to an exterior wall.

Natural earth colors make attractive walls, and the warmer, lighter colors, such as the earthy yellows, are often more pleasing than the cold grays. This is especially true in areas where the weather gets very cold or there are many gray days in the year. Colors seem less bright on a sunny day. That is probably why the somewhat brighter colors are used more successfully on houses in southern climates than in the north. The advantage of using a light grayed color for a house is that it makes a good background for colored trim and for the planting for which it forms a background. In designing a house, one should consider the patterns which the shadows of the projections will form against the walls, for they are important elements in design. The broad expanse of a practically plain surface makes it possible to enjoy thoroughly the shadows of trees in summer and the pattern of the branches in winter.

An example of misplaced emphasis in a building is seen when roofs are conspicuously spotted with shingles of different colors or strong contrasts of light and dark. Figures 71 and 84 are reminders of this disturbing practice. The house illustrated in figure 19 shows another type of over-emphasis. This house combines a poor structural design with five conspicuous window treatments and a band of spotty brick work at the base of the house, all of them competing with one another for attention. A comparison of the two houses in figures 18 and 19 shows that there should be rest spaces in the design of an exterior, for when the walls are all broken up by windows and trim there is an effect of confusion due to over-emphasis. Another poor window plan that has been made even more obvious with the use of white paint is seen in figure 80. *When the openings and the details of a house are not beautiful, and particularly when they are not well proportioned, they should be painted the same color as the body of the house.* If it is desired to have them another color, they should be practically the same value (degree of lightness or darkness) as the house itself. Never pick out shapes on the walls of a house with a contrasting value unless those shapes are beautiful;

and even then be sure that there are not so many of these openings that they will create too much emphasis. Some well-painted wood trim is shown in figures 18, page 17; 97, page 96; and 335.

Emphasis in planting   There is the same need for simplicity in the design of the planting around the house as applies to the design of the house itself. The effect should be simple even though many trees, shrubs, and flowers are desired. Simplicity and a feeling of organization can be secured by grouping the plants at structural points; specifically, around the base of the house and out at the boundaries of the yard. (See figure 225.) Well-planted grounds, whether large or small, need plenty of clear, open spaces. Plants or bushes and flower beds scattered about over the lawn create confusion in a yard and make a poor setting for the house, which should, after all, be the center of interest.

Emphasis in interior design   Nowhere are the effects of overemphasis so trying as in the home. In rooms in which people remain over long periods of time, a subtle type of decoration can be appreciated, whereas a more dramatic decorative scheme is suited to rooms in which one spends but a short time. In the tea room or game room a dramatic scheme is enjoyable, but not many would care to spend their lives in an atmosphere so stimulating. The amount of emphasis suitable for interiors cannot be stated definitely. It must vary with the room and with the people who live in it. The proportion of emphasis to rest space in a room should be approximately the Greek proportion of two parts to three—that is, two parts of attraction in pattern or color and three parts of quiet space. This does not mean that with two pieces of figured upholstery fabric, one of which has a quiet surface pattern of two tones and the other a striking design in strong color, we should use two parts of either one against three parts of plain background. It means that a very much smaller amount of the striking pattern should be used as compared to the simpler pattern, because as a whole there should be two parts of attraction, not of pattern.

Distribution of emphasis in a room   With the approximate amount of plain and pattern space in mind, the designer will decide where and how to make the distribution. There are so many different possibilities in this matter of distribution, as to eliminate all danger of houses becoming stereotyped.

Suppose, for example, that one decides to take three parts of plain space in walls and rug. That leaves the possibility of selecting figured draperies and furniture covers, pictures, and decorative objects, so adjusted in their various attractions that the sum of them all will be less than the restfulness of the background. If the walls and the rug have pattern, it would be essential to choose draperies and furniture covering whose interest lies in good color and texture instead of figure. The additional pattern would be limited to use in such areas as the decorative details might supply. The first plan of plain walls and floor is chosen more frequently for living rooms, because it affords an opportunity to make more individual choices in the smaller things. Figure 138 shows that figured paper makes a poor background if one wishes to enjoy the objects placed against it. How many people would notice the pair of seven-branched candlesticks on either side of the vase? The candlesticks have no chance for attention against this striking background; even people would be eclipsed in this room. If such a paper were used, it would take great skill indeed to get enough plain space into a room to keep the Greek proportion of two parts of emphasis to three parts of rest space. Compare this arrangement with that of figure 139, where the emphasis is used to produce greater enjoyment. This is a room in which there is a pleasant distribution of plain and figured surfaces. The most definite pattern here is found in the slip-covered chairs, the curtains, and the decorative objects. Against the plain walls one sees easily the subtle details of the objects that are used above the fireplace and on the shelves of the open cupboards. Flowers, too, can be fully enjoyed in a setting of this kind. Since it is well to limit the amount of pattern in a room, one should decide where it will be enjoyed most and then subordinate the other objects in the room so that the pattern may be appreciated. Although ordinarily one thinks of using figured materials to secure variety in room furnishing, the same interest can be obtained by using plain fabrics. If plain fabrics differing in color and texture are skillfully arranged in fairly large areas, they create the impression of pattern. In such rooms there should be a blending and contrast of colors so that the pattern formed may be effective and individual. (Figure 232A.)

Figure 138. Confusion results from the use of a background that is as striking as the objects placed against it. The candlesticks on each side of the vase
have almost lost their identity because of the overpowering pattern of the
background. The vase can be seen as it is a large solid mass, darker than the
general effect of the background, but its design cannot be fully appreciated
because the designs around it are so emphatic.

It is desirable to have one principal center of interest in every
room, but each wall should have its own focal point so that the
room may be agreeable to look at from any position. For the sake
of comfort to the eye these points should be balanced across the
axes of the room.

As in the exterior of a house, the rooms should have just enough
rest space to give an effect of reserve, and enough emphasis, used
adequately yet sparingly, to show imagination and individuality.

To see how a view has been made the center of interest in a
house, turn to figures 140A and B. These photographs show how a
splendid view of meadow, trees, and water have been made a dramatic center of interest from all across the front of the house. Although the house is completely opened toward the view on this
side, the back of the house, which faces the street, has small windows for privacy. Compare this plan with one in which large win-

Figure 139. (Architect, Clyde Smith. Decorator, Levoy Studios.) Emphasis is gained by using a background less conspicuous than the objects shown against it. Notice how the shape as well as the detail of each object can be fully appreciated against a plain background.

dows open toward the street, exposing the living areas to passers-by. In order to achieve any degree of privacy in such a plan, it is necessary to keep the windows covered with curtains or blinds. This defeats the reason for choosing large areas of glass. When it is desirable to place an expanse of window facing the street, it is possible to achieve a degree of privacy by using a band of windows above the eye level of the person on the street instead of using glass from floor to ceiling. In figure 140A the overhang is wide enough to control the amount of sun that enters the house and to form a roof over the terrace. From within, a free-standing fireplace becomes a secondary focal point for the entire living area as well as for the master bedroom, which is slightly above and behind the living room, and can be opened by a wide sliding door. Notice that the narrow wood strips of the ceiling have been so laid that the eye will be led directly toward the outdoors, and so the house and the land-

Figure 140A and B. (Architects, Charles Eames and Eero Saarinen. Photographs by Julius Shulman.) Views become important centers of interest when a house is planned so that the outdoors is an integral part of the interior. It will be noted that these "view windows" do not expose the rooms and their occupants to the passer-by on the street.

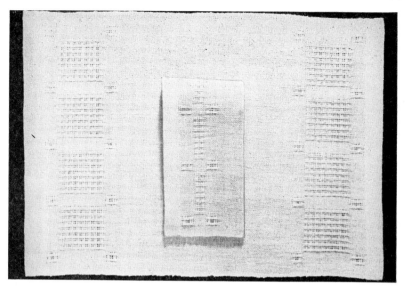

Figure 141. (Woven by Ruth Ross.) This place mat has sufficient reserve in its design to make it a suitable background for dishes and silver.

scape are really one. Here is an instance of a center that never loses its interest.

We have applied this principle of emphasis to the largest objects and to the smallest; to the walls and to the vases; to the furniture and to the things to be used with it. Where in this scheme should the linens be placed? Are they background, or are they decoration? If a background is something against which other things are seen, then they belong to the background, for when linen covers are used on a chest of drawers or a table, they have objects placed upon them. Because there is a certain amount of interest in the texture of some household linens, such as in damask napkins and tablecloths, they are usually finished with just a narrow hand-sewed hem, and the interest is attracted to the texture and the pattern of the fabric. Sometimes a decorative design is desired for a runner or a doily or place mat as an additional note of interest. Such designs are shown in the place mats in figures 141 and 165.

So much time and work are spent in the preparation of meals

Emphasis in table setting

Figure 142A.

Figure 142A, B, and C. Serving food attractively is an art. When simply garnished and pleasingly arranged on the plate it becomes more appetizing. In A the emphasis is on the food. Adequate space has been left around the edge of the plate, the dishes are simple, and the linen is plain. B, a figured cloth in colors that look well with the food makes a table gay and informal. Here the china is plain enough to separate the well-arranged food from the emphatic background. (Stainless steel in A, courtesy of Van Keppel–Green.)

Figure 142B.

154

Figure 142C.

C, a table set with over-garnished food, placed upon decorated dishes and patterned place mats, gives an impression of confusion.

that they should be presented with all the beauty at the home-maker's command. There is something stimulating about the simplest meal if it makes an appeal to the eye. Food should be served so that it looks natural, but some foods are lacking in sufficient contrast to make them appear appetizing and require the addition of some color interest. A mistaken idea of beauty makes people over-decorate food or use too much garnish. The standard for good service is to place enough food on a plate or platter so that it appears adequate, but never too full. The rim of the plate should be clear, or nearly clear, as in figure 142A. B shows the maximum amount of food that would be attractive; and the tomato extending over the rim of the platter is merely the garnish to be considered as pattern against the plain colored border. It is easy to picture the appearance of the entire table on which each of these plates is placed. In A the plain table cover and the simply designed plate focus the interest on the centerpiece and the food. While the tomato aspic and broccoli supplied color contrast, the serving became more attractive when a little parsley gave emphasis to the shrimp and a dark olive to the cheese. In B the plaid tablecloth suggests an informal supper. The brown and dark green of the stuffed peppers are accented by the slices of tomato and hard-cooked egg and the yellow of the melted cheese on top of each pepper. Dishes with only a plain colored border and plain napkins of a color appearing in the tablecloth would help to keep this table from having too much emphasis. In C this one service shows the effect of overemphasis, and we can imagine the confused appearance of the entire table. The dark wood showing under the place mat has started the confusion. The decoration on the dishes adds another note of emphasis further built up by the pattern made by the toasted coconut shreds on the cake.

Emphasis in dress design   In dress the idea of background is just as important as it is in any other problem where taste is involved. Here the wearer is the chief center of interest, and the clothes are the background. For that reason the amount of emphasis that can be used in dress depends, first of all, upon personality, and, second, upon the occasion for which the clothes are chosen. Some people are so striking, so brilliant or dramatic, that they are able to appear to advantage against a great deal more emphasis in their dress than the average person. Regardless of personal qualities, however, the law of harmony—suitability to occasion—sets certain standards which are observed by people of taste. To meet these standards, street and business clothes, though smart and individual, should be quiet in effect; sports clothes may be as striking as one's personality will permit; the amount of emphasis in evening dress for women will be governed by the personality, the income, and the occasion. Clothes which must be seen day after day by the same group of persons should be less conspicuous than those which are to be seen occasionally. Stout people should avoid suit or dress fabrics of very pronounced designs, and should not use striking colors or contrasts of light and dark in large areas.

In the ideal plan for an ensemble, the face will be the chief center of interest (figure 143). The most successful design is one which, through the choice and arrangement of colors and lines, leads the eye to the face. Man's dress follows this principle, for his collar and tie center the attention upon the face. The average man is conservative and does not often use conflicting centers of interest, such as

Figure 143. Costume of the period of Louis Philippe. This charming costume from the past summarizes the essentials for emphasis in dress. It is simple. Attention is directed to the face by the hat, the collar, and the line of buttons. The scallops on the skirt form a secondary center of interest, and the cuffs give a minor accent.

occur when white or very light shoes are worn with dark clothes, making the feet the center of interest. That particular mistake is made much more frequently by women, and one often sees all the emphasis centered upon an expanse of unusually light hosiery with no repetition of the light value in other parts of the ensemble. In view of the fact that attention is attracted and centers of interest are created by the use of any of the five means stated under "How to Emphasize," it is well to consider what one wishes to emphasize and proceed accordingly. For example, the woman who has a graceful walk and attractive feet might have decoration placed at the bottom of her skirt when fashion suggests the use of decoration there, or if her hands are her best feature she may employ a note of emphasis at the cuff.

While the ideal costume is the one that centers interest chiefly at the face, many other arrangements are very successful. The important note of emphasis may occur at the waistline and an echo of it be brought up around the neck for a secondary center; or there may be a decorative band at the bottom of the skirt and a repeating note around the face, while the rest of the dress is kept simple. Again, the sleeves may be chosen as the individual note, with minor

Figure 144. Lucrezia Panciatchi, by Bronzino, 1502(?)–1572.
A beautiful sixteenth century costume that shows the main center of interest around the face, with subordinated centers at the belt and wrists. (Courtesy of Anderson, Rome.)

centers at other places on the dress. Scattered forces of equal emphasis give an unpleasant "hit or miss" effect. The important thing is to choose one place for the main center of interest and keep the rest of the costume subordinated to that. Above all, make sure that the garment has the distinction that results from the right amount of emphasis for the individual, placed where it will bring out her best features.

The sixteenth century costume in figure 144 shows how a dress may help to enhance the beauty of the wearer. The contrast of the light yoke has centered the interest near the face so that one is more conscious of the wearer because of the dress. When a costume is a background to this extent, it has fulfilled one of the most important requirements of good dress design. The belt makes a second and subordinate center of interest in this costume, and the lace at the wrists, giving a transition from the dark sleeves to the light flesh tone, brings a third and even less striking point of emphasis. The jewelry this aristocratic young woman is wearing is simple for the period in which she lived, but today only one of the two necklaces would be used. Jewelry should be worn sparingly, and then only when it helps to complete a costume. This means that jewelry should be judged for its fitness to the particular costume rather than for its intrinsic value. When patterned beads, necklaces, or brooches are worn against figured or embroidered materials the same effect is produced as when the candlesticks in figure 138 are seen against the figured background. To quote the words of a lecturer on interior design, "Do not forget that a spot on a spot makes a blur."

In a word, success in dress design depends largely upon restraint. Simplicity should be the aim, with enough emphasis to give the design individuality and distinction. Nothing in the way of emphasis should be added to a dress unless it is clearly needed to complete and beautify it.

In planning store displays the window decorator has three groups of people to attract: *Emphasis in store displays*

1. *The people across the street*
2. *Those who are passing in front of the window*
3. *Those who have stopped to examine the display.*

For the first class there must be one simple forceful effect to attract attention and make the pedestrian wish to cross the street and see the rest of the display; that effect would correspond to the chief center of interest as stated in the definition of emphasis. Those who are passing will be attracted by this one big note and also by the items of secondary importance. For those who stop there must be some interesting details. All of this emphasis must, of course, be carefully directed to the end that the interest aroused will lead more or less directly to a desire to purchase the merchandise.

The four window displays in figures 145 to 148 show how emphasis may be secured in the store window. Figure 145 illustrates the attention value of contrast in light and dark as well as of grouped forms having a main center of interest and subordinated

Figure 145. The timeliness of this display and the simplicity with which it is carried out make this a good holiday window. The white tree forms a motif around which the dolls are grouped to create a main center of interest. Subordinate centers are established, and the dolls are seen in an organized pattern against a contrasting background. (Courtesy of the Dayton Company.)

Figure 146. When the eye encounters many objects of equal importance it does not see any of them clearly. There is a loss of power in this window because the objects are scattered, and there is no main center of interest.

Figure 147. (Photographed by "Dick Whittington.") Effective lighting has selling power. The shafts of light in this window center the attention on the mannequins and the mermaid. The groups of small details, introduced to carry out the theme of the window, are carefully subordinated to the merchandise. (Courtesy of Bullock's Westwood.)

centers. Compare this effective window with figure 146 where there is no organization in the arrangement and no center of interest. It is plain that the appeal of the merchandise in the crowded window has been lost. Although not many more dolls are shown in this window, the display has lost its force because they are not grouped.

The value of light used for emphasis is seen in figure 147. More and more, people are coming to recognize the vast potentialities of light as a medium for store display. Not only are colors enhanced by the correct choice of lights, but the plastic quality of light is being used to create illusions of pattern and volume. According to the wish of the display man, forms can be strengthened or flattened; and parts of the display, by the proper use of lights and shadows, can either be made dramatic or be blotted out. The display illustrated here is made up of a number of small objects which would, in spite of the skillful grouping for a chief center with subordinate centers,

Figure 148. (Photograph by "Dick Whittington.") The figured materials in this window arrest the attention because they are shown against a plain background. Even as much pattern as is seen in the stone wall in figure 147 would give a confused effect here. (Courtesy of Bullock's Westwood.)

have been much less compelling without the use of the directed light. Here, in a different field from that pictured in the photogram in figure 133, we see a way of "painting with light."

In the window display in figure 148, a plain background was used to emphasize the patterned fabrics. Unless these materials were separated by plain spaces, it would not be an effective way to advertise. There is interest value in the fabrics along with the original designs that inspired the patterns, and all are dramatized by the use of a quiet background.

Emphasis in advertising

In any type of advertising, as in store display, there is the same need to arouse the desire to possess a product. Two important facts must be recognized by the advertiser no matter what the field in which he may be working. First, very few people deliberately start out to read his advertisement; and second, he has only a limited time in which to tell his story.

The amount of time allowed to him varies with the type of advertising he is doing; for example, the billboard must be positive enough to convey its message almost instantly to the people who rush past in street cars and automobiles. While the billboard and the car-card need a dramatic note, the newspaper advertisement may be much quieter, for it has more time in which to make its appeal. Nevertheless, any advertisement must have a certain amount of emphasis in order to arouse interest. Too mild a statement will pass unnoticed, and even the quiet message must therefore have something positive about it. When there is competition for attention, that positive note must become more compelling. (But even here overemphasis is as serious as underemphasis.) The dramatic use of the contrast obtained by unusual or unexpected lines and colors is an aid to the advertiser who wishes his product to stand out from those of his competitors as shown in figure 149.

To such an extent has business sought the aid of the ablest artists *Packaging* for industrial design, that good design is now coming to be expected in all industrial products. The packages in figure 150 are not isolated examples. Just one small shelf at the corner grocer's furnished these and many more examples of such forthright designing. These few illustrations demonstrate the qualities that should be inherent in

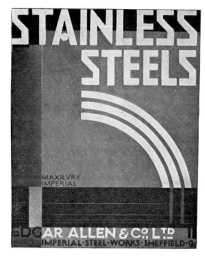

Figure 149. (Design by Leonard Beaumont.) Three silver arcs against a deep blue ground lead the eye forcefully from the product to the firm's name on this design for the cover of a brochure. (Courtesy of Art and Industry and Edgar Allen and Company, Ltd.)

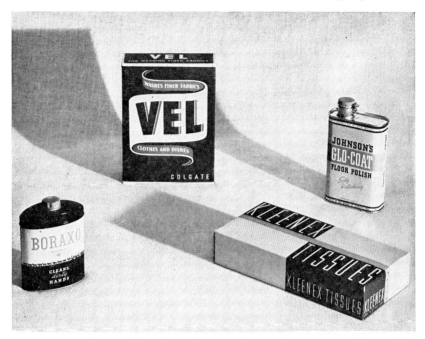

Figure 150. Successful package designs rely greatly upon an understanding of emphasis: contrast in color, preferably in light and dark; clearness of design and lettering; an unusual treatment of an idea; and, above all, simplicity.

any advertising. They are good advertising, and by the same token, good emphasis, because the designs are planned for their suitability to the product they contain, in the striking contrast of their color, in the amount of plain space that sets off the name of the product, and by the simplicity and directness with which their story is told.

WHERE TO EMPHASIZE

Centers of interest

    The diagrams in figures 151 to 156 will be found useful in determining where to place attractions. In order that each person may adapt this plan to his own field, the drawings are kept abstract and spots are used, so that they may be thought of as representing any object with which one may be working.

    If an object on a horizontal plane is to be seen from all sides, it

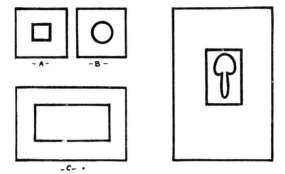

Figure 151A, B, and C. *Objects on a horizontal plane that are to be seen from all sides may be in the center of the space on which they are placed.*

Figure 152. *(At the right.) The center of interest looks well if placed slightly above the exact center when it is to be seen in a vertical position, as a mounted picture, a show card, or a design on a printed page.*

should be placed in the center of the space, with borders of equal width on all sides. This is agreeable because the object then looks the same from any direction (figure 151). The placing of a cover and a bowl of flowers on a table is an application of this plan.

When a design is to be seen in a vertical position, figure 152 suggests an appropriate placing for the center of interest. In this case the lowest margin is wider than any of the others in order to overcome the optical illusion which makes objects in this position appear to drop in space. (See Law of Margins, figure 186, page 241.) Applications of this kind of placing are used in designing or mounting compositions, or planning a page of written or printed matter. The size of the margins would vary according to the emphasis of the object being used. If it is very striking, it may need a large mount, as shown here. A sheet of written or printed matter would follow the same relative proportions, but the margins would be smaller. When planning compositions it should be remembered that the greater the emphasis of the object, the larger the plain space around it should be.

Figures 153A and B suggest positions for centers of interest where the lines of the object carry the eye off toward the right and toward

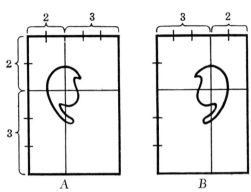

Figure 153A and B. A, If the lines of the center of interest have a tend-ency to carry the eye toward the right, the most interesting position for it to occupy would be slightly above the center and slightly toward the left. This plan may be used when placing an object against a background or an illustra-tion on an advertisement or a poster. B, When the eye is carried toward the left it is agreeable to have more background space on the left side.

the left. It will be observed that the eye enjoys more resting place on the side toward which it is being led. (See figure 297, page 442.) The positions for these centers of interest were determined in the following manner: the top and one side of the mount were divided into five equal parts; because the relation of two parts to three re-sults in beautiful spacing, lines drawn through points 2 or 3 made interesting divisions in the rectangle; the points where these lines cross each other give four points on which centers of interest could be placed. To state it briefly, *the center of interest should be above or below the mechanical center, and to the left or right,* depending upon the direction in which the lines of the composition carry the eye. It is not necessary actually to measure these spaces; an ap-proximate division will be as pleasing as an accurate one.

Figure 155 illustrates a method for placing three centers of inter-est in a composition—to be seen either vertically on a flat surface, or on a horizontal plane where depth and volume are involved. It is often necessary to group three objects, and if one knows this sim-ple plan it will help to suggest arrangements for some of the puz-zling problems in informal balance, such as arranging flowers, making designs for embroidery, placing groups of objects on a stage,

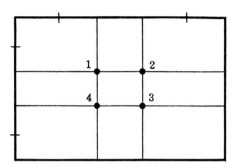

Figure 154. The intersections in this diagram indicate four spots, upon any one of which a main center of interest might well be placed to avoid the mechanical center of the composition.

a store window, or a table. The same plan as for figure 154 was used to start with, and two of the objects are placed at points 1 and 3, although 2 and 4 could have been used instead. These relative positions are chosen so that both objects will not be on the same straight line. In this diagram (figure 155), 1 and 3 were selected for the first two spots. In placing the third spot one should avoid the following three classes of lines: (1) any horizontal line or (2) vertical line running through either of the first two spots, because the arrangement would be monotonous if there were too many

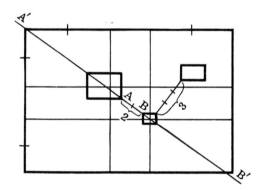

Figure 155. A simple method of placing centers of interest for informal balance. Two objects may be placed at points corresponding to 1 and 3, or 2 and 4, on Figure 154; the third object may be placed anywhere except on the horizontal or vertical lines passing through the two spots, or on a line connecting the centers of the two spots (A′B′). Counting the distance between the first two spots as two parts (AB), the third spot may be placed three parts away.

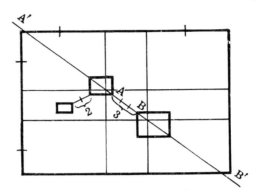

Figure 156. *This arrangement is similar to figure 155, but in this case the distance between the first two spots (AB) has been considered as three parts, and the third spot placed two parts away.*

parallel lines; (3) the diagonal line that runs through the center of the first two spots, for then there would be a lack of rhythm because the eye would immediately be carried out of the picture. It can be placed anywhere in the space except on the lines mentioned. The next step is to decide how far away to place this third spot. A knowledge of proportion tells one that it should not be the same distance from either spot (1 and 3) as the space between 1 and 3; and that a position that is more than one-half this distance, but less than two-thirds, will be interesting. If the distance between spots 1 and 3 is considered as constituting the two parts, then the third spot will be in an interesting position if it is placed about three parts away (figure 155). If it seems desirable to have it closer to the other, the space between 1 and 3 can be considered as the three-part of the ratio, and the third spot would then be placed only two parts away, as shown in figure 156. In a three-spot arrangement one of the spots will be the chief center of interest, and the other two will be subordinated.

Chapter Eight

HOW TO KNOW COLOR

THE APPEAL of color is universal, and one of our greatest enjoyments is the ability to use it beautifully. Some people who know nothing about the nature of color have a gift for using it well but have no idea why their work is good and so can not share their ability with others. It is possible to copy color schemes in a "recipe" manner, but such workers are not likely to feel any confidence when they attempt to do independent work, for they have done nothing to train their color judgment. If we wish really to understand color and to know why it is better to choose some colors rather than others for a particular use, we would do well to learn something of the nature and language of color.

The study of color may be approached from any one of five angles: that of the physiologist, the chemist, the physicist, the psychologist, or the person who works with pigments. Each one of these workers has his own point of view, which is quite different from that of every other one. The physiologist is concerned with the way in which the eye receives the sensations of color. The chemist studies the chemical properties of the natural and the artificial coloring materials used for the manufacture of dyes and paints. To the physicist the significance of color is merely its wavelengths and its intensities. The study of optics, which is a branch of physics, explains the effect of colored lights as they combine with each other, although the actual seeing of color is a psychological experience. The psychologist shows how a person is affected by the colors he sees and how colors are affected by one another. The fifth group, those who mix paints and dyes, find that mixtures of colored pigment behave differently from mixtures of colored light; they differ also from the way the colors of materials mix in the eye. Although the scientific explanations of these phenomena are complicated, each of these fields has given us a group of simple, easily understood facts to enable the practical worker in color to achieve success.

The average person uses color for various purposes. He has frequent occasion to mix colors as well as to judge the effect of colors upon one another and their becomingness to people. Most people have learned something about color from having mixed paints and dyes and colored crayons, and so they know what is commonly called the "artist's color theory." When one wishes to work with colored lights he must learn how colors combine in light. If a person uses combinations of colored materials, he should learn how the eye is affected by the colors it sees. These are everyday problems, and they touch upon three fields of color—color in light (sometimes spoken of as color in physics, sometimes as optics), color in vision (psychology), and color in pigment. In general, the principles which guide one to use color beautifully are the same in these three fields. The outstanding difference of concern to the worker is a difference in the colors that complement each other in these three mediums— light, sight, and pigment. Even that difference is not marked in the fields of vision and of pigment, because the complementary colors in these two fields are so similar, and because the effect upon the eye of two colors which are nearly complementary is very much the same as the effect of true complements. When a problem arises needing absolute accuracy for color mixtures, it is very easy to turn to the table of complementary colors in that particular field. The color theory of pigments is the one usually learned first, and it serves satisfactorily enough for most practical purposes.

At the end of this chapter will be found brief statements and diagrams to show the fundamentals of the use of color in light and of color as it affects the eye. The physiology and chemistry of color are not discussed here, for they do not bear so directly upon the ordinary problems in the use of color.

Of the many theories of color in pigment, two are in very common use. These are generally known as the "Prang System" and the "Munsell System." For the sake of avoiding confusion in the mind of the beginning student, the Prang theory only will be used when explaining the properties and classes of color. Following the discussion of the Prang System, the Munsell System will be explained and the fundamental differences between the two systems noted. When speaking of colors in "How to Use Color" we shall employ the popular name for the color, with the Prang and Munsell symbols which represent it.

THE PRANG COLOR SYSTEM

There are three properties or qualities which may be called the *dimensions* of color, and which are just as distinct from one another as the length, breadth, and thickness of an object. These color dimensions are:

How colors differ from one another

1. *Their* warmth or coolness (*the hue or name of the color*)
2. *Their* lightness or darkness (*the value of the color*)
3. *Their* brightness or dullness (*the intensity or chroma of the color*).

All three of these dimensions—hue, value, and intensity—are present in every color, just as every object has length and breadth and thickness.

HUE (SYMBOL H)

Hue is the term used to indicate the *name* of the color, such as red, blue, or green. The difference between blue and green is a difference in hue. Just as soon as green turns bluish it has changed its hue and would be called blue-green instead of green.

Very early in our study of physics we learn that light travels in waves of different lengths and at different rates of speed and that these waves produce in the eye the sensation we call color. Objects have a property called "color quality" which makes it possible for them to reflect some of these wave lengths and to absorb others. The

Light—the source of color

color of an object is determined by the wave lengths it does not absorb. For example, an object that we see as white in daylight appears white because it has reflected all wave lengths equally to our eye and has not absorbed one set more than another. But one that appears green has not absorbed the green rays of the white light as much as it has absorbed the others, and so by this reflection of the green wave lengths we see its color as green.

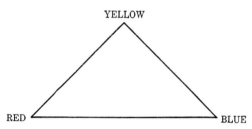

Figure 157. *The three primary colors in pigments: Red, Yellow, and Blue.*

Normal colors

If a prism or a diamond is held in the sunlight, the white of the prism or the diamond will be broken down and separated into all the colors of which white light is composed. If white light is broken down against a white background a spectrum appears, in which all the rainbow hues are spread out in a band. These colors, just as they appear in the spectrum, are commonly called *normal colors*.

The neutrals— black, white, and gray

Black results from the absence of color or of light. A surface that absorbs all color or all light rays will appear black. White is a combination of all the colors in light. A surface that reflects all colors equally will appear white in white light. Gray is a neutral resulting from a mixture of pigments. Pigments, unlike light rays, absorb white, and when mixed they leave black or gray instead of producing a clear white. In other words, a pigment absorbs everything from white but its own color, and the combination of red, yellow, and blue pigments absorbs all the wave lengths from white. The whole mixture, having absorbed all the wave lengths, makes gray. If the pigments are concentrated, they will give black.

Classes of color

Colors may be divided into five classes: *primary, binary, intermediate, tertiary,* and *quaternary.* All colors may be obtained by mixing in various proportions three fundamental hues: red (R), yellow (Y), and blue (B). These are called the three *primary* colors, because they are the elements in the use of pigment. They are the only hues in pigment that cannot be obtained by mixing other hues. (See figure 157.)

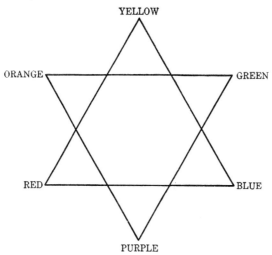

Figure 158. *The six standard colors of the Prang Chart. These are the three primary colors, Red, Yellow, and Blue, and the secondary or binary colors, Orange, Green, and Purple (Violet.) The colors which are opposite each other are complements.*

When two primary colors are mixed in equal amounts a different hue will result. This new hue is called a *binary* or *secondary* color. There are three of these binary colors—purple (P), called violet (V) in the Prang System, made by mixing red and blue; green (G), made by mixing yellow and blue; and orange (O), from red and yellow. (See figure 158.)

The primary and binary colors together are commonly called the *six standard colors.*

When a primary and a neighboring binary are mixed an *intermediate* hue results. In appearance, the intermediate is halfway between the two colors. There are six of these intermediate hues: yellow-green (YG), blue-green (BG), blue-purple (BP) or blue-violet (BV), red-purple (RP) or red violet (RV), red-orange (RO), and yellow-orange (YO). So far the twelve hues that constitute the typical color chart have been placed (figure 159). However, there is room between each one of the intermediates and its neighbor for an indefinite number of gradations. For example, one can easily imagine a color halfway between the blue and the blue-green on the chart. These hues may be indicated by repeating the name of the more conspicuous one. Thus, the hue called peacock blue, which is between blue and blue-green, would be called blue-blue-green (BBG). Next on the spectrum would appear the blue-green (BG); then green-blue-green (GBG), and green (G). Obviously, it is possible to make more and more detailed charts recording steps between the standard and intermediate hues.

When two binary colors are mixed a *tertiary* results. The tertiary colors are yellow, blue, and red, much neutralized. Tertiary yellow resembles a smoky yellow, the blue is known as slate blue, and tertiary red is the color of old red brick. The following analysis illustrates how tertiaries are obtained: Tertiary yellow is a mixture of green and orange. Green is $B + Y$ and orange is $Y + R$, and when they are mixed the color will be predominantly yellow with some purple from the red and blue. This purple will neutralize part of the yellow leaving the color a grayed yellow. Tertiary blue is a mixture of purple and green, for $R + B + B + Y$ gives principally blue dulled by orange from the $R + Y$. Tertiary red is orange mixed with purple, for $Y + R + R + B$ gives red dulled by green from the $Y + B$.

A mixture of two tertiary colors gives a *quaternary*. The quaternary colors are green, purple, and orange, much neutralized. They are sometimes spoken of as olive, prune, and buff. Quaternary green is a mixture of the tertiaries yellow and blue. Tertiary yellow $(B + Y + Y + R)$ added to tertiary blue $(R + B + B + Y)$ gives this sum of colors—three parts of yellow, three parts of blue, and two parts of red. The result of the mixture is green, from the predominance of yellow and blue, and it is much dulled with the red. The quaternary purple is a mixture of the tertiaries blue and red. $R + B + B + Y$ and $Y + R + R + B$ make three parts of red and

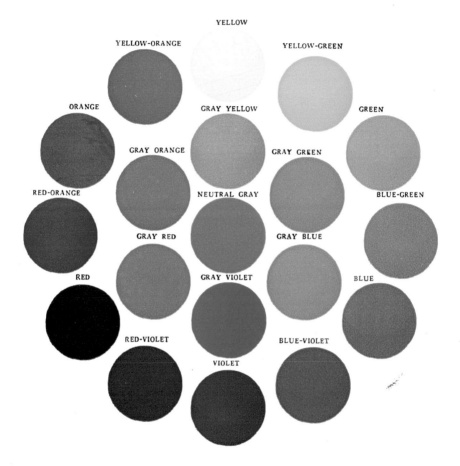

Figure 159. The Prang Color Chart.

three parts of blue, giving purple, with two parts of yellow to dull it. Quaternary orange is tertiary red $(Y + R + R + B)$ mixed with tertiary yellow $(B + Y + Y + R)$. This makes three parts of yellow and three parts of red, which give orange, and the two parts of blue neutralize the orange.

It will be noted that many familiar color names do not appear in this list of hues. Tan and brown, pink, lavender, henna, beige, and atmosphere are only a few of the names given to different values and intensities of the standard and intermediate hues. Every season brings a new list of names for the fashionable colors, but each of these can be described accurately by using the name of the hue it matches in the spectrum, with its correct value and intensity. To illustrate: Tan and brown are the names commonly used for the duller tones [1] of yellow, yellow-orange, orange, and red-orange, the tans being the lighter tones, or tints, and the browns, the darker tones, or shades; pink is a light red; and lavender is a light purple, light red-purple, or light blue-purple. *Popular names for colors*

If a person wishes to change the hue of a color, he will mix with it some of a neighboring or adjacent hue. For example, some red added to blue paint will change its hue to purple. A change of hue may be accomplished by dyeing, or by putting a semitransparent fabric over another color. Blue can be turned toward purple by putting red or red-purple under or over it, and toward green by the use of yellow or green. Some very beautiful effects may be obtained if this is understood. Frequently a slight change of this sort will make an unbecoming hat or dress entirely satisfactory. *How to change hues*

Imagine a band of spectrum colors brought around to form a circle, as shown in the outer ring of figure 159. Place yellow at the top, in the center, and purple will fall directly opposite on the same vertical line. The hues will fall into two large groups, one on either side of the vertical line. The colors at the right of the line near the blues are the cool hues, and those on the left side of the vertical line, around red and orange, are the warm. Red and orange are the warmest of all the colors, and they seem to advance the most and *Warm and cool hues*

---

[1] "Tone" is a general term that may be applied to the hue, the value, or the intensity of a single color or a group of colors. It is the most inclusive term in color use.

be the most conspicuous. Blue and blue-purple are the coldest hues, and they seem to recede and become inconspicuous. Green is between heat and cold, but it gets warmer as it grows yellowish, and cooler as it grows bluish. This quality of warmth and coolness is the most important thing to remember about hues. There is a harmony among the warm colors because they are related to one another, and the same harmony or family quality exists among the cool colors; but the warm and cool colors are strangers to each other. As white complements black and heat complements cold, so are warm and cool colors complements; they contrast rather than harmonize.

Advancing and receding hues

The warm advancing hues will make objects appear larger and nearer to the observer, while the cool hues, which seem to recede, will appear to reduce size. The landscape gardener may create the illusion of a larger space than he actually has to work with if he plants his bluish flowers in the background and his red and orange flowers in the immediate foreground. If he desires to bring some distant point nearer, he can do it easily by planting flowers or shrubs which show the warm, advancing colors. The stout woman needs to note this effect of color. If she wishes to conceal her size, she should select the most becoming of the receding colors and leave the conspicuous, advancing hues to the small, slender figures.

Hues and the seasons

Certain hues seem to be particularly appropriate to the different seasons of the year, and window decorations and advertisements, stage costumes and settings, may be made to suggest the seasons if colors are chosen according to the following plan:

Spring—Starting with blue, through blue-green to green
Summer—Green, yellow-green, and yellow, approaching a yellowish orange toward the end of summer
Autumn—Orange, red, and red-purple
Winter—Purple, blue-purple, and blue.

Effect of different hues

Hues have a decided effect upon one's feelings, and it is important to know how people react towards color schemes. People tire more quickly of the six standard colors—clear green, yellow, orange, red, purple, and blue—than they do of the intermediates—yellow-green, yellow-orange, red-orange, red-purple, blue-purple, and blue-green. Warm colors are more cheerful and stimulating than cool colors, which are calm and restful. Too much warm color may be exciting and "loud," while too much cool color may be depressing. Experiences in two tea-rooms designed to appeal to the same class of patrons illustrate this point. One tea-room had walls of a light dulled yellow-orange (sand-color) and cheerful red-orange (tea-rose) candle shades. The other room had cold, light gray walls and purple candle shades. In the yellowish room conversation seldom lagged, and there was an air of geniality. When the same people entered the gray and purple room they began to whisper. Although the gray room had an ideal location, served excellent food, and charged the same prices as the yellow room, it failed after a very short time.

A knowledge of hue, the first dimension of color, should enable the color user to accomplish the following:

Summary of hue

1. *Give the color its proper name*
2. *Recognize related colors and contrasting colors*
3. *Recognize advancing colors and receding colors*
4. *Place a color in one of three groups*
   a. *In a warm group; as a cheerful, an aggressive, or an exciting color*
   b. *In a cool group, where it may be either a cool, calm, restful color, or a depressing color*
   c. *On the border line between warmth and coolness, with something of the cheer of the warm colors and the calmness of the cool.*

VALUE (SYMBOL V)

Value, the second dimension, describes the *lightness* or *darkness* of a color. There are many degrees of light and dark, ranging all the way from white to black, but, for the sake of convenience in use, nine typical steps are selected. Dr. Denman W. Ross gave these nine steps names and symbols to aid in visualizing them. White is the highest value, and no hue can be as light as white. Black is the lowest value, and no hue can be so dark. Halfway between black and white comes middle value. (See figure 160A.) The value scale begins with White at the top (symbolized by W). The next step is High Light (HL); then come Light (L), Low Light (LL), Middle (M), High Dark (HD), Dark (D), Low Dark (LD), and Black (B).

The value of any hue may be named by comparing it with one of the steps on the value scale of neutral grays in figure 160A.

If the color chart is compared with the value scale, it will be seen that the hues change gradually in value with the lightest at the top and the darkest at the bottom. The table below gives the value equivalent of the normal colors:

$$HL = Yellow$$
$$L = Yellow\text{-}Orange \ and \ Yellow\text{-}Green$$
$$LL = Orange \ and \ Green$$
$$M = Red\text{-}Orange \ and \ Blue\text{-}Green$$
$$HD = Red \ and \ Blue$$
$$D = Red\text{-}Violet \ and \ Blue\text{-}Violet$$
$$LD = Violet$$

How to change values

Values can be changed by adding white or water to lighten and by adding more pigment or black to darken them. Every hue is capable of being lowered to a value just above black, and of being raised to a value just under white. Values that come above Middle are commonly called high values and those below Middle are the low values.

Tints and shades

A value that is lighter than the normal color is called a *tint*, and one that is darker, a *shade*. It will be noted that since normal yellow comes at High Light on the value scale its tints would not be included in this chart, although they would be visible to the eye (figure 160A). Similarly, the shades of purple, which comes at Low Dark, do not find a place upon the chart, although they, too, are distinguishable to the eye (figure 160A).

Effect of different values

A comparison of figures 160C, D and E shows the part that value plays in color use. In E the same color has been printed against white, gray, and black, while in C and D a combination of colors is printed against backgrounds of white and black. The color looks darker against white, paler against black, and against a gray

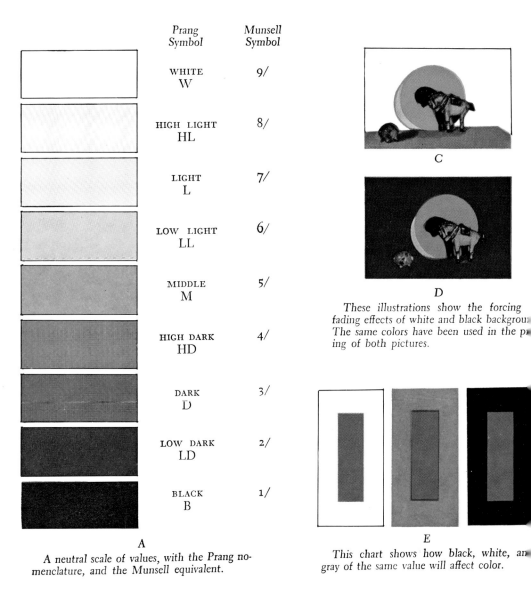

Prang Symbol	Munsell Symbol
WHITE W	9/
HIGH LIGHT HL	8/
LIGHT L	7/
LOW LIGHT LL	6/
MIDDLE M	5/
HIGH DARK HD	4/
DARK D	3/
LOW DARK LD	2/
BLACK B	1/

C

D

These illustrations show the forcing fading effects of white and black backgrou The same colors have been used in the p ing of both pictures.

A

A neutral scale of values, with the Prang nomenclature, and the Munsell equivalent.

E

This chart shows how black, white, an gray of the same value will affect color.

B

The five principal colors in the Munsell System at spectrum value, with their tints and shades.

Figure 160.

with just the same value as its own it blends and becomes very inconspicuous. Large sums of money are wasted in advertising and in displays because this fact is not recognized. Many people dress unbecomingly and decorate their homes badly because they do not know when to choose dark, light, or middle values.

Light values seem to increase the size of an object. Small rooms may be made to appear larger if they are decorated in light colors, and a person looks larger in white or very light clothing. Besides appearing to increase the size, light values create the impression of distance. For that reason a room appears higher if its ceiling is light than if it is dark.

White and other very light values reflect color and seem to intensify the color of the objects seen against them. (See figure 160C.)

Black and dark values seem to decrease the size of an object. Therefore dark colors would be a poor choice for the background of a small room, and a good choice for clothing for large people. While white and light colors suggest distance, dark colors suggest foreground, or nearness. For that reason dark values are particularly appropriate for floors and rugs because they give to the room an impression of stability. In store display dark values should be used below, rather than above light values, for if they are seen above the light colors the display will appear unstable.

Black and very dark colors absorb the color of objects seen against them (figure 160D). Black also has the power to unify colors and helps to bring harmony into an arrangement when a number of bright colors are used together. For example, in a ballroom the gay colors of the women's gowns are harmonized by the masses of black of the men's clothes.

Close values are those which are very much alike. They are subtle and very quiet in their effect. (See figure 160E.) In most cases it will be found that when light backgrounds are to be used, the most beautiful effects will be obtained when the general color value is rather light. When backgrounds are dark, the colors should be relatively darker, and when the background is of middle value, the general scheme should approach that tone. If the use of close values, particularly in closely related hues, is carried to an extreme, the result may be decidedly monotonous.

In house furnishing, close values are agreeable if many colors are to be used. While several colors may add interest to a room, one may go so far in the direction of variety that unity is sacrificed. The remedy may be found in keeping the color values similar enough to give reserve to the arrangement.

A strong contrast of light against dark or dark against light is more conspicuous than the strongest hue contrasts in equal values. For example, blue is the coldest color, and orange is one of the warmest, and for that reason they are as unlike as two hues could be. To test these contrasts, choose a bright blue and a bright orange of exactly the same value. The brightness of the orange must not be mistaken for its true value. (Anyone who has difficulty in determining values should almost close his eyes and look at the colors through his lashes; there is a point when hue and brightness nearly disappear and a correct judgment can then be formed as to relative amounts of light or dark in colors.) If a piece of the blue is placed against the orange, and an equal amount of black against white, it will be discovered that value contrasts have a more striking dissimilarity than hue contrasts. Therefore, in choosing backgrounds for advertising or for window displays one should consider this property of color very carefully, for a dark background can neutralize the effect of dark objects so much that most of the selling power of a window or a poster will be lost. If a closely related color scheme seems to lack interest, the introduction of a contrasting value will supply the needed accent.

Objects contrasting strongly in value with the background become silhouetted and call sharp attention to their shape. Therefore, objects which are beautiful in shape may be used against a background of very different value. But when an object is not beautiful —if it is clumsy, or too large—and it is desired to call the least possible amount of attention to its outline, it should be placed against a background which is very nearly its own value.

Since close values produce quiet effects, and strong contrasts have the opposite result, it will be found that where many objects are to be used together, they will appear more harmonious when they are similar in value than when they show sharp contrasts.

From this discussion on value, the second dimension of color, it will be seen that:

1. *White seems to add color and to increase size because it reflects light*
2. *Black seems to take away color and to reduce size because it absorbs light*
3. *Gray seems to neutralize, and the closer the value of the gray to the value of the color seen against it, the stronger the neutralizing force*
4. *White on black is less conspicuous than black on white because white reflects color while black absorbs it*
5. *Strong value contrasts have a tremendous power of attracting attention; and if not used wisely may produce a very restless and confusing effect*
6. *Close values are restful*
7. *Strong value contrasts call attention to the silhouette of an object.*

INTENSITY (SYMBOL I) OR CHROMA (SYMBOL C)

Intensity or *chroma* is the dimension that tells the *brightness* or *dullness* of a color—its strength or its weakness. In other words, it is the property describing the distance of the color from gray or neutrality. Intensity is the quality of color that makes it possible for a certain hue—such as red—to whisper, to shout, or to speak in a gentlemanly tone.

The colors at full intensity are very striking and form brilliant and interesting effects when they are used with discretion. The colors in the lower intensities are more subtle, and for general purposes they are enjoyed in the large areas with the colors of full intensity used for accents.

The colors in the outer circle of the color chart in figure 159 are said to be of full intensity because they are as bright as each color can be. As colors go down in their brightness and toward neutral gray, or no-color, they are said to be of *low intensity* or *chroma*. Changes in the intensity of a color may be brought about through the admixture of its complement, which lies opposite it on the color chart. Complementary colors complete a balance of warmth and coolness. When complementary colors are mixed they neutralize each other, and when mixed in certain proportions they completely destroy each other and produce gray or neutrality. When a color has had enough of its complement mixed with it to make it half as bright as it can be, and it is halfway between full intensity and neutrality, it is said to be one-half neutralized (½N) or one-half intense (½I). The inside circle on the color chart shows the six standard colors one-half neutralized. There are, of course, many steps in the intensity of each hue, between full or spectrum intensity and neutrality. Halfway between full or spectrum intensity and the one-half neutralized stage the color would be one-fourth neutralized (¼N), or three-fourths intensity (¾I). Going further toward the center, the half step between ½N and neutral gray is three-fourths neutralized (¾N) or one-fourth intense (¼I). These four steps form a simple basis for ordinary use, although additional fractions may be added between full intensity, ¼N, ½N, ¾N, and gray. Note that on the chart the intensity of a color decreases as it leaves the circumference and moves toward the center of the circle.

Complementary colors in the Prang System   It is easy to find the complement of any color without the aid of a color chart if it is remembered that in order to have neutral gray it is necessary to combine all the spectrum colors. In other words, there must be equal parts of red, yellow, and blue, which are the elements of the spectrum as it would be reproduced in pigment. In order to neutralize the primary color red, for example, it would be necessary to add the other two primaries, yellow and blue. The mixture of these two primaries produces the binary, green. Therefore it may be stated that the complement of a primary is the binary which results from the mixture of the other two primaries. To neutralize a binary it would be necessary to add the primary color that does not enter into its composition. Thus, the complement of green (which is yellow plus blue) is red. The complement of an intermediate is a mixture of the complements of the hues of

which the intermediate is composed. For example, the complement
of red-orange would be blue-green, made from green (which is the
complement of red), plus blue (the complement of orange). The
complement of a primary is a binary; the complement of a binary
is a primary; and the complement of an intermediate is an intermediate. The following pairs of complementary colors are seen on
the Prang color chart:

> *Yellow and Purple—Y and P*
> *Yellow-Green and Red-Purple—YG and RP*
> *Green and Red—G and R*
> *Blue-Green and Red-Orange—BG and RO*
> *Blue and Orange—B and O*
> *Blue-Purple and Yellow-Orange—BP and YO*

If paints or dyes of opposite, or complementary, colors are mixed,
they will destroy each other, but instead of making pure white, as
colored light would do, paints will leave colorless or neutral gray.

Neutral gray, at the center of the chart, shows by its position
that it is the result of mixing any pair of complementary colors.
Neutral gray itself has a neutralizing effect and may be used instead
of a complement to dull a color.

A color may be emphasized in the following ways:

How to make colors appear more or less intense

1. *By placing it next to its complement. In the discussion of Hue
   it was stated that when warm and cool colors are placed side
   by side they intensify or emphasize each other. The complements have the greatest power to force or intensify their op-
   posites when they are both bright. As one or both colors
   become dull, the tendency to force the complement is less-
   ened.*

2. *By combining the color with a neutral. Black or white will
   emphasize color more than does gray.*

3. *By repeating near it a large amount of the same hue in a
   lower intensity. For example, a little bright green surrounded
   with dull green would become more emphatic.*

4. *By repeating in some other part of a composition a small note
   of the same hue in a brighter intensity.*

A color may be made to appear less intense by the following means:

1. By combining a large amount of a very bright color with a dull or delicate color. These must be of the same or very similar hues. Since a bright color creates an after-image of its complement on the retina of the eye, the large area of bright color next to a dull color of the same hue will make it seem even duller. (See page 192.)

2. A bright color may be made to seem less intense if it is combined with a very dull color about the same value and slightly different in hue. To illustrate this point, let us take the problem of subduing the strong yellowish tone in the woodwork of a room. If a faintly pinkish tan (RO ¾N LL) were chosen for the walls, it would be observed that the yellow in the woodwork would blend with the yellow in the tan, and a slightly reddish tone would be the color that would be most apparent.

A color may be neutralized or destroyed by mixing it with its complementary color, or gray.

Complementary colors placed side by side tend to intensify each other. However, if the areas of the complementary colors are very minute, as in the threads of a woven fabric, they will at a distance seem to blur or blend. In that case the effect upon the eye will be that of neutralization.

Texture and intensity Texture plays so important a part in color use that it cannot be ignored. Surfaces having more or less roughness reflect light in tiny accents and throw little shadows that have the effect of dulling the intensity of a color. There is something mellow about the surface of a plaster wall which has sufficient texture to create a vibration of color, while the smooth and shiny painted wall gives a harsh and glaring effect. It is interesting to notice how the texture of a rough surface seems to blend colors used together and give the appearance of vibrating color instead of the clearness of the colors on a shiny surface.

If a material with a rough weave or a high pile were dipped into the same dye bath as a smooth fabric, it would appear to be duller in color because of the softening effect of the rough texture. For this reason a color in a shiny texture is more trying to the complexion than the same color used in a texture that has a soft, irregular surface.

Intensity is the dimension of color which expresses the taste and refinement of the color worker, and it is the property able to give the effect of Coney Island or of a Quaker meeting-house. Intensity, then, is a tremendous force, and bright colors need to be used most carefully if the result is to be beautiful.

Taste shown through choices of intensity

Everyone who has studied color is familiar with what is called "The Law of Color Areas"—sometimes known as "The Law of Backgrounds." That well-known statement says that the larger the area to be covered, the less intense the color should be and the smaller the area, the brighter the color may be. It is interesting to observe the interpretation of that statement in the different periods of art. Fashions effect changes in our point of view on color, and what seems beautiful to one generation may appear quite different to another. Houses decorated in the Mission period with colors their owners regarded as restful appeared dull and drab to eyes accustomed to the fresh clean colors that resulted from the popularity and influence of such painters as Cézanne, Van Gogh, and Matisse. Accordingly when we are considering the Law of Color Areas, we realize that we must interpret it in terms of the time in which we live. We find that it should not be thought of as a law or a rule, but rather as a principle, in other words, as a flexible guide. Although people turned away from the drabness of too much dull tan and brown, they found that the principle underlying the Law of Areas still held. For when clear bright colors for clothes were in fashion it was still a mistake for a very stout woman to wear an entire costume of bright red, and even when gay and sprightly colors were used commonly in house decoration, there would be little sense of comfort to the eye if walls and floors and furnishings were all of such bright colors that there were no areas of background color to point up the gay colors or no quiet surfaces where the eye might feel a sense of rest. And so in each fashion cycle we interpret the so-called Law of Areas and understand why it is the foundation upon which good work in color is based.

A knowledge of intensity, the third dimension of color, leads one to recognize that:

1. Some colors are more forceful than others
2. Each color as it is seen in the spectrum is as strong as that color can be
3. Colors may be made duller or less intense by mixing with them some of their complementary color
4. Colors may be made to appear more intense by placing beside them some of their complementary color
5. A bright color creates an after-image of its complement which will affect the appearance of the colors seen near it.

In the Prang notation a color is expressed as follows: Hue, Value, Intensity. Hue is indicated by the name or the initials of the color, as Red or R. Value is denoted by the name or the initials of the step to which it corresponds on the value scale, such as Low Light (LL), or Dark (D). Intensity is expressed by a fraction that shows its degree of neutralization, as ¼N, or by a fraction showing its degree of intensity, as ¾I. Thus, a red of fullest intensity, in the value in which it is seen on the color chart, would be written R HD Full Intensity. Red that is High Dark in value and one-fourth neutralized would be written R HD ¼N, or R HD ¾I.

The preparation of a color chart and a value scale offers excellent training for the color sense. Any colored materials may be used. A good-sized diagram should be made, similar to that on which the colors on Chart 159 are placed. There should be a space on it for each of the hues and for four of the intensity steps of each hue. A prism should be used for throwing the clear spectrum colors on something white and an attempt made to match these colors for the hues in the outer circle. Printed color charts are seldom, if ever, accurate. While they serve satisfactorily enough to establish certain color relationships, the student is urged to study the spectrum, which can so easily be produced by means of the beveled edge of a mirror, a diamond, or a prism. As a color is found it should be cut out and pasted in its proper place on the chart. One can paint these colors, or use papers, ribbons, silk, wool, or cotton dress goods, yarns—anything that shows the right color. It will be found that analyzing many colors for their correct hue, value, and intensity develops skill in matching colors and in identifying them. A trained color sense is of the greatest value to everyone, and it can be secured only through exercise.

THE MUNSELL COLOR SYSTEM

A. H. Munsell worked out a color system that eliminates much of the guesswork in color study. It will be exceedingly profitable to the reader to study Munsell's *Color Atlas* and *Color Notation* and *A Practical Description of the Munsell Color System* written by T. M. Cleland, in order to supplement this very brief description of the Munsell color system.

In the Munsell plan the dimensions of color are shown upon a *The color* sphere (figure 161). The hues appear around the circumference of *sphere* the sphere. Values in neutral gray are shown upon a vertical pole— the axis of the sphere. The "North Pole" is white, and the "South Pole" black. As the hues become lighter in value, they are placed higher on the sphere; as they grow darker they appear lower, toward the "South Pole." Chroma, or intensity is represented by paths or arms running from no-color, or Neutral Gray, out to the circumference and beyond it.

By intensive research Munsell found that if the hues were in *Hue* proper balance around the sphere and this sphere were rotated *(Symbol H)* upon its neutral axis at a high rate of speed, the hues would blend together to form a neutral gray. Because of this discovery he definitely discarded the previously accepted division of the hues into three primaries—Red, Yellow, and Blue—and the three secondaries —Orange, Green, and Violet—as this gave an excess of Orange and Yellow in the circumference of the sphere. He therefore chose hues that were spaced so as to eliminate the excess orange and yellow. He decided to use five principal hues in order to make use of the decimal system. The chosen hues were named Red, Yellow, Green,

Blue, and Purple. The hues intermediate between these were named Yellow-red, Green-yellow, Blue-green, Purple-blue, and Red-purple. He discarded the names of Orange and Violet because they were not distinctive as color names but were also related to names of flowers and fruits.

Instead of the twelve-hue circle we now see ten major hues, divided into five principal hues and five intermediate hues. The symbols for the five principal hues are: R, Y, G, B, and P, and for the five intermediate hues: YR, GY, BG, PB, and RP.

Use of numerals to denote gradations between hues

Numerals are used to designate the hues lying between the principal and intermediate hues. The principal and intermediate hues are always 5. Principal blue would be 5B; the intermediate hue blue-green would be 5BG. The hues lying between 5BG and 5B are designated as follows: 6BG, 7BG, 8BG, 9BG, 10BG (the midpoint between 5BG and 5B), 1B, 2B, 3B, 4B, to 5B. The 6BG has a little more blue in it than 5BG; 7BG is another step nearer to principal blue; 8BG has still more blue; 9BG is four steps from 5BG and six steps from 5B; 10BG is just halfway between BG and B. The other steps—1B, 2B, 3B, 4B—all show more blue and less blue-green until they reach 5B. It is possible to distinguish 100 steps in the hue circuit at five value and five chroma. These again fall in line with the decimal system and are designated in the following manner: 1R, 2R, 3R, 4R, 5R, 6R, 7R, 8R, 9R, 10R, 1YR, 2YR, 3YR, etc. At stronger chromas it is possible to distinguish more hue steps, and they are designated simply by dividing the symbols again into tenths as: 1.2R, 1.3R, etc. This will take care of any hue difference it is possible for the human eye to see.

Value (Symbol V)

Values, in the Munsell plan, have numbers. Ten steps are charted between black and white. Absolute black (which the eye cannot see) is 0, and is written N 0/. Absolute white is N 10/. Halfway between black and white is *Middle Value*, or N 5/. (See figures 160A and 161.)

Chroma (Symbol C)

The full strength of the weakest hue—blue-green—determines the circumference of the circle, and all other hues extend beyond the circumference in the degree of their relative strength. Each hue has its own chroma or intensity scale, just as it has its own

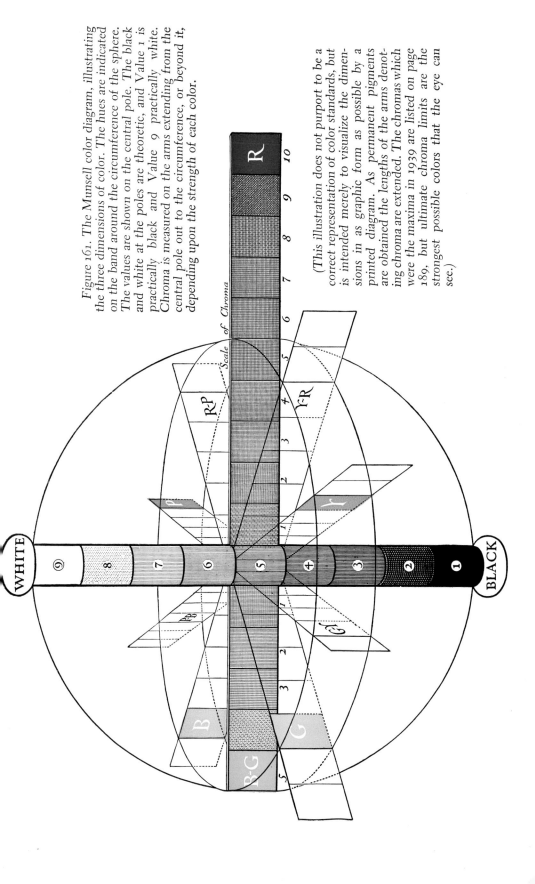

Figure 161. The Munsell color diagram, illustrating the three dimensions of color. The hues are indicated on the band around the circumference of the sphere. The values are shown on the central pole. The black and white at the poles are theoretic, and Value 1 is practically black and Value 9 practically white. Chroma is measured on the arms extending from the central pole out to the circumference, or beyond it, depending upon the strength of each color.

(This illustration does not purport to be a correct representation of color standards, but is intended merely to visualize the dimensions in as graphic form as possible by a printed diagram. As permanent pigments are obtained the lengths of the arms denoting chroma are extended. The chromas which were the maxima in 1939 are listed on page 189, but ultimate chroma limits are the strongest possible colors that the eye can see.)

value scale. Red displays the strongest chroma of all the hues. One is unconsciously familiar with the contrast between the strong red of vermilion and a weak red as seen in old brick. Vermilion probably has a chroma of 10 or more while "old brick" is around 2 chroma. One may think of chroma as passing from the grayish red of "old brick" through medium red of let us say "rose," out to the strong red of vermilion and on to the most vivid red possible for the human eye to see. The notation for chroma is written after a line that divides it from the figure used for the value, e.g., /10. Thus a scale of red chroma is written R/1, R/2, R/3, etc. /1 chroma is an almost neutral gray but is recognizable as a warm gray, and each succeeding step is nearer to the strongest visible red (figure 161).

In the Munsell notation color symbols are expressed as follows: Hue ^{Value}/$_{Chroma}$. Hue is denoted by the name or the initials of the color, as Red or R. The value is expressed by the number on the value scale to which it corresponds, and is written with a line after it: 5/. Chroma is expressed by the number of the step on the chroma scale and is written after a line. The line is there simply to separate the value and the chroma notations. Thus, the five principal hues as they appear in the fullest intensity now obtainable with permanent pigments would read as follows: R 4/14, Y 8/12, G 5/8, B 4/8, P 3/12. The five intermediate hues would read: YR 5/12, GY 7/10, BG 5/6, PB 3/12, and RP 4/12. It should be noted that the ultimate chroma limits of the Munsell System are the strongest possible colors the eye can see. However, the charts are limited by lack of permanent pigments. As stronger colors and dyes are found they can be added to the Munsell Charts and will find their place beyond the present material limits. Thus, the printed chart is a changing rather than a fixed record of color.

Just as explained in the case of hue it is evident that additional steps of value exist between each consecutive pair on the value scale and that additional steps of chroma exist between each consecutive pair on the chroma scale. These may all be designated by decimal system so that a very exact color determination might read (1.1R 4.5/5.2) or (5.5YR 6.5/8.5) etc.

Complete color symbols of the Munsell Color Notation

The Munsell System is based on ten major hues reading as follows:

> Red and Blue-Green—R and BG
> Yellow and Purple-Blue—Y and PB
> Green and Red-Purple—G and RP
> Blue and Yellow-Red—B and YR
> Purple and Green-Yellow—P and GY

An understanding of the various chroma strengths is important for successful balance in the use of color. For example, since red is much stronger than its complement, blue-green, it would be necessary to use a much larger amount of the strongest blue-green to obtain enough force to give the equivalent of the attraction of strong red.

VISUAL PERCEPTION OF COLOR (PSYCHOLOGY)

The experiments of psychologists have shown us three aspects of color in vision: First, that colors can affect the mood of an individual; second, that colors have the property of seeming to advance or to recede; and third, that colors have very definite effects upon each other.

Colors and the emotions   Colors can have such strong effects upon the emotions that color therapy is now used with remarkable success in the treatment of nervous disorders. The diagram in figure 162 shows how the various colors affect a person. It will be seen that the group of cool colors, that is, those related to the blues and greens, have a quieting influence, and as the color grows colder and darker it may become really depressing. On the other hand, the warm colors—those grouped around the red and orange hues—have a cheerful, comforting effect, which may increase to stimulation and excitement when the colors become very bright and near to red.

Receding and advancing colors   The cool colors, which are really the colors of distance in nature, always carry with them an illusion of distance, and thus objects which are cool in color seem to recede. A mass of blue placed at the end of a room may make the room appear to be longer than it really is. On the other hand, the warm colors, especially the fiery ones, seem to advance, and it is possible to make a room look shorter than its actual length by using warm colors at the ends of the room.

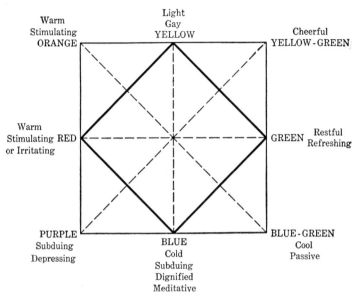

Figure 162. *The Psychologist's Color Chart. The colors which are complementary in vision. There are four primary colors: Yellow, Green, Blue, and Red. The four secondary colors are Yellow-Green, Blue-Green, Purple, and Orange. The complementary colors are opposite each other.*

In pigment and in light there are three primary colors, but in vision there are four colors that are primaries, or elements. That is to say, there are no colors which, when mixed in the eye, will produce red, yellow, green, or blue. Since the psychologist has four primaries, his color chart is built upon the plan of a square instead of the familiar triangle of the two other systems. The secondaries are orange, yellow-green, blue-green, and purple (violet). The colors which are complementary to each other in vision are not the same as those found to be complementary in the mixing of colored pigments or in the mixing of colored lights. Figure 162 shows the

The effect of colors upon each other

pairs of complementary colors that neutralize each other in the eye and form gray. These complementing pairs are as follows: red and green, yellow-green and purple (violet), yellow and blue, and orange and blue-green.

After-image

We know, through psychological studies, that the visual effect of one color upon another placed near it may be so strong that in the eye of an observer other nonexistant hues will appear. A new color, called the "after-image," appears in one's eyes about half a minute after he has gazed fixedly at a color. This after-image is the complement of the original hue, and it will change the appearance of that original color, even while one is looking at it. This is explained by the fact that when the sensitive nerves of the eye which permit us to see color become tired from looking too long at one hue, the nerves register the color less and less vividly. Not only does the original color become duller, but there remains in the eye the impression of the complement—the sum of all the other colors of the spectrum left after this particular color has weakened or disappeared.

It is very easy to try this out for one's self and to discover the complement of each color. If, for example, one looks fixedly at a spot of bright orange color for about half a minute, and then looks at a white surface, a bluish-green spot, the exact shape of the spot of orange, will appear upon the white surface. Actually, the color seen in this after-image is the remainder of the colors that would be needed to produce gray after the orange was subtracted from the spectrum hues. The blue-green would be particularly bright if the orange was very bright, but weaker if the orange was not a strong color.

Since each color has its after-image, the color one has just been looking at will affect the appearance of every other color seen near it. That is why colors give one impression in a certain combination and quite another effect in a different scheme. This phenomenon explains why it is necessary to arrange colors in such a way that those which affect one another unpleasantly are separated, either by neutrals or by colors known to supply good background or harmonizing colors.

COLOR IN PHYSICS

The physicist regards the seeing of color as a psychological sen- *Colors in light*
sation which provides a more-or-less crude and inaccurate indication
of the relative intensities of the wave-lengths to which the eye
responds. Because the color sensations which these wave-lengths
arouse in the eye are only approximately correct, colors in physics
are denoted by their intensities and by their wave-lengths rather
than by color names. Of all the colors, red has the longest wave
length and violet the shortest. The physicist determines the quality
of light radiation by spreading the wave-lengths present in light
into a spectrum, and he measures the intensities of the different
wave-lengths. By this method he obtains a clear and physically
complete analysis of the quality of light radiation. Experiments in
the field of optics, the branch of physics which explains the effects
of colored lights upon one another, illustrate the fact that colored
lights, when mixed, do not produce the same results as would be
secured by mixing paints of the identical hues. In the case of lights
one is working with light rays, whereas paints are colored matter of
either mineral or vegetable origin.

A colored surface absorbs or subtracts from white light the wave- *The effect of*
lengths of all the colors except its own, and so one receives the *pigment mix-*
impression of that particular color, since it is the only color left. *tures*
A yellow pigment, for example, takes the other two primaries, red
and blue, out of white light and leaves the impression of yellow.
Each pigment subtracts wave-lengths or light from white, and so
when two colors in pigments are combined, the result is usually
less brilliant than either of the colors would appear if seen by
itself. Finally, when all of the colors of the spectrum have been
mixed, the brilliance of the white has been absorbed, and the result
is a dull, colorless gray, or black, depending upon the concentration
of the original colors.

Colored lights may be mixed to form any number of brilliant *The effect of*
colors, or white. When colored lights are combined, the light waves *mixtures of*
supplement each other, so that the sum of the wave-lengths keeps *colored lights*
on increasing. As the wave-lengths pile up with the addition of each

color, the mixture becomes more brilliant. When it reaches a point where the wave-lengths of all the colors of the spectrum are present in the mixture, the colors neutralize each other and produce white. White, therefore, is more brilliant than any of the separate colors.

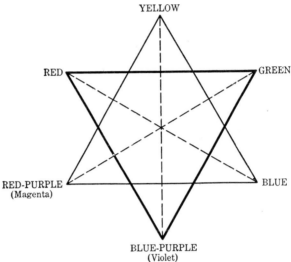

Figure 163. The Physicist's Color Chart. *The colors which are complementary in light. The three primary colors are Red, Green, and Blue-purple (Violet). The secondary colors are Yellow, Blue, and Red-purple (Magenta). The colors which are opposite each other are complements.*

It is found that, in the mixing of colored lights, all the hues, as well as white, can be secured from three primary colors, but they are not the same three colors the painter must use as primaries in pigments to secure all the hues. In colored lights, red, green, and blue-purple are the three primaries instead of the red, blue, and yellow of the painter. The three secondary colors, as they are seen in light, are yellow, red-purple, and blue. These secondaries are produced as follows: yellow light is secured by mixing red and green lights; red-purple results from a mixture of red and blue-purple; and blue light is made by mixing green and blue-purple. The terms "magenta" and "violet" are often used in this field to indicate red-purple and blue-purple.

Figure 163 shows the colors that are complementary to each other in light. These complementary pairs are red and blue; green and red-purple; and blue-purple and yellow. Each of these pairs of colored lights will neutralize each other when combined and will produce white light. This may be demonstrated by throwing lights of complementary colors upon a white screen.

When one understands how colored lights affect color in ma- *The effect of* terials, colors may be emphasized, changed, or made actually to *colored lights upon colored* vanish when the proper lights are thrown upon them. Window *materials* decorators and lighting experts in the modern theaters accomplish wonders in the transformation of backgrounds and costumes through the application of colored lights.

In the theater it is not uncommon to paint two entirely different scenes on one canvas, and then to separate the scenes by obliterating one of them by means of colored lights. In this way a blue-purple object that is a conspicuous center of interest in one scene in which the light is white, can be made to disappear in the next scene by means of a blue-purple light. The effect of the blue-purple light upon the same color is to cause it to fade into the background and thus eliminate it from the sight. In a third scene this blue-purple mass can be made to appear dark gray or black if yellow light, which is its complement, is thrown upon it.

In some of the more spectacular examples of the transformation of scenes and costumes, the artist makes use of his knowledge of chemistry as well as optics. Samoiloff, for example, found that several pieces of red material that matched perfectly under white light, changed very differently under colored lights. Chemical analysis shows that one fabric contained radium bromide, another phospherine, and the third zinc. By throwing especially prepared lights upon them, he could change the colors in different ways, according to the chemicals they contained. By this method he was able to make a costume elaborately embroidered with materials that contained these chemicals take on various colors and patterns; and then, when he wished, he could make it look like a plain dress, merely by turning a white light upon it.

Chapter Nine

HOW TO USE COLOR

THE SUCCESSFUL use of color is an extremely complex matter. Different individuals and different cultures may seem at first to have entirely different and apparently conflicting standards. If, however, we make a study of successful color schemes in all their various combinations, we find that they have certain factors in common. First, the colors are beautiful for the purpose for which they have been chosen. Second, they are so combined as to enhance one another's beauty.

At the outset it should be realized that there is no such thing as an ugly color. Every color is beautiful if it is used in the right place and in the right amount. The "right place" may be a floor covering in one case or a decorative bowl in another. The "right amount" may be a broad sweep or a tiny dot. The object of color study is to become so sensitive to color relationships that the recognition of "right place" and "right amount" becomes intuitive.

In the course of daily living everyone must choose colors and use them, and for that reason everyone should know something about color effects and combinations. One hesitates to say that certain colors may not be used together, for as soon as a dogmatic color statement has been made, a genius comes along and takes the condemned colors and, by choosing certain values and intensities of those colors and combining them in the right amounts, makes a thing of beauty. This chapter, however, is for the average person who wishes to learn what constitutes good taste and beauty in the use of color. In order to develop judgment in regard to colors one must learn what effects colors have upon one another when they are used in different quantities and in different degrees of brightness and lightness. The statements made in this chapter should be regarded as guiding principles rather than rules, and they are worthy of consideration because they have proved helpful to many people.

Unfortunately one cannot learn to apply color principles after merely reading about them once or twice in a book. They must be studied, and they must be consciously applied every time a color is used. The first step toward intelligent color work is a careful study of the color chart and the value scale in order to gain the ability to visualize colors in their different degrees of lightness or darkness (value); to recognize colors in various degrees of brightness or dullness (intensity); and to be able to picture the additional hues that appear between the colors shown on the color chart, such as a yellower yellow-orange between yellow and yellow-orange, and a redder red-purple between red and red-purple.

One may be inclined to think that the principles of design apply to line only. This is not true. Every one of the principles applies to color use: *balance*, or rest; *proportion*, or beautiful sizes; *rhythm*, or easy movement; *emphasis*, or centers of interest; *harmony*, or unity; and *contrast*, or variety. All of these contribute to beautiful color effects.

PRINCIPLES OF DESIGN IN THE USE OF COLOR

Balance, or a feeling of rest, is the first essential for good color arrangements. It is the principle underlying the well-known "Law of Areas," which states: Large areas of color should be quiet in effect, while small amounts may show strong contrasts; the larger the amount used, the quieter the color should be, and the smaller the amount, the more striking the contrast may become. These contrasts may be due to a decided difference in hue, in value, or in intensity.

Balance in color: The Law of Areas

The Munsell color chart in figure 161 shows that some colors are quieter than others even when each color is as bright as it can be. For example, blue-green has only six chroma steps as compared

Balance of bright and dull colors

to the ten of red. The length of each arm of the chart shows the strength of that color as compared to all the others.

Munsell found that any colors which are alike in value and are /5 chroma will present the same amount of attraction to the eye and will therefore balance each other. Examples to illustrate this are often found in fine oriental rugs, where colors are usually about the same value and are commonly used in /5 chroma. Since all colors of equal value and /5 chroma balance, it is found that just as soon as one uses any color brighter than that in a combination, he should use it in a smaller amount in order to retain the balance. On the other hand, if a duller color than /5 chroma is used in such a combination the amount would be correspondingly increased. This is another way of stating the "Law of Color Areas."

Balance of light and dark colors

Value, or dark and light, is as important in color balance as brightness. While equal amounts of color of the same value at /5 chroma will balance each other, it is found that if there is a difference in value there must be a corresponding change in the amounts used, in order to give the effect of repose. Thus, a small quantity of a light value will balance a large amount of a dark value, or small amounts of dark balance large areas of light.

Balance of hues: Complementary colors

Complementary colors—the hues which lie directly opposite each other on the color chart—form a natural balance because they complete or complement each other in the eye. (See figures 159, and 162.) It is a well-known fact that one can rest any one set of muscles in the body by using another set, as occurs when one changes occupations. The same thing is true of using those nerves of the eye which make color vision possible. On the retina of the eye there are a great many tiny nerves which are sensitive to various colors, but are capable of growing tired and refusing to work. Psychological experiments may be made in order to discover what happens when one fatigues the nerves that respond to each color. Take, for example, a piece of bright red paper. Hold this against a piece of white paper, covering some of the red with the thumb. Sit in strong daylight and stare at the red paper for some time. After a short while the paper will seem to grow duller. To prove that this has happened, lift the thumb and it will be seen that the spot which was covered appears much brighter than the piece at which one has been looking. One set of nerves was registering the color of the thumb, and the red nerves at that spot in the eye did not become fatigued. After looking still longer at the red paper, take it away and look at the spot on the white paper where the red had been and an after-image of green will be seen, which is the complement of red in color vision. Green is the color left in the eye after these red nerves refuse to act. Thus it will be seen that if a touch of complementary color is used in an arrangement it brings all of the nerves of the eye into use and prevents any one set from becoming overtired.

To illustrate the balancing of hues, imagine a room furnished in tan and brown with accents of bright red-orange. Unless there were a cleverly balanced distribution of light and dark areas in this analogous scheme the room might become monotonous. Add some of an opposite hue, such as blue, green, or blue-green, and it will be seen that the effect will be more satisfying through the introduction of the balancing color. If the bluish colors were bright, the room would need only a small amount, such as could be supplied through figures in draperies, a vase, or a picture. Complementary colors produce such strong contrasts that only a small touch of a bright opposite color is needed to give balance.

There are two ways to balance colors. The first way, as has just been seen, is through the selection of the varied amounts of bright and dull colors, according to the "Law of Areas," and the second is through the arrangement of these colors. Colors or values can be balanced by repeating some of the same colors or values in various parts of an arrangement, and this repetition—sometimes called "crossing"—has a tendency to give a feeling of rest. To illustrate balance by crossing, let us imagine a dining room in which the walls and woodwork are ivory-white and the furniture mahogany. Suppose that some draperies in which blue-green predominates are hung at the windows on one side of the room. The concentration of the only blue-green in the room on that one wall would make the color scheme seem incomplete. If some echoes of the blue-green were to appear in the accessories seen against the

Balance through "crossing" or repetition

other walls and if possibly a note of it were repeated in chair seats or in the rug, there would be a pleasant effect of color balance. A second illustration may be drawn from the field of window decoration. In the window something of the same hue (not necessarily in the same value or intensity) could be used on both sides of the center to create balance. A purple dress at one side would be balanced by a purple hat on the other side, farther away from the center, since the hat is smaller than the dress; if the hat were much brighter than the dress it might balance it at the same distance from the center.

Since each color has the power of attracting attention through its hue, value, and intensity, that attention must be considered as the "weight" of the color, and the color arranged according to the principles used in placing large and small objects.

Proportion in color   The study of proportion showed that interest may be gained through a subtle variety in proportion, while monotony results from too much repetition. Since this principle applies to color as well as to sizes, color combinations are more beautiful when the amounts are varied than when they are equal. A dress or a hat, for example, made of more than one color would be more interesting if unequal proportions of the colors were used than if the amounts were alike. In any arrangement, if the colors to be combined are equal in their power to attract attention, the Greek proportion of about two parts of one to three or five or seven of the other will be a good distribution. However, if the colors are very different in their forcefulness, they should be arranged according to the "Law of Areas," and the brighter colors used in smaller amounts.

Rhythm in color   In color use, rhythm and balance through "crossing" or repetition are very closely related, for both imply an arrangement of colors along which the eye can move easily from one color to another. In both aspects of color arrangement there is a sort of interlacing rhythm not unlike the rhyme found in the structure of the sonnet. An example of such a composition is shown in figure 112, page 112, in the chapter on Rhythm. Notice how the arrangement of the blacks leads the eye easily throughout the picture. When colors are skillfully repeated in several places in a room or in a costume, the eye travels rhythmically as it follows these colors. Rhythmic color also results from the use of gradations in hue, value, or intensity. This, too, is seen in the print, where there is a gradual change from the lightest colors through the grays to black.

Emphasis in color can be gained through contrasts of hue, light and dark, and brightness. *Emphasis in color*

In any color arrangement there should be one outstanding color effect. Whether the scheme be very quiet and simple, or complicated, one should be conscious of a main color, perhaps in different degrees of distinctness, or in various values and intensities. For example, there may be an effect of a yellowish tone running through a group of orange and green tones, or bluish through greens and purples. The effect of every other color used in that arrangement should be subordinated to the main color in order to prevent confusion. If only black and white and grays are used, the same principle would be followed, and one value would predominate.

In the chapter on Emphasis one of the most important principles in color use was discussed. This principle is as follows: *Backgrounds should show less emphasis than the objects placed against them.* Colors to be used as backgrounds in rooms and in store windows should be quiet, because the quieter they are, the more effective are the objects seen against them.

Color combinations giving the most pleasure are likely to be those having harmony or unity. They give the impression that all the colors really belong together, and yet at the same time there must be sufficient variety to avoid monotonous arrangement. *Harmony in color*

The color chart in figure 159 shows that there are two large groups of color, the warm colors, including the reds and yellows, and the cool colors, which lie around blue. There is a certain family likeness —a natural harmony—among the warm colors, and a similar kinship or unity among the cool colors; therefore, if one wishes to obtain color harmonies he will combine warm colors with warm, and cool colors with cool. If contrasts are desired, some cool color may be used in a warm scheme, or a warm color note introduced into a cool scheme. There are, however, degrees of warmth and coolness within the warm and cool groups. Blue of full intensity is colder than a somewhat neutralized blue, since the neutralizing orange has also warmed it. Blue-green is warmer than blue because it contains yellow. Therefore, if it is desired to use a cool color as an accent in a warm scheme, a tone of blue-green or a somewhat neutralized blue will be more harmonious with it than a clear, cold blue. Similarly, if one were bringing a fairly large amount of a warm color into a cool scheme, it might be better to use the yellow, yellow-orange, and orange tones than a full intensity red-orange or red. If the warmest of the warm hues were used, they should be utilized in small amounts or else they should be neutralized, since the addition of the complement tends to cool them. Instead of interesting variety, discord is apt to result when extremely warm colors are combined with cold colors, unless one follows the "Law of Areas" and uses these contrasts in small amounts. If they are skillfully combined, contrasts are arresting and stimulating, but be sure there is no confusion in the mind of the worker between what is gay and what is crude in color use. Greens and purples come halfway between the warm and cool colors, and so they prove to be excellent hues for tying other colors together. In embroideries, especially, one frequently finds that a great variety of hues may be harmonized by the intermingling of partly neutralized greens or purples.

Background colors

The most unifying colors are the colors of light—yellow, yellow-orange, and orange. When these colors are dull enough, as in warm grays and tans, any hue looks well against them, and therefore they make the most useful colors for backgrounds. It will be found that the grayed warm hues, which are somewhat advancing, have a tendency to unify the colors placed against them. The cool hues, which recede, have a tendency to separate colors seen against them.

Beauty in color schemes

The most beautiful color schemes are those which give a single impression: an impression of warmth, with perhaps a note of coolness for variation; or of coolness, with an accent of warmth. It is particularly desirable to follow this order when one is planning colors for anything as large as a room or a store window. For example, in a window display of suits and dresses of cool colors—blues, blue-greens, and greens—it would be interesting to bring in just a little orange and red-orange in scarfs or hats for the warm accents. A typical example in house furnishing may be visualized through the description of a color scheme for a bedroom. The colors are suggested by a Japanese print that hangs in the room. The colors are mainly warm with some accents of cool color. The walls and woodwork are a soft ivory tone.[1] The drapery material with its conventionalized floral design has a cream-colored background with a pattern showing masses of sunny golden-yellow,[2] and pinkish tan,[3] with a touch of tomato red,[4] and some bits of purplish blue and green which give contrast and add distinction to the room. The blue is dark,[5] and the green is slightly yellowish [6] and the same value as the red. The rug is inconspicuous with a grayed coppery tone, dull and dark enough to make a good background. The bed cover is light copper color,[8] and the furniture is mahogany. Some of the cool colors of the draperies and the Japanese print are repeated on the fourth side of the room in pottery, pictures, and in a painted box. Here, then, the first impression is of a group of colors related to the orange family, with points of cool colors for interesting variation.

A combination of several colors is said to be *keyed* when each color has something in common with every other color. A fine colorist is likely to say that this keying of color is the secret of his success. Colors may be keyed to each other in the following ways: *Keyed color*

1. *By neutralizing them*
2. *By mixing them to introduce a color in common*
3. *By glazing, veiling, or topping them*
4. *By tying them together by means of a neutral color*
5. *By the use of a rough texture.*

Since all the hues are present in a neutralized color, it is apparent that all neutralized colors are keyed, because they have something in common. It will be seen that many colors may be used together if they are somewhat neutralized. *Keying by neutralizing*

The admixture of a common color will key two rather widely separated colors. Yellow and blue are brought together by the use of green, and green and purple are keyed by combining blue with them. *Keying by mixing*

[1] (YO 7/8N HL) (YR 8/1).
[2] (YO 1/4N LL) (YR 6/7).
[3] (RO 7/8N LL) (RO 6/2).
[4] (RRO 1/8N M) (6R 5/8).
[5] (BBV 1/4N D) (7PB 3/8).
[6] (GYG 1/8N M) (4G 5/6).
[7] (RO 1/3N HD) (RO 4/6).
[8] (RO 1/3N LL) (RO 6/6).

Keying through glazing, veiling, and topping   One color placed over the top of a group of colors will key them. In painting, this method is called glazing, and a golden-colored varnish, or a flat wash of one color over a picture, will unify all the colors in the composition. In dress, this result is achieved through placing a transparent or semitransparent fabric over several colors. Chiffon or georgette over a figured material, or over the many-colored flowers on a hat, will key the colors. When this method is used in dyeing it is called topping. A piece of embroidery with inharmonious colors may be keyed by dipping the piece in a weak dye bath of some beautiful color.

Keying through tying   Colors that are not entirely agreeable when placed next to each other may be tied together or harmonized by the use of a neutral tone between the two colors. In addition to the neutrals, black, white, and gray, an intermixture of silver and gold can serve to tie colors. It is well known that tan will bring colors together, and when green and purple are partly neutralized they have a tendency to harmonize a group of colors with which they are combined.

Keying through texture   A rough texture will have a tendency to key colors because of the variations in light and shadow over its surface. For example, bright colors printed on terry cloth would appear softer than the same colors on glazed chintz, for the rough weave of the terry cloth would tend to melt the colors together.

SOURCES FOR COLOR HARMONIES

There are two common sources for ideas on color arrangements:

1. They may be adapted from a beautifully colored picture or fabric, and fitted to a special need
2. They may be made by combining related or contrasting colors according to the principles of color use.

The enterprising color worker keeps his eyes open for good color suggestions, and he has a collection of reference material that he is always changing. His taste improves as he studies, and while there are frequent additions to his file, there are also many subtractions. Sometimes a magazine cover will offer a wealth of suggestions for color arrangements. Quite frequently beautifully colored illustrations and advertisements appear in the magazines. Other sources are: fabrics, such as cretonnes, chintzes, printed linens, and silks; pottery; fine book illustrations and reproductions of good paintings, which are becoming readily available. Even the inexpensive magazines often have color reproductions of the works of such fine colorists as Cézanne, Van Gogh, Matisse, Georgia O'Keefe, Diego Rivera, and many others whose paintings will offer rich suggestions for color work. Very often one may select a portion of one of these colored plates to follow. If only a small section is being chosen from a composition, it is important to make sure that balanced colors are being selected. There is a tendency, in working from such illustrations as have been mentioned, to overlook the balance of bright and dulled colors. There must be enough of the background colors to make an effective setting for the bright colors. When the sizes are increased, as would be the case if a room decoration were planned from a small illustration, there probably should be a proportionately larger amount of background color and smaller amounts of bright than is shown in the original picture. In adapting these beautiful color schemes the worker must be able to preserve the same delightful color relationships. If the appealing color is blue-green, and it is next to a beautiful tone of orange, the colors should be kept in similar positions. If the blue-green were placed next to a purplish blue, which, in the picture, is separated from it by a large area of grayed color, the result will not have the beauty the worker had hoped to secure. Remember that the fine quality in a color scheme may be due to the values used, while sometimes it is due to the balance of grayed and bright colors. One must discover what has made the original beautiful before attempting to adapt it to another purpose.

Certain color combinations give pleasure to the eye, and others offend. Until one has had a great deal of practice in combining colors *Standard color harmonies* it is helpful to follow those harmonies which have been used successfully by artists for many years. It may seem at first glance that a list of color harmonies will give everything one needs to know about combining colors. Unfortunately, this is not true. As a matter of fact, some of the least beautiful as well as some of the most beautiful color arrangements can be made by following the so-called standard color harmonies. All they can do is to present a framework upon which to build, but careful attention must be given to the principles of good color use lest the results prove unfortunate. These standard harmonies will help to carry one along to color combinations which might otherwise be overlooked, and so, for the stimulation they may give to the imagination, they deserve our attention. The standard color harmonies may be divided into two main groups:

A. *Harmonies of related colors*
B. *Harmonies of contrasting colors.*

RELATED HARMONIES

Related color harmonies are those in which the colors are similar. They include the *one-hue harmony* and the *analogous harmony.* The simplest of these is the one-hue harmony.

One-hue harmony

(This is also called *one mode,* and *monochromatic.*) (See figure 198D, page 296.) In instances where only one color is used, there may be different values and intensities. A one hue harmony is always a safe one to use but is more effective for dress, or for a comparatively small area, such as a rug, or even walls and rugs. It may become tiresome if carried out in an entire room, as was described in the paragraphs on Color Balance. In one-hue harmonies additional interest may be gained if there is a contrast in the textures to be combined, as smooth wool with pique, or rough wool with leather. A man's apparel would show a one-hue harmony of blue in different values and intensities if he were wearing a dark blue suit, a white shirt with stripes of a lighter and brighter blue, a dull blue tie, and black hat and shoes. *The neutrals black, white, and gray may be used in any harmony.* In matching colors for a one-hue harmony, be very sure that you are getting the exact hue; a greenish blue is unpleasant with a purplish blue, and a reddish purple—crimson, for example—is disagreeable with reddish orange—such as scarlet. In matching colors it is safer to try them both by daylight and by artificial light, since some colors take on an entirely different hue in artificial light.

Analogous harmonies

When colors are used which lie next to or near each other on the color chart, they form analogous harmonies. They are usually most agreeable when they are limited to those colors falling between the primaries, and they may include any or all of these adjacent hues. For example, between the primaries yellow and blue such combinations as G and BG; Y, YG, and G; or YG, G, BG, and B, might be used. An analogous harmony shows one color running through the entire group; as green running through YG, G, and BG; or orange through YO, O, and RO. (See figure 198E, page 296.)

In using analogous harmonies, the colors should always be in different values or different intensities; or they should differ both in value and intensity. If they are too nearly alike it will seem as though an attempt had been made to match the colors, but that the result just missed being pleasant. Three adjacent combinations which are exceedingly difficult to manage are the colors on either side of a primary. These pairs are: RP with RO; BP with BG; YO with YG. It is difficult to use blue-purple with blue-green, or yellow-green with yellow-orange, and it takes genius to combine red-purple and red-orange beautifully, because the colors in these pairs are neither different enough to form good contrasts, nor are they sufficiently related to create harmonies. In peasant or folk art one frequently finds beautiful combinations of red-orange and red-purple, and one wonders why they are so rarely pleasant when they are used by the modern amateur. In order to discover how the effects have been secured it would be profitable to study such combinations of these hues as is seen in the old Mexican embroidery illustrated in figure 4. In many instances, the colors have been produced with vegetable dyes and thus lack the harshness of some of the aniline dyes. In most examples, the red-orange and red-purple are found in small areas and are frequently combined with transitional hues which harmonize with both. Colors often used for this purpose are: blues, greens in their varied hues of yellow-green, green, and blue-green; purples in dark values; tan; silver or gold; and the neutrals—black, white, and gray.

Analogous harmonies are apt to be quiet and restful, and they show more variety than one-hue harmonies. They may be used for any purpose, although, we repeat, they are not likely to be so completely successful for the color scheme of an entire room unless interest has been provided by changes of values and intensities or a variety of textures to supply some of the contrast otherwise obtained through changes of color.

HARMONIES OF CONTRASTING COLORS

The contrasting harmonies are:

1. *The complementary harmony*
2. *The double complementary harmony*
3. *The split complementary harmony*
4. *The triads.*

Combinations of opposite colors are more difficult to use than those of neighboring colors. When they are well done, however, they are richer than related harmonies and more satisfying to the eye for rooms, window displays, or any purpose where large amounts of color are to be used. The addition of a contrasting color to a color scheme is like adding pepper to food, and therefore the "Law of Color Areas" should be the guide when contrasting colors are used.

Complemen-
tary harmonies
When colors directly opposite each other in the color circle are used, they form complementary harmonies. In the Prang circle they are Y and P; B and O; R and G, etc. In the Munsell circle they are Y and PB; B and O; R and BG, etc. In the psychologist's color chart, they are R and G; YG and P; Y and B; O and BG.

Complementary schemes may be most pleasing, or they may be the least satisfactory, depending upon how they are used. The reddish hues, in particular, need careful handling, because they are so much stronger than their complements. Either they or the complement should be dull, or very light or dark, or else only a small note of the opposite should be used. Of all the contrasting colors, red and green are perhaps the most difficult to combine beautifully. Their tints, pink and green, usually lack character when placed together. The complements as seen in the Munsell chart—red with blue-green, or green with red-purple—are apt to be more pleasing. (See figure 198A, page 296.)

Double com-
plementary
harmonies
Two directly adjacent colors and their complements, when used together, form double complementary harmonies. Examples on the Prang chart are: P and RP with Y and YG (see figure 198C, page

296); R and RO with G and BG. In using a double complementary harmony, there should be one outstanding hue, which would be the largest amount used, and it should be the dullest of all the colors; the next color may be a little brighter, but should still be dull; the third color, used in only a small amount, ought to be about one-half neutralized; the fourth color, for the smallest accents, may be in or near its brightest intensity. To illustrate: a plum colored suit (dark, dulled purple) might be worn with an egg-shell blouse (light, dulled yellow) and a fuchsia-colored hat (fairly dark, somewhat neutralized red-purple) with a band of egg-shell, plum color, and chartreuse (rather light and fairly bright yellow-green). This combination of colors completes the double complementary harmony of P, RP, Y, and YG.

Combinations of a primary or an intermediate color with the colors on either side of its complement form split complementary harmonies, as for example, Y with RP and BP; or YO with B and P. As the term implies, one "splits" or divides the complement of a hue into its component parts, using these parts only, and omits the complement itself. Thus, the Y, RP, and BP combination is secured by splitting the complement of Y, which is P, into RP and BP. These are the colors on either side of P which, when mixed, form purple. Since a primary is an element, it does not have component parts. The colors on either side of it do not enter into its composition. Therefore, one cannot start to plan a split complementary harmony with a binary color, because its complement is a primary, and it is impossible to split a primary because there is only one color in its composition. The colors sometimes mistakenly combined as split complementary harmonies are YG, RO, and RP; P, YO, and YG; O, BP, and BG; in all of these combinations the effect is likely to give an impression of discord rather than harmony. A true split complementary scheme is a harmony of similar colors with a note of a contrasting color. The amounts of the different values and intensities should be adjusted as in any other contrasting harmony. *Split complementary harmonies*

On the Prang color chart, equilateral triangles create four triads. These are: the Primary Triad, made of the three primary colors, R, B, and Y; the Binary or Secondary Triad—G, O, and P; and the two *Triads*

Intermediate Triads—(a) YO, BG, and RP (see figure 198B, page 296), and (b) YG, BP, and RO. On the Munsell color chart the triads are as nearly equilateral triangles as can be made with ten hues in the circle. The hues forming the points of the triad triangle should always be at least three hues apart on the color chart. Thus every triangle will have three spaces on two of its sides, and four spaces on the third side. To find the Munsell triads, draw a diagram of the ten-hue circle. Then put a piece of transparent paper over the diagram and draw these triangles, locating each one of the triads. Starting with RP and counting three hues toward the right, draw a line to Y; from Y count three points farther to BG, and draw another line; connect the BG and RP, and you have the RP, Y, and BG triad. A second triad including RP can be made by counting four hues to the right, to GY, and three hues beyond it to B, resulting in RP, GY, and B. The third triad with RP is located by counting three hues to Y, four to B, giving RP, Y, and B. Any similar triangles on the chart will locate triads.

While triads are the richest of all the harmonies if they are well used, they are the ones which need the most careful treatment.

How to combine contrasting colors

When three unrelated hues have to be combined, the color worker feels as if he were handling high explosives. Although no unqualified answer can be given for color combinations, he usually follows some such plan as this: The color chosen to occupy the largest space is of the lowest intensity, and though the degree of neutralization must be determined by the use for which the scheme is planned, the color is likely to be definitely neutralized; the next amount will still be neutralized; the third may be bright, and a proportionately small amount would be used. Imagine a cretonne showing the YO, BG, and RP triad; the background is YO, so grayed that it would be called a straw color; the larger amount of the design is a darker, dulled YO, and a dulled BG, and there are small figures of bright RP. These colors balance each other because they use all of the color nerves in the eye; and, because they are so varied in degrees of brightness and in amounts, they give pleasure.

Chapter Ten

SOLVING AN ART PROBLEM

THREE CHARACTERISTICS mark the person who is prepared to make suitable designs or wise purchases: First, he is able to measure his choices according to the principles of art in order that his selections may have beauty; second, he knows enough about the materials and processes used to be able to judge good workmanship; and third, he has a certain store of related information—such as some knowledge of science and economics—which has a more or less direct bearing upon his problem. These qualifications make it possible for him to form a good judgment upon:

1. *Whether the object should be purchased or made*
2. *The factors which affect good quality*
3. *The right price to pay in relation to the income, considering the other demands made upon it*
4. *The time and strength consumed in making the object in the light of the return it yields (this return may be measured in increased skill, or in the satisfaction resulting from the finished object)*
5. *The time and strength it will take to maintain it in good condition.*

Only when a problem in purchasing or in designing has been worked out to satisfy all these requirements, may it be called a *related art problem*. The ability to apply this related information should give one a sense of relative values and of appropriateness. Furthermore, it will help to bring art into close terms with everyday life.

THE STEPS IN SOLVING AN ART PROBLEM

The plan suggested here can be applied to the solving of any art problem. Since it is based upon the generally accepted steps in solving a problem, one does well to think through the various stages or jot down his conclusions before making or buying anything that has to be lived with and looked at for a length of time. This plan for solving a problem has four steps:

1. *Recognizing the problem—that is, setting up a definite aim or purpose to be accomplished*
2. *Making a plan for working out the problem, which involves collecting all the information related to it*
3. *Carrying out the plan*
4. *Testing the results and making a final judgment of the success or failure of the plan before accepting it or discarding it to make another.*

SELECTING A RUG

In considering a typical problem, such as the selection of a rug, the details of the plan would be filled in somewhat as follows:

THE PROBLEM

The aim is to select a suitable rug for the living and dining room illustrated in figure 164A.

THE PLAN

Some of the factors which will need to be considered before a satisfactory rug can be selected are: *the room*—its purpose, size, shape, wall treatment, furnishings, and the people who are to use it; *textile information*—such as weave construction, properties of fibers used for rugs, and textures suitable for a floor covering, for the use of the room, and for the type of furnishings; *art information* —standards of structural and decorative design, and of color; eco-

Figure 164A. (Photograph by Julius Shulman.) If one were considering the purchase of a suitable rug for this room his choice might be a rug similar in type to figure 164B.

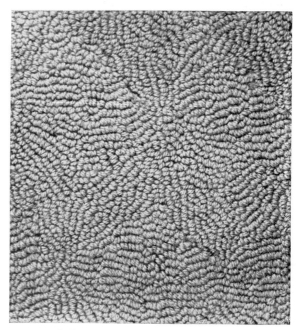

Figure 164B. This is a good type of patterned rug because the design, which is created by the direction in which the looped yarns were placed, is flat in effect.

nomic aspects—amount that should be spent, time and effort required to keep the rug clean, reduction of cost of maintenance by wise selection, effect of buying good materials and colors, and reliable shops or makes of rugs.

CONSIDERATIONS IN CARRYING OUT THE PLAN

The room   The room is a living and dining room, 14′ × 24′; the walls are light gray (HL); the furniture wood is blond oak; the casement cloth curtains tone into the color of the wood; the upholstery in the living room is beige; accents in the room are saffron yellow (YYO ⅛N LL), persimmon red (RRO ⅛N) and black. The family consists of two adults who have simple tastes. This characteristic is already expressed in the choice of the furnishings in the room which indicate their owners' ability to enjoy the beauty resulting from good line, good construction, and restraint in decoration.

Textile information   Materials should be chosen for appearance and economy. The fibers used for rugs are—wool, linen, cotton, hemp, jute, grass, and synthetic fibers. Worsted yarn and some synthetics give longest wear. The two principal types of weave construction in floor coverings are the flat weave and the pile weaves, cut and uncut, including chenille, Wilton, Brussels, and Axminster, as well as those in which surface yarns are cemented upon a base. Textures should be sturdy and the pile high and dense to withstand wear. The much-used dining area needs a texture that is serviceable. The character of the furniture and the decorative objects in this room suggest an intermediate texture and a substantial fabric.

Art information: 1. Structural design   The shape of the rug should harmonize with the shape of the room. It is desirable to have it large enough to appear to cover the floor space adequately. Usually the margin of plain floor left around the rug is in about the proportion of one inch to each foot of floor space in the room. Therefore, in a room of this size—14′ × 24′—a rug measuring about 12′ × 21′ would be suitable. This size would be available in broadloom carpeting and in some ready-made rugs. A rug which serves as a good background for furnishings is quiet in effect; that is, it is inconspicuous and appears to stay flat

2. Decorative design

upon the floor. The type of design should be in harmony with the furnishings. These considerations call for a plain rug or a well-packed geometrical or conventionalized surface pattern. If the rug is to be chosen for its background qualities, quiet colors and not much contrast between the lights and darks should be selected.   3. *Color*

In this instance there is a sufficient amount of money to buy   *Economics* a rug of good quality, but not enough to have it sent to the cleaner frequently, and it cannot soon be replaced. Therefore the rug must be of a fiber and weave which will wear well, and of a pattern and color which will not show spots easily. Since it requires more experience to judge the qualities of a rug than the average person has, it is desirable to know what makers of rugs are reliable, or which stores are dependable.

CARRYING OUT THE PLAN, OR MAKING THE SELECTION

After one has acquired the necessary information concerning the factors listed, and has applied it to the particular problem, he is able to make a satisfactory selection. He might choose a rug, then, similar to the one in figure 164B, which is described as follows: size —12′ × 21′; fiber—wool; yarn—worsted (long, parallel twisted wool fibers); weave—loop pile with securely anchored loops close together, so as to make a firm body; design—an all-over pattern which results from the way the rug is made rather than from the use of yarns of different colors; color—gray, keyed to the color of the wall but darker in value, ranging from low light to middle value because of variations in the texture.

THE FINAL JUDGMENT

The final judgment can be made only after the rug is used. The success of the choice will be measured by the degree of satisfaction derived from the use of the rug.

SELECTING A PLACE MAT

The following paragraphs are included to show how one might plan for the choice of each detail in a room just as he would for the purchase of something so important and costly as a rug. Here, the problem is to choose or make place mats for a dining room table (figure 165A). *The plan* involves these considerations: *the room,* its furnishings, and the people who will use it; some *textile information* having to do with the materials which are available and suitable for a washable place mat; *art knowledge* which will give standards by which to judge good structural and decorative design, good color, and consistent texture. The *economic aspects* of the problem are the amount of time or money that should be spent on the mats and the question of whether they can be cleaned satisfactorily.

Starting out on the plan, it is recognized that an undecorated place mat, well chosen for size, color, and texture, makes a beautiful setting for table appointments, food, and flowers. However, sometimes one wants to use some decoration and the problem becomes that of finding or making mats which have character and individuality. Figure 165B shows two mats that were chosen for the same table: one, a sage-green linen, is embroidered by machine with black, white, and dark green threads. The other is oyster-white linen, hand-embroidered with brown and orange threads.

There are times when one would like to make place mats: for example, if the ready-made ones are too small to hold adequately one's own place setting; or if the table requires a size somewhat different from the usual one in order to seat a desired number of people. As the points in the plan are considered, we see that both mats are suited to an informal room and to the undecorated dishes and silver. The colors, too, go well with the sandy beige tone of the pottery and with the colors in the room. The design has been placed out at the ends of the mats, and for the one with the more striking band, the napkin has been left plain, while a small, embroidered motif, harmonizing with the shape of the folded napkin, has been used on the napkin for the mat with the narrow border.

It does not seem unreasonable to predict that the owner of these mats would feel that they are well designed for her purpose, for they seem to fit into their setting as a natural adjunct in the entire scheme. This last consideration is, after all, of the utmost importance in the solving of an art problem.

Figure 165A and B. (Machine-embroidered mat by Esta James. Pottery by Denwar. Silver by Allan Adler.) A, the place setting for which a mat was to be selected. B, a machine-embroidered mat and a hand-embroidered mat and napkin which were chosen according to the essential qualities to be considered in the selection of a place mat for these appointments.

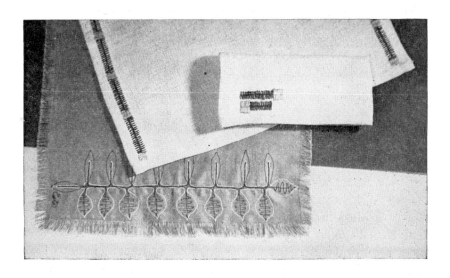

Chapter Eleven

MAKING AND JUDGING DESIGNS

THE MAKING of a design comes spontaneously to the person who has native ability. He has an unconscious feeling for organization, and designing for him is a completely creative experience. This chapter is not meant for the designer who knows instinctively how to convey his message in a good design. Rather, it is for the person who is seeking a method by which he may learn a basic way of thinking in terms of design. The designing process is a form of organization in which the elements are a collection of units. These units, in the art field, happen to be sizes, shapes, and colors. A good design is built up as logically as any other type of organization and may be compared to a form for the movements of a sonata or to the plan of a city made up of blocks and lots.

A knowledge of a logical process for making a design is of interest to the consumer as a matter of intelligent appreciation of the things he uses. To the person who would make designs it shows an easy, consistent method of working. By observing the principles of art described in the previous chapters, anyone can learn to make orderly, acceptable designs. Since design is a form of self-expression one may expect to add quality and individuality to his work in the measure of his appreciation and his imagination. There is no better way to develop imagination, good judgment, and fine standards of taste than through a thoughtful study of good designs. If, at this time, the principles of art are a conscious or unconscious part of one's thinking, they are being used as a standard for measuring quality. It must be remembered that mere correctness—adherence to the principles of design—will not insure beauty. A design may show the application of all the principles and still be lacking in character or style. On the other hand, if it has character and shows the strong feeling of a creative mind, a design may be significant even though some, or conceivably, all of the recognized measures for judging it are missing. Students are frequently reminded of this statement, attributed to Beethoven: "I have learned all the rules so that I may *know how* to break them." It is usually discovered that those great artists whose work seems to defy the conventions of formal structure have built their work upon a background of thorough training in these very conventions. In spite of breaking them, these artists are able to achieve beauty through the sheer force of style and character. In this chapter and throughout the book, will be found many designs made by primitive artists who knew nothing about methods of working or standards for judging their designs. A careful scrutiny will reveal that their unconscious feeling for order was so vital, and their work so sincere and teeming with creative invention, as to have real beauty.

The designer is urged to invent—to "play with his pencil"— until something interesting appears on the paper. Remember that uninfluenced ideas are best if one really has something he can say in terms of design. However, if ideas do not come, the next suggestion is to look at many excellent designs in order to store away myriad impressions. This will usually make it possible to create something of one's own that does not resemble anything that has been seen, yet the design could not have come from any but an inventive or a well-furnished mind. If a designer goes to one source only, his work may become mannered. That is as undesirable as the work of a designer who has only one idea of his own and copies that too long. The subsequent material is included for the person who wants to make a design for something but does not know how to start.

Although the different uses for designs will impose different limitations for working them out, the same general method may be followed in making designs for any purpose. The working plan outlined here is followed by an application of the plan to many familiar problems, such as how to make a design for a woven runner, a room, a costume, how to mount a picture, and how to letter.

There are two considerations in every design: first, the shape of the object itself, called the structural design; second, the enrichment of that structure, or the decorative design. Before one can be a successful designer he must get rid of the idea that design includes only the decoration added to an object. The structural design is of the greatest importance and should have the designer's first consideration.

OUTLINE OF PROCEDURE IN THE MAKING
OF A GOOD DESIGN

A. *Kinds of design*
  1. *Structural design (see Chapter II)*
     The size, form, color, and texture of the object
        Note. Since the structural design is the fundamental or essential part of an object, it must be beautiful in itself.
     Structural design is conditioned by—
     a. *The use to which the object will be put*
     b. *The person for whom the object is planned*
     c. *The surroundings in which it will be used*
     d. *Standards for good design*
  2. *Decorative design (see Chapter II)*
     The enrichment of the object
        Note. Decorative design may be omitted. If it is included it should be used to enhance the structural design.
     Decorative design is conditioned by—
     a. *The structural design*
     b. *The use to which the object will be put*
     c. *The person for whom the object is planned*
     d. *The surroundings in which it will be used*
     e. *The personality of the designer (which determines the character or quality of the design)*
     f. *Standards for good design*
     g. *The amount of decoration desirable*
     h. *The nature of the design—motif or idea:*
        (1) *Sources—abstract or geometric lines or masses, symbolism, or nature forms*
        (2) *Treatment—conventionalization, or adaptation to the materials used and the use to which the object will be put; pictorial or naturalistic. (Suitable for pictures, but not*

appropriate on articles for use such as clothing, house furnishings, decorative objects, etc.)

Note. An essential requirement for good decorative design is character or "decorative quality."

B. Method of working out a design

1. Structural design
   a. Plan the size, shape, and color of the object, according to the principles of design:
      (1) Proportion
      (2) Harmony—shape, texture, ideas (suitability to purpose), and color
      (3) Rhythm
      (4) Balance
      (5) Emphasis
   b. Execute the structural design.

2. Decorative design.
   Geometric plan or "layout"
   a. The aim in the layout is to secure an orderly arrangement.
   b. Within the structural design the principal masses of form and color of the decoration are indicated by sketching or "blocking in" the sizes and shapes in their positions. (See figure 166.) Now the design is in an experimental state. One should play freely with shapes and colors, for here one desires inventiveness. After something has been put down, the design may then be judged according to:
      (1) Emphasis
      (2) Proportion
      (3) Harmony
      (4) Rhythm
      (5) Balance

3. The details of the decorative design
   The objective at this step is to secure beauty and character.
   Arrange and judge forms and colors according to:
      (1) Emphasis
      (2) Proportion
      (3) Harmony
      (4) Rhythm
      (5) Balance
      (6) Individuality

Designs that have been worked out in this manner have coherence, and the worker is enabled to perceive relative values if he uses

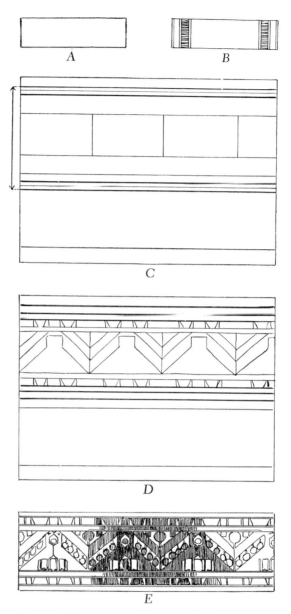

Figure 166A, B, C, D, and E. An illustration of
the process of building a design.

Figure 166F. Blue and white towel, Italian, Umbrian, XV Century. This conventional design is adapted to the process of weaving. Observe the fine pattern created by the sizes and shapes in the border and the decorative quality in the interpretation of the bird and plant forms. (Courtesy of the Minneapolis Institute of Arts.)

this process: first, planning his structural design; second, blocking in the entire area the decoration is to occupy; and third, breaking this area up into details that are related to each other and to the entire structure. It is important to form a habit of looking at any design from the standpoint of, first, the whole effect and, second, the details. It is the mark of the amateur to judge or to make designs by working from the details to the whole. The effect is likely to be that of unrelated units designed without reference to the whole.

A concrete example of the process of building a design is illustrated in figures 166A, B, C, D, E, and F. In order that all the steps of this problem may be considered, let us assume that the designer of the blue-and-white runner chosen for this analysis has planned to use it on a chest of drawers in a particular bedroom. The furniture is mahogany, and there is much white in the room,

Analysis of the making of a design

so that a white runner will not stand out too conspicuously, and the blue of the pattern will make an interesting color contrast.

The structural design

First step (figure 166A): The objective is to show a well-proportioned border of wood on each side of the runner on the top of the chest and to have the scarf hang down over the sides so that an oblong of interesting shape may be seen against the side of the chest. The top of the chest measures 20″ × 34″, so the structural design will be an oblong measuring approximately 15″ × 54″.

The position of the decorative design

Second step (figure 166B). It is decided that the ends of the runner are to receive the decoration. The space it is to occupy is then blocked out on the structural design as at B. This space is compared with the remaining background areas and adjusted if necessary in order to gain good proportions.

Breaking the space

Third step (figure 166C): The big space which is to contain the design is subdivided. These new shapes and spaces are tested to see that the proportions are beautiful and the shapes harmonious with the big oblong within which they are placed.

Filling the spaces

Fourth step (figure 166D): The spaces are broken up still further, and the general movement the eye is to take is now determined. It is at this stage that the designer is urged to experiment with the utmost freedom. Sketches, so quickly made that one would not be reluctant to discard them, will help the worker to try out several ideas. After a sketch has been made the tests for the art principles are applied, and the designer asks himself if his design adequately fills the space; if it looks orderly; if an easy, rhythmic movement is created by the leading lines; if the proportions are agreeable; and if the background shapes, as well as those of the design itself are beautiful and in harmony with each other.

Determining the character of the design

Fifth step (figure 166E): It is at this point that the character of the design is established. The motif may have been selected before the design was started, or it may be chosen at this stage in the process. The work will gain individuality according to the amount of inventiveness that goes into the interpretation of the motif or idea. The person who finds that he cannot originate a good design may select a good idea, interpret it to suit his own taste, and change it in whatever manner he finds advisable in order to adapt it to his design and its purpose. The libraries and museums hold a wealth of inspiration for young designers. Valuable illustrative material can be found in the designs of Persia, Java, Mexico, Guatemala, Sweden, Central Europe—in short, all folk art is likely to yield rich inspiration for design. Some of these designs may furnish an idea for the plan or the "geometric lay-out," while others may suggest interesting details. The motifs chosen for this design are flower and bird forms. These ideas were adapted to the shapes "blocked in" in D. The forms were stylized or conventionalized in order to make them suitable for use and adapted to the process of weaving. The background shapes were as carefully studied as the shapes of the pattern, for they are just as important a factor in the effect of a design.

Sixth step (figure 166F): After the details are added and refined, the design is judged again. When it is beautiful as well as orderly in its arrangement it is declared finished and is ready to be woven.

Adding and beautifying the details

Seventh step: The colors and threads are selected and the design is woven into the fabric.

Applying the design

Let us suppose that, instead of making a design for weaving, it was desired to make a simple design to be embroidered on the ends of this runner (figures 167A and B). The designer would proceed in the same manner as has been diagramed in figure 166 from A, the structural design, through C, breaking up of the space for decoration. The change in the design appears at this point, and figures A and B parallel figures C and E. The same procedure as

Figure 167A and B. The process of making a simple design for embroidery is illustrated, in order to show that the same procedure is followed whether a design is to be simple or complicated. The aim is always to break up the spaces into interesting shapes. The layout in figure 166C has been used as a foundation for this design. The procedure in figure 167A parallels figure 166C, while that in figure 167B parallels figure 166E.

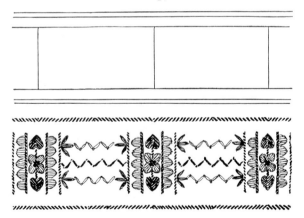

explained above would be followed for filling the spaces, determining the character of the design, and beautifying the details. The only outstanding difference is that the design needs to be planned so that it can be embroidered rather than woven.

THE INTERPRETATION OF IDEAS

A study of Ruth Reeves' printed linen in figure 168B and the original abstract painting of West Point (figure 168A) from which she took the idea will reveal that the character of a design is determined not so much by the source which inspired it as by its intended use. Observe how the surface repeat was built for the textile design and how the black, white, and blue tones are distributed so that they are beautiful in themselves and do not depend upon any rela-

Figure 168A. Abstract Study at West Point by Ruth Reeves.
This painting was used by Miss Reeves as her "start-off" for the hand-blocked linen called "West Point." (Courtesy of Ruth Reeves.)

tionship to the forms found in the painting. The reader can follow still another stage in creative imagination if he attempts to visualize the appearance of a photograph taken at the point from which this painting was made. He can then appreciate how much invention and interpretation went into the abstract painting which suggested the still more abstract design in the printed linen.

Because the term "decorative design" applies to any decoration on an object, it will be recognized that a decorative design may be good or poor. The decorative design in figure 169 is poor because the worker lost sight of the fact that any decoration for useful objects

Figure 168B. "West Point" by Ruth Reeves.
Hand printed in blue and black on white linen. This fabric shows how the painting in figure 168A was used as an inspiration for a surface pattern and adapted to the technique of block printing. (Courtesy of Ruth Reeves.)

Figure 169. A table runner printed in blue, pink, and green. The design and the color scheme of this runner lack "decorative quality." The vine and the birds are imitations of nature, and the design is unorganized. Compare this runner with figures 166F, 170, and 171.

should be a simplified pattern rather than an attempt to copy nature. He was so concerned with making his theme recognizable that he imitated the bird and plant forms as closely as he could. Meanwhile, the more realistic his design grew, the more it lacked character, and the less appropriate it became. Compare with this weak treatment of nature forms the Mexican Indian designs shown

Figure 170. Otomi bag, State of Hidalgo, Mexico. The striking contrast of the white design against a black ground and the inventive, simplified treatment of the motifs account for the "decorative quality" of this woven bag.

Figure 171. Embroidery made by the Indians of Toluca, Mexico. Used as a hanging, the pattern of an embroidered textile of this sort may add character to a room. Such motifs and massing of lights and darks as are seen here offer interesting suggestions for designs for needlework.

in figures 170 and 171 and see the difference between designs which have, and those which lack, character. The Mexican designs were made for objects intended to be used, and they show very clearly the Indian's idea that nothing is too small or too simple to merit being made beautiful. Figure 170 is a woven black and white woolen bag used for many practical purposes. Figure 171 is an embroidered headdress worn by the Indians of the Sierras at their fiestas. Observe that these untutored people have some quite unconscious instinct which keeps their art simple and strong and filled with an innate sense of abstraction. These designs are direct, and the interpretations of natural forms and colors are vigorously handled. In each of the designs there is a strong feeling for rhythm and balance and a keen appreciation for the rightness of design for material.

Although one might truly say that all beautiful designs are more or less conventionalized or adapted to the materials and use, it does not follow that all conventionalized designs are beautiful. Both of the conventionalized designs in figure 172 are poor because they are commonplace. To be sure, by avoiding the fault of the imitation of nature, they are a step in the right direction, but they show that the designers lacked imagination. A successful treatment of a theme similar to those in figure 172 is shown in figure 173. The embroidery on this runner has gained some distinction through the contrast of the dark blue thread on the white linen cloth and through a certain individuality in the treatment of the motifs. While it cannot be said that this design has "decorative quality" to a marked degree, it is excellent for its purpose.

Turning to the designs for printed textiles on page 232, it will be seen that color, or light and dark, and drawing go hand in hand to produce character in design. The chintz patterns in figures 174A and B show a transition from design approaching the naturalistic to one that comes very close to abstraction. In A the colors have been conventionalized and, although the flower and leaf forms clearly resemble their sources, they are not imitative for they are quite stylized in their drawing and arrangement, and the color is entirely conventionalized. Furthermore, its charm gives the design individ-

Figure 172 (Above). Although both of these designs may be said to be conventionalized, they lack character. The details are weak, and the effect of the decoration as a whole is commonplace.

Figure 173 (Below). The design on this runner is good. The motifs carry the eye smoothly along the border, and the individual details are interesting.

uality. The modern design, B, taken from a Swedish peasant theme, has purely imaginary shapes and colors. They are really symbols invented from familiar forms which have been used until they have become traditional. Each of these chintz designs is good in its type. They all show good organization and a creative treatment, although they would be chosen for entirely different rooms.

The plate in figure 175 with its floral wreath falls into a class of design which would parallel the striped fabric in figure 174A. It is conventionalized and "decorative" both in design and color and offers a suggestion for a good type of design for the person who likes a gay and informal note in her tableware. What this designer did in the way of stylizing flower forms was carried even farther in figure

Figure 174A and B.
Two good designs in
curtain fabrics which
show varying degrees of
conventionalization in
color and drawing.

A

B

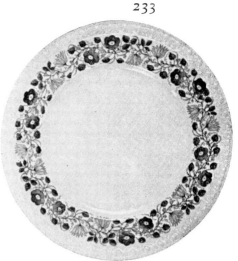

Figure 175. In this design the flower forms are decorative and the colors are conventionalized so that they are suitable for table ware.

176 in the bird and plant motifs. Here, grown-up designers have adopted the fanciful approach that a child might take toward design, and we are interested and amused at the naïveté of the design. How much better for children would be designs like these than the poor one on the plate in figure 177! In the latter, the decoration

Figure 176 (At left). Plate from Tonola, Mexico. The free technique and the simplified shapes in this design give it a feeling of sincerity and spontaneity.

Figure 177 (At right). How different from the stylized design in figure 176 is the poor, imitative design on this plate. Its influence upon a child would be in the direction of lowering rather than developing his taste.

suggests comic design without being either clever or amusing. This is an inferior design which would not stimulate a child's imagination or help to develop his taste. If a good design for a child's dish is not available—and frequently they are hard to find—it would be so much better to buy gay dishes of an attractive solid color or with brightly colored borders.

Making food attractive is one of the activities in which design is involved that frequently puzzles the homemaker. Sometimes she does not quite know how to begin or where to stop. It is all so simple if the fact is recognized that food is material for design and the same standards are used here as for any other composition. The best single standard is restraint. Any food which gives the impression of having been overtrimmed is distasteful to most people, and so even for the most festive occasions the hostess will be wise if she avoids over-emphasizing decoration. Ordinarily, one enjoys most the accent produced by the combination of natural materials. For example, chopped pimentos in cheese, or the green of a lettuce leaf with white cheese would make a pleasant color pattern for a sandwich

Figure 178. Undecorated cakes are always in good taste. If decoration is added it should be simple and quite abstract. In these cakes natural color has been added in single well-scaled spots of cherry, jelly, strips of angelica, and nuts, and they show a high standard for the decoration of food. (Courtesy of Ivey's.)

and would be enjoyed by the most fastidious person, whereas the same cheese colored with pink or green artificial coloring results in an effect that discriminating people consider very bad. The cookies in figure 178 are good in design, and illustrate the interest to be obtained with natural materials. On this plate the accenting colors have been supplied with cherries, strips of green angelica, drops of jelly with chopped pistachio nuts, and the pignolia nuts in which these macaroons were rolled. Some of the cakes were formed with a pastry tube, but all of the shapes are simple. This is about as much decorating as the homemaker will do if she has a sense of the value of her time. In figure 179 we see still another example of the handiwork of the Mexican Indian. In Mexico there is always an attempt to please the eye as well as the appetite, and these little cookies, sold in the market at Toluca, show a keen sense of design, but certainly no consideration of time! However, some of the simpler designs among these cakes could be done rather quickly, and for

Figure 179. A Mexican market place offered these entertaining designs. They are done with an instinctive sense of order and pattern.

Figure 180. These small cakes show types of design that might be chosen if one wished to give an air of festivity to a party. There is as much decoration as one would use, yet they are stopped short of looking overdone, and the colors used suggested natural, wholesome food. (Courtesy of Richards-Treat.)

Figure 181. Decoration that is too imitative, too bright in color, and too large marks these cakes as poor design.

special occasions one might sometimes be justified in using the extra minutes necessary. The cakes in figures 180 and 181, found in two food shops, show very different standards of design in still another type of decoration. In figure 181 the decoration is very poor. The flowers and leaves are not adapted to the idea of a cake, and the colors—bright pink, sharp light green, and "baby blue" frosting with too-bright flowers and leaves on top, show poor taste. In figure 180 there is reserve in the decoration and the colors, chocolate, butter yellow, fruit-juice pink, pistachio green, and white, are appetizing, for they suggest wholesome food.

In this search for character in design we turn to a very different field. The decorative animals in figures 182 and 183 would be of a type chosen by anyone who not only knows good design but enjoys

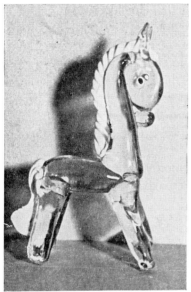

Figure 182.

Figures 182 and 183. There is character as well as play spirit in the amusing glass horse, the fantastic zebra, and the sturdy pottery horse. Decorative figures of this type can add wit and sparkle to the room into which they fit.

Figure 183.

Figure 184. The nearer this figure came to being a literal reproduction of a dog, the more it lost its value as a decorative object. One should distinguish between a likeness of this type and a creative design.

Figure 184.

fun. The whimsical glass horse and the humorous spotted one go along with the improbable zebra to make a collection showing character and decorative quality. The little dog in figure 184 would have more of this character had it looked less like somebody's real dog and more like no dog that ever was or could be.

Photographers who see with the eye of an artist have gone beyond mere picture making and are using the camera as a tool for creative work. Amateur photographers are searching to find beauty in the world about them, and in this search they are learning the arts of selection and elimination. By omitting what is irrelevant and stressing the important features in his picture, the photographer is able to portray the essential beauty and the character in his subject. In this connection it is interesting to analyze the two photographs in figures 185A and B. In A it is clear that the photographer recognized the character in the personality of the subject, but the photograph did not convey enough of the quality that he thought of as "character in design." By selecting from the original negative only that portion of the photograph which seemed to him to be significant and dramatic, he has shown us how to make a distinguished design.

Figure 185A.

Figure 185A and B. (Photographs by V. P. Hollis.) Enlarging the most significant feature in a picture is like throwing a spotlight on the important character on the stage. Notice how aware one is of a beauty that is insufficiently emphasized in the photograph of the entire figure.

Figure 185B.

In preparing a list of the requirements for good designs in various fields, one would find certain essential qualifications which apply to all. In judging any design one should consider its suitability for its service, the orderliness of its arrangement, the individuality of its treatment, and the beauty of its pattern and color.

It must not be assumed that a design is made only when a new form is created. When furniture and the decorative and useful ob- *Steps in designing a room* jects that go into the furnishing of a room have been placed, a design has been made. The main structural design is the size and shape of the room. This may be represented by figure 166A. Other structures—rugs, furniture, and various other objects—must then be placed within that form. The largest pieces are placed first, as in figures 166B and C. Arranging the smaller objects, such as movable chairs and the larger pictures, would correspond to figure 166D. Figures 166E and F, translated into terms of house furnishing, would be the arrangement of the books and the decorative details upon these larger forms already placed in D. The designer's appreciation of art would be shown in the choice of every object and color and in the manner in which the objects were grouped.

*Steps in de-
signing a
costume*
In dress design, as in house furnishing, the structural design is given to the designer. He must use as his basic plan the human figure, wishing to make it as beautiful as possible. Upon this structure other structural designs are placed—hats, dresses, shoes— which, in their turn, may receive the addition of some decorative design. The tests of orderly arrangement and beauty are applied. As in any design, there should be harmony. No unit exists for itself but should be an integral part of the entire costume. The more completely each detail is subordinated to the effect of the whole, the finer its quality becomes.

HOW TO MOUNT A PICTURE

*The Law of
Margins*
The design problem of planning margins enters into such everyday tasks as writing letters and invitations, lettering display cards and posters, and planning the margins of a mat for a picture. One may start out with a card or a piece of paper of a certain size and shape and arrange his composition within that shape; the size and shape of the mount become the structural design, and the block of writing or decoration corresponds with decorative design and is planned in the same manner as any other design. Or, on the other hand, one may be obliged to select a mount for a picture, which necessitates choosing a good structural design upon which to place the decorative design—the picture.

The principles of design to be observed in mounting pictures or written matter are: shape harmony, balance, and proportion. These principles are embodied in what is commonly called "The Law of Margins," as follows: *In a vertical oblong the bottom margin should be the widest,* the top next, and the sides narrowest; for the horizontal oblong the bottom should be the widest, the sides next, and

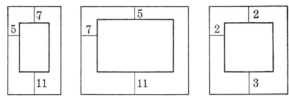

Figure 186. The "Law of Margins" applied to the mounting of a vertical oblong, a horizontal oblong, and a square. This method suggests a means of adding beauty and interest to the mounts of pictures, layouts, and written matter. The margins should give the impression of the approximate ratio of 5:7:11, but actual measurements will rarely give this effect, due to the varying forces in lines and colors.

the top narrowest; in a square the bottom should be the widest, and the sides and top equal to each other. (See figure 186.)

"Objects which are seen in an upright position have a tendency to appear as if they are dropping in space." This is a statement of the familiar "Law of Optics," and it is obvious that the art principle of balance is involved here. When mounting an object it is agreeable to counteract this illusion by placing it above the mechanical center of the area, so as to have more space below rather than above it. (Compare figures 187A and C.) *The Law of Optics*

Harmony of movement and of shape are reasons for the difference in sizes between the tops and sides in the horizontal and vertical oblongs. A horizontal oblong will lead the eye cross-wise, rather than up and down. Therefore the most harmonious movement will be secured if the margins on each side are somewhat wider than that at the top. This may readily be seen by studying figure 188. In the case of the vertical rectangle, it becomes more agreeable to have the top margin wider than the sides in order that the eye may be assisted rather than hindered in the upward and downward movement. (See

Figure 187B.

Figure 187C.

Figure 187A. A vertical oblong well mounted. Observe that the use of the widest margin at the base gives a sense of balance; that the next wider margin at the top enables the eye to carry along in the general movement of the picture without seeming to meet the top too suddenly and harmonizes the shape of the mount with the shape of the picture; and that all these margins follow approximately Greek proportions.

Figure 187B. A vertical oblong badly mounted. The shape of this picture demands that the eye travel with its height, but the wide margins at the sides carry the eye across, and there is a consequent sense of discomfort. (See figure 187A.)

Figure 187C. The "Law of Optics" was disregarded in mounting this picture with all the margins of equal width. Since mounted objects appear to be dropping in space, the use of a wider margin at the bottom than at the top would correct this unpleasant optical illusion. Compare these margins with those in figure 187A.

Figure 188. Painting by John Huseby.
Correct margins for a horizontal oblong. When the side margins are wider than the top the eye is carried in a horizontal direction, emphasizing the shape of the picture. This makes for shape harmony. The bottom margin is enough wider than the top to keep the picture from seeming to drop in space.

figure 187A.) In both instances the resulting shapes enhance and are harmonious with the oblong being mounted. A square looks best with its widest margin at the bottom; but the sides and top are most pleasing when alike, producing a rather close harmony between the shape of the picture and its mount (figure 189). If Greek proportions are used in determining the width of each margin, there will be a subtle variety in the spaces. In addition to margins for material placed symmetrically on a mount, as exemplified by the illustrations so far (figures 186–189), there is the type of arrangement

Figure 189. A square well mounted. The picture is balanced in the space because the bottom margin is wider than the top. The mount harmonizes with the square because the top and side margins are alike.

in which backgrounds are to be planned for a mass that is to be placed off-center. Here the question of informal balance is involved, and all masses and background spaces need to be carefully adjusted according to the weight of the attractions. When one is balancing material which is off-center, as in figure 153, or placing masses out at the edge of a page, as in the square and the lettering in Frank Lloyd Wright's splendid design for a magazine cover (figure 191), he must be aware of the relationship of all the spaces so that they will be beautifully proportioned.

In order that the mount may not appear meager, the size of the entire mat should be large enough to make an adequate setting for the picture or other material to be mounted. (See figure 189.) When the bottom margin is decided upon, each side that follows will be about two parts to three in relation to the previous space, or in the ratio of about 5:7:11. (See figure 186). This cannot be taken as a rule because the optical illusion created by the direction of the lines within the subject may seem to change the appearance of its actual size and shape. For a wide oblong or a picture with horizontal lines one would use a relatively wider mount, and for a long vertical shape with strong vertical lines a longer mount would be chosen. This is illustrated in proportion in figures 76 and 77 on pages 75 and 76.

Since the mount is to serve as a background its color should be in harmony with the general color scheme of the picture.

LETTERING

Good lettering is a matter of good designing. The selection of an appropriate style of alphabet together with well-planned arrangement and spacing depends solely upon one's knowledge of design, while good letter construction is due to good design plus practice. In lettering it is far more important that the design be good than that the letters be faultless in construction. In fact, letters which are so mechanically correct as to look like printer's type lack the individuality so pleasing in lettering done by hand.

The process of lettering is similar to that of making any other kind of design, and in lettering a poster, a place card, or a notice to post upon a bulletin board, the same method would be followed. To illustrate the procedure in lettering for any purpose, we shall follow through each of the typical steps as they would be taken in lettering the notice in figure 190D.

First write the material to be lettered, in order to gain a general idea of the amount of text. Make the writing approximately the same size as the lettering will be. Then decide what tool will be used for forming the letters. Among the tools likely to be useful for various sizes of letters and layouts are charcoal, crayon, soft pencil, brush, and the flat- and round-nibbed lettering pens. *Estimate the size of the letters and the mass, and select the tool*

The second step is to select an alphabet that is attractive and suitable in style, size, and weight to the idea to be expressed and to the tool which is to be used. A lighter type of alphabet should be chosen to write about such delicate things as laces and art objects *Select the alphabet*

Figure 190A.

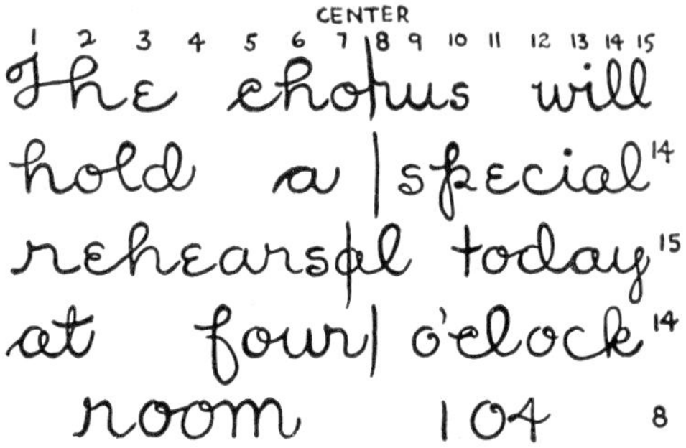

CENTER

1 2 3 4 5 6 7 8 9 10 11 12 13 14 15

The chorus will
hold a |special [14]
rehearsal today [15]
at four| o'clock [14]
room   1 O4   8

Figure 190B.

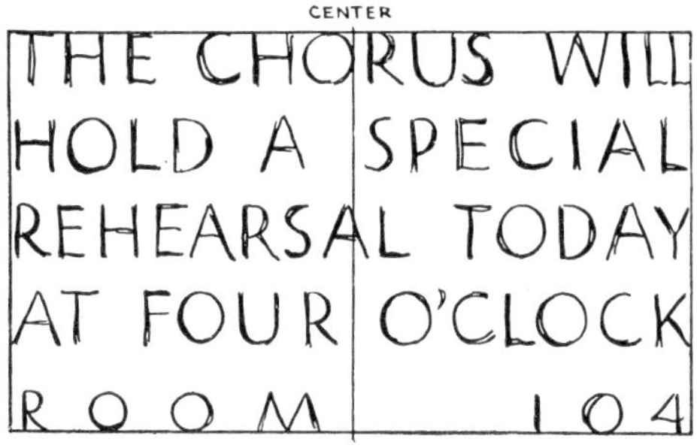

CENTER

THE CHORUS WILL
HOLD A |SPECIAL
REHEARSAL TODAY
AT FOUR| O'CLOCK
R O O M | 1 O 4

Figure 190C.

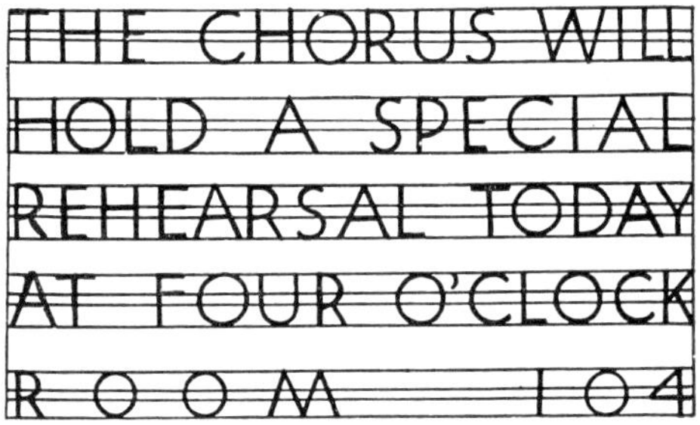

THE CHORUS WILL
HOLD A SPECIAL
REHEARSAL TODAY
AT FOUR O'CLOCK
R O O M   1 O 4

Figure 190D.

THE CHORUS WILL
HOLD A SPECIAL
REHEARSAL TODAY
AT FOUR O'CLOCK

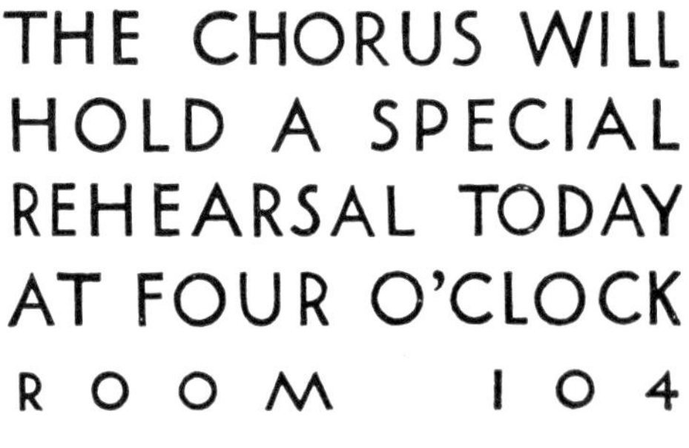

*Figure 190A, B, C, and D.
Four typical steps in lettering.*

R O O M   1 O 4

246

than would be selected for hardware. The alphabet should be simple and easy to read. One may use all capitals, or capitals with lower-case letters, or all lower case. An alphabet should be chosen in which the letters are well balanced and in good proportion. Letters will appear in better balance if the division lines in B, E, F, and H are placed slightly above rather than below the center. Since the degree of difference between the upper and lower divisions is a matter of good proportion, this difference will not be exaggerated, but will follow the Greek standard (figure 192).

The next step is to select the size, color, and texture of the card or sheet of paper on which the lettering will be placed. *Choose the paper*

Decide whether the rectangle is to be vertical or horizontal, and plan a well-proportioned oblong, with the margins drawn according to the "Law of Margins." (See figure 186.) *Plan margins*

In order to obtain a good arrangement, the shape of the entire mass of lettering must harmonize with the shape of the rectangle. The first written paragraph should be studied and so divided into lines that the lettering will be balanced on the page. Count the letters, in order to have the same number on both sides of the center line. The space between each word should be counted as a letter. Then, using a medium pencil, so that the work can easily be erased, sketch the letters very lightly. This step is merely to place the letters, not to form them, for adjustments will be necessary later. *Lightly sketch in the letters*

Since lettering is designing, the space between letters, the spaces between words and those between lines become a problem of the fine adjustment of masses of dark against light, and of keeping as orderly and harmonious a shape as possible for the outside edges of the block of lettering. If the lines do not have the same number of letters, the letters may be brought closer together, or they may be extended to fill the space. Frequently, however, it is desirable to re-word the material. Figure 190 shows the letters in some lines to be extended, and they are made more compact in others so as to retain the shape of the rectangle. The spaces between letters should be so arranged that the word will seem a unit rather than a collection of separate letters. The way to do this is to adjust the background spaces so that there appears to be the same amount of back-

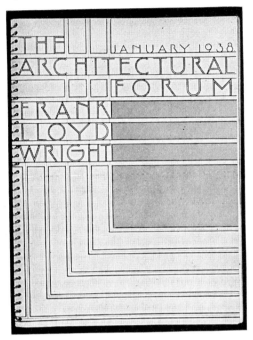

Figure 191. *The position of a red square gave unusual interest to this composition. Notice the beautiful balancing of the square and the lettering on the page; the subtle variations in the background spaces; and the way the letters have been adjusted to fit the size of the spaces. (Courtesy of The Architectural Forum.)*

ground around each letter. Since some letters are wide and some narrow, some light and others heavy, the spaces between letters should not be alike. If the spaces are alike, the narrow letters, such as I and J, will appear crowded, while such letters as A, T, V, and W, which have a great deal more background space, will seem too far apart. The spaces between words are usually the size of an ordinary letter, as the letter o. If words are much closer to one another than such a space, they are difficult to read. They may be somewhat farther apart, but not too far or else the eye must jump from one word to the next and the effect of unity is lost. The space between the lines is usually a little more than half the height of the capital letter, but this is variable. The space between lines should be just wide enough to make it easy to read the text, but narrow enough to make the block of lettering appear as a unit—a well-distributed pattern which makes an even gray tone against the background. This pattern may have the effect of a light gray if the letters are delicate in line and in form, or it may be a rather dark gray if formed

Figure 192. (By Barbara Warren Weismann.) A simple free-hand alphabet.

of sturdy letters. But the spaces should be so well adjusted that the sheet looks balanced and of an even tone when it is held off at a distance or looked at through half-closed eyes. (See figures 191 and 194.) If it seems "spotty" and shows irregular paths of light among the darks, the page will lack rhythm.

After the preliminary sketch has been made to show shape harmony in its general mass, balance in all its parts, and easy, rhythmic *Guide lines* movement, it is ready to be trued. The first step in the finishing process is to draw guide lines. Measure the height of the lines of lettering and the spaces between, and draw these lines very lightly, using a ruler. If they are faint enough, they will not interfere with the legibility of the lettering and may be left if the work is to be finished in pencil. It is well for the beginner to draw either three or four guide lines for each row of letters. When four lines are drawn, the base and the top lines indicate the height of the capital letters, and the tallest of the lower-case letters, b, d, f, h, k, l, and t. The two inside guide lines mark points somewhat above and somewhat below the center line, so that the proportions of the letters will follow the Greek standard. (See figure 190C.) The upper of these inside lines—the one drawn slightly above the center of the space—will indicate the height of the upper division of the capital letter B;

the cross-bars of E, F, and H; and it will locate the swing of the S, and points for the strokes of K, W, X, etc. This line also marks the top of the lower-case letters, such as a, c, e, n, and o, the cross-bar of t, and the body of the letters b, d, h, and k. The lower of these inner guide lines—the one slightly below the center—establishes the place for the cross-bar of A and G; the meeting point for K, M,

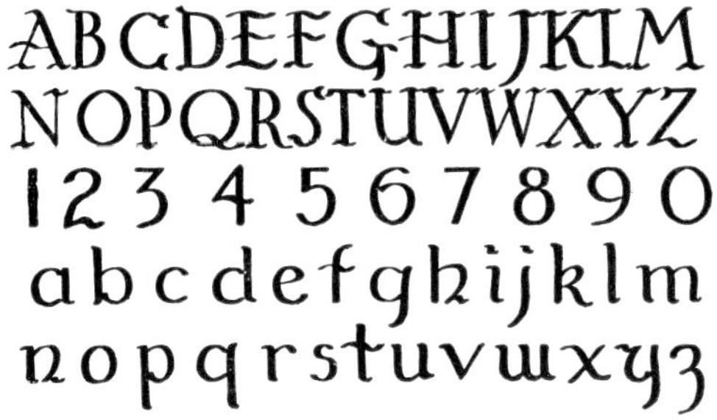

ABCDEFGHIJKLM
NOPQRSTUVWXYZ
1 2 3 4 5 6 7 8 9 0
a b c d e f g h i j k l m
n o p q r s t u v w x y z

Figure 193. (By Barbara Warren Weismann.) A simplified alphabet for manuscript writing.

and Y; and the point for the termination of the lobe of P and R (figure 192). For the lower-case letters, this line is used to locate the cross-bar of e and points on k, s, and x. The descending lines of the lower-case letters g, j, p, q, and y are somewhat shorter than the height of the stems of b and d as they rise above the body of the letter.

When three guide lines are used, the center line serves merely to assist the worker to judge spaces, and the divisions of the letters should be drawn slightly above or below that center line. It is important to remember that all divisions should appear to be on the same line above or below the center.

Carefully draw letters and space letters and words

The last step in lettering is to give careful attention to the construction of the letters. (It is well for the beginner to refer to a model alphabet constantly.) The faint sketch will help to place the letters, so that the entire attention may be given to the proportions of the letters and to the final adjustment of spaces. It is important to see that the width of the letter is in good proportion to its height; that the cross lines divide the letters into well-related spaces; that all the cross lines above the center follow the same line; and that those below the center are on a line, so that when the eye follows

Figure 194. Facsimile of the First Psalm from the Fust and Schoeffer Psalter. Printed on the Gutenberg Press in 1457. The dark and light massing of the lettering and the composition of this page can serve as an inspiration, whether one is using the simplest alphabet or a more complicated one of the manuscript type. (Courtesy of the Cuneo Press.)

along the rows of letters it travels an easy, orderly path. All lines intended to be vertical and horizontal should be really so; if the letters are to slant, they should all incline at the same angle.

A simple alphabet is illustrated in figure 192. This type of alphabet is easy to learn, and it may be varied in many ways. The letters may be made taller or broader, and serifs may be added if desired. It is a useful model, suited to a great many purposes. After one has experimented for a time he will develop his own style of alphabet, based on the forms he likes best. The simplified manuscript alphabet in figure 193 offers a suggestion to those who may wish to work in still another manner. Manuscript writing is done with a flat-nibbed pen, and figure 194 shows the richness and dignity inherent in this type of lettering.

Chapter Twelve

DRESS DESIGN

I. CHOOSING CLOTHES FOR WOMEN AND MEN

THERE ARE many reasons why people wish to dress well. Some get satisfaction out of enhancing their personal charms. Some desire to impress their audience of friends. Some acquire a feeling of security and poise from knowing that they are correctly and becomingly clad. But whatever the reason, the fact remains that the appearance of well-dressed men and women brings pleasure to all who see them.

Most people will agree that clothes should be chosen to enhance the individual and his personality, and perhaps the first thing for us to do if we wish to make the most of ourselves through our clothes is to learn how to judge dress and to determine which values are important. If we are willing to put thought to it, every one of us can dress so that our clothes may be attractive and our best points enhanced.

Besides being good to look at, becoming, and in keeping with one's mode of life, successful clothes meet the additional standards of health, comfort, and economy. We can find definite reminders of the means for achieving beauty in design and color in clothing by turning back to the paragraphs on dress design in each of the chapters on the principles of design. From these we gather, for example, that simplicity, which is a factor in securing smartness and individuality, results from understanding how to use emphasis and subordination, while suitability to the individual and to use are applications of the principle of harmony.

WOMAN'S DRESS

The word *style* has been used in three different ways in this book. First, to denote character or distinction in design—a quality which does not change with the passing of time. For example, the sculptured panel on the Bayon (figure 17) may be said to possess style even though the particular manner which marks this carving may have gone out of use shortly after it was done. Examples in other fields having style in this meaning of the word are the functional house in figure 20, the Cézanne painting in figure 275, the Milles statue in figure 280, and the dress in figure 195. Style in a second sense means the original manner of expressing an idea in terms of some medium. For example, an individual's style or that of a period or a nation is a characteristic way of using words, paint, or the materials of dress, architecture, or furniture. We speak of Shakespeare's style and Rembrandt's, of the Empire style and the style of the Egyptians. A third use of the word style is linked with fashion and the terms style, fashion, and fad are here associated with the idea of a prevailing mode. In this sense, a style is understood to reflect a general tendency in design which continues for a relatively long period. In the field of dress, a style cycle is likely to last for about three years, whereas a fashion is of shorter duration. Fashions occur within a style cycle and involve some aspect of it. A fad is understood to be a transitory feature of a fashion. To illustrate the use of these terms in the field of millinery, one might say that the tendency to favor small hats over a rather long period of time would indicate a style. Within this style cycle of the small hat, it might be the fashion in one season to use a military note and in the next there might be a popular emphasis on the use of flowers. Fads are short-lived fashions, and within the seasonal trends some hat designs may appear which suddenly become extremely popular. These may be exaggerations of the fashion, but they need not be. However, as soon as they are seen too often, these capricious designs are dropped by people who are fashion-conscious, and they come to be known as fads. These brief vogues or fads can be illustrated in the fashion

Style, styles, fashions, and fads

trends described within this particular style cycle through the over-use of one striking motif, such as a large metal arrow, during the period when military effects are fashionable, or by great numbers of hats so small as to appear extreme.

To appear well dressed one needs to understand the relation of personality to clothes. The person who is interested in following fashions should realize this important truth: No one mode is suitable for all types, but there are so many possible adaptations of a fashion that every woman can make the right selection for her personality.

In analyzing anyone's personality such questions as the following are pertinent: Is she conservative or an extremist? Is she of the athletic type, suggesting a tailored style of dress; or is she exceedingly feminine, calling to mind dainty ruffles and soft materials? Is she dramatic and forceful so as to be able to wear striking designs and colors and still be seen as a personality distinct from her clothes, or is she quiet and retiring? If she is very quiet she may be eclipsed by clothes and designs that are too striking. The quiet person will be most attractive in clothing that is not too conspicuous, but she should wear accents in color, or light or dark, in order to supply some of the sparkle she seems to lack. Occasionally a conflict between what a person looks like and the way she feels, or may desire to look, results in the choice of a type of dress that appears inconsistent for the wearer. In these instances it would be well to avoid choosing clothes with a pronounced expression of the type that is so different from her appearance and to select those suggesting only enough of the desired characteristic to make them enjoyed by the wearer and her friends. If one is a combinative type and has, for example, both feminine and dramatic traits, she may choose to dress in such a manner as to accentuate the attributes she prefers. The mood of one occasion might lead her to emphasize her feminine qualities, and at another time she may lay stress on her dramatic characteristics.

Just as there are designs for every personality type, so are there colors particularly suited to the various personalities as well as to an individual's coloring. Thus, in order to make one's clothes the best possible self-expression, it is worth while to put careful thought into color selections.

When a costume appears suited to the wearer, the first requirement for appropriate dress has been fulfilled. The second requirement is that all the garments worn at one time should appear to belong together. Frequently in an impulsive moment a woman buys an attractive, becoming hat. It may not look well with the other things she has, but she does not think of that. Next, a handsome pair of shoes is purchased. They are not quite right for anything in the wardrobe, but they are "good looking." A dress is selected on the same basis—it fits well and is beautiful in color, but it is not right with the hat or the shoes. Then comes an occasion when the short-sighted buyer needs to wear her new hat, shoes, and dress. She looks at the things she has purchased and suddenly realizes that they cannot be worn together. When she sees her mistake, she has learned the first principle of good buying (which is also the first principle in design), namely: *things to be used together should be harmonious.*

Since a wardrobe should be a unit, all the clothes that are to be worn for at least one year should be included in the plan. The economical person will look ahead to two years, or in some cases, even to three if an expensive winter coat is being chosen. The long-time plan is especially important when the color of the coat is being decided, because it ought either to establish the basic color of the wardrobe for the length of its wear or else it should be beautifully related to the scheme. It is easy to select a basic color for a wardrobe in the case of a person who falls into a definite color type, because if the colors included in the wardrobe of a pure blonde or brunette are becoming, they are very likely to be keyed to each other. It requires more thought to plan for the intermediate type who can wear warm or cool colors with equal success and who may shift from a brown coat to a dark blue or black. Such a transfer will either necessitate different dresses and accessories or very careful planning to ensure being well dressed at all times during the period of transition. If the wardrobe is small, the best colors for coats, and suits as well, are black or dark or neutralized tones because they combine with many colors. A coat of strong color limits the number of other colors

Planning a wardrobe

that can be worn with it, and it becomes, from the standpoint of the wardrobe as a whole, a relatively expensive garment. In budgeting one's clothing expenditures it is wise to put as much as can well be afforded into the more permanent garments. Choosing a good quality for the main costume will make it possible to add individual but inexpensive accessories which will give stimulating changes to a basic wardrobe.

The size of the wardrobe depends upon one's social and occupational requirements. The average person needs clothes for five types of occasion. The school or college girl and the woman who has few social demands may have fewer requirements than this. The types of occasion for which clothes must be chosen may be grouped in this way:

1. At home
2. Sports—active and spectator
3. Street, business, school, or travel
4. Luncheon, tea, five-to-seven o'clock, informal dinner and evening
5. Formal dinner and evening.

The four factors which make for difference among the costumes for these occasions are the design, color, material, and trimming or decoration on the dress. The idea of fitness to purpose would lead one to see that the garments chosen for the various occasions would have some of the following characteristics:

At home   Clothes for work at home should be easily laundered, simple, and trim looking. The choice of clothes for lounging is determined by the manner and scale of living. The decision between the richer and more perishable negligees and serviceable, tailored robes should be made on the basis of which will be more suitable to the personality and to the surroundings in which they will be worn, in addition to a consideration of the cost of their upkeep and replacement.

Sports, active and spectator   Such special sports as skiing and riding have their own type of costume, while for general sports wear flat-heeled shoes are required, and a tailored suit of sturdy tweed or a similar fabric is an excellent choice. If clothes are to be used for participation in a strenuous game, they may be more rugged than those needed by a spectator at a game. The spectator type of sport clothes would be appropriate also on the street, or for school, business, or travel.

For these occasions a tailored suit or tailored dress and coat are particularly appropriate. If they are conservative in line and dark or rather quiet in color, they may be supplemented in many ways. Blouses, hats, scarfs, bags, or costume jewelry are some of the details which may add smart accents to these costumes and give enjoyable variety. *Street, business, school, or travel*

This is a transitional type between the work and the formal evening dress. A suit that is not definitely a sports suit, worn with an appropriate blouse, or a more-or-less tailored dress may be used for these occasions. Dresses for five-to-seven o'clock wear may be street length or the length that is the current fashion for that hour. The advantage of the street-length skirt is that one may wear a coat of street length with it. The hat should be selected in relation to this costume since it is usually kept on when a suit or an informal dress is worn. *Luncheon, tea, five to seven o'clock, informal dinners and evenings*

The formal evening or dinner gown is often decolleté, sleeveless and of floor length, although its cut and length and even its fabric may be influenced by fashion changes. This type of gown with a jacket, if they are in the mode, may be worn for a less formal dinner and so made to serve for two occasions. *Formal evening wear*

The design and the adjuncts of a costume more than its material determine its character. For example, a silk dress might be designed with fine accessories, and it would serve for such purposes as the luncheon and informal dinner or evening dress. The same fabric cut on simple lines with tailored accessories would be suitable for business and street wear. The latter dress could be worn also as an informal evening dress if the accessories were interchangeable, and it would be even more useful if it were made so that a scarf or a decorative piece of costume jewelry could sometimes replace a collar. With a simple, smart suit or tailored dress and another less tailored costume in her wardrobe a woman can be appropriately dressed for all but very formal occasions. The person of taste will never be overdressed. If there is any question in her mind as to the *Clothes for the limited wardrobe*

Figure 195. Costume of the Italian Renaissance, XV Century. This dress is distinctive and beautiful in its simplicity. There is harmony in its structural design, and in a general way it follows the lines of the figure. Its decorative design is appropriate in treatment, reserved in amount, and it is so placed that it enhances the beauty of the structural design of the dress. It is only when fashions are far enough in the background that they are likely to be looked at impersonally and judged as any other work of art is judged. Historic costumes are the main source of inspiration for costume designers, and for that reason it is important that they should be judged according to their design merits.

proper choice for an occasion, she will choose the simpler costume.

Health and comfort in dress

These two essentials, health and comfort, are quite as important in dress as the aesthetic requirements. A person cannot be truly well dressed if she is conscious of her clothes. It is always difficult to forget one's dress if there is a feeling of inappropriateness or of discomfort. The physical discomfort of wearing unhealthful clothing is as disturbing as the consciousness that one is unsuitably dressed. Skirts, sleeves, belts, and shoes that are tight are unhealthful because they hinder the free movement of the body. Furthermore, since tight clothing interferes with graceful, rhythmic movement, it lacks beauty.

Economy in dress

Problems involving economy must be answered by the individual, for dress should be consistent with one's means and be regulated by the customs of the community in which one lives. Everyone tries to look as well as possible, but it should be recognized that good taste and extravagance are not synonymous. Economy is determined very largely by the relation of the cost to the number of times an article is worn with satisfaction. If the material wears out too soon, if the dress does not harmonize with the rest of the wardrobe, if it quickly goes out of style or proves unbecoming, so that it is discarded before it has rendered the maximum amount of service, the article is relatively expensive. It is economical to plan a costume so that a change in accessories will make it useful for more than one type of occasion. However, for hygienic reasons, no wardrobe should be so limited that one dress would be worn every day. The intelligent application of design standards will help to solve the problem of economical dress so that both one's desire for beauty and the need for economy may be satisfied. The study of several historic costumes with the idea of discovering what makes the clothes look queer and old-fashioned, will show one that this does not result from the decoration, but from the silhouette—the structural design. (See figure 195.) If one were to paint out every bit of the detail and keep only a black silhouette, a grotesque costume would still look queer. If several of these silhouettes are compared, it will be found that in all the costumes where the structural design follows the lines of the body in a general way—that is, where the silhouette does not go in suddenly at unexpected places or out eccentrically at others, the clothes will look well even though they are much older than some of those that appear very old-fashioned. Thus it is seen that if the silhouette or the structural design is so planned as not to be extreme it will look well over the longest possible time. It is said of some dressmakers that one can always count on their costumes looking well for at least three years, which is the typical duration of a style cycle. Studying the clothes made by these dressmakers one discovers that the effects are not due to genius—the same thing may be accomplished by anyone if fairly conservative styles and colors are chosen. By "conservative style" is meant one in which extremes are avoided. The degree of conservatism in dress may be somewhat influenced by the material and by the occasion for which it is planned. For example, a dress design that is a modified version of a fashion would be selected for such a fabric as wool to be used more than one season for business or street wear, whereas a dress of inexpensive material that will last but a short time may reasonably be more extreme in design.

The thoughtful person who dresses on a limited income avoids strictly seasonal fabrics and colors for they are not economical. While most materials may be worn throughout the year, fur trimmings and a few fabrics, such as velvet and organdy, seem more suit‑ able for certain seasons and limit the usefulness of a dress.

MAN'S DRESS

If a man understands the principles relating to line and color effects, he will have no difficulty in choosing becoming clothes. He will recognize that from the point of view of color, line, or pattern, there is no basic difference in selecting clothing for men or women. He knows, for example, that lines and colors can be manipulated so that they will add or detract from apparent height or width and that plaids or other large patterns have the effect of increasing the impression of size in any figure. Men put a great deal of emphasis upon being correctly dressed, and, since all communities and social groups do not follow the same conventions in dress, the man who does not wish to be too different follows the local customs. What will be included in his wardrobe depends upon his social needs and the requirements of his work. The typical wardrobe includes clothing for sports, business, or school, semi-formal daytime and evening wear, and formal wear for daytime and after six o'clock. Some of these garments have definite limitations. Clothes for certain active sports are likely to be limited in their use, whereas spectator sports clothes may be worn at school and for some work. Social usage is definite when evening wear is concerned, and convention also determines the clothes for formal daytime wear. However, many men limit their wardrobe to one type of suit, and if they are to feel well dressed for every occasion such suits should be conservative in line and inconspicuous in color.

As a reminder of some of the devices a man may use to bring out his best points through his choices in clothing, these specific suggestions are listed.

Narrow stripes, such as herring-bone patterns, make a man look *Fabrics* taller and more slender. Definite plaids make him seem shorter and broader. Bulky materials give an impression of added weight.

A light coat worn with dark trousers adds breadth to the upper *Coats* part of the body and shortens the entire figure. The shorter than hip length coat gives height to the figure. A close-fitting coat calls attention to the silhouette and would be unbecoming to a stout person. A coat with a deep yoke, pleats, and a belt widens the figure. A coat with a long, narrow lapel makes a man look taller than one with a short, wide lapel. Since all details should be in scale with the figure, stout or very large men should wear lapels of medium width or slightly wider. A double-breasted coat gives a horizontal effect and so adds more width to the figure than one that is single breasted. Heavily padded shoulders make a man seem broader and somewhat shorter. Large patch pockets add width to the hips.

The longer the trousers, the greater will be the impression of *Trousers* height. Wide trousers add bulk and so make a man look heavier. A high waist line in the trousers lengthens the legs and shortens the upper part of the body, whereas a low waist line shortens the legs and adds length to the trunk.

Shirt-bosoms that show in a narrow, long line add height and *Shirts, collars* slenderness to the figure. Pointed collars modify the too-broad lines *and neckties* of the face. Long lines such as those of a four-in-hand tie will lengthen the face and features while the cross lines of a bow tie will appear to broaden them.

High crowns add height to the figure and length to the face. *Hats* Broad brims widen the face and shoulders. Unusually narrow brims make a large face and figure seem larger by their contrast. Unusually wide brims look out of scale with a small or very narrow face and make it appear smaller. Turned-up brims are good for a short stature and a short neck. Rolled brims are becoming to a small face. To modify a broad face and square jaw, tilt the hat slightly for a transitional line.

Single-breasted overcoats with narrow lapels add height. Double- *Overcoats* breasted overcoats with wide lapels add width and decrease height. If economy is a factor, conservative lines and colors should be chosen and conspicuous plaids and stripes avoided. Black, dark blue, and dark gray overcoats can be worn with almost any suit. Brown is limited in its use except for the man who uses brown as a basic color.

CHARACTERISTICS OF A WELL-DRESSED PERSON

From the foregoing discussion we may arrive at some general conclusions. People who wish always to appear well dressed will not plan a wardrobe entirely on the principles of what other people are wearing, but will study their own personality, figure, and coloring, so that in a sense they may set their own fashion. The most satisfactory plan for building an economical wardrobe is to avoid the extremes in fashion and to select, instead, the more conservative and good-looking lines and colors reflecting the tendencies of the prevailing mode and, at the same time, expressing the individual. Perhaps if three of the most important factors that mark the well-dressed man or woman were listed they would be good grooming, correctness, and the ability to wear well-chosen clothes with an air.

Chapter Thirteen

DRESS DESIGN (*Continued*)

II. HOW TO PLAN A DRESS

USUALLY THE first concern of the well-dressed person when she is making or buying a dress is that it contribute toward making her appear distinctive—a rather intangible quality difficult of definition but very easily recognized. Distinction in dress has nothing to do with cost, but is usually evident when clothes look as if they really belong to their owner and to the occasion and are being worn with confidence and enjoyment. Sometimes just the way a garment is worn will make it appear distinguished, or it may take its special character from one smart decorative accessory worn against a dramatically simple costume. A distinctive dress will not be eccentric, but it will be individual, and above all, the details in the costume will have been selected with the idea that they look well together.

When selecting a dress one should consider the occasions for which it will be used, and the accessories, such as the hat, shoes, gloves, and bag to be worn with it. Since all the details of an ensemble should be related in idea as well as in texture and color, the dress fabric cannot be well chosen without regard to the items mentioned.

The materials chosen for a dress should be suited to its use and to the type of its design. For example, stiff wiry fabrics adapt themselves best to tailored effects, while soft fabrics, which do not easily fall into the straight lines of pleats, take flowing lines successfully. Textures which are flattering to the skin should be considered when selecting a dress and its accessories. For example, pearls and delicate silks are in harmony with a skin of fine texture and are so inhar- *Selection of fabric*

Texture

263

monious with a rough skin that the face will seem harsh by contrast. A hard, lustrous fabric would be unbecoming to a stout person, since it would catch the lights and make the figure look larger. It might also be unbecoming to an older woman because its severity accentuates the angles of the face and figure and emphasizes the lines in the face. It takes an average or a slender figure to wear very shiny surfaces successfully, and a fresh, or youthful face. On the other hand, soft and lusterless fabrics temper the lines of the face and appear to reduce size if chosen in the proper colors. In combining different materials there should be a nice adjustment of textures, for those that are too much alike may be monotonous, while extremely different ones are likely to appear incongruous. For example, a coarse cotton collar would not be used on a fine dress, though organdy or batiste would be good. There are no hard-and-fast rules for combining textures, and success depends very largely upon a sense of fitness.

Plain and figured dress fabrics   After texture has been considered, one should decide whether the dress is to be made of plain or figured material, or a combination of the two. While one always enjoys looking at dress materials which show no movement, it is sometimes desired to have a design either woven in or printed on the fabric. Everyone can wear plain fabrics, but when a printed one is preferred there are many factors to be considered. If the person selecting the dress is well proportioned and would like to have an attractive surface pattern, she will wish to know that a good design for a printed fabric will have interesting drawing in the details and character in the color. (See figures 196A and B.) She should know, too, that fairly small details, similar in value and placed close together, will produce a design of quiet effect. Designs in dress materials become more striking as they increase in size and in value contrast, and to wear very striking patterns one needs to have a well-proportioned figure and an outstanding personality. The combination of a plain color with printed material often adds character to a dress. The color may match one of the colors in the design, or, if it is in different values of one hue, the plain color may be chosen in a contrasting hue. In selecting figured material one should look for a design in which the shapes

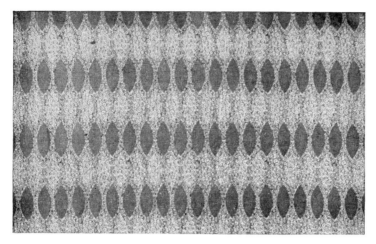

Figure 196A and B. Surface patterns which are suitable for dress fabrics. In A the forms are geometrical, the design is well distributed, and the colors are sufficiently close in value to give a quiet effect. In B the drawing of the conventionalized flower and leaf forms is inventive and the design has character. As the drawing in fabric designs more nearly approaches the appearance of realism, their beauty comes to depend upon character in their color.

are harmonious. A fabric spotted at intervals with large triangles and circles, or similarly unrelated shapes and arrangements, gives a sense of disorder which destroys harmony. If the material is figured, the design should show a beautiful proportion in the sizes of the details, and the scale of the design should be suited to the size of the person. One would associate dainty patterns with the small person, while the larger, more dashing individual suggests larger, bolder figures. However, the person who is too large will not select materials with too definite a pattern, because they will make her look larger.

If the proportions of the person are not ideal, the dominant lines of the design may be chosen to help bring the proportions more nearly to those of the average figure.

What may be considered good taste in the amount of emphasis in the design of dress material varies with the size and personality of the individual, the occasion for which the dress is planned, and the changing fashions. It is recognized that a design which appeared conspicuous in one season may seem more reserved at another time when the mode has swung toward more extreme pattern in dress fabrics.

Color in dress fabrics

The colors used in the costume should be becoming to the wearer. Values should be selected to bring out the wearer's best points and subdue undesirable ones. The choice of intensity in color will be influenced by the person's coloring, age, size, personality, income, and the occasion for which the dress is to be worn. Its use will vary with the person, as well as with the surroundings in which the dress is to be seen and the number of times it must be worn. The colors should be combined in such a way as to beautify each other. (See Chapter XVI.)

Selection of a design for a dress

Having decided that the dress to be chosen is to be of a certain type, as, for example, a school dress or an evening gown, and having also selected the materials with this type in mind, one is ready to choose a definite design. In order that this discussion may be helpful in planning an economical as well as beautiful wardrobe, some of the specific considerations discussed in the chapters on the principles of design are repeated here. The art principles should be applied in the selection of the design, whether one intends to buy the dress ready-made, or have it made, or make it oneself. When starting a plan for a dress design the general lines are considered first and the decoration later. These two steps are called the structural and the decorative designs. Shape harmony is the most important consideration in planning any beautiful and economical structural design. When the dress is seen in silhouette it should bear some resemblance to the human figure. A study of the most beautiful dress designs will show that somewhere the dress is likely to follow the contour of the figure rather closely—for example, if the skirt is very full, the bodice will be fitted. Variations from the lines of the figure should be more in the nature of transitional than of contradicting shapes, and they should come at logical points, as at the shoulders, hips, or bottom of the skirt. The separate shapes making up the structural design, such as the divisions of the skirt, and the waist with its sleeves, belt, collar, and similar divisions, should all have enough in common so that they appear at first glance to belong to the same unit. The lines forming the edges of these shapes should be consistent with one another and should bring out the best features of the individual for whom they are being selected.

The size of every part of the structure of the dress should have a fine relationship to every other part. The length of the waist should be interesting in combination with the skirt; for example, one should avoid the position of a waist line that divides the dress into two equal parts and should seek a more subtle proportion for this important structural division. If the dress is for a very large person, the details would be on a larger scale than if it is for a small person, and if the material is of a coarse nature, the scale of the parts, such as tucks and cording, would be larger than would be necessary for a very fine material.

The costume as a whole should be studied in order to note the direction in which the eye travels in looking at it. For example, if it is desirable to add height only, it is well to see that a vertical movement predominates; and if there are a number of vertical lines, they should be neither so close together nor so far apart that the eye travels across the figure, thus increasing the width.

Since the human figure is made up of curved lines, the most beautiful lines for a dress are usually those showing some slight degree of curve. In every costume it is pleasant to be conscious of one dominant direction of line with the other lines, used for variety, subordinated.

If a dress must be worn for more than one season, extreme cuts in the structure should be avoided because they seem to stamp the date upon a dress and make it go out of fashion quickly. When plain materials are used one may enjoy more complicated lines in the construction of the dress than if the fabric is definitely figured.

The guiding principle in planning the structural divisions of a dress is to work up to the individual's desirable points and away from those to which one does not wish to direct the attention. For example, if the bust is large it should not be emphasized by a structural line or by pulling in the waist; rather the waist may be built out—working always for a structural design that will make the figure look as nearly like the average figure as possible. Where it is not possible to disguise a defect, call attention to an asset by placing a note of emphasis there.

The figure should appear to be balanced when the person is standing, sitting, or walking, and the structural design of the dress is of great importance in securing this effect. The figure should balance on both sides of the center line as well as above and below the center.

The structural design of a dress, then, should be made up of shapes and sizes beautiful in themselves and in pleasing relation to the human figure; if it is to bring out the best qualities of the person for whom it is designed, it will have its dominating lines so skillfully placed that they will subordinate less attractive features and emphasize the good.

Decorative design in dress   If a dress is to be beautiful it is essential that the structure of the dress be beautiful. A good structural design with interest in color and texture needs little if any decoration. If decoration is desired it should be so planned that it will enrich the dress and flatter the wearer. Unless a person wishes especially to avoid calling attention to some feature, any place that seems to be consistent for decoration may be selected for the principal and subordinate centers of interest.

Beautiful decorative effects in dress may be secured through the use of well-planned tucking, cording, or bands of the same material as the dress. This "self-trimming," as it is sometimes called, is always good, and if economy is a consideration it has the advantage of being inexpensive. Simplicity and smartness may be secured in this way; they can never be gained by the use of cheap lace and trimmings. Similarly, some decorative embroidery, when it is in the mode, may add much to the attractiveness but little to the cost of a dress. The methods and materials for decoration matter far less than the fact that fine quality, simplicity, and individuality are desired. A decorative design should appear to grow out of the structural design, and not look as if it had been dropped there, or had been grafted on from some foreign source.

After having decided how much design should be used, one must plan the relationship of all the parts within the design itself. The design and, if embroidery is used, the stitches should be in scale with the material used. Heavy materials require a bold, free treatment, and delicate designs suggest a correspondingly finer texture. Care should be taken that beads or threads and stitches are not so fine that the result looks thin and weak for anything so large as a dress. The position of the decorative designs on the dress should help to preserve the balance of the whole costume. The design of the dress as a whole should appear unified, but not spotted or confusing, and the decoration should be so planned that the eye will be carried to the different parts of the costume in the order in which it is desirable to emphasize them.

Elimination is often the secret of achieving smartness in the costume. Frequently one finds an inexpensive dress that has good lines and materials but looks cheap because of its poor buttons, buckles, or other trimming notes. The person with a practised eye will see its possibilities and can have a smart dress by removing the trimming entirely or by supplying a substitute that has character.

In short, when there is something distinctive in a dress it has been lifted out of the commonplace and made individual. Distinction may result from many factors such as the cut of the dress, or from a decorative note found in an interesting vest or collar and cuffs, an unusual belt, or attractive costume jewelry. The distinctive note should serve the purpose of making the dress smart and should make it seem definitely to belong to the wearer. Appropriate, becoming, and individual clothes give one self-confidence, enhance one's personality, and make a favorable impression upon other people.

Chapter Fourteen

DRESS DESIGN (Continued)

III. HATS, HAIRDRESS, AND ACCESSORIES

A COSTUME can give complete satisfaction only when its adjuncts appear to belong together. A sense of fitness is nowhere more apparent than in the choice of one's hairdress and of the accessories that make up an ensemble.

Year in, year out, the selection of a becoming hat is one of the most puzzling decisions a woman has to make. The swing of the pendulum in hat fashions and fads covers a large area from enormous flower gardens and aviaries settled on wide plateaus to little fur pompoms tied on with ribbon. Many a woman has trudged drearily from store to store trying to find some piece of headgear which will even remotely look as though it belonged on her particular head, and yet which will conform to the current trend.

How many women really know how to select a hat? Each season brings so many changes—the crowns are higher or lower than on last year's hats, the brims are wider or narrower, and turned up or turned down, so that it is difficult to know what to select, unless experience has shown that there are certain lines and some sizes which always seem to be particularly becoming. There are, however, some basic principles a woman can learn, if she has not already discovered them for herself, which will serve as a guide in making a choice of hats. A reproduction of a newspaper advertisement showing some of the wrong hats for the different types of women is shown in figure 197. One can draw many conclusions from a study of this picture, and, in observing what not to do, get help in finding out what to do. It will be seen that the following facts are generally

Figure 197. *This is a forceful illustration of the way lines and shapes are accentuated by the use of lines that repeat them or lines that contradict them. In every case here the use of transitional lines—those halfway between repetition and contradiction—would have modified the peculiarities of these women. (Courtesy of Stronge, Warner & Co., "Unbecoming hats of 1894." Drawn by Alice E. Hugey.)*

true: Large faces are best in hats that do not fit too closely but give an adequate frame or setting for the face. Lines that suggest circles in the shape of a hat or in its trimming, make the face look rounder. If a dominant line of the face is repeated either in the hat or in its trimming, that line will be emphasized; therefore drooping lines, extremely long lines, or any outstanding feature, such as a long nose or chin, should not have a repetition of that particular kind of line in the hat. When these lines are conspicuously contradicted the undesirable line will be emphasized just as much as if it were repeated, and the best way to remedy the effect is to use lines just between the two extremes. People who wear glasses have the same problem as those whose features are overprominent. They, too, will find that trimming at the front of the hat looks well because it seems to throw the features back. A hat with a brim would be a good choice if it is selected with reference to the height and width of the figure. Faces with stern or sharp features do not look well in turned-up brims. These faces, too, need the softening influence obtained from the shadow of a brim. Faces that are too broad should not have trimming placed on both sides, but there should be a suggestion of height not so extreme as to make a striking contrast, but with lines tending that way. Similarly, the very long narrow face should avoid the flat hat, and the extremely high hats. Round faces look well in hats with the brim turned up slightly at one side, so that a varied line is given. Small faces do not look well in hats that are too large because they make the face appear smaller than it really is. The person with an oval face and regular features can wear almost any attractive shape.

Deciding upon the lines of the hat is only one step in the selection. Another is to see that the well-chosen hat is well placed upon the head. Tilting the hat slightly toward the right eye is becoming to many women. The drawings show that when the hat sits too high on the head it looks strange because it is seen by itself and not as a frame for the face. Too large a crown is just as bad, for it gives the impression that if the ears did not stop it, the hat would settle down over the eyes! The crown should appear to be securely placed upon the head, and then the lines of the brim may vary as seems best for the lines of the face and the figure. Small, closely fitted hats are worn most successfully by the person whose features are regular and whose head is well proportioned for her figure. If any feature is irregular or too prominent, such as high cheek-bones, prominent eyes or nose, very small hats should be avoided, and more or less of a brim should be chosen. However, the hairdress may change the effect of a close hat, for if the hair is built out becomingly it may supply the needed width to frame the face.

The arrange-
ment of the
hair
The size of the hairdress and the lines of its arrangement modify the lines of the face in very much the same way the hat does. The size of the head is the unit by which the eye measures the proportions of the figure, and for that reason it is important that the hair be so dressed as to suggest the most flattering proportions for the entire body. The average figure measures seven and one-half heads high, and when an artist desires to express unusual refinement in a drawing he makes the head smaller than the normal unit and constructs a figure that measures eight heads high. On the other hand, cartoonists who wish to show the opposite of grace and refinement secure that effect by making the head lengths go into the body about four and one-half or five times. Therefore, a person who wishes to gain the maximum amount of grace in her figure will dress her hair to make its contour conform rather closely to the head. This is especially important for one whose head is larger than average. A person whose head is too small for her size would build out her hairdress just enough to bring the head into scale with her figure.

One should watch the pattern created by the lines of the hair. A person who has regular features and a head of average proportions may dress her hair in any beautiful style in scale with her figure. If, however, there are lines or proportions to be modified, it will be remembered that the shape and the lines of the face are emphasized when they are repeated or contradicted and are modified by the use of transitional lines.

Moreover, one's hair should be dressed in a manner suited to one's personality. A style that would be becoming if only the lines of the face are considered, might be entirely unsuited to the type of person. Obviously, a woman's activities and the amount of time she can afford to spend on the arrangement of her hair will be an important factor in choosing a style of hairdress.

Later in the book suggestions are given for modifying the effect of irregular features and proportions through the lines of the hairdress. It is easy to recognize the design reasons for the suggestions, and when they are understood the reader will be able to modify other features not included in this list.

Shoes may mar an otherwise successful costume if they are not *Shoes* well chosen, and too frequently they do not give a sense of being suited to the occasion. Shoes intended for street wear should not only be comfortable, but they should look comfortable. Shoes with high, slender heels are planned for afternoon and evening dress and look out of place with sports or school clothes. Shoes should appear to belong in their line, color, and material, to the costumes with which they must be worn.

The hosiery is as important a note in costumes as the shoes, and *Hosiery* perhaps the most outstanding single principle that should be followed in its selection is to keep the stockings a unit in color with the entire ensemble. Although the color range for hosiery changes each season, it is usually possible to find warmer or cooler tones which will be harmonious with a costume and becoming to the wearer, so that the stockings will not be seen as unrelated spots.

In planning an ensemble, one would begin by choosing the basic *The ensemble* garments—the suit, or the coat and dress. If the hat matches an accessory, the effect of an ensemble will still be retained when the coat is removed. This repetition of a note in a costume is an important technique in creating an ensemble. When there is too much repetition the costume becomes spotty and loses its smartness. (See Chapter XVI, pages 289 and 305.) The well-dressed woman wears simple clothes having an individual note which expresses her personality and distinguishes her from those around her; her shoes, hose, gloves, bag, and jewelry are fitting accessories, and, while not calling undue attention to themselves, they serve to make the wearer and the costume a perfect unit.

Chapter Fifteen

DRESS DESIGN (Continued)

IV. A TABLE OF SUGGESTIONS FOR PERSONS WHO HAVE UNUSUAL PROBLEMS IN DRESS

OBVIOUSLY, as fashions change, some of the specific terms and modes included in the following lists will not be pertinent, but if one will think beyond a particular detail to the principle involved, it will be easy to transfer the fundamental idea to the fashion details of the season.

THE STOUT FIGURE

Becoming	Unbecoming
One material or color, used throughout the costume, rather than breaking it up into separate parts.	Lustrous fabrics. Taffetas, and other stiff fabrics. Plaids, or any large or outstanding surface pattern.
Soft yet not clinging fabrics.	Heavy, bulky fabrics.
Fabrics with dull surfaces.	Fabrics that take round lines.
Dull colors in large areas.	Bright colors in large areas.
Black, or very dark colors if the silhouette is good. If the outline of the figure is poor, use fairly dark colors to reduce size, but not so dark that they will call attention to the silhouette.	
An unbroken silhouette, if the figure is normal.	Unnecessarily full, long garments. Foundation garments that produce bulges above and below the garment.

276

Becoming	Unbecoming
Semifitted, rather than tight effects in the dress as a whole but molded to the hips with some fullness below.	Very full or tight garments. Ruffles.
Transitional lines in the dress rather than extreme curves or angles.	Horizontal movement in the lines of the dress.
Vertical movement in the lines of the dress.	
The emphasis on the dress up and down the center front, with the principal accent at the throat and, if possible, a subordinate one at the bottom of the skirt.	
A long diagonal line in the waist is excellent for a stout figure, provided the diagonal is not directed too far out toward the hips. Carried too far it will broaden the waist and hips.	Exaggerated curves or angles, for the curves repeat the lines of the figure and the angles contradict them, therefore both call attention to the size.
Panels of moderate width. Pleats, panels, etc., that start above or below a point where the figure is large.	Very wide, or extremely narrow panels. Panels, pleats, or overskirts that spread or flutter as one walks. Pleats, panels, or any trimming ending or starting at a point where the figure is large. Very narrow lines of trimming. Thin pipings. Fluffy fichus. Large circles on hats or dresses.
Comparatively long skirts. Skirts that flare a little in center front with a straight silhouette.	Short skirts. Skirts which flare all around. Yokes on skirts.
A normal waist line or slightly above or below it.	A high waist line, since it makes the waist appear broader. An extremely long waist line, for it makes the upper part of the figure too heavy for the lower part.

Becoming	*Unbecoming*
No belt or narrow belt.	Belts or sashes which are conspicuous in width or in color.
Slim, long set-in sleeves. Normal armhole, or a trifle higher if the shoulders are broad. Sleeves that are slit vertically to show the length of the arm and only a portion of the width.	Entire sleeve tightly fitted. Flowing sleeves. Transparent sleeves. Sleeves lighter than the dress. Kimono sleeves which give an effect of breadth, owing to looseness under the arm. Ribbons or trimming extending beyond or hanging from the sleeves. Sleeves ending at a place of unusual width on the figure. Wide, light cuffs on a dark dress, for the eye will travel across the figure, adding width.
Simple neck lines, preferably long lines and long collars.	Tight broad collars, or short collars.
Short jackets the same color as the skirt. Long coats and jackets.	Short jackets that contrast with the skirt.
Flat, short-haired furs. Dark furs.	
	Freakish or conspicuous shoes. Shoes with slender, high heels.
Hats of moderate size. Hats that suggest an upward movement. Hats with irregular lines in the brim and a rather high crown. Hats with transitional lines rather than extreme curves or angles.	Small hats. Big hats. Flat hats. Round hats. Hats with long lines or brims drooping on both sides.
	Contrasting colors and values in hats, hose, and shoes.
Hair dressed high. Hair well groomed. It may have a	A low or broad style in hair dressing.

Becoming	Unbecoming
wave with rather large undulations.	Small tight waves or "bushy" hair.
	Thin or very small pieces of jewelry.
	Tiny trimmings for hats and dresses.
	Very small accessories.

THE THIN FIGURE

Becoming	Unbecoming
Lustrous materials, unless the person is too angular.	
Materials that stand out somewhat from the figure.	
The silhouette of the dress showing a broken, rather than a long clinging line.	Severely straight lines. Angles in the lines of the dress. Long, narrow skirts.
Broken lines and curved lines.	
Loose clothing.	
A horizontal movement in the lines of the dress.	
Fluffy laces on the waist and soft fichus.	
Short collars.	
The soft, full lines of drapery in the waist.	Flat tight waists.
Wide and contrasting girdles and sashes (for the tall person).	
Kimono sleeves.	Sleeves so short that the bones of the arms are conspicuous.
Full sleeves.	
Full sleeves gathered into tight cuffs.	
Patch pockets.	
Suits with contrasting jackets.	
Bolero jackets slightly below the waist line.	
Loose, or full coats.	
Circular capes.	

Becoming	Unbecoming
Light furs, if becoming to the complexion.	
Long-haired furs. If the person is small, the scarf must not be too large.	
Hats with low crowns.	High hats.
Hats with drooping brims.	Angles in the lines of the hat.
Hats of average size.	Stiff trimmings as wings or quills
Hats with irregular lines.	standing out from the hat.
	A high coiffure.

NARROW SHOULDERS

	A panel or vest effect that starts wide at the waist or hips and becomes narrower toward the neck. This makes a triangle with the point at the neck and the base at the waist and hips, thus narrowing the shoulders and broadening the waists and hips.
Padded or broadened shoulders.	
Broad lines in yokes, collars, and lapels.	
Armhole seams placed slightly out (or lower than normal).	Armhole seams placed higher or farther in than normal.

BROAD SHOULDERS

Lengthwise pleats, folds, or tucks extending from the shoulders to the waist, placed somewhat toward the center line in order to narrow rather than broaden the figure.	Wide or horizontal structural lines in yokes, collars, and lapels.
Hat with a relatively high crown and a fairly wide brim.	Very small hats.

Becoming   Unbecoming

ROUND SHOULDERS

Set-in sleeves.
The shoulder seam placed about one-half inch back of the normal shoulder line.

Kimono sleeves.
Raglan sleeves.

Collars that will appear to straighten the curve of the back. Either have the collar long enough to hang loose from the neck to below the highest point of the curve, or have it short enough to fill in the space between the neck and the beginning of the curve. Then build out the waist line by having the waist full and loose in order to fill in below the prominent curve. This may be done by the use of a panel that hangs from the neck to the waist, turning back under a loose belt, or by the use of a bolero jacket.

Collars that end at the curve of the back.
Collarless dresses that are tight at the waist line.

Hat with a long drooping brim in back that forms a continuous line between the crown and the curve of the shoulders.

LARGE BUST

Panels or vests.
Silhouette built out at waist and hips if not already large.

The waist line drawn in.
High fitted waist.
Wide belts.

A yoke line, jewelry, or some other conspicuous line that stops above or below the bust line.
Long flat collars and jabots.

Trimming at, or near, the bust line.

Becoming	Unbecoming

FLAT CHEST

Full, soft collars.
Jabots and fichus.

Fullness over the chest by means   Tight waists.
of tucking or shirring the material
into the shoulder seam.

LARGE HIPS

Emphasis up and down the center   A one-piece, beltless dress hanging
front of the dress.   straight from the shoulders.
Oblique lines from hem to waist   Pockets at the hip line.
that end slightly at one side of the   Horizontal lines in the skirt placed
center front.   near the hip line.
Narrow belt placed slightly below
natural waist line.

Average amount of fullness in the   Short skirts.
skirt.   Tight skirts.
The skirt flared slightly from the   Very full skirts.
hips.   Skirts that are narrowest at the
hem.

A slight blouse at the waist line.   Tight, closely fitted waist.

LARGE WAIST AND HIPS

Built-out shoulders.   Broad panel effects.

The center of interest kept at the   Sashes or wide girdles.
face and away from the waist and
hips.

Long skirts, in order to add height.

Hats of average size or slightly   Small hats.
larger.

LARGE ABDOMEN

Waist slightly bloused.   Waist and upper part of skirt fitted
tightly.

Becoming	Unbecoming
Long, simple jabot of moderate fullness or revers that end slightly below the waist line.	Sash or belt tied at the center front.
Coats that build out the sides of the figure.	

LONG WAIST, SLENDER FIGURE

Becoming	Unbecoming
The effect of a slight blouse at the underarm seam.	A long, diagonal line in the waist. Tight bodice.
Long lines in the skirt.	

SHORT WAIST

Waist line dropped below the normal line, especially for people whose hips are low.	Built-up waist lines.

SWAY BACK

Blouse at back of waist.	Garments fitted tightly in the back, including tightly belted dresses.
Fullness between the waist line and the hips.	
Belts which swing from loops at the side and which do not hug the waist line too closely.	
Devices which build out the waist line in the back, as bows.	
Thick jackets.	
Boleros which come down far enough to conceal part of the back.	

LONG NECK

Collars with high or medium roll.	Collarless, without a necklace.
Round neck lines, especially those	V-necks.

Becoming	Unbecoming
which fit closely to the base of the neck.	
Fluffy collars or fichus or furs.	
High close collars.	
Scarfs.	
Short necklaces, especially bulky ones.	
	Hat with upturned brim.
	Hat with high trimming.
Hair worn low at the neck.	Hair worn high.
Hair worn over the ears.	

SHORT OR THICK NECK

Becoming	Unbecoming
Flat collars.	Collars with high roll.
Collarless dresses.	Broad neck lines.
V-necks.	Necklace worn close around the throat.
Flat furs.	
Narrow-brimmed hats.	Drooping hats.
	Hats with broad brims.
Hair dressed high.	
Hair worn to show the ears, or at least the base of the ears.	

LARGE FACE

Becoming	Unbecoming
Hats sufficiently large to form an adequate frame for the face.	Hats smaller than the widest part of the face.
	Trimmings that are too small.
A hairdress of moderate size.	Too large a hairdress, since it may make the head look too heavy for the body.
	Too small a hairdress, which will emphasize the size of the face.

Becoming	Unbecoming

SMALL FACE

Becoming	Unbecoming
Hats that are rather small.	Large hats.
Trimmings that are rather fine in texture and in scale.	Heavy hats.
A relatively small hairdress.	Too large a hairdress, for, by contrast, it will make the face seem too small.

SQUARE OR BROAD FACE[1]

Becoming	Unbecoming
Hat with an irregular line.	Lines in the hat or at the neck that repeat the lines of the face. Lines that oppose the lines of the face.
Hair dressed rather high and with a soft, irregular line.	Hair dressed wide over the ears. Hair parted in the middle.
Rouge placed in toward the center of the face and blended up and down.	

ROUND FACE[1]

Becoming	Unbecoming
Collar or scarf worn close to the neck in back and with a long line in front.	
Necklines that give an oval effect.	
Hats with slightly irregular effects. Hats with lines that carry the eye upward.	Hats with round shapes and lines that repeat the curves of the face.
Rouge placed rather high toward the nose and blended down.	
Hair worn in an irregular line.	Hair parted in the center and drawn tightly back.

[1] For becoming necklines see page 44 and figure 47.

Becoming	Unbecoming
Ears covered unless neck is short. In that case leave the lower part of the ear exposed.	Hair dressed wide over the ears.
Hair parted toward the side and arranged in an irregular line. Hair dressed high.	Hair dressed in rounded shapes and lines.

NARROW POINTED FACE [1]

Short necklaces.	
Hat with medium-sized brim. Hat with slightly drooping brim. Soft crown on the hat.	High hats. Tall, angular trimmings.
Hair worn low on the forehead and in soft irregular lines. Moderate size in hair dress. Hair worn back from the cheeks.	Hair worn in a high, pointed knot at the top of the head. Hair so dressed as to cover some of the cheeks.
Rouge placed high out on the cheek bone and blended toward the nose and quite close to the hair.	

RETROUSSÉ NOSE

A hat with a brim.	A hat that turns away from the face.
Lines of the hair that do not repeat the line of the nose.	

PROMINENT NOSE

Hat with a brim. The brim may be somewhat wider in the front. Trimming in the front of the hat.	Turbans. Severe, tailored hats.
Hair built out in a soft, rather large mass. Hair built out over the forehead, in	Hair parted in the middle. Hair drawn straight back from the forehead.

[1] For becoming necklines see page 44 and figure 47.

Becoming	Unbecoming
order to balance the nose. Hair parted on the side.	Hair dressed high on the head. The large mass of the hair directly opposite the nose, so that the eye moves across that line when the profile is seen.

PROMINENT CHIN AND JAW

Becoming	Unbecoming
Rather large hats. Hats with soft, irregular lines.	Small hats. Severely tailored hats.
Hair worn in a large mass at the top of the head and wide at the sides, above the ears.	Hair puffed out below the ears.
Rouge placed high on the cheeks and toward the nose.	

RECEDING CHIN AND SMALL JAW

Becoming	Unbecoming
Hats of average size. A hat with a brim.	Large hats. Hats that turn sharply away from the face.
A very small amount of rouge on each side of the chin.	
Small hairdress. Hair worn low at the neck.	Hair dressed to widen the upper part of the head and face.

PROMINENT FOREHEAD

Becoming	Unbecoming
Hat with a brim. Hat worn low on the head.	
Hair dressed low over the forehead to conceal some of it. A broken irregular line in the hair dress.	Hair pulled straight back from the forehead. Hair dressed wide over the ears and temples.

Becoming   *Unbecoming*

LOW FOREHEAD

Hair drawn back from the fore-
head.
Hair dressed rather high.
Hair parted in the middle.

SHARP ANGULAR FEATURES

Becoming	Unbecoming
Hats of medium size.	Severely tailored hats.
Irregular lines in the hat.	Sharp, angular trimmings, as wings,
A brim that droops very slightly.	quills, and sharp bows.
	Stiff fabrics.
	Harsh textures.
Hair worn in a soft, irregular line.	Hair drawn severely back.
Soft, large waves in the hair.	Hair in tight waves, because it emphasizes harshness by contrast.

LARGE FEATURES

Becoming	Unbecoming
	Small hats.
Hair worn in a broken line around the face.	Hair curled in small, close waves.
Hair worn smooth or in large, loose waves.	Hair drawn tightly back.
Coiffure rather large.	Coiffure extremely large.

GLASSES

Becoming	Unbecoming
Hat with a brim.	Hat turned sharply away from the face.
Hair worn in a soft, irregular line over the forehead.	Hair drawn severely back from the forehead.

Chapter Sixteen

DRESS DESIGN (Continued)

V. COLOR IN DRESS

AN IMPRESSION of fine color in dress will be gained if the colors are becoming to the person who is to wear them, if they are right for the occasion, and if they are selected and arranged so as to make a pleasing ensemble.

The "Law of Areas," which states that the larger the area the duller a color should be, applies quite generally to clothes for street and business wear, but it is apt to be modified when one is selecting a costume for evening or sports wear. In these circumstances it is quite suitable that the costume be bright in color if the wearer is not too large and if she has a striking enough personality to avoid being eclipsed by her clothes. *Color balance in dress*

Colors in a costume should be so distributed that they will balance. When a woman wears a light blouse with a dark skirt the skirt may appear to overbalance the blouse; however, if some of the value (not necessarily the same hue) of the skirt were repeated as on the blouse in a tie or a string of beads, the balance would be somewhat better; and it would be still better if a jacket or scarf were worn, which would bring a larger amount of the value of the skirt into the waist.

One obtains rhythmic effects in color for dress in two ways. First, by the repetition of a color. This process is so closely akin to balancing through crossing or repetition that one cannot differentiate between the two. Care should be taken to distribute these contrasts in value and hue so rhythmically as to avoid a tendency toward spottiness. This type of rhythmic arrangement would be *Rhythmic color in dress* illustrated in an ensemble built around navy blue and amber colors if the suit, shoes, and bag were blue, the blouse amber, the hat blue with an accent of amber, and the gloves either blue or amber. The second way to secure rhythmic color is by the use of a transitional hue, value, or intensity to modify the strong contrast between two different hues, between very light and dark colors, or between dull or dark and very bright colors. For example, a bright red-purple blouse and a dark blue suit, hat, and shoes would be unified and made rhythmical by the transitional tones of gray gloves and silver beads or brooch.

Interesting proportions for color use

If the colors to be combined in a costume are quite subdued, the Greek proportion of two parts to three in area will prove to be an interesting distribution. If, however, they are bright, or contrasting in value, it will require but a small amount of one to produce this effect of two to three parts of attraction.

Emphasis in color for dress

In dress the individual should be the center of interest, and the costume a background. The amount of emphatic color that can be used successfully varies, therefore, with the individual.

Harmonious color in dress design

Harmony in color depends very largely upon the application of all the other design principles, for as soon as any one of the principles is violated the unity of the whole costume is likely to be destroyed. In order that costumes may be beautiful their colors should be balanced or keyed, and the entire color scheme should be related to the coloring of the individual.

COLOR FOR INDIVIDUAL TYPES

The aim in choosing colors for individual types should be to select those which will bring out the person's best points and subdue the less attractive ones. Some of the factors influencing the choice of colors are the following:

1. *The effect of light*
2. *Texture*
3. *The age of the person*
4. *The size of the person*
5. *The personality*

6. *The complexion*

7. *The occasion.*

As daylight is very much more brilliant and trying to the com- *The effect of light*
plexion than artificial light, colors need to be chosen more carefully
for daytime wear. Colors selected for evening wear should be seen
by artificial light; yellowish lights, for example, will neutralize or
destroy their complements, the purplish colors, and will put more
yellow into their neighboring colors; the greens will look more
yellow-green, the blues will look greenish, and the orange and red
hues will look more yellowish.

The way a cloth is woven, the structure of its yarns, and its *Texture*
finish determine its texture and all have such an important effect
upon color that they must be recognized for successful color choices.
A certain hue in a soft texture, such as velvet, fur, wool, flat crêpe,
or tulle is easier to wear than the same hue in the brilliant hardness
of satin or lustrous velvet. Similarly, white organdy or linen worn
near the face is becoming, while white satin, because of its sharp
lights, is more trying. The bright reflections of satin accentuate
every curve of the figure and therefore appear to add to its size;
for that reason it should be avoided by stout women or those with
pronounced curves. Thin women should not choose fabrics that fall
in long, straight folds, thus making them look thinner. They should
use fabrics similar to soft taffetas which break into lines taking several directions and appear to increase their size.

As much interest may be gained in dress through contrasts in
texture as through color contrasts; for example, smooth wool may
well be combined with satin, and crêpe with fine tweed. Textures
that are very similar, but not alike, such as two kinds of crêpe, are
not interesting together.

Older women should not wear such harsh bright colors as sharp *Age of the person*
blue and orange or vivid purple. Since bright colors have a tendency
to harden an older woman's face small amounts of these colors
would be more flattering.

If a large woman's complexion requires warmth in color, she *Size of the person*
should choose the duller warm hues. A woman who is stout and

of good figure should choose low values which will give the appearance of reducing her size. If the silhouette is poor she should select the values around high dark which will not call attention to the outline of her figure. Stout women should avoid strong value contrasts or color contrasts in the design of their dress materials, and they should not wear contrasting jackets or light blouses with dark skirts, because a difference in value seems to cut the figure in two.

Personality   People who lack color and have a quiet and retiring manner are eclipsed by large amounts of bright color, and are effaced by too much dull color. Dramatic persons can wear any colors which are becoming to them and suitable for the occasion.

Complexion   So few people are perfect blondes or perfect brunettes that a table stating merely that blondes should wear certain colors, as blue, purple, etc., and that brunettes should wear other colors, as red, yellow, etc., is often misleading. There are so many variations in individuals, and each spectrum hue has so many different effects through its three properties, that a mere table of colors will not solve the problem. For example, it has always been said that a blonde can wear blue; yet the intensity and the value of the blue are very different in their effect. If she is a very pale blonde, shall she wear a bright blue? or a very dark blue? This problem of color for individual types can be solved by knowing how to classify people and by understanding what colors do to each other.

EFFECT OF VALUES UPON THE INDIVIDUAL

Dark values take away color. Pale people find that plain black worn next to the face makes them look tired and more sallow. On the other hand, light skin or very light hair become dramatic in juxtaposition to black. If one has too much color and wishes to tone it down, then black or other dark values are a good choice.

Very light values seem to add color. If a person wishes to bring out the color in the complexion and hair, it would be advisable to wear white or some very light value next to the face.

Values that are alike or similar blend into each other. Men and women who have light hair and eyes and not much color in the cheeks seem to lose every particle of individuality when they wear tan or light gray clothes. Sometimes it is possible to place a dark value near the face and, if the person is not too colorless, by this accent bring sufficient contrast to relieve the monotony. Middle values blend with the values of the average background and do not call attention to the outline of the figure.

Since colors may force either their opposite or their neighboring hues, those colors should be chosen that will bring out the desirable hues in a person's complexion. An intense color forces its complement. The duller a color becomes, the less power it has to force its complement and the more it tends to emphasize, through repetition, the colors like it. *How intensity affects the coloring of an individual*

Complementary colors force each other, so any desirable color in the complexion may be emphasized through their use. For example, a slightly rosy flush on the cheeks will be intensified by the use of the greenish colors. On the other hand, if a person has any undesirable color in his complexion, he should avoid wearing the intense complement of that color. To illustrate, if a person's face were inclined to be suffused with a reddish-purple flush, any of the bright contrasting colors containing large amounts of green, yellow-green, or blue-green would intensify that flush. Similarly, if there were an undesirable amount of yellow in the skin it would be forced by contrast if bright blues or purples were worn in large areas. *The effect of intensity on contrasting colors*

The color of the hair, eyes, or any color in the complexion can be emphasized through the repetition of the same hue. This may be accomplished by wearing a large amount of the same hue in a lower intensity than the color to be stressed, or a small amount of the same hue in a bright intensity. For example, blue eyes will be emphasized by a large area of a dulled blue, or a small amount of bright blue near the face. If, however, a larger amount of bright blue were worn it would make the eyes appear less intense than they really are. This is explained by the fact that a bright color throws an after-image of its complementary color into all the colors seen near it, and so a bright blue dress would cause so much of its complementary color to envelop the face that the eyes would appear to *The effect of intensity on related colors* be dulled, while the yellow and orange tones in the skin would become more pronounced. As a color becomes neutralized, power to force its complement decreases, and, through repetition, it calls attention to the colors that are like it. That explains why the eyes will appear to be more blue when a duller blue is worn. Similarly, one may accentuate an attractive hint of red-orange or red-violet flush in the cheeks by wearing some of the same color in a dulled tone. The yellow of a sallow skin would be unpleasantly emphasized through its repetition in such colors as the yellowish tans.

How to sub-
due color

A color may be subdued by combining with it a slightly different hue (an analogous color) which is rather low in intensity. To illustrate this point, let us take the problem of subduing the yellow in a sallow complexion. If the exact hue of the skin were repeated, one would be conscious of the presence of a great deal of yellow. But if a dulled red-orange (reddish-brown or henna) were worn, the yellow of the skin and the yellow in the red-orange would tend to blend with each other, and the odd hue, the red, would be the color that would stand out. Such a color would have a flattering effect upon the skin.

The detracting effect of a trying color may be remedied by the use of a becoming color worn between it and the face or by make-up.

TYPES OF COMPLEXION

People may be grouped according to type of coloring and classified in three main groups with many variations within these groups. These classifications may be designated as: *the cool type, the warm type,* and *the intermediate type.*

These terms "cool" and "warm" as applied to the hair and complexion are only relative, but it is essential to have an idea of what the terms denote as applied to individuals. All hair and flesh colors are more or less warm, because they fall on the warm side of the spectrum, with the exception of gray hair and blue-black hair, which are distinctly cool; brown eyes are warm, blue eyes are definitely cool, while bluish-gray and greenish-gray eyes are cool.

By turning to the color chart and looking at the warm colors it will be seen that although all the colors between yellow and red-purple are warm, they are not equally warm. Red and red-orange are the colors of flame and are the warmest of all the colors; even the orange is distinctly warm. Then looking at the yellow, one recognizes that while it belongs in the same group with red and red-orange, it is decidedly cooler; the yellow-orange, which would come next to yellow and toward orange creates a much less positive impression of heat than orange and red-orange; likewise red-purple is a cooler variation of red than red-orange, or flame color. These hues—yellow, yellow-orange, and red-purple—are the cooler tones of the warm hues which, when combined with some blue, produce the coloring of a blonde, distinctly cooler than the brunette's which includes yellow-orange, orange, and red-orange. When this difference is recognized one has a basis upon which to start a classification of the cool and warm types of individuals.

Keeping in mind the color comparisons that have just been made, compare two entirely different groups of people:

1. Think of the people in the south of Europe—especially of the Gypsies and the Italians—with their entire color scheme composed of the warmest colors: orange and yellow-orange skins, with a red-orange flush on the cheeks; the hair a rich dark red-orange (brown), and the eyes brown. Their coloring is characteristic of the warm type of person. (See figure 198E.) The presence of still more of these orange-toned pigments produces the rich deep flesh tones of the Oriental, the Indian, and the Negro.

2. In comparison, think of the people in the north of Europe—especially in the Scandinavian countries—with their cooler coloring: fair skins, showing the cooler pink which really is a tint of red-purple; yellow or yellow-orange hair (called golden and ash blonde), and blue eyes. (See figure 198D.)

These types illustrate the essential differences between the representative examples in the warm and cool groups.

In order to become accustomed to differentiating the types it is very helpful to classify the people one sees. As a general rule the combination of hair and flesh color, including the flush on the cheeks, will be the determining factors in placing one in a warm or cool group. The eyes will serve further to place a person in one group or the other, but the hair and skin are the principal considerations. In order that the reader may proceed with the classification the typical examples in the warm and cool types and in the intermediate group are described:

The cool type:
(1) The cool
coloring with
golden hair

Picture a typical blonde: the general flesh color is commonly called "fair"—a pale yellow-orange with just a tint of blue around the temples, nose, and mouth; the flush on the cheeks suggests red-purple—it is a delicate pink which is slightly tinged with blue, rather than a pink tinged with yellow (figure 198D).

(2) The cool
coloring with
blue-black
hair

This type is frequently seen among the Irish. The cool complexion is the same as in the first group—the fair skin with the cheeks showing a pink tinged with blue, blue or gray eyes, and blue-black hair. This coloring may be even cooler in its effect than the blonde's (figure 198C).

Figure 198 (facing).

A. The warm type with red-orange hair. The hair is bright, the skin warm and "creamy," and the flush of the cheeks is red-orange. A complementary color harmony of blue-green and red-orange is seen in this costume.

B. The intermediate type which suggests neither warmth nor coolness in any striking degree, but has some of the characteristics of both. Her costume shows a triad consisting of yellow-orange, red-violet, and blue-green.

C. The cool type with blue-black hair. This coloring shows a cool fair skin, blue-black hair, blue eyes, and the red on the cheeks tinged with violet. The costume is a double complementary harmony of violet, red-violet, yellow, and yellow-green.

D. The cool type with "golden hair." The typical blonde, with fair skin, light yellow-orange hair, blue eyes, and the reddish flush, slightly tinged with violet, on the cheeks. The costume shows a monochromatic harmony of different values and intensities of blue.

E. The warm type with dark brown hair. The typical brunette with warm brown hair, brown eyes, warm skin, and a red-orange flush on the cheeks. This costume is in an analogous color harmony of yellow-orange, orange, and red-orange.

Note that black, white, and gray may be included in the various color harmonies.

A

B

C

D

E

M.M.
TEUBNER

There will be variations of both these examples, where the general color scheme is cool, yet the individual may have special problems to consider, such as sallowness, flushed face, etc. These examples will be discussed under the topic "Complexion Difficulties to Overcome."

This person is the warmest example of this group. The hair is bright red-orange, commonly called "red hair"; the eyes are brown; the skin is yellow-orange, or creamy, and the flush on the cheeks is red-orange—pink tinged with yellow rather than blue. A variation of this type, and one more frequently seen, is the person with blue or gray eyes and fair skin with red-purple in the cheeks. While these are cool features, the color of the hair is so much more conspicuous that it should be considered first in the color plan (figure 198A). *The warm type: (1) the warm type with red-orange hair*

This is the typical brunette: the hair is brown, the eyes are brown, and the skin is a more or less deep yellow-orange with red-orange showing in the flush in the cheeks (figure 198E). *(2) The warm type with dark brown hair*

Variations in this group include persons whose general color scheme is warm, but who may be pale or sallow, and the opposite variant—the deep dark skin of the Oriental, the Indian, and the Negro. They all belong to the warm group but have special characteristics to consider.

The Intermediates are just between these two groups and have some of the qualities of both types. Characteristically, the skin is neither distinctly warm nor cool—it may be called "fair"; but there may be a rather wide variation in the color of the skin. The eyes may be blue, brown, or gray; the hair is usually medium or light brown, suggesting neither warmth nor coolness in any striking degree (figure 198B). *The intermediate type*

The people in this group who have good complexions, eyes that are not too light, and value contrast between their hair and skin can choose the warm or cool hues or black for their basic wardrobe colors. As the coloring of a person in this group verges toward the cooler tones, the blues and the cooler greens will prove especially becoming, while those who have more warmth in their complexions will find the browns and the warmer greens successful basic colors. The person of the intermediate type looks well in a combination *Colors for the intermediate type*

of warm and cool colors, and the concern should be to distribute
them so that their proportions and arrangement are pleasing.

*Colors for the
cool type*
Since cool colors harmonize with cool colors, good basic colors
for the cool type would be black and the cool hues—blues, blue-
purples, purples, blue-greens, and greens in becoming values and
intensities. (See figures 198C and 198D.) Accessories may be
chosen from the contrasting colors on the warm side of the spectrum. When reds are chosen for these people, let them be reds
tinged with blue rather than yellow, so that they will harmonize
with the flush on the cheeks; such a color as dark American Beauty
(RRP D) (1R 3/6) is good, while the color commonly called
henna (RO D) (7R 3/6) is poor.

Since the coloring of the blonde is delicate, it requires careful
discrimination to choose just the values that will bring out the fine
qualities of the complexion. Since blondes have little value contrast,
it is well to supply some contrast in the costume. Values just like
the hair are likely to be uninteresting, either lighter or darker values
being more becoming. This is especially true when the color also
is similar to the hair in hue. When blondes wear light colors a dark
note near the face will add interest. If a person is rather pale, something very light, preferably white, should be used near the face when
black or dark colors are chosen. Blondes are somewhat limited in
their choice of intensity because their coloring is so delicate that it
does not appear to advantage against many of the bright colors. The
most becoming bright colors for them would be the cooler hues.

The cool people who have blue-black hair have value contrast in
their coloring and so are able to wear a wider range of values than the
blondes. They are also able to wear more bright colors because their
own coloring is not easily destroyed. They look well in black and
such cool colors as purples, red-purples, blue-purples, blues, blue-
greens, and greens. In fact, they can wear any color that does not
clash with the red-purple flush in the cheeks.

*Colors for the
warm type*
The warm type of person is not so delicate in coloring as the
cool type and can wear brighter colors. Black, although difficult,
may be worn if it is relieved near the face by a becoming color or
by a low cut neck. When white is chosen, let it be a warm white, as

cream color or ivory, to harmonize with the warm tones of the complexion. The colors on the warm side of the spectrum will be becoming: yellow, as in old gold; yellow-orange; orange; red-orange, as flame color; red; and often a dulled dark red-purple. (See figures 198A and 198E.) The related hues called brown, particularly the reddish-brown, and the bronze-greens (YG D) (YG 2/1) for the basic colors and bluish-greens for contrasting colors, are among their most successful hues. If grays are used they should be warm rather than bluish-grays. The bright reds should be chosen from among the reds and red-oranges, rather than from the bright red-purples, in order that they may harmonize with the color in the cheeks and emphasize it. The deep warm tones of the skins of the Oriental, the Indian, and the Negro are enhanced by all of the warm colors, especially in their richer and deeper tones. When browns are used a hue or value of a color different from the color of the skin should be worn near the face. Particularly unbecoming colors are pale blue, bluish pink, lavender, harsh blue, and all of the values of bluish gray.

Auburn or "red-haired" persons must determine the extent to which they wish to force the color of the hair. The warmer colors give a pleasing related harmony with the exception of bright red-purple, which is seldom pleasing with the brighter red-orange. If the red-orange of the hair is to be suppressed, then the dull dark browns will be best because they make a close harmony. To emphasize the color of the hair, choose the contrasting colors, keyed to yellow or orange, as green, bluish-green, or the brownish-greens. Avoid large areas of clear cold blue, blue-purple, or cold grays, for the contrast is too harsh to be beautiful. The person with red hair who has fair skin and blue eyes can wear the partly neutralized tones of blue, for they will emphasize the blue eyes by the repetition of the color and the warmth of the hair through contrast.

COMPLEXION DIFFICULTIES TO OVERCOME

The problems likely to be found in any group may be too much yellow in the skin, pale eyes, pallid cheeks, flushed face, and lack of value contrast in the hair, skin, and eyes. In these cases one should emphasize the person's best feature or features and attempt to suppress less attractive ones.

Women can solve some of their complexion difficulties by the discriminating use of make-up, but men do not take this advantage. Both, however, have some problems whose successful solution depends upon knowing how to use color. The following suggestions are given as aids in solving some of the questions that may be met:

To subdue yellow in the skin For the person who is inclined to be sallow:

Wear colors that are neither too similar to the color of the skin nor too unlike it.

Choose colors that are warm enough to be harmonious with the skin, yet are different enough in hue and value to give interest and variety.

Avoid unrelieved black near the face. (Black absorbs color and makes a person appear pale.)

Avoid unrelieved tans and grays too near the value of the skin.

Avoid colors in light or middle values in which yellow, yellow-orange, or yellow-green predominate. (Color is emphasized by the repetition of a similar hue.)

Avoid bright purples, red-purples, blue-purples, or blues. (A color is forced by a strongly contrasting or complementary hue.)

If the person is a warm type with a sallow skin, the warm colors should be chosen, such as rich dulled orange, red-orange, and red. The colors commonly called reddish brown, henna, and mahogany are especially good, for they are warm enough to harmonize with the complexion but are not so much like it as to appear monotonous.

If the person is a cool type with a sallow skin, the duller cool colors will be best, such as the duller blues, blue-greens, greens, and purples.

It is well to wear cream white near the face to relieve a very dark color or black. Although it is desirable for sallow people to wear somewhat dulled colors for the large areas in their costume, they should attempt to secure interest in their dress by using accents of bright colors.

This may be done in three ways:

By wearing white or cream-white near the face.

By the use of the complementary color.

By using the same color as the cheeks, or a neighboring color—red, or red-orange for the warm type, and red-purple or purple for the cool type. The color that is chosen should be duller than the color of the cheeks if it is to be used in a large amount, but if it is an accent, it may well be bright.

To force the color in the cheeks

This may be done by wearing dark values, as black or any very dark color except the complement.

To subdue the color in the cheeks

For large amounts, as in a dress or suit, use a darker and duller color of the same hue as the eyes.

To force the color of the eyes

A small touch of a color brighter than the eyes used near the face will intensify the color of the eyes.

The complementary color of the eyes will force them; thus, yellow and orange will force blue eyes. While attempting to bring out the color of the eyes, one must be very careful not to choose a hue that will force an unpleasant color into the face. Therefore a person with very cool coloring may prefer to force the blue in the eyes by using a cool color, such as blue, for the large areas, with just a small note of the complement (the yellowish and orange tones) near the eyes, while a person with warm coloring and blue eyes could use the complement in a large area.

This may be accomplished in three ways:

By using value contrasts; for instance, black or white or any color that is darker or lighter than the hair.

To force the color of the hair

By using a duller color of about the same hue as the hair and having it lighter or darker than the hair.

By using the complementary color.

In making a final choice, one should be sure to bear in mind that the complexion should not be sacrificed to bring out the color of the hair.

This is desirable only in the rare cases where a person wishes to subdue the red-orange in the hair, and it may be done by using the same hue, or a neighboring hue, at about the same value as the hair.

To subdue the color of the hair

Realizing that complementary colors force each other, the person who wishes to subdue the color of the hair will avoid all bright contrasting colors.

To relieve monotony in the hue and value of hair and skin Colors for people with gray hair

Value contrasts are needed, especially near the face. A garment of a becoming hue or a small note of intense color placed against a dulled background may be very successful.

As one grows older it is found that the hair and complexion change, and so each person adds certain colors to his list of becoming ones and eliminates others. As the skin takes on more of the yellow, one eliminates colors having a tendency to force yellow. As the hair grows gray one may change his color list, for gray hair is cool, and thus a person who always chose rather intense warm colors when the hair was warm brown and the skin warm, can frequently add some of the dulled cool hues to the list of most becoming colors. Purple and lavender are generally accepted as becoming colors for people with gray hair, but these colors must be carefully chosen, because the bright purples force yellow, yellow-orange, and yellow-green.

Men and women who have black hair turning gray should avoid gray clothes of the black and white mixture commonly called "pepper and salt," when these are just the same value as the hair. These colors have a neutralizing effect upon the individual. If they are chosen they should be combined with a dark or bright accent near the face. A person of this coloring will look much better in clothes that are lighter or darker than the general effect of the hair.

Colors generally becoming

It will be found that if a color is dark enough or dull enough nearly everyone can wear it. Dark colors that are generally becoming are:

Dark blue, in the color called Midnight Blue (B LD) (B 2/3).
Dark grayed blues, as Dark Cadet Blue (B 1/2 to 3/4 N D) (B 3/2)
Dark green (G 1/2 to 3/4N D and LD) (G 3/2)
Dark yellow-green, called Dark Bronze Green (YG 7/8N LD) (YG 2/1)
Dulled blue-green (BG 1/4 to 3/4N HD) (BG 3/2)

Dulled blue (B 1/2N HD)

Dark orange and red-orange in the colors called Dark Seal Brown, African Brown, and Dark Red Brown (O and RO 1/2 to 3/4N D and LD) (O and RO 3/1 and 2/2).

Dark red, called Dark Maroon, Dark Wine, and Prune (R 1/2 to 3/4 N D to LD) (R 2/3 and 2/2)

Dark purple and red-purple, called Plum and Raisin (P and RP 1/2N LD) (P 2/2 and RP 2/2)

Warm dark grays about the color of moleskin

Black.

Light colors that are generally becoming are:

White and creamy white

Light blue-green, called Turquoise and Robin's Egg (BG 1/4N HL and BG 1/8N L) (BG 8/3 and BG 7/4)

Light red-orange in the colors called Flesh, Apricot, Salmon, and Shell Pink (RO 1/4N HL) (7R 8/5).

Certain colors stand out as being trying to most complexions, the colors that are particularly difficult to wear being:

Colors difficult to wear

Bright blues, around middle value

Bright yellow-greens (mustard color)

Light dull orange, called tan

Bright purple

Bright blue-purple

Bright red-purple (cerise).

COSMETICS

Rouge, well chosen and applied with taste, may give a person the much-to-be-desired appearance of health, and sometimes it can be used to moderate the effect of a trying color in a costume. One's first concern when buying cosmetics is that the ingredients are not harmful, and the next, that they enhance the appearance. Make-up will bring out a person's natural coloring if it is keyed to the color of the skin, and it can be used to modify the shape of the face and features if it is cleverly applied. One must realize that light and dark rouge will produce opposite effects, for light rouge will emphasize fullness, whereas dark rouge creates shadows. The drawing of an ideal face illustrated in figure 208 will reveal the proportions toward which one works when applying make-up. Cutting a spot of color out of pinkish paper and moving it around on this diagram will show that the position of the rouge will seem to effect changes in the face, and it will explain some of the suggestions that follow.

Applying light rouge in relation to the facial structure

1. The Oval Face. Apply rouge to follow the natural flush in order to emphasize the contour. The natural flush is usually above the center of the cheek.

2. The Round Face. Blend the rouge from a fairly high point close to the nose, downward in a slightly lengthened line.

3. The Broad Face. Place rouge close to the nose and blend it lightly in an up-and-down direction as well as outward over the cheeks toward the side of the face.

4. The Long Slender Face. Apply rouge far out on the cheeks and high on the face, blending it toward the nose and toward the ears.

5. The Mature Face. Place the rouge relatively high on the face and blend it up and out toward the temples. Avoid putting rouge over the lines about the nose and mouth.

Applying lipstick

Put the color at the center of the lips and blend it out toward the corners and the edges of the mouth, but do not extend it beyond the edges of the lips. If the lips are of more than average fullness, keep the color well inside the edges and use very little on the under lip. Lipstick should be used moderately by the person who has an unusually large mouth.

Hues for powder, rouge and lipstick

Powder should match the natural color of the skin. Rouge should match as nearly as possible the hue of the natural flush that shows on the cheeks after violent exercise. Rouge that is red tending toward orange will blend well with warm skin tones and complexions that show red-orange, while rouge with a bluish tinge harmonizes with a really fair skin and red-violet coloring in the cheeks. Since red comes between red-orange and red-violet, red rouge can be used by many types and will harmonize with more costumes than either of the other hues. The lipstick may be a little darker than the rouge, but should match it in hue. Occasionally the color of a particular costume is not harmonious with the hue of rouge ordinarily worn. In such cases one should substitute another color of rouge. For example, a person with warm skin may successfully wear a purplish costume if red or red-purple rouge were substituted for the red-orange that she would normally use. Similarly, one with a cool skin may wear the red-orange tones if orange or red-orange lipstick and rouge are chosen. Since attention is drawn to the part of the face where color is applied, it will be seen that a careful analysis of one's features is of first importance. Suggestions for altering the appearance of particular features by the position of rouge are given under the specific headings in Chapter XV.

COLOR SUGGESTIONS FOR THE ENSEMBLE

If in planning a wardrobe one adheres to a basic color, it will prove to be convenient since all of one's clothes will look well together. Furthermore, it will be economical because fewer accessories will be needed. In working out such a plan, the first question is when to choose related colors and when to use contrasts; second, if contrasts are to be used, how they may be supplied; and third, which garments should be selected for these contrasting accents. The size of the person will influence the choice between related and contrasting colors, for if a person is large for her height, such areas as jackets and skirts should be kept the same or very similar in color. A slender and well-proportioned person may afford to break the length of the figure by the use of contrasting jackets and skirts, but when this is done, the color of the skirt should, if possible, be repeated at the neck or on the hat. Perhaps the following suggestions may be helpful when one is selecting contrasts for an ensemble: If the basic color of the dress or suit is rather bright, it may well be accented with merely a change of texture or a neutral; if a dress or suit is a dull color, accent it with a bright one; if it is dark, use bright or light colors, or both; if the basic color is light, accent it with a bright or a dark color, or a combination of the two. When economy is a factor, use the odd color in the details of the costume rather than in the structure of the garment. Details like scarfs and belts are inexpensive to change and give an appearance of newness to the ensemble.

Colors that harmonize with some of the basic wardrobe colors becoming to the warm and cool types of complexion are here included in lists that are merely suggestive and not intended to be complete. It should be recognized that the values and intensities in which these hues are chosen will make the colors more or less becoming. For one individual some of the colors might be chosen in small accessories or accents, whereas another person whose skin color might be clearer could wear the same colors in large areas.

SOME BASIC COLORS AND SUGGESTED COMBINATIONS FOR VARIOUS TYPES

THE WARM TYPE

BROWN *with one of the following colors:* green, blue-green (peacock-blue), yellow-green (mustard) (bronze), yellow (gold) (maize), yellow-orange (cream) (beige) (amber), orange (copper) (tangerine), red-orange (rust) (henna) (lacquer red), warm gray.

THE INTERMEDIATE TYPE

DARK BLUE *with one of the following colors:* red, red-orange (henna) (coral) (scarlet) (shell pink), red-purple (cherry) (American beauty) (dubonnet) (bluish pink), orange, yellow-orange (gold), yellow-green (chartreuse), warm gray, cool gray.

GREEN *with one of the following colors:* brown, yellow-orange (cream) (beige), red-orange (rust) (henna), red-purple (egg-plant), gray.

BLACK *with one of the following colors:* green, blue-green (peacock-blue), yellow-green (emerald) (chartreuse), yellow (gold), yellow-orange (cream) (beige) (apricot), orange, red-orange (scarlet) (lacquer red) (coral) (shell pink), red, red-purple (cherry) (American beauty) (bluish pink), warm gray, cool gray.

THE COOL TYPE

DARK BLUE with one of the following colors: blues that match exactly in hue, green (light or bright green), yellow-green if skin is clear (chartreuse) (emerald), yellow if skin is clear, red-orange in flesh color, red, red-purple (dubonnet) (American beauty) (bluish pink), white, gray.

BLACK with one of the following colors: blue-green (robin's egg) (peacock), green, yellow-green (emerald), red, red-purple (cherry) (amethyst) (American beauty) (dubonnet), purple, blue-purple (periwinkle), white (blue-white or cream), gray.

To illustrate the technique of creating a pleasing ensemble by repeating a color from one part of the costume to another, some suggestive color combinations are given below. These colors have been assembled from the basic wardrobe colors just discussed. Obviously, one might substitute other articles for many of the items mentioned since a sweater, for example, would supply the same color area as a blouse. In all of the following combinations, it will be noted that some of the areas show the repetition of one color and, in addition, a balancing of contrasting or transitional colors.

1. Basic color *brown*: brown coat, suit, shoes, and bag; cream, gold or turquoise blouse; cream or brown gloves; an accent of the color of the blouse on the hat.

2. Basic color *gray*: gray suit and gloves; black or gray coat, shoes, and bag; periwinkle-blue blouse; periwinkle-blue or gray hat.

3. Basic color *brown*: brown coat, hat, shoes, and bag; green dress; beige gloves.

4. Basic color *dark blue*: dark blue coat, shoes, bag, and gloves; cherry-colored hat; dark blue dress with cherry-colored belt.

5. Basic color *black*: black coat, suit, shoes, and bag; coral or aquamarine blouse; black and ivory hat; ivory gloves.

6. Basic color *black*: black shoes and bag; black coat with gray fur; bright blue or red-purple dress; black or gray gloves; black hat with gray and a note to match the color of the dress.

In order to turn all of this theoretical knowledge into immediate, practical working equipment, one should try colors on themselves or other people, watching the changes that seem to take place in the coloring of the person. Make the first experiments with the extremes in color, working:

1. *From the coldest color to the warmest, for example from clear cold blue to red-orange, and then trying on the dividing hues, as green and purple and their neighbors*
2. *From white to black and then to the middle values*
3. *From the brightest to the dullest colors and then to the middle intensities.*

In this way the most striking effects become apparent, and the eye will gradually recognize the more subtle changes brought out by the different colors in the hair, eyes, and complexion of the individual.

After having learned how colors affect each other and change one's appearance, one will be able to determine the best colors for any person and to suggest changes, such as color at the face to relieve harshness, or the addition of a color note or value contrast, a darker or lighter collar, scarf, or tie that would transform an unbecoming garment into a becoming one. Very often the addition of just such a small note of color or value contrast makes an altogether successful costume out of one that would otherwise be unbecoming and commonplace.

Chapter Seventeen

DRESS DESIGN (Concluded)

VI. HUMAN PROPORTIONS AND FIGURE CONSTRUCTION

ONE OF the aims in dress design is to make the figure look as nearly as possible like the normal figure. A knowledge of the proportions of the normal figure is a necessary aid to this end, for it gives a standard for judging human proportions. In addition to this knowledge one should gain skill in the use of lines and color in dress, so that width may appear to be added to portions of the figure that are too slender, and height to parts that may be too wide for perfect beauty.

When the proportions of the human figure are being estimated, the unit of measurement is always the length of the head, measured from the top of the skull (not including the hair) to the base of the chin. Fashion designers usually use a figure which is eight heads high, but some costume illustrators use figures measuring as many as nine or ten heads high. These models have unusual style and elegance, but a person who is selecting a dress design shown upon one of these figures should consider her own proportions before she makes her choice. The dress will have a very different effect when it is worn by one whose head goes six and one-half times into her total height. *The head the unit of measurement*

In the attempt to find the number of head lengths in the average woman's figure, the authors have made careful measurements of the proportions of 350 women. The average number of head lengths of the first hundred and fifty who were measured was 7.493, while the average for the three hundred and fifty was 7.5009. It is not likely *Average proportions* that there would be any marked variation if the numbers were greatly increased, and so we may say that the average woman's figure measures approximately seven and one-half head lengths.

Figures of three different proportions have been included in this chapter: the average woman's figure, which measures seven and one-half head lengths; the fashion figure of eight head lengths; and the young girl's figure measuring six and three-fourths head lengths, which are the proportions of the average girl of high-school age. All of these measurements are taken from the crown of the head to the soles of the feet. When the figure is drawn in perspective, as it generally is, this measurement comes to the ball of the nearer foot. The average figure of seven and one-half lengths is the most useful of the lay figures because its proportions are graceful enough to enable one to make attractive costume drawings, and the proportions of a costume planned upon it look as they would on the average person. (See figures 200, 201, 204, and 205.) The figure of eight head lengths is used for fashion illustrations because its greater height and slenderness give an impression of smartness and grace to the clothes drawn upon it. (See figures 202, 206, and 207.) Since fashion illustration is in the field of advertising, the fashion illustrator attempts to make his lay figures follow the proportions favored in the current modes. When a style cycle brings widened shoulders and narrowed hips, the fashion illustrator draws his lay figures so that broad shoulders and narrow hips are stressed. When waist lines are unusually high, the fashion figure reflects the new tendency. Thus it will be seen that the proportions of the fashion figure may vary rather frequently, whereas a change in the proportions of the average figure is a matter of a slow evolution brought about by such factors as changes in the diet, exercise, and manner of living of great numbers of people.

Methods of determining an individual's proportions
A simple way to secure a lay figure for an individual is to pin a large piece of paper on the wall and to have the person stand against it while someone makes a pencil or charcoal drawing of the outline of the entire figure. One's proportions may easily be studied from such an outline, and a dress design may be sketched upon this life-size drawing. If desired, a smaller sketch may be drawn to scale

(figures 199A and B). In determining all the proportions, the head length should be used as the unit for measuring, and all measurements written down in terms of one head length (1 H. L.), one and three-fourths head lengths (1¾ H. L.), etc. Then, using a ruler, and taking one inch as equal to one head length, it will be a simple matter to translate these proportions into inches and fractions of an inch, and to show them in diagram form as illustrated in the table of lengths and widths in figure 199B.

A second method of securing measurements for the drawing of a lay figure is to have the person who is to be measured stand perfectly still while the person who does the measuring holds a ruler in the hand stretched out as far as the arm will reach. (The reason for always having the arm outstretched as far as possible is to make sure that there is no variation in the distance of the ruler from the subject, while the measurements are being taken.) The person who is measuring should walk toward or away from the subject until the length of the head (measuring from the chin to the top of the head, but not including the hair), is exactly one inch. All the measurements shown on pages 314 and 315 should be taken and drawn as shown in figure 199.

Photographs are very satisfactory to use as foundation figures for dress design. They may be secured for a comparatively small cost, since they do not need retouching. It is convenient to have the head, in the photograph, measure one inch in height. Since the aim in the photograph is to secure a model that will show the natural silhouette, it is necessary to wear garments which follow closely the lines of the figure.

The person who has average proportions may trace a good lay figure and design costumes upon it, but one who has any unusual proportions may wish to know a simple method of constructing a figure of her own proportions, so that she can design her clothing upon it. A simple method of building up a lay figure is illustrated in figures 200A to H. Here the proportions of the average figure are used, but it is obvious that they may be altered to suit individual requirements. Before starting to draw one should become familiar with some of the outstanding proportions, in order to have a stand-

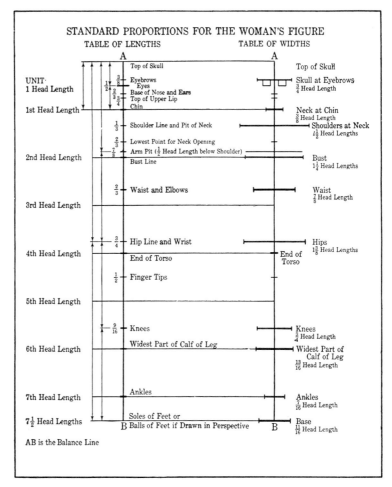

STANDARD PROPORTIONS FOR THE WOMAN'S FIGURE

TABLE OF LENGTHS   TABLE OF WIDTHS

A   A

Top of Skull   Top of Skull

UNIT· $\frac{3}{8}$ Eyebrows   Skull at Eyebrows
1 Head Length $1\frac{1}{2}$ $\frac{2}{2}$ Eyes $\frac{4}{5}$ Head Length
                                          Base of Nose and Ears
                                     $\frac{3}{4}$ Top of Upper Lip

1st Head Length   Chin   Neck at Chin
                                                                 $\frac{5}{8}$ Head Length

                         $\frac{1}{3}$ Shoulder Line and Pit of Neck   Shoulders at Neck
                                                                 $1\frac{1}{2}$ Head Lengths
                         $\frac{2}{3}$ Lowest Point for Neck Opening
                         $\frac{7}{8}$ Arm Pit ($\frac{1}{2}$ Head Length below Shoulder)
2nd Head Length   Bust Line   Bust
                                                                 $1\frac{1}{4}$ Head Lengths

                         $\frac{2}{3}$ Waist and Elbows   Waist
                                                                 $\frac{7}{8}$ Head Length

3rd Head Length

                         $\frac{3}{4}$ Hip Line and Wrist   Hips
4th Head Length $1\frac{3}{8}$ Head Lengths
                              End of Torso   End of
                                                    Torso
                         $\frac{1}{2}$ Finger Tips

5th Head Length

                         $\frac{9}{16}$ Knees   Knees
                                                                 $\frac{3}{4}$ Head Length
6th Head Length   Widest Part of Calf of Leg   Widest Part of
                                                             Calf of Leg
                                                         $\frac{13}{16}$ Head Length

7th Head Length   Ankles   Ankles
                                                                 $\frac{7}{16}$ Head Length
$7\frac{1}{2}$ Head Lengths   Soles of Feet or   Base
                         B   Balls of Feet if Drawn in Perspective   B $\frac{11}{16}$ Head Length

AB is the Balance Line

Figure 199A. A table of standard proportions for a woman's figure. Scale—one-half inch equals one head length.

ard for judging a well-proportioned figure. These proportions are shown by the group of lines with arrowheads at the left of the line on which is marked the table of lengths for the woman's figure in figure 199. By drawing no more than the correct divisions of the figure, one will have a useful framework upon which to build a dress design.

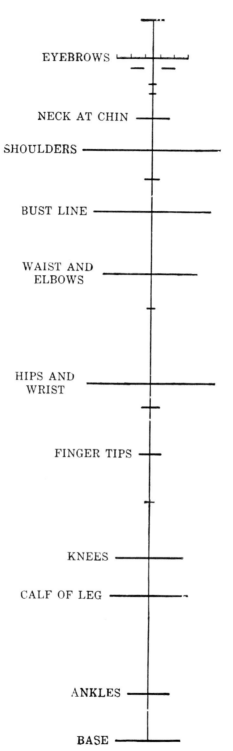

EYEBROWS

NECK AT CHIN

SHOULDERS

BUST LINE

WAIST AND
ELBOWS

HIPS AND
WRIST

FINGER TIPS

KNEES

*Figure 199B. The
lengths and widths of
the woman's figure,
measuring seven and
one-half head lengths,
as diagramed in figure
199A. Scale—one inch
equals one head length.*

CALF OF LEG

ANKLES

BASE

Proportions of the woman's figure   In the average figure, the line of the hips and wrist divides the body into two equal parts. The armpits divide the upper half of the body into equal parts, while the knees come halfway down the lower half of the body. The eyes come halfway between the chin and the top of the skull.

The "balance line"   In drawing the figure the lengths and widths are marked off on a "balance line" (AB, figure 199). The balance line coincides with a plumb-line that would follow through the center of the front-view or the back-view figure. In three-quarter-view figures the balance line comes through the center of the column of the neck and waist, and to the ball of the foot on which the weight is resting; or it comes between the feet, if the weight is equally distributed.

Proportions of average figure   If the total height of the figure measures seven and one-half heads the normal proportions are as follows:

TABLE OF LENGTHS OF THE WOMAN'S FIGURE

Top of skull to chin				1	head
" " " " shoulder line and pit of neck				1⅓	"
" " " " "modesty line," the lowest point for neck opening				1⅔	"
" " " " armpits (½ H. L. below shoulder line)				1⅞	"
" " " " bust line				2	"
" " " " waist and elbows				2⅔	"
" " " " hip line and wrists				3¾	"
" " " " end of torso				4	"
" " " " finger tips				4½	"
" " " " knees				5⁹⁄₁₆	"
" " " " widest part of calf of leg				6	"
" " " " ankles				7	"
" " " " base (soles of feet, or balls of feet if drawn in perspective)				7½	"
The length of the hand				¾	"
Top of skull to eyebrows				⅜	"
" " " " eyes				½	"
" " " " base of nose and ears				⅔	"
" " " " top of upper lip				¾	"
" " " " base of chin				1	"

The average woman's head length is 8½ inches.

TABLE OF WIDTHS OF THE WOMAN'S FIGURE

Skull at eyebrows	¾ head
Neck at the chin	⅜ "
Neck at the base (slightly above the pit of the neck)	½ "
Shoulders at the pit of the neck	1½ "
Bust	1¼ "
Waist	⅞ "
Hips	1⅜ "
Width across knees	¾ "
" " widest part of calves of legs	1³⁄₁₆ "
" " ankles	⁷⁄₁₆ "
" " base of feet, front view	1¹⁄₁₆ "
Width of arm at elbow	¼ "
Width of widest part of arm (forearm, slightly below elbow)	⅓ "
Width of wrist, side view	³⁄₁₆ "

The eyes are the width of an eye apart, and there is the width of an
eye between the eye and the edge of the face. The features are
parallel to each other.

HOW TO DRAW THE LAY FIGURE

First step

The first step in drawing the figure is to draw the balance line, and
to mark on it all the important lengths and widths of the body, as
shown in figure 200A. The drawing of this table will be facilitated
if the balance line is divided first into the correct number of head
lengths. If one makes an accurate table, using clear black lines, it
will not be necessary to draw a new table of lengths and widths every
time a costume is to be designed. This drawing will show through
thin paper, and a figure may be drawn over it. A full-size drawing of
this table is shown in figure 199.

Refer to figure 200B.

Second step

1. Swing in an oval for the head.

2. Draw the shoulders. Carry a curved line from the chin to the
end of the shoulder line, as if it were a continuation of the side of the
face. This makes an easy curve for the shoulders.

3. Draw the torso. From the ends of the shoulders, swing a slow

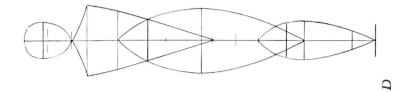

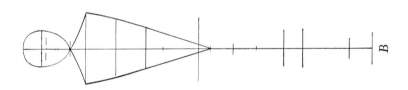

316

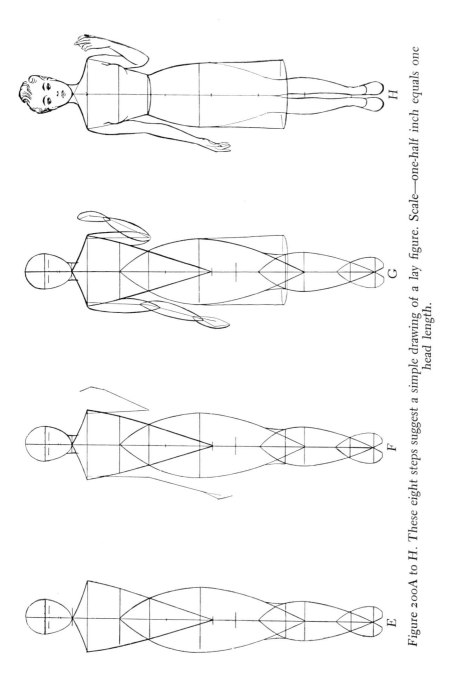

Figure 200A to H. These eight steps suggest a simple drawing of a lay figure. Scale—one-half inch equals one head length.

curve down to the end of the torso. Have this curved line touch the end of the bust line and the waist line.

Third step   See figure 200C. Draw the upper portion of the legs. Draw curves from the middle of the bust line, touching the ends of the waist and hip widths, and extend these lines to the 6th head length on the balance line, to complete a graceful curve.

Fourth step   See figure 200D. Draw the lower portion of the legs. From the point on the balance line which marks the 5th head length, draw curves which touch the ends of the lines showing the broadest part of the calf of the leg, and the ankles. Continue the curve to the base line. To complete the outside outline of the leg, connect the upper and lower portions of the leg with a gentle curve touching the end of the line which represents the width of the knees.

See figure 200E. Draw the feet.

Fifth step   1. Draw the outside lines of the feet with a swinging line by connecting the ends of the lines showing the width of the base line and the width of the ankles.

2. The lower part of the foot is drawn with two slightly curved lines meeting at a point to form the toe of the shoe.

Refer to figure 200F.

Sixth step   1. The bone of the upper arm. From ⅛ H. L. within the shoulder line, draw a line to the elbow line, to indicate the bone of the upper arm.

2. The forearm. From the elbow to the wrist, draw a line for the forearm.

3. The construction lines of the hand. From the wrist, draw lines for the thumb and the bent lines to indicate the hand.

4. Draw the curves of the neck, widening them slightly toward the base.

Indicate the pit of the neck.

Refer to figure 200G.

Seventh step   1. Width of the arm. Mark off widths of ¼ H. L. at the elbow, and ⅓ H. L. slightly below the elbow for the widest part of the arm.

2. Swing in the upper arm with a curve from the end of the shoulder line, touching the elbow width on the outside, and continue the line until it meets the bone. On the inside, start at a point

about ⅛ H. L. inside the bust line, and continue the line beyond the elbow width.

3. The curves for the forearm begin somewhat above the elbow, touch the elbow width, and the width of the forearm, going down to the wrist, which, side view, measures about ³⁄₁₆ H. L.

4. Draw the hands, studying your own hand for general proportions and for form. Keep the hands slender.

5. Indicate the curves between the knees.

6. Draw the inside line of the leg with a curve from the widest part of the calf to the ankles.

7. Draw the lines to show the shoes. Work within the outline of the foot.

8. Draw the waist line and the bottom of the skirt. These are curved lines, the ellipses of circles seen below the level of the eye.

See figures 200H and 208. Draw the features and hair.

1. Eyes. Have the upper lid cover a little of the iris so that the *Eighth step* eyes will not look staring. Leave high lights at corresponding points on both eyes.

2. Nose. Keep the lines indicating the nostrils nearly horizontal. If they approach vertical lines the nose looks tilted.

3. Mouth. The mouth may be indicated by a line which curves downward slightly toward the center; then use a very short, flat U shape for the top of the upper lip, and a much flatter one for the base of the under lip. High lights may be indicated on the upper and lower lips by means of a break in the line.

4. Ears. Usually the ears are covered, but if the base of the ear shows it comes on a line with the base of the nose. The top of the ear is on a line with the eyebrows.

5. Hair. The hair should be drawn very simply. An outline is sufficient. The line should be easy and graceful. The hair should not extend much beyond the skull.

(Remember to keep all the features parallel.)

THE THREE-QUARTER-VIEW LAY FIGURE

The method of drawing the three-quarter-view lay figure is, first to swing in the outline of the head, then the trunk, the legs and

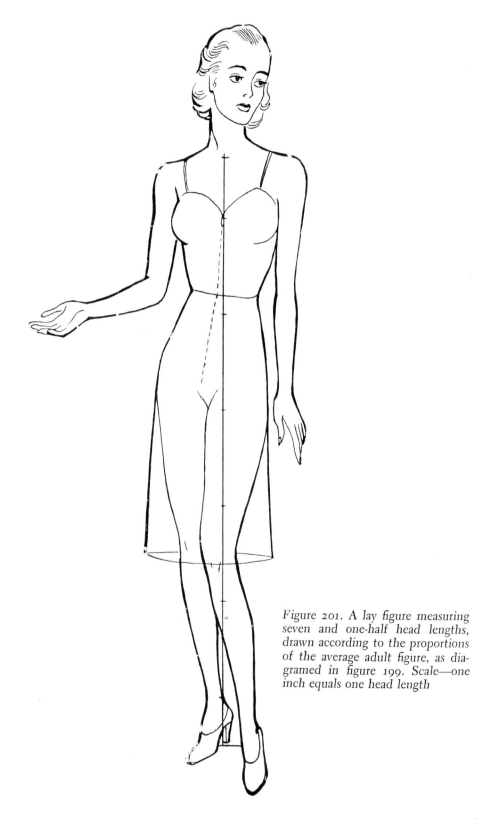

Figure 201. A lay figure measuring seven and one-half head lengths, drawn according to the proportions of the average adult figure, as diagramed in figure 199. Scale—one inch equals one head length

Figure 202. This lay figure, measuring eight head lengths, shows the proportions of the fashion figure. Scale—one inch equals one head length.

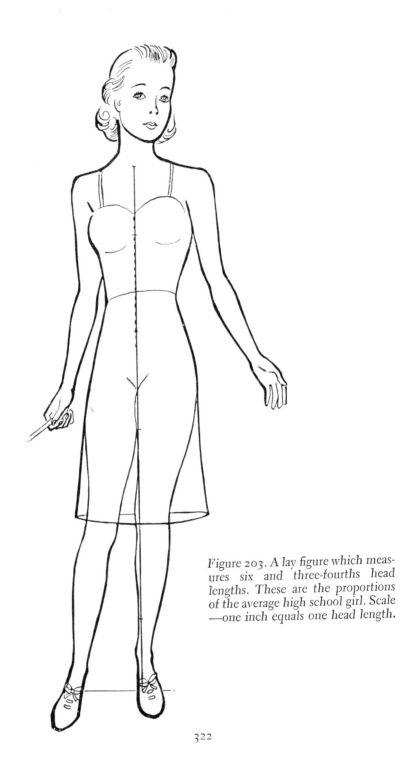

Figure 203. A lay figure which measures six and three-fourths head lengths. These are the proportions of the average high school girl. Scale —one inch equals one head length.

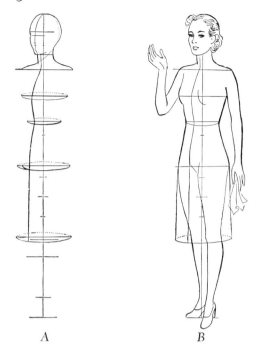

Figure 204A and B. A simple method of drawing a three-quarter view
lay figure.

feet, and the arms and hands. No details are drawn until the entire
figure has been sketched in. This method of drawing will produce
an effect of greater unity than one in which the work is finished part
by part.

Refer to figure 199. The balance line with its widths and lengths *First step*
is drawn or traced from the table of lengths and widths, as for the
front view.

Refer to figure 204A. The oval for the head is drawn next. *Second step*

1. Lightly sketch an oval as for the front view, with the width at
the eyebrows equal to ¾ H. L.

2. Draw a slight depression for the eye on the outline on the
farther side of the face. The cheek bone comes just below this eye
socket.

3. Build out the chin slightly on the same side, to complete the

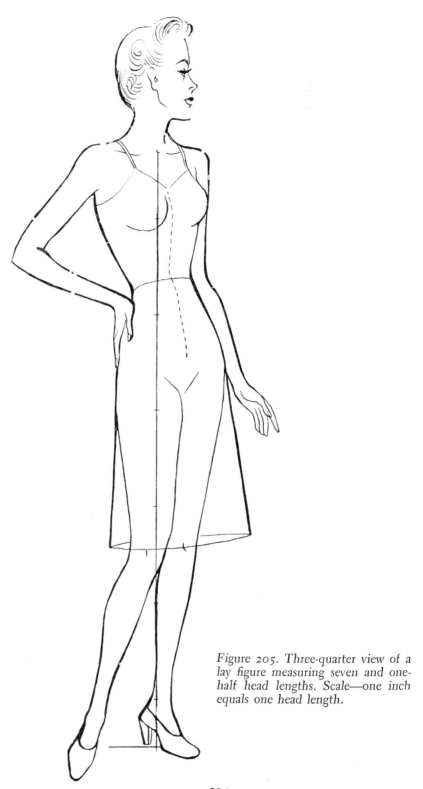

Figure 205. Three-quarter view of a lay figure measuring seven and one-half head lengths. Scale—one inch equals one head length.

outline of the farther side of the three-quarter-view face. The line of the original oval at the chin should be erased when the new chin line has been drawn.

4. Add ⅟₁₆ H. L. to the width of the head at the eyebrow line, on the nearer side, for the additional width of the skull as seen at this view. This amount should slope off in a gradual curve to the top of the head, and downward, until it reaches the line of the original oval, at a point opposite the base of the nose; it should be continued in a gradual curve until it reaches the balance line at the base of the chin.

Refer to figure 204A. Draw the neck and shoulders. *Third step*

1. Add ⅟₁₆ H. L. to the nearer half of the line which represents the width of the neck at the chin.

2. Erase ³⁄₁₆ H. L. from the farther side of the shoulder line.

3. Draw the farther shoulder. Swing a curved line from the nearer outline of the skull to the new shoulder point, ³⁄₁₆ H. L. inside the original shoulder line.

4. Draw the nearer shoulder. This is a curved line which starts from the skull at a point opposite the line of the mouth, carries downward until it touches the end of the line marking the width of the neck, and then swings down and outward to the end of the shoulder line.

5. Draw the farther side of the neck. This is a curve which is almost a straight line. It begins at the end of the line which shows the width of the neck at the chin, and goes just a little below the new shoulder line.

Refer to figure 204A. *Fourth step*

1. Erase ³⁄₁₆ H. L. from the farther side of the hip line.

2. Draw ellipses for the bust, waist, hips, and bottom of the skirt, keeping them in correct perspective.

Figure 204A. Draw the center front line. To find the line for the *Fifth step* center front, divide each of the ellipses into four equal parts, and indicate these divisions by dots on the outline of the ellipse. Divide the neck into four equal parts and place a dot between the balance line and the farther line of the neck. Draw a vertical line through this dot from the line of the chin to the pit of the neck on the shoulder line. Then connect each of the dots on the ellipses with curved lines indicating the contour of the body.

See figure 204B. Draw the outlines of the figure.

1. For the farther side of the figure. Connect the end of the shoulder line on the shortened side with the end of the bust, waist, and hip lines, and carry the line downward in a straight line to indicate the skirt, as it falls below the hips.

2. Draw the nearer side of the figure by connecting the end of the shoulder with the end of the bust, waist, and hip lines, and carry the line straight downward toward the bottom of the skirt.

See figure 204B. Draw the legs, feet, and arms.

1. Draw the legs and feet. Note the position of the balance line and the lines which mark the knees and ankles, and draw the three-quarter-view legs and feet in the same relative position as shown in figures 204B, 201, and 205. It will be seen that the outline of the farther knee comes ⅛ H. L. inside the line showing the width of the knee, on the balance line. The outside of the nearer knee is ³⁄₁₆ H. L. beyond that line. The contour of the legs and feet may be copied from this drawing.

2. Draw the arms and hands. The lines marking the center of the arms are started ³⁄₁₆ H. L. within the shoulder line. If they are swung away from the body, the elbows and wrists will come slightly higher than the position marked on the balance line. In the three-quarter-view, the armhole of a garment is an ellipse which would be about three-quarters of a circle, and its diameter is the distance between the shoulder line and the bust line. The width of the arm at the elbows is about ¼ H. L.; the side view of the wrists measures about ³⁄₁₆ H. L.; and the widest part of the arm, which is slightly below the elbow, measures between ⅓ and ¼ H. L. The arms and hands may be copied from one of these drawings or one's own hands used as models.

Refer to figure 204A.

1. Divide the eyebrow line of the original oval into four equal parts. Through the point next to the balance line, on the farther side of the face, draw the new center line for the face as it would appear in the three-quarter-view. This line is a curve which begins at the

balance line on the top of the head and swings down to the second division of the eyebrow line; from there it continues to swing out in a curve to a point a little above the line of the nose, and then back to the middle of the chin, halfway between the balance line and the outline of the neck.

2. Continue the lines marking the divisions of the face from the balance line until they cross the new center line. Then erase the balance line with its divisions, so that it will not be confusing. The new center line is not to be erased until the head is finished.

3. Draw the features. The features should be drawn parallel to each other, and centered upon the center line. However, since the face is seen in perspective, the farther half of each feature will appear somewhat narrower than the nearer half. The nearer eyebrow and eye end at the balance line, or a trifle beyond. The inside of the farther eye is hidden by the new center line, which, at that point, marks the bridge of the nose. The nearer nostril appears slightly larger than the farther, and, as in the front view, is nearly a horizontal line, so that the nose will not look tilted. The nearer half of the mouth is somewhat wider than the farther half. The ear is placed slightly inside the outline of the skull. The top of the ear comes on a line with the eyebrows, and the base of the ear is on a line with the base of the nose. The beginning of the line for the jaw comes at this point, two-thirds of the way down the head. The hair begins at about ⅙ H. L. down from the top of the head, and extends very slightly beyond the face, on the farther side; and it covers most of the ear on the nearer side. The hair should not extend much beyond the skull.

A STRAIGHT LINE FASHION FIGURE

Proportions for the figure measuring eight heads

Refer to figure 206A.   *First step*

1. Draw a vertical line for the balance line, and mark 8 heads lengths upon it. It is convenient to use 1 inch to represent 1 Head Length (H. L.).

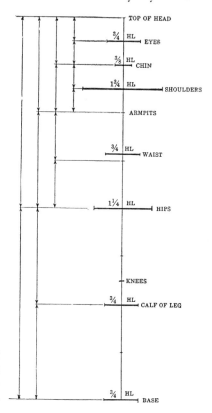

Figure 206A, B, and C. A method of drawing a straight line lay figure measuring eight head lengths. Scale— one-half inch equals one head length.

A

2. Halfway down the balance line is the hip line. (Until one becomes familiar with these proportions it would be well to write lightly on one side what the marks indicate.)

3. Halfway between the hip line and the top of the head is the location of the armpits.

4. Halfway between the hip line and the base of the figure marks the location of the calves of the legs.

5. Halfway between the top of the head and the armpits comes the chin, or the end of the first head length.

6. Halfway between the chin and the armpits marks the shoulder line.

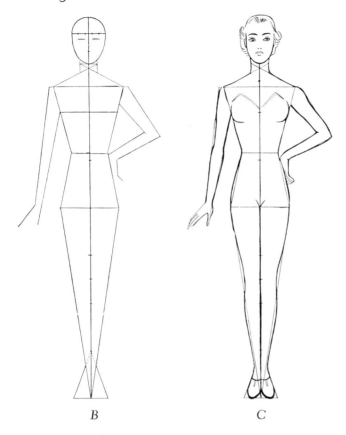

B   C

7. Halfway between the armpits and the hips marks a rather low waist line. One-eighth head length above this point is the waist line used in these drawings.

8. Halfway down the head marks the position of the lower eyelids.

9. About two-thirds head length above the base line locates the ankles.

10. One-half head length above the calves of the legs marks the knees.

Refer to figure 206A. Mark off the widths on the balance line as illustrated.   *Second step*

1. The width of the head at the eyes is slightly less than ¾ H. L.
2. The width of the neck is ⅜ H. L.
3. The shoulders are 1¾ H. L.
4. The waist is ¾ H. L.
5. The hips are 1¼ H. L.
6. The calves are ¾ H. L.
7. The base line indicating the width of the feet is ¾ H. L.

Third step   See figure 206B. Draw the contours of the body.

1. Mark off ⅛ H. L. on each end of the shoulder line. From these points draw straight lines to the waist line.

2. Connect the waist line and the hip line.

3. Draw lines from the hip line converging at the base of the balance line.

4. Draw lines from the ends of the base line to the ankle line.

5. Draw lines from the points marked on the shoulder line to the opposite end of the neck line at the chin.

6. Draw the base of an oval from the line of the eyes, touching the chin line.

7. Draw vertical lines for the neck, connecting the oval and the shoulders.

Fourth step   Draw the arms.

1. For the outside line of the arms, draw a straight line from the end of the shoulder line, at any angle desired. The length of the arm equals the distance from shoulder to hip. The length of the arm to the elbow equals the distance from the shoulder to the waist line. The arm may be bent at the elbow.

2. For the inside of the arm, draw a line from the armpits, leaving a space of about $\frac{3}{16}$ H. L. for the width of the wrist.

3. Draw hands, if desired. For the outside of the hand, draw a line from the wrist, ¾ H. L., at any angle desired.

4. For the thumb, draw a line from the wrist, ½ H. L.

5. Draw straight lines for the inside of the thumb, and for the inside lines of the hand. Keep the hand and thumb slender. These inside lines may be omitted if desired.

The figure may be used at this stage as a foundation upon which costumes may be designed.

See figure 206C. Draw the feet.

1. For the outside lines of the feet, draw lines to cut off a small triangular piece from each end of the base.

2. Cut off smaller triangular pieces on each side of the balance line for the inside lines of the feet.

3. Draw flattened V-shaped angles touching the balance line, to indicate the vamp of a shoe, or the top of a pump.

See figures 207 and 208. Draw the head.

1. Draw the top of the head oval.

2. Halfway down the head the line has been drawn for the lower eyelids. Divide this line into five equal parts to indicate the space between the eyes and the width of the eyes.

3. $\frac{3}{8}$ of the way down the head draw a line for the eyebrows.

4. Draw the hair, simply. If desired the features may be omitted, and the head oval and the hair only may be drawn.

5. The line locating the eyes has been divided into five equal parts. The central division marks the space between the eyes, and the outer divisions mark the spaces beyond the eyes.

6. Draw the iris of the eye. Its diameter is $\frac{1}{2}$ the width of the eye.

7. Draw the pupil, $\frac{1}{3}$ of the diameter of the iris.

8. The top of the upper lid is indicated by a line drawn just above the top of the pupil.

9. Draw the eyebrows as nearly straight lines across the width of the eye, and, at the ends, slanting them downward.

10. In a large head, repeat the shape of the upper lid by lines drawn a short distance above the eye. This may be omitted in a small drawing.

11. The tip of the nose is $\frac{2}{3}$ of the way down the head. Its width at the base is slightly less than the space between the eyes. If the drawing is large, indicate the nostrils with short lines at the outside, and short lines slanting slightly toward the center. Draw a short, nearly horizontal line across the balance line to indicate the tip of the nose. In a small drawing, two short lines, nearly horizontal will suffice.

12. The mouth is placed so that the top of the upper lip comes

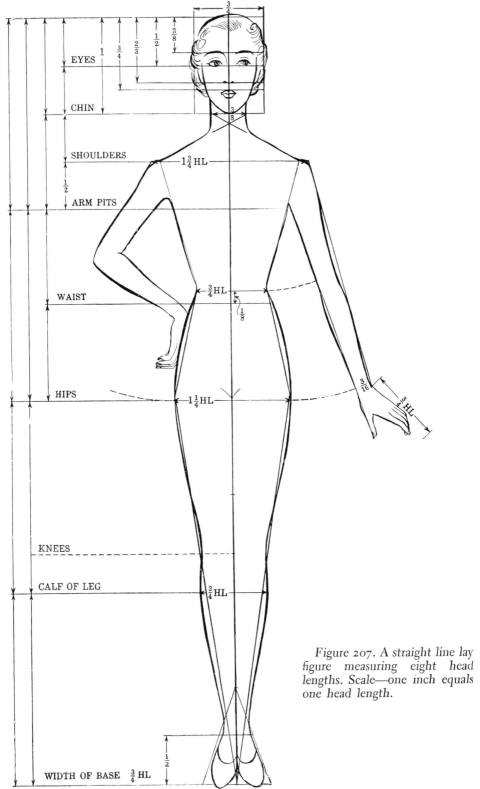

$\frac{3}{4}$

1    $\frac{3}{4}$ $\frac{2}{3}$ $\frac{1}{2}$ $\frac{3}{8}$

EYES

CHIN

$\frac{3}{8}$

SHOULDERS $1\frac{3}{4}$ HL

$\frac{1}{2}$

ARM PITS

WAIST $\frac{3}{4}$ HL

$\frac{1}{8}$

$\frac{3}{16}$

HIPS $1\frac{1}{4}$ HL $\frac{3}{4}$ HL

KNEES

CALF OF LEG $\frac{3}{4}$ HL

Figure 207. A straight line lay figure measuring eight head lengths. Scale—one inch equals one head length.

$\frac{1}{2}$

WIDTH OF BASE $\frac{3}{4}$ HL

332

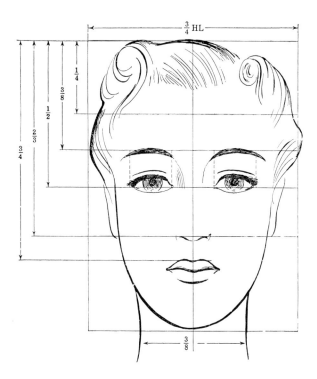

Figure 208. A method of drawing a head for a lay figure. Scale—three inches equal one head length.

at a point ¾ of the way down the head. The line between the lips is mostly horizontal, interrupted by a short V shape in the middle. The lower lip is a short, flat U shape with a slight curve at the base. The width of the mouth is slightly greater than the space between the eyes.

A book on anatomical drawing will be valuable as an aid in figure drawing, but there is nothing so helpful as experience in drawing from life. In these life drawings one should not work for details, but rather aim to learn proportions, and to discover the rhythm in the body. One should study to see how one line relates to another, how graceful and unified the figure is; and attempt to put this rhythmic quality into the sketches. As one learns to see the rhythm in the lines of the body, the lay figures will take on beauty and charm and will add interest to the costumes which are designed upon them.

Chapter Eighteen

INTERIOR DESIGN

I. PERSONALITY EXPRESSED THROUGH CHOICES

WHEN WE choose an object to be put into our house, we are doing two things. We are gratifying some need or desire, and we are, through the qualities possessed by this object, unconsciously stating our personality to everyone with the power and insight to interpret the meaning behind our choice. Our home, our clothes, our pictures, books, and furniture all mutely proclaim to the world just what sort of person we really are. They tell of our interests; they prove or disprove our sincerity; they display our imagination or lack of it. We should, therefore, make a definite effort through knowledge and appreciation gained therefrom, to express in our choices our best personal qualities. Walt Whitman, in his "Leaves of Grass," says:

> *There was a child went forth every day,*
> *And the first object he looked upon and received with wonder,*
> *pity, love, or dread, that object he became,*
> *And that object became part of him for the day, or a certain par'*
> *of the day, or for many years, or stretching cycles of years.*

Mere belongings have a tremendous influence in forming character. It would take an unusually strong character to remain true to high ideals of truth and sincerity if dishonesty were the keynote of the home surroundings. Such things as wall paper and metal made to simulate wood; too shiny fabrics imitating costly damasks—all these would be avoided if their significance were understood.

Unfortunately, quality in things is more or less intangible—as difficult to define as personality in an individual—but the outstanding features can be recognized and classified. With the eyes opened one very quickly reaches the point where every picture, every piece of furniture, or drapery pattern speaks its note of social grace or friendly domesticity, vigor, or fineness. Louis XIV, Louis XV, and Napoleon told as much about themselves in the furniture and decorations with which they liked to surround themselves as we are able to learn from historical records. Similarly, we are better acquainted with people after a short time spent in their home, surrounded by their own things, than we should be in a long time spent with them in a hotel or any other impersonal setting.

If the reader happens to be one who has never realized that the things people choose tell about their character and their ideals, let him think for a few moments about impressions which he has received at the theater. The curtain rose, let us say, upon a living room; before anyone came on to the stage the audience formed a very definite idea of the kind of people who would be at home in that room; and, if the stage decorator understood his craft, the people would prove to be just about what was expected. If a stage setting shows a living room with glaring lights, florid wallpaper and rugs, showy lace curtains, and overdecorated lamps, one expects the people who live there to come on the stage in flashy clothes and using a great deal of common, unpicturesque slang. Suppose, however, that the setting shows a room with soft and mellow lights, yellow walls, rugs with subdued and harmonious coloring, thin white glass curtains with attractive chintz overcurtains at the windows, well-designed furniture, with some comfortable chairs in front of an open fire, plenty of books, flowers, a few good pictures and decorative objects that catch the light and create points of interest. The audience would expect the people who live in this room to be tastefully dressed, well bred, and charming.

It would be interesting if everyone would ask, "What would my home express if it were shown on the stage?" One would then stand off in a detached and impersonal way and judge every detail. Has the choice of pictures expressed qualities to be approved or regretted? Have the lamps, vases, candlesticks, and other decorative objects been chosen for their beautiful shape and color and refinement of decoration, or are they overornamented? Are these decorative objects placed where they are needed—to relieve a bare spot, to create interesting shapes and spots of color, or to balance some other object? Or, on the other hand, are they put up for show purposes? Are they so numerous that they do not enhance one another or the object on which they are placed, but add to the confusion of an overdecorated room? Does the furniture express the kind of person its owner would like to be? If the result is not entirely satisfactory, it would be a good plan to find out just what is the matter.

Furniture, hangings, pictures, and decorative objects may suggest either a masculine quality, a feminine quality, or they may be intermediate. Usually the same things would not be chosen to furnish a bedroom for a very feminine girl, a man's room, and a guest room. While it is undesirable to have the girl's room look weak, a feminine quality will result from the selection of a little lighter type of furnishing—a slightly smaller, finer pattern in the drapery material, and a little more grace in the lines of the furniture and other objects. The colors in a feminine room should be somewhat different from those in a man's room; they should not be lacking in character, but the colors may well be lighter and the textures finer. A man's room need not be dark or heavy to be masculine in quality, but it should have no appearance of "daintiness"; it ought to be more solid than a woman's room, and somewhere a forceful note of contrasting color would be found. A guest room should be intermediate—that is, just between the masculine and feminine—so that either a man or a woman will feel at home in it. A transitional quality should be present, which may be achieved by selecting furnishings neither distinctly light nor heavy, patterns neither very small nor very large, and colors neither dainty nor heavy.

Masculine, feminine, and intermediate furnishings

The illustrations in this book, if studied with a view to visualizing the owners, would suggest that the bedrooms in figures 209 and 210 belong to women. In each there is a feeling of delicacy as compared to the boldness of a man's room. The furniture tends to be light in scale and there is an impression of fineness in the decorative accessories as well as in the textures and designs of the fabrics.

Figure 209. This bedroom is informal and domestic in spirit. It implies its feminine ownership largely through the pattern and textures of the fabrics and the accessories. (Courtesy RKO Radio Pictures Inc.)

Figure 210. (Architect, Burton Schutt. Photograph by Julius Shulman.) The lightness of scale gives to this room an impression of femininity. The richness of the furnishings and the fabrics convey a social spirit.

338

While these two illustrations show a feminine quality, they show very different personalities; one could not imagine that the owner of one would feel perfectly at home in the other's room. Turn to the drapery material in figure 243, page 371. One would say at once that this pattern seems to belong in a woman's room, for it has the lightness in scale that one associates with furnishings for a woman. Masculine personalities stamp the rooms in figures 211 and 212. These rooms seem to suggest sturdiness as compared with the women's rooms; they have a more severe line, and while the details are as thoughtfully worked out as in the other rooms, they are a little larger in scale all the way through. Similarly, the fabrics in figures 244, page 372, and 245 are distinctly masculine in type, for they show more vigor in pattern and color than seems to be consistent for a characteristically feminine room. Turning to figure 213, we should say that this room expresses neither a strikingly masculine nor a feminine quality. It is the type of room that makes a suitable guest room. The furniture is neither so light in scale as to appear frail to a man, nor so large that a woman would think it heavy. The drapery material has strong enough character to appear sufficiently forceful to a man and is light enough in scale to be pleasing to a woman. It is through striking a middle ground in form, pattern, and color that one secures a room in which either a man or a woman would feel at at home.

In addition to expressing a masculine or a feminine quality, objects may give a social, or a domestic feeling, or be impersonal. Domestic quality is the outward expression of the love of home and family and is usually informal. The social idea is usually expressed more formally than the domestic. When the term "social" is used to define one of these group expressions, it must be understood that the more limited sense of the word is intended, as referring to the characteristics resulting from an interest in the conventions of formal society. This expression will vary according to the social standards of the individual. If he is a person of taste, if he is sincere and his standards are high, grace and charm and fine quality will be reflected in the choice and arrangement of his furnishings. If, on the other hand, he is insincere or a social climber, that will

Domestic, social, and impersonal qualities as ex pressed in the home

Figure 211. (Photograph by Richard Averill Smith.) The design of the furniture and the choice of the accessories in this room show that its owner is a man. The decorative map, which gives a clue to his interest in the sea, and a simplification of details strike the keynote to the spirit of the room.

be apparent in the things he selects, for they will be ostentatious.

It should be understood that questions of expense, of good or bad taste, of richer or poorer materials never enter into these attributes of objects—the social or domestic, the masculine or feminine. It is simply the individuality of an object, just as it is individuality which gives distinct character to each of four different types of person. One person is devoted to the home and to the family; the second is interested in social life; the third has some of the traits of both; and the fourth is a colorless individual with no imagination. Although the actual furnishings of the houses of these four persons would change with their changes of fortune and their acquisition of taste, the essential quality would always be the same. The possessions of each individual would reflect his personality because he could not help surrounding himself with things that reflected him.

Let us go back to the four persons whose characteristics are described and see what their houses would express under various conditions. It has been noted that the outstanding characteristic of the first is a keen interest in the home. If, in addition, he has good taste

Figure 212. (Architect, Richard J. Neutra. Photograph by Julius Shulman.) There is a masculine quality in this bedroom. It is denoted particularly by the substantial furniture, the ruggedness of the textures, and the boldness of all the designs.

Figure 213. *The furnishings in this room are intermediate in scale and texture and so are right for a guest room to be occupied by either a man or a woman.* (Courtesy of House Beautiful and Pan-Pacific Press.)

and average means, one would expect him to choose a house very much like figure 214. The first impression that is made is one of domesticity. Its homelike quality is expressed in several ways. The low lines of the structure, which tie the house to the ground, make it seem secure and snug, and this impression is heightened by the

Figure 214. (See page 343.) *(Architect, Cliff May. Photograph by Maynard Parker.) The domestic quality of this house is due in part to the informal treatment of the building materials and the openings, which are arranged around the needs of the interior rather than according to a formal, symmetrical plan. The low pitched roof and the planting seem to make the house a part of the landscape.*

Figure 215. *(Photograph by Julius Shulman.) This informal living room suggests the same spirit as the exterior shown in figure 214. The choice of furnishings, the convenient way in which they are arranged, the easy availability of books, magazines and records all give one the feeling that people would enjoy living here.*

Figure 214.

Figure 215.

343

planting at the base of the house. There is an unmistakable air of friendly hospitality and a complete absence of affectation. The same domestic quality that is expressed in this exterior is shown in the living room in figure 215. Here, the emphasis is on informality, and the casual friendly air of the exterior is found in the furnishings and their arrangement. A feeling of companionship has been suggested by the presence of comfortable furniture as well as plants, books, records, and accessories that stimulate interesting thoughts. The larger house in figure 216 is just as domestic and sincere in spirit as the small one, and the living room in figure 217 has the same inherent character that is found in the little living room in figure 215. In spite of its large size, there is a feeling of intimacy that has been brought about by arranging the comfortable furniture for easy general conversation; by the big, friendly fireplace which

Figure 216. *The domestic, homelike effect of this house is achieved largely by the irregular contour, the low pitched roof, and the planting. In spite of its large size, there is an expression of simplicity and a feeling of sincerity in the structure and the details of the house.*

Figure 217. (Decorator, Adele Faulkner, A.I.D. Photograph by Robert C. Cleveland.) Informality is evident in this large domestic living room. The comfortable furniture grouped in front of the fireplace invites relaxation and conversation. The room expresses the same spirit as the house shown in figure 216.

dominates the room; and by the use of patterns, accessories, and textures that are sturdy and informal. The most domestic of all the historic period styles are the early English periods, especially the Tudor and the Jacobean, but the two houses in this group show that a homelike atmosphere can be achieved in contemporary as well as in traditional styles. Furthermore, they make clear that the characteristic quality of a house does not depend upon the amount of money expended but upon the choice of the textures and designs and their arrangement.

It will be found that even though a domestic person has poor taste he will express himself just as decidedly as, although less beautifully than, the person reflected in the rooms illustrated. The rooms of the domestic person who lacks taste may not be beautiful, but they will be comfortable and have a homelike appearance.

A study of figures 215 and 217 brings one to the conclusion that

Figure 218. (Architect, David Ludlow, Summit, New Jersey. Photograph by Jane Margaret Ream.) The "social" expression, illustrated in the more formal architecture of this adaptation of the English Regency period, is largely due to the design of the entrance, the arched windows, and the measured symmetry of the design. Figures 219 and 220 picture interiors that would be suitable in this type of house. (From House and Garden. Copyright 1938, The Condé Nast Publications, Inc.)

while there is a difference in the amounts of money spent in these rooms the owners have one idea in common—a love of the home and of home activities resulting in the spirit we may call "domestic."

The conventions of more formal society have influenced the second type of person more than they have the one who has been described as domestic. This person is typical of the "social" group, and the English Regency house in figure 218 reflects the influence that would express this social personality. Compared with figures 214 and 216, it is seen to be more formal and more conventional

Figure 219. (M. B. Lucas, Decorator. Photograph by Emilie Danielson.) The grace and formality of a social atmosphere appear in these furnishings. (From House and Garden. Copyright, 1938, The Condé Nast Publications, Inc.)

Figure 220. (Photograph by Robert C. Cleveland.) This dining room, with its fine eighteenth-century furniture and rich upholstery, is social in type.

Figure 221. (Photograph by Maynard Parker.) This social room is too ornate. There is a sense of confusion here due to the overuse of pattern and curved lines in the furnishings.

Figure 222. The room below looks dull and unimaginative. There is nothing to indicate that a family enjoys living here. Poor taste is seen in the choice of an animal's head used as a vase and a badly designed piece of painted china on the low table.

than either of these domestic houses. Some of the characteristics that help to mark this house as a social expression in architecture are: the symmetrical plan, the sharp contrast of dark shutters against white walls accentuating the formal balancing of the openings, the round-headed arch over the windows, the studied grace in the design of the entrance, and the formal placement of the planting.

One cannot say that one type of expression in architecture is more beautiful than the other. These types—social, domestic, and impersonal—are so different that no attempt should be made to compare them. Just as the classicism of Greek architecture particularly appeals to some people and the romanticism of the Gothic to others, so things that are domestic satisfy one group of people, while the social expression pleases others. One's choice between these is a matter of temperament, and it should be one's desire to show his personality in the most consistent and the most beautiful way possible.

In a house of the formal type just discussed, one would expect to see furnishings similar to those shown in figures 219 and 220. There is beautiful restraint in the furnishing of these rooms, and with their richness they have an air of simplicity. Everything is formal and social, and one associates a distinguished type of entertaining with its occupants.

Not all the social expressions are so sincere and so fine as these, and if a person were without social background as well as "ambitious" and without taste, the social quality would express itself in showy things. If he had wealth he would select new and shining reproductions of palace furniture, such as that of the periods of the Italian Renaissance and of Louis XIV, and he would use it in all its grandeur, in spite of the fact that his life was not regulated on the scale and manner of royalty. If he did not have a great deal of money to spend, he would secure this display in some less expensive way, and such rooms become merely pretentious. Figure 221 is a social room that shows the unfortunate effect of using too much pattern and too many curved lines. Although some of these objects are good, the room gives one the feeling that it has been furnished for the sake of its appearance and is not really lived in. All of this creates

Figure 223.

Figure 224.

Figure 223. (See page 350.) (Architect, Reinhard M. Bischoff.) Houses based on the Colonial styles of the eighteenth century are apt to combine social and domestic qualities. The symmetrical arrangement of the openings and the classic doorway have helped to make this small house more formal than the exterior shown in figure 214. (Courtesy of The Architectural Forum.)

Figure 224. (Photograph by Robert C. Cleveland.) One feels that this living room would be particularly right in a house such as illustrated in figure 223. A restrained use of classic detail gives to this simple domestic room a slightly social atmosphere. It might be noted that lamps designed for electricity would be more consistent than these which, obviously, were made to burn oil.

Figure 225. (Architect, Edwin H. Lundie.) More social in feeling than the house in figure 223, but more informal than the one shown in figure 218, this house might be said to come just between the "domestic" and "social" expressions in architecture. The front of the house is illustrated in figure 37, and some of its interiors are seen in figures 226, 227, 239 and 257. All of these illustrations are listed in order to show a unity of impression that runs throughout a consistently furnished house.

the impression that the room is inferior in quality to the room in figure 219, yet it is just as social.

The personality of the third individual in this group of types is a combination of the first two, with the social and domestic inclinations balanced. The desire for comfort will be apparent in the home, and there will also be some formality. Figures 223 and 224 might be the home of this person if he had simple means and good taste; if it were to be larger and a little more costly it might look something

Figures 226 and 227. The furnishings in these rooms are in keeping with the effect suggested by the exterior of the house seen in figure 225. Elements of both social and domestic qualities are in evidence. For example, there is a certain air of formality in the classic details of the architectural background and in the richness of some of the textures used. On the other hand, the Victorian sofa and chairs in the living room are quite informal, and the early nineteenth century furniture in the dining room and the chintz curtains are intermediate in type.

Figure 227.

like the exterior in figure 225 and the rooms in figures 226, 227, and 257. In both these houses there is a suggestion of the formality of the social rooms in figures 219 and 220, but in addition, there is something of the intimacy and informality of the domestic room in figure 215.

Figure 228. (Architect, Gregory Ain.) This well-designed, small house is a good example of the "impersonal expression" in architecture.

Figure 229. (Cliff May and Chris Choate. Interior by Peggy Galloway. Photograph by Maynard Parker.) These furnishings, which are impersonal in type, might have been selected for the house in figure 228. The choices show an awareness of utility and good taste.

The fourth individual represents the type most unlike the other three. He is the unimaginative person; he has no outstanding personality and is colorless and uninteresting. Since he has no imagination he follows the crowd. In the days when the dullest houses were built upon a high foundation of cement blocks, roofed with flat asphalt shingles with no interest in their texture, and covered with cold gray stucco, his would have been like that. When the common type was pseudo-half-timber, his would be one of these, standing in a long row of others like it. And his rooms would be as stereotyped and lacking in personality as the room pictured in figure 222. There would be nothing to induce interesting thoughts or encourage conversation, no charm, no books and magazines—no impression that people enjoyed living there.

The distinguishing features of the social and domestic types of expression have been illustrated here in both traditional and twentieth-century modern houses. The so-called "functional" houses of the early twentieth century were extremely impersonal, but as the modern movement developed, houses became less cold. However, because of the simplicity in line and surface and reserve of decoration, the twentieth-century houses tend to be more impersonal than the typical traditional house. (See figures 228, 229, 230, and 231.) That does not mean that they lack the amenities of traditional living, but rather that they are not tied to the conventions of the past. Although the contemporary house is likely to be intermediate in character, it can, through the choice of textures and furnishings, become formal or informal and be suitable either to a man or to a woman. In addition, it can be domestic or social as well as impersonal in expression. Once more it is seen that cost has no bearing upon these characteristics. The exteriors in figures 228 and 230 are equally impersonal, and they suggest the modern family with its life of many outside activities and interests, leading to a corresponding simplification of the furnishings within the home.

It is interesting to see that masculine, feminine, and intermediate qualities, or domestic, social, and impersonal characteristics are so definitely expressed. A comparison of these rooms has shown how one expresses his personality in the things he chooses, and how, in

Figure 230. (Designer, Millard Sheets. Photograph by Maynard Parker.)
Simple lines and reserved decoration make the twentieth-century house
more impersonal in feeling than the typical traditional house. Designs of
this period may tend slightly toward the domestic or social types, depending
upon the details of the design and the textures that are used.

addition to having personality, a room shows good or bad taste.
One's aim, therefore, should be to acquire good taste, remembering
that appreciation based upon knowledge will aid in discriminating
between honesty and sham, between simplicity and ostentation. It
will also lead to an understanding of fine quality, so that one may
express his individuality in the most beautiful way.

Figure 231. (Architect, Rodney Walker. Photograph by Julius Shulman.) Subtle colors and quiet backgrounds have made this room appear spacious and restful. The warm colors give the house a friendly feeling and, along with the simple, textured wood and brick walls, serve to emphasize the pictures, fabrics, and books. The background and the furnishings in this living room express the same spirit of functionalism as is seen in the exterior in figure 230.

Figure 232A and B. (A, Architect, Gregory Ain. Photograph by C. W. Totten. B, Designer, Arthur Lawrence Millier. Photograph by Robert C. Cleveland.) Contrasting colors are used in both of these living areas planned for small houses. The harmony in "A" consists of a subtle green with purplish and orange hues appearing throughout the scheme. The balancing of these colors from one room to the other creates an impression of unity. The color scheme in "B" shows large areas of warm hues ranging from yellow-orange to red-orange against which the cool green folding curtain forms a pleasant contrast. The grayed warm tones in the walls and rug make an excellent background for the colorful sofa and the pictures in the room.

Figure 233. Flowers that are rich in color are effective when seen in a mass. The hand-made pottery vase is especially appropriate for the sturdy texture of zinnias.

Figure 234. A floated arrangement seems particularly suitable for these beautiful blossoms, since their stems are very fragile.

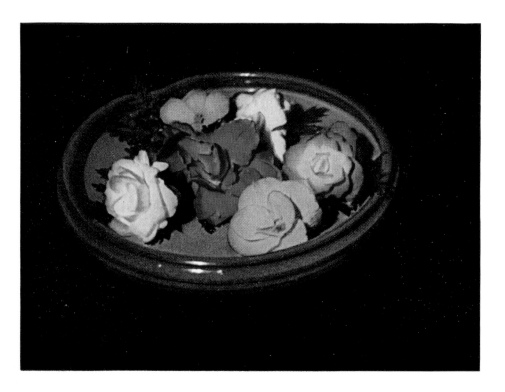

Chapter Nineteen

INTERIOR DESIGN (Continued)

II. THE ROOMS OF A HOMELIKE HOUSE

A "HOMELIKE EFFECT"—one of the rarest qualities a house can possess—depends almost entirely upon the basic idea of enjoying the home. It has nothing to do with architectural style or with so-called "interior decoration." The most important single factor toward accomplishing a homelike house is to have it so planned and furnished that it will not only fulfill the requirements of the particular family but will look as if it does. The selections of all of the furnishings and even the way they are placed reflect the life and interests of the family. Having about the things the family enjoys not only makes a house comfortable and livable but makes it appear so.

Geography has a far-reaching effect on the design of the house as a home. Despite the fact that modern heating systems, insulation, and air-conditioning are fast reducing the physical discomforts of winter and summer, people in cold climates still enjoy the appearance of a cozy, weather-tight house, while those in warmer regions naturally prefer a home which gives the impression of openness, simplicity, and a generous supply of moving air. Architects in the north, whether they be designing modern houses or those in traditional style, still follow the old custom of placing the great open areas of windows and doors toward the southern exposure and keeping the openings on the north reduced to as few as possible and those small in size. In figure 236 the spacious living room of a northern house suggests delightful evenings when the family and its friends come together around the open fire. Interiors and exteriors

Figure 235. (Architect, Frank Lloyd Wright.) In the planning of this house, as well as in the house below, the architect has used a minimum amount of window area on the north and opened the plan toward the south. This is a good practice in many localities and is especially desirable in northern climates.

Figure 236. (Architect, Frank Lloyd Wright. Photograph by Ezra Stoller.) This livable room expresses beautifully the spirit of a home in a northern climate. Nearly solid walls protect it from the cold of the north, but it has ample window space on the south side.

Figure 237. (Architect, Richard J. Neutra. Photograph by Julius Shulman.) Among the features that make this house comfortable in a warm climate are the orientation of the house to catch the prevailing breezes, a wide overhang that cuts off the rays of the summer sun and gives protection from the rain, a large expanse of windows planned for through ventilation, and a terrace for outdoor living.

like these provide happily for the requirements of indoor pleasures in the winter and outdoor living in the summer. (See figure 235.) On the other hand, in the warm countries, the architect will plan large windows and shady porches, and will pay special attention to ventilation across the rooms and through the house in order to utilize every available breeze. (See figures 237 and 238.)

In our planning it is extremely important to keep in mind continually the idea of the home as a setting for a happy family life.

Figure 238. (Architect, Carl Maston. Photograph by Julius Shulman.)
An open plan and an impression of an almost exaggerated simplicity are
ideal qualities for houses in warm climates.

There is danger sometimes that we may lose sight of the broad idea of the house as a home and think about room decoration as an end in itself. If we ask ourselves "How will it work?" as well as "How will it look?" houses will be livable: service rooms will be convenient and compact for the most economical use of time and strength; the sleeping rooms will have privacy and quiet so as to conserve nervous strength; the living rooms will be as spacious and hospitable and cheery as we are able to make them; and in all the house there will be found such healthful, comfortable considerations as good light, ventilation through the house as well as across the rooms, and such well-planned arrangements of rooms and furnishings that passageways will not infringe upon areas which should be kept free for work or conversation. These are fundamental requirements for any livable house, whether it is a closed-room plan in the traditional manner or the open plan of the new architecture.

Figure 239. This inviting, spacious hall, planned for the practical requirements of connecting the rooms and floors of the house and providing a
place for wraps, tells much about the rooms that open from it. (See figures
226 and 227.) Besides serving a useful purpose the hall gives a delightful view
into the garden beyond.

The character of the hall establishes the keynote to the spirit of   The hall
the house, for it is there that one receives his first impression of the
atmosphere which, he assumes, represents the home. The hall may
be just a passageway large enough to hold the fewest pieces of furni-

ture, such as a small table and mirror, or it may be large enough to accommodate a large table, some chairs, and a chest or chest of drawers; but in any case it should be useful, connecting the rooms of the house and providing a storage place for wraps. It should have a hospitable, yet not too intimate air; simple but not meager; and it should suggest that beyond it are rooms carrying out the spirit it promises. A hall in keeping with the character of the house is shown in figure 239. The rooms opening from this hall are pictured in figures 226 and 227.

The living room

The homemaker or the decorator who has succeeded in putting a livable quality into a room has done something really invaluable for the family and its friends. This intangible, homelike quality nearly always needs to be supplied by the owner, for the decorator usually plans and places the larger and more structural objects and stops short of showing the more intimate characteristics of the owner's personality in order to give the family the opportunity to express itself. A room has individuality when it is so lived in that it appears to belong to one person or to one family. Many factors help to make a room livable; among them perhaps the first two are comfort and convenience. Many instances will come to mind of families who have moved into fine new houses, and, after a few weeks of unaccustomed splendor, the mother or the father has fitted up a bedroom, or a room in the basement or the attic, with some comfortable chairs, books, and magazines, and a well-placed reading lamp, creating the only homelike room in the house.

An appreciation of the homelike quality in other people's houses may help one to introduce it into his own if it is lacking. If a room is not simple enough, everything not essential for comfort or necessary to complete the design should be eliminated; but it must be remembered that frequently objects of no practical use are needed to bring color or pattern into a particular space.

Grouping furnishings for comfort and convenience

After simplicity come comfort and convenience. A woman who says that her house is always disarranged after visitors leave unconsciously admits poor management in her furniture arrangement. If chairs and sofas are grouped for conversation, if lamps are placed where they are convenient, and if clear passageways are left between doorways and the various centers of activity in the room, the furniture and lamps will not have to be moved every time they are used. In the living room there should be a place for intimate talk, requiring thoughtful grouping of chairs as in figure 40; there should be places for each member of the family to read, with comfortable chairs and convenient, well-designed lamps (figure 336 on page 490); there may be a place for writing, calling for a desk or table and a good light. It is desirable to place the desk away from the conversation group if this is possible. There may be a music group; it, too, should be separated from the conversation center and from the desk. A sofa may be placed at right angles to a fireplace if it is desired to suggest the separation of one large living room into spaces to be used for different activities such as a dining area or a place the children may call their own. This device is almost as effective as a screen or a partition to shut off the space behind the sofa. However, it reduces the potential size of a social group. If it is ever desirable to have a group enlarged, it would be pleasanter to use comfortable chairs in that position instead of a sofa, for they could easily be moved. Unless the area behind a sofa is used for some desirable purpose, placing it out in the room is likely to be an extravagant use of floor space.

Having planned the various groups for a room in relation to their use, the next step is to arrange them in an orderly design. The large *Order in furniture arrangement* pieces of furniture should be placed to follow the lines of the room and to balance each other against the four walls. This will leave the center free and create the maximum impression of space. The shape of each piece should be in harmony with the wall space against which it is seen so as to form a pleasing pattern against the background. After the larger pieces in these convenient groups have been placed so that the room appears balanced, the smaller objects may be arranged to relieve bare places. A picture or an interesting fabric, a small table or a bowl of flowers may add a delightful accent to a space that seems too empty. Too many large, bare places in a room may have a chilling influence, but enough clear free spaces should be left to give the restful feeling we like to associate with modern living. (See figures 211, 231, and 250.)

Figure 240. Books are very much like people and will bring a spirit of companionship into the home when they are placed so as to be easily ac· cessible. Books also give color and an effect of pattern to a room.

The impor- After the room has been furnished to this point, the time has come
tance of books to think about the intimacy and the individuality to be gained
and accessories through the smaller things, such as the books, pictures, and other useful or decorative objects. It is through well-chosen accessories that the greatest amount of charm and intimacy comes into the home, although, to be sure, much individuality is expressed in the selection and grouping of the furniture. Easily accessible books and magazines will do more than anything else to make the living room seem homelike. (See figures 2 and 240.) Books are always more inviting if they are placed on open shelves instead of being shut off behind glass doors. They should be placed so that they are convenient for use, and if there are interesting books and magazines on small tables, in addition to the generous shelves, it will add immeasurably to the enjoyment of the room. Good pictures in the

room will also help to give a delightful atmosphere. In order to secure a satisfying living room the objects used for decorative purposes
should be beautiful and suited to the owners, to the room, and to
the space in which they are placed. The large part details play in
making a room look homelike is seen in figures 56, 215, 224, and
232B. Good pictures, plants, flowers, or winter berries when fresh
flowers are not easily obtained, something to read, ottomans, and
simple, well-designed lamps conveniently placed, will help to make
a room not only comfortable but pleasant.

The appearance of a room can be radically changed if the color Color for walls
of the walls is changed. Small dark rooms with dark-colored walls
may be made to seem larger and lighter if the walls are changed to
a light color, and light rooms will appear smaller and darker when
the walls are darkened. Warm colors will bring cheer and the effect
of sunshine into north rooms which receive no sun or to rooms
which are difficult to heat. Cool colors will temper the glare of too
much sunshine and may give an illusion of greater comfort in a
room that cannot be kept cool. Obviously, then, the size of the
room, the number of windows, and the direction of the light will
influence the choice of the colors for the walls.

Light walls and woodwork are likely to suggest furnishings of
rather slender proportions. Rooms with fairly dark walls and woodwork are usually more informal than light rooms, and their furnishings may be proportionately sturdier. The darker color schemes
must be enlivened and enriched by the use of some bright colors
and notes of fairly light colors. Isolated spots of white in dark rooms
are usually to be avoided because they create such striking contrasts.
However, if they are cleverly balanced the effect may be smart. A
comparison of figures 241 and 242 shows how a decorator altered the
background colors when he wished to change the character of a
room. In figure 241 the sand-colored side walls tone into the mellow old wood color of the pine paneling and make a consistent setting for the substantial furniture with its homespun upholstery. A
richly colored map and a hooked rug add their note of domesticity.
When he wished to create a more formal room, the decorator had
the wood paneling painted white and the walls covered with light

Figures 241 and 242. (Courtesy of Wm. A. French and Company.) The effect of a room may be greatly altered by changing the color of the background. In figure 241 the sand-colored walls and the pine paneling make a consistent setting for the informality of Early American and French Provincial furniture. Notice, too, how five well-related pictures have been hung to make a consistent group. The two small pictures on either side of the large one were hung close enough together to be seen as units; and these units, in turn, were placed near enough to the central picture to form a shape that harmonizes with the wall space and with the long table.

In figure 242, the white paneling and the light walls have made a suitable background for the delicate colors and graceful contours of the furnishings.

paper. Over the fireplace the delicacy of an eighteenth-century portrait gives the keynote of the new decorative scheme. In this room the textures are finer, the colors grow more delicate, and the designs become more sophisticated. The frank lines of the unassuming furniture and the wrought-iron andirons in the pine room are not suited to the new plan. Here a lighter touch is carried throughout the furnishing scheme. It is marked in the flowing lines of the sofa, in the slenderness of the andirons, in the fine scale of the lamps, and summed up in the feminine, social character of the drapery and the upholstery fabrics. The thoughtful person will make use of this property of color when he wishes to create an effect of formality or informality. If his problem is one of redecorating, these two pictures show that the type of furniture owned would condition the lightness of the walls. If the furniture is to be purchased for a new house, the kind of atmosphere one wants to live in will be the deciding factor. There is no difference in the quality of these rooms. They are equally beautiful, but there is a vast difference in their personality.

Grayed colors make good backgrounds against which other colors may be seen to advantage. Especially good background colors are the dusty yellows, called beige (figure 232B); grayed green (figure 232A); the yellowish greens (figure 1); and the natural wood tones as seen in the room in figure 231. The color may be lighter or darker, depending upon the size of the room, the number of windows, and the design and number of the pieces of furniture. When the outstanding color of the furnishings—particularly the rugs and upholstery materials—is distinctly warm or definitely cool, the walls would contain some note of that warmth or coolness if harmony is desired; and should a contrasting effect be preferred, the color for walls may be chosen from the opposite group of hues. White walls may be made to take on warmth or coolness by the use of color in window shades and curtains through which the light will enter the room. All the colors in a room will seem to be keyed or harmonized by the use of sunny yellow blinds or curtains. (See figure 3.)

When the furniture is beautiful in line and in its arrangement, light walls will emphasize these points; but if the room must be rather full, and the pieces are large or not ideal in line or proportion, it is well to have the walls of about the same value as the furniture, so that the latter will not stand out prominently. A comparison of figures 241 and 242 will show that when the values of the furnishings and the background are similar one does not particularly notice the outline of each piece, but that when there is contrast of dark against light every line stands out.

Although the designer has much latitude in his selection of hues and values for the living room walls, he is more limited in his choice of intensities. Background colors of rather low intensity permit the people and the furnishings in a living room to be seen to good advantage.

Pattern for walls   Shall we have plain or figured walls? There are many things to consider before this question can be answered satisfactorily. First, it must be decided whether one wishes to use pictures and decorative objects and fabrics to supply the pattern for the walls, or to have the decoration of the walls supplied by the paper. A room becomes bewildering if too much pattern is used, but the decision as to amount is a very personal matter. If pictures are to be used, the walls should be plain, or quite subdued, in order that the details of the pictures may be seen. If a picture is to be used on walls showing a distinct pattern, it must be very large, and its frame or mount needs to be wide enough to set it apart from the decorative background. If it is decided that there are to be no pictures and no pattern in drapery materials, the walls may well supply the decoration. There is a type of wall that, in its emphasis, lies between the plain surfaces and the paper with definite figures. This is the textured surface such as grass-cloth and sand-finished plaster; these make ideal walls, often chosen by people who enjoy a slight vibration of color yet wish to use patterns and pictures in the room. The pattern of a figured wall paper that will be generally useful as a background should be in scale with the size of the room and its furnishings; it should appear to lie flat against the wall and show no perspective; the hues and the values should show very little contrast; and the design should be conventionalized or stylized. The beautiful scenic papers used so successfully in the eighteenth century gave the effect of murals and were not considered as backgrounds for pictures. (See figure 220.)

When one wishes to secure the greatest possible appearance of spaciousness along with economy in lighting, the ceilings will be kept as nearly white as will look well. Dead white ceilings are pleasant in white rooms and with such cool colors as blue and green. Usually it is agreeable to add a little of the color used in the wall to the white paint for the ceiling so that it will be keyed. Ceilings which are darker than the wall seem to make a room look lower. A room may be very attractive with a ceiling of a beautiful contrasting color or painted with one of the colors found in the wall paper or carpet. Since dark colors absorb light, it is more costly to illuminate rooms in which the ceilings are dark.

The woodwork is a part of the background of a room, and the tendency in modern houses is to eliminate the wood around the doors and windows or to reduce the amount to a minimum. If the woodwork in a house has beautiful proportions and the doors and window openings are so placed that a pleasing pattern is made against the walls, the trim may be made to contrast with the walls. Usually, however, it is better to call little attention to woodwork and to keep the color and the value of the wood a part of the background.

The average person likes floors and floor coverings to be dark enough to appear to give a room a good foundation. If the rooms are light, he likes to see relatively lighter floors. Unusually light or dark floors are not practical because they show footprints and are not easy to keep looking well. Rugs may harmonize or contrast in color with the walls. If a contrasting hue is chosen it is usually desirable to repeat some of that color in curtains, pictures, or a hanging so that the room may appear to be balanced in color. Plain rugs or those having an interesting texture always make perfect backgrounds, but if a surface pattern is chosen the design should be conventionalized; the surface should be evenly covered, there should be no outstanding spots or medallions, and the colors and lights and darks should show very little contrast. (See figures 226 and 164B.) A plain carpet, with not even the lines of a border to break up the floor space, will give a room the maximum appearance of size. A plain rug that leaves but a narrow border of wood comes next in this effect of increased space, and small rugs make a room look smaller. The furnishings of a room will be drawn together through the use of one unobtrusive rug or carpet.

If the walls of a room are definitely figured one should select plain curtains. Plain materials should also be chosen for rooms with walls that are plain or have a comparatively inconspicuous pattern if there are many pictures and much pattern in the furniture and rugs in the room. Plain curtains the same color as the walls will seem to become a part of the walls and will enlarge the background. This kind of curtain is particularly successful in small rooms with many windows, because the greatest possible impression of size is gained. In choosing curtains with pattern, one should take into consideration the size of the room, the general color of the furnishings, and the personality expressed in the room. Designs for the material for overcurtains should be judged by the same standards as those applied to any surface pattern. When material is being selected it should be arranged in folds as though it were hanging in the windows, for frequently designs which look spotted or show too much line movement when the fabric is flat, "hold together" when the material is hung in folds. (See figure 244.) In addition to trying the curtain fabric in folds, it is advisable to hold it against a window to see how it will look when the light shines through. Also be sure to try a sample in the room where it will be used to see what effect its colors will have on the other furnishings. Light coming through some fabrics makes the color clearer and more luminous, while in other materials the color cannot be seen because of the weight or the weave of the cloth. Curtains which lose their beauty when seen against the light should be lined so that the light inside the room will make it possible to enjoy the design. It is important to select colors for curtains and for linings that will look well with the color of the exterior of the house. An ivory tone is the conventional color for linings, but frequently it is pleasant from the inside as well as the outside to see curtains lined with some other color. However, one should keep the glass curtains or the curtain linings very much alike on all the windows that are seen from the street.

The scale of the pattern should be adapted to the size of the room and to the size of the windows. A pattern like figure 243 is

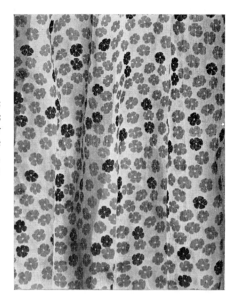

Figure 243. Patterns, as well as rooms, have personality. This drapery design, printed on sheer linen, is quaint and small in scale and suggests a feminine setting. (Courtesy of Dan Cooper, Inc.)

suitable for a small room with light pieces of furniture, while figure 246 requires a large room. If there are many windows in ·the room, the pattern should be less striking than if there are only two or three.

The type of design one selects depends upon the general character of the room. If it is large and very social and formal, a pattern similar to figure 246 would be suitable. For an informal room in which the furnishings are domestic, the design might have the general character of figure 245. Figure 243 is feminine in feeling, and the three fabrics pictured in figure 244 are of the type that could be used in a man's room. Figures 247 and 248 are quite impersonal patterns; figure 247 suggests a guest room; and figure 248 calls to mind the rooms in a modern house.

Even the person who has a very small furnishing budget feels that there are two places in her furnishing scheme where she can afford to play with color and pattern. If she must economize, she can get beautiful colors in paint for her walls and do them herself, and if she is ingenious she can find some smart material at very low cost and make her curtains. However, she should not economize

Figure 244. (Photograph by Emilie Danielson.) Bold weaves and vigorous designs are appropriate for the fabrics in a man's room. (Courtesy of House Beautiful.)

on the amount of material she buys because curtains ought to be of sufficient fullness to appear ample if they are drawn. The question of what type of pattern to choose for curtains may be answered by turning back to the suggestions for selecting designs for curtain materials on page 370, and to the illustrations shown in figures 174A and B. Well-selected curtains provide one of the best means for the introduction of pattern or color into a room, and rooms that otherwise might seem too plain may appear well furnished by the addition of interesting curtains.

Some rooms require curtains next to the windows for privacy or to soften the light. For this purpose thin curtains, spoken of as glass curtains, may be chosen, or perhaps split bamboo or Venetian blinds may be preferred. Each has its advantage. Thin curtains

Figure 245. Strong drawing and directness in design express the spirit of either a domestic room or a man's bedroom. (Courtesy of Dan Cooper, Inc., Textiles, 30 Rockefeller Plaza, New York.)

look fresh and crisp, and if they are made simply they are easily kept clean. Venetian blinds can be adjusted so as to admit degrees of light and air and are very satisfactory. Split bamboo blinds are an attractive and inexpensive substitute for Venetian blinds, but they are not adjustable and would not be so satisfactory in the sleeping rooms of persons who are sensitive to light. The modern taste is for very simply curtained windows. Frequently the glass

Figure 246. This social type of design shows the use of such familiar period motifs as cupid's heads, tassels, flower baskets, and the dove, combined in an arrangement with the formal festoon. A pattern of this type would be limited in its use to a fine fabric in a large formal setting.

curtains are omitted, letting overcurtains and Venetian blinds or window shades supply the window dressing. Materials for glass curtains and for overcurtains are available in so many types that a myriad of appropriate fabrics could be found in the dress fabrics department of a store as well as in the curtain department. While figured overcurtains may supply good color or pattern they are not indispensable, for pictures and decorative objects in the room will serve the same purpose, and much interest can be given to the windows through the choice of plain colors with the interesting weaves and textures that are easily available. If windows are numerous, it may be desirable to use a plain material there and let the view or the objects in the room furnish the emphasis.

It is better design to let the curtains hang straight than to loop them back tightly, and they should extend to a structural line in the room. (See figure 36, page 33.) A good line is created when the curtains hang to the floor, as in figure 226, although in informal rooms it is consistent to have them come to the sill, as in figure 262.

The hanging of curtains

Figure 247. An impersonal character in the stylized design of this textile makes it suitable for a man's room, a woman's room, or a guest room. (Courtesy of Dan Cooper, Inc., Textiles, 30 Rockefeller Plaza, New York.)

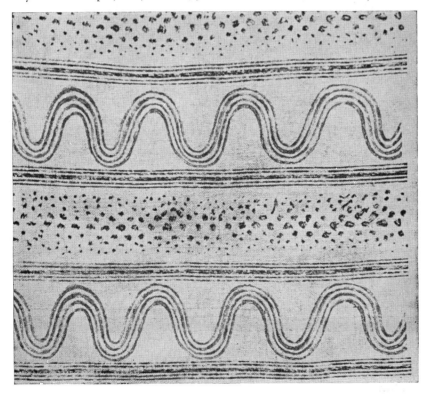

Figure 248. (Photograph by Emilie Danielson.) Unusual textures, nubbed weaves, and simplified impersonal patterns would make these fabrics fit especially well into the modern or functional house. (Courtesy of House Beautiful.)

Curtaining the windows becomes more puzzling when the openings in the room are not uniform. Short high windows, french doors, and radiators underneath windows complicate the problem. The usual solution is to hang the curtains to reach the floor on all but obstructed openings, as in figure 253, and to the top of the radiator or to the shelf, when the window is above a bookcase (figure 102). Curtains so long that about a foot of the material lies upon the floor are used only in very formal and social rooms. Curtains may be hung inside the wood trim or outside, depending upon the effect desired. They should be hung to cover the trim if it is advisable to secure the maximum amount of light, if the woodwork is unattractive, or if the proportions of the window or group of windows would be improved by the effect of additional width. Whether curtains are made with or without a valance depends upon the shape of the windows. Valances tend to make the window appear shorter and wider, and they will make a unit of a group of windows. If it is desired to make windows appear longer, the curtains should be long and the valance omitted, or else used in the form of a valance frame hung above the casing of the window, covering it completely. In that way the actual length of the curtain will be increased as well as the apparent height of the window. In most homes the straight valance is the best type. Draped valances are suited to formal rooms, but when they are used in modest homes they appear pretentious.

There are many good ways to plan a beautiful color scheme for a house but in the end it seems largely to be a matter of deciding *Planning a color scheme* first on the kind of effect one likes and then understanding how to make colors and textures give that effect. If one is at a loss for an idea to start a color plan it is always easy to build a scheme around a drapery fabric, a rug, or a picture which is to occupy an important place in the room. The color plan is likely to be pleasing if the backgrounds are selected so that they give an impression of a fairly close relationship among the large areas with enough accents in the accessories to enliven the scheme. The room in figure 2 illustrates a color plan in which the few colors that are used range in value from white to black. The white walls emphasize the slight warmth of the natural wool color of the rugs and upholstery and of the bleached cork table tops. The warmth of the rug is accented by the mellow color of the gold in the antique Japanese screen. Darker variations of these warm hues are seen in the books and in the pre-Columbian sculptured figures and bowls. There is a small note of strongly contrasting blue in the bands of the two cushions, and the window curtains are of a blue that has been neutralized until it is very close to gray. Black, too, has been used for contrast, and its distribution throughout the room is marked by a reserve in which the color composition has played as large a part as the quality of the objects in the furnishing scheme of the room.

Backgrounds play a prominent part in a furnishing scheme when natural wood and brick are used, for they bring color and texture into a room. In figure 231, the warm tones of the wood in the paneled walls and the ceiling and the brick of the fireplace established a base for the color and texture pattern which are carried throughout the principal rooms of this house. The yellow in the room is keyed to the warmth of the background tones and is repeated rhythmically in the large chair, the pattern of the sofa, and the two plaid chairs. This is a closely related color scheme which would be classified as analogous, for the hues lie between red-orange and yellow in the spectrum. A pleasant variety has been introduced by the use of gray and black, and the dark values have been balanced throughout the room in such a way as to create an impression of stability in the color arrangement. A glance back at figure 3 will show another analogous scheme, but here, painted walls provide the background color. The hues are similar to those in figure 231, but the effect is quite different because in one room the walls are light and the floor is dark, whereas in the other room the values are reversed. Practical considerations would help one to decide whether to use a dark or a light floor color, since either one may be attractive.

Figure 1 illustrates that even such strong contrasts as complementary colors can be selected in values and intensities that will create a quiet color scheme. Furthermore, one sees that the way the color is distributed will affect the appearance of a room. This room in a small house is used for general living and for sleeping. Generally, an impression of maximum size would be desired for this purpose, and this effect was accomplished by using one color for all of the backgrounds—the walls, fireplace, woodwork, and carpet. With the idea of relaxation in mind, it is natural that a restful color would be chosen, and the subtle tones of the grayed greenish color that is seen in the background has provided this feeling of repose. Since there is no other room where one may go for a change of environment, colors were selected to provide enough stimulation to keep the room from looking monotonous. The use of the darker greenish tones of the ceiling and the stronger, brighter green of the chair at the right has broken the monotony of only one value in a room that has a single dominant color. However, the addition of the contrasting hue in the grayed reddish upholstery material on the chair and the ottoman at the left in the photograph has created a complementary harmony. Then, to bring more interest into the color pattern, there are varying tones of these contrasting hues in the decorative objects as well as in the books—colors that add life to the room without detracting from its essential restfulness.

Two additional color schemes in small houses are seen in figure 232A and B. Contrasting color harmonies have been used, and both houses show how the principles of color and design were applied to secure a pleasant impression of space and of balanced color. In "A," when the sliding wall between the living-dining room and the den-bedroom is open, the cool, receding color of the light green wall seems to send the eye farther than the dimensions of the floor plan would indicate. The color scheme is approximately a triad, with subtle colors that suggest orange, green, and purple producing a comfortably balanced effect. It is interesting to see how the hues have been carried across the two rooms to give them a sense of unity: the greenish hue of the wall is repeated in stronger tones (at the table) in the green chair and the covered jar, and the two pictures are large enough so that their colors are effective in "crossing" the hues from one room to the other. Notice the attractive pattern created by the color and placement of the cushions on the sofa. Although this triad harmony has been handled in a manner that is not too literal, it produces a comfortable balance between stimulation and relaxation.

It is clear that the charm and livability of the house in figure 232B owes as much to its color as to the discriminating choices of the furnishings and the well-related texture combinations. Whereas in "A," the architect used a sliding wall as a device to divide the two small rooms, the designer of "B" separated the kitchen-dining area from the living room with a folding screen. The windows under the eaves give a sense of space, and by means of a window wall, the living area has been opened so that the garden fence seems to mark the boundary of the room. Although most of the colors in the room are keyed to warmth, with red-orange and yellow-orange predominating, the large area of green in the folding screen has created a contrasting harmony. The cool green has been balanced rhythmically around the room in pictures and in small accessories. Because the curtains are plain and continue the color of the walls, they make the small room look more spacious. The wall color has the characteristics of an excellent background for pictures: it is sufficiently light in value to emphasize any color seen against it, its slightly warm hue unifies colors, and it has been neutralized to a degree where it will neither conflict nor compete with other colors.

The basis for determining the type of color scheme to choose for a room should be governed by the owner's preference. It does not matter whether all of the colors in a scheme are warm or cool, or if there is a combination of both. All may be pleasant. But whatever one's preference may be, a room is most likely to be beautiful if the large surfaces for the backgrounds and some of the furniture covers are rather closely keyed to each other, and the contrasts are kept for the smaller areas.

Lighting   Much of the comfort as well as the charm of a room depends upon successful lighting. A great deal of research is being done in the field of lighting for health and comfort, and it is advisable to keep informed on the findings of these studies, for the designs and materials for lamps are steadily being improved. The simplest room may take on an air of comfort and friendliness when the lamps are well chosen for color and well designed and placed for the correct intensity and distribution of the light. The most thoughtfully furnished room will seem uncomfortable and uninviting if the light is too glaring. There are two types of illumination—general and local. General illumination is useful when general activities are being carried on. It may be secured with ceiling lights, but well-distributed lamps with shades open at the top will also provide general illumination. A kitchen is one of the rooms where general illumination is used, but here, too, it may be desirable to supplement it with some local lighting. Concentrated illumination is secured through the use of local lights at those places in a room where such close work as reading, writing, or sewing is to be done. The standard for lighting a room, from the point of view of eye comfort as well as beauty, is a softly diffused light that has much the effect of a well-lighted room in daylight. It is neither beautiful nor healthful to look into a bright light or to see lights at the side within the line of vision. The eyes become very fatigued when some parts of a room are in deep shadow while other parts are brilliantly lighted. Experiments have shown that in order to reduce eye fatigue no local light should be more than ten times as bright as the general illumination in the room. It is particularly important to follow this ratio when one is reading or doing close work, for it is injurious to the eyes to have a sharp, undistributed light in an otherwise darkened room, such as the light which would fall upon a surface around a lamp with an opaque shade. Lamps should be well distributed so as to provide adequate light at every chair or point where people will read or work in addition to a fairly even light throughout the room. This type of lighting affords an opportunity for pleasant coloring and, by throwing parts of the room into soft shadows, creates an air of intimacy and hospitality not to be secured with the uncompromising evenness of a strong general illumination.

Lamps If it is remembered that the design of a lamp should suggest its purpose, all eccentric shapes will be avoided. The lamp base should be beautiful in structure and well balanced. From the point of view of the appearance of the room, the lamps should be low enough to group with the furniture and will be most attractive if all are the same height. However, the correct height for each lamp depends upon how it will be used. The light should always be above the line of the vision. Accordingly, if one is working on a table or desk, the bottom of the shade should be about nineteen inches above the surface of the table. If one is sitting beside a table and reading or sewing, it is not necessary to have the lamp so high. The light from a lamp should also be so well diffused as to avoid glare on a paper or other working surface. The shade should be in good proportion to the base and so shaped that it throws the light upward and as far out as may be desired. The use of a white shade or a white lining will add appreciably to the amount of light reflected. In selecting colors for lamp shades, these points should be considered: first, the color effect in the room in daylight, for it should fit into the general color scheme; second, the color effect in the room at night. A warm, cheerful lamp light will suffuse an entire room with a soft glow. Hard, bright colors, such as red and bright rose, are not pleasing for lamp shades. If white shades can be made to fit harmoniously into the room they will be the best choice. Creamy white will nearly always harmonize in a color scheme if white will not. Other good choices are the very light, softened tints of yellow-orange, orange, and red-orange, in the hues commonly called yellow-beige, straw color, and pinkish-beige. Another important consideration in lighting is the effect of the color at night upon the people in the room. Blues, purples, and greens make people look like ghosts. In short, the best colors for lamp shades are those which, in themselves, suggest the color of light. If several lamps are used in a room, the colors in the shades should be alike or similar in hue or made to blend with the background against which they will be seen.

Furniture   Good furniture will give many years of satisfaction and for that reason should be bought deliberately. Every piece of furniture should be studied from the point of view of its construction and suitability to its purpose and surroundings. If the piece is one in which comfort is a factor, it ought to be distinctly comfortable. Simplicity in structural and decorative design is desirable. Since the average house is small, it is important to consider scale when selecting furniture and furnishings. Although people who themselves are larger than the average in size look and feel more at home if their furniture is fairly large in scale, the small house owner cannot successfully use the larger, heavier pieces of furniture that may look so well in his neighbor's big house, for they will crowd his rooms.

The living room should contain enough comfortable pieces of furniture to accommodate each member of the family. It is not necessary that furniture be costly to be comfortable, but it must be designed to fit the body. Before a chair or a sofa is purchased it should be tried by those who are to use it to see if the height of the seat in relation to its depth and the angle of the back provide the desired comfort. Deep soft chairs are luxurious and relaxing to most people, but no chair or sofa should be so deep and soft as to make a person appear awkward when seated or in arising from it.

Selecting furniture for the living room

Much of the traditional furniture in America has been adapted from Italian, French, and English models. Most Italian and French styles are very formal, and these are suitable only for formal and rather imposing houses. Not all French and Italian furniture is formal, however; some of the provincial furniture of these countries has much in common with early American Colonial style. They are quaint but sober interpretations of the formal styles, with a quality of sincerity which is strongly akin to the modest dignity of the American Colonial types. This is seen especially in figure 241, where the French provincial chair at the right of the fireplace seems to go naturally into the Colonial room. The English styles and the American Colonial styles that were adapted from them are unpretentious and are particularly appropriate for the American home. The American Colonial period shows a wide variety of styles ranging from the solid, durable, serious examples of the early Puritan work to the finer and more classic work of the period of the Revolution.

When one attempts to trace the source of the twentieth-century furniture, he sometimes finds faint reminiscences of the Empire and Directoire periods of France and, occasionally, a slight likeness to Chinese furniture. But on the whole the style is original and is designed particularly for the quickened tempo of life in the "age of the machine." In this style there is a wide range of expression. Most examples have a marked appearance of reserve, but a few poor pieces indulge in erratic shapes and decoration. (See figures 23 and 24 on page 21.) The best modern work has a straightfor-

ward, logical beauty resulting largely from the fact that it is so direct.
The best work does not follow any set manner, but in every case
the designs of the building, the interior, and the furnishings are determined by the likes and the needs of the owners, by the use to
which they will be put, and by the materials employed. It is significant that the twentieth-century furniture designs and interiors
are planned for the twentieth-century architecture. The spirit of this
style is impersonal; when it is handled on a light scale, with delicate
colors, it may be feminine in its character, but more frequently it
has a rather masculine note. Most modern rooms show subdued but
unusual colors, a frequent use of the horizontal line varied occasionally with the curve, and a restful effect secured by means of
empty spaces.

Just as modern houses are planned for modern living conditions
and new materials, so the rooms pictured in figures 236, 249, and
250 illustrate how the designs for the modern interiors and furnishings are planned for the new achitecture. In these rooms there
is an air of simplicity so striking that it may be said to be the first
consideration. In the contemporary house everything that could be
eliminated has been abandoned. The wood cornices and picture
moldings have disappeared, and the wooden frames around the
doors and windows are frequently replaced by a narrow line of
metal treated as is the wall so that it is not apparent. In the few
examples where wood is used, the paneling of the former styles,
with its lines of moldings, has been replaced by large plain panels
made from sheets of wood veneer. There is no ornament, and the
room never appears crowded. As much of the furniture as can well
be is built in, and the movable pieces of furniture are constructed
on exceedingly simple lines. The distinguishing features of modern
furniture are seen in figures 249 and 250. Various metals are sometimes used instead of wood for the structure, and when wood is
used, it is handled in a logical way. The structural lines of the
furniture are simple and clearly defined. The grain of the wood and
the excellence of its finish have taken the place of applied decoration as seen in the cabinet in figure 164A. In order to preserve
the natural beauty of the wood, it usually receives no other finish

Figures 249 and 250. (Architect, Richard J. Neutra. Photograph by Julius Shulman.) These two views of the living-dining area of a small house show the spirit of the mid-twentieth century. The informal furnishings harmonize with the textures of the background.

than extremely careful rubbing, and, at the last, a transparent coat of wax. Figure 86 shows some interesting examples of twentieth-century informal furniture of a type that fits comfortably into the traditional as well as into the modern houses, and in figure 56 we see a pleasant combination of well-scaled traditional furniture combined with modern pieces.

The modern style makes exacting demands upon the designer. He needs to know, first, how to adapt designs to suit the personality of an individual. If he does not, his client must make his manner of living suit the new home, and that immediately defeats the ideals and the purpose of modernism and becomes affectation. Furthermore, if the house is to have meaning, every element will have a proper relationship to every other one. That is to say, the house will be suited to its surroundings; the interior architecture will be consistent with the exterior; the furniture and all the accessories will be in the spirit of the house and show the necessary reserve and quality of design; and, as a final note, the color schemes will have the characteristic quality of vitality and freshness.

The homemaker should not be so much interested in securing an authentic period style or a room in which all the furniture is historically correct, as in pieces that are beautiful in design and combine well in size and texture.

After the room has been successfully furnished to the point of having good backgrounds and furniture that is comfortable, suitable, and beautiful in line and color, the owner should bring into it the things he particularly enjoys looking at or handling. Using one's favorite colors in a textile or pieces of pottery; having vases of flowers, and plants or bulbs; displaying the collection that marks a hobby or a pleasant journey; placing the magazines and books one is reading, or likely to read, on convenient tables—these are some of the ways of making a room homelike.

The dining room The character of the furnishings for the dining room depends somewhat upon where the room is located. If it is a separate room, the traditional dining room furniture, consisting of the table, chairs, a buffet, and serving table, may be used; but if the room is an ell or a dining alcove adjoining the living room, or is actually a part

Figure 251. (Decorator, Bob Brown, A.I.D. Photograph by Maynard Parker.) The restraint in this dining room expresses the spirit of a typical twentieth-century interior. All of the furnishings are well designed and attractively arranged. The grouping of the flowers with the candlestick makes a striking center of interest in this individual room.

of the living room, it is more interesting to use less usual pieces—a highboy or a chest of drawers, for example, and a table that does not look too much like the conventional dining room table.

The average person wishes to have a restful time at meals, and it is difficult to do this in a room which does not look restful. If there are many objects and much pattern in the room, it will seem confusing; and when the large number of pieces of silver, china, and glass making up the table service are brought in they will increase the unrest. The first thing to do, then, in order to obtain a restful dining room is to keep the background simple; second, to display only a few objects; and third, to place the table appointments in an orderly arrangement at meals. On the other hand, there

Figure 252. (Architect, Kenneth Lind. Photograph by Julius Shulman.)
The successful placement of the storage wall provides this small house with
three distinct centers: living, dining, and study-sleeping areas. All of these
appear to be unified because the furniture is so well harmonized. There is a
strong impression of character, good taste, and sincerity in this inexpensive
home.

are some people who desire a stimulating rather than a restful dining
room and who enjoy patterned walls. If one wishes to use a rather
striking figured wall paper it is better to use it in the dining room
than in the living room, for the dining room is not used for so long
a period. Furthermore, one may more easily dispense with other
decorative objects in this room and be content to let the walls themselves supply the decoration.

The furnishings of the modern dining room shown in figure 251
would be suitable either in a separate room or in the dining end of a
living room. The furniture is well designed and all of the selections
have character. Seen against a plain background, the table appoint-

ments have become dramatic in the room. Another pleasing effect in the otherwise quiet scheme is achieved by the use of the patterned curtain and the indefinite stripe on two of the chairs.

In figure 252 we see the dining area of a small house. The amount of space used in this dining area would be inadequate for a separate dining room, but as it is used here, it creates a feeling of size because it is an extension of the living room. The room divider, useful for storage, suggests a partition at that end of the room but allows the

Figure 253. With space at a premium, small house-builders are wise to plan combination rooms. Here the dining room, used for such short times during the day, has been happily combined with a study.

eye to travel above and beyond it, creating the illusion of space. The light-weight screen can be used to close off the dining area from the living room or from the kitchen, and it can be used to give privacy to the study-sleeping area when that is desired. There is a homelike quality in this well-designed interior, as well as a sense of sincerity and charm: the light-scaled furniture is excellent in design and is well arranged; the informal textures harmonize with the furniture; the pictures are good, and well hung; the books, flowers, and plants give warmth to the room.

Owners of small houses are reluctant to use too much floor space for a dining room since it is used for so short a time in the day; and one good solution of this question is seen in the dining room-study combination in figure 253. There is plenty of storage space for dishes, silver, and linen behind these cupboard doors, and when the roomy table is not being used at meal time it makes a fine study table. This plan gives the privacy desirable both for study and for meals.

The kitchen   A vital center in the homelike house, the kitchen may be a room of many aspects. In some houses it is small and efficient, solely a place for work. In other homes, where living is very informal, it is larger and is a friendly and hospitable room. In the winter it may be the warmest and most inviting room in the house and so become not only a center for work, but a place where children play and the family relaxes. It is clear that there is no one formula for the satisfactory kitchen, for it depends so entirely upon the manner of life in the particular family. However, a few points stand out prominently: whether it is large or small, the ideal plan for the kitchen is one in which the work areas are so grouped that the homemaker does not need to take unnecessary steps. The size of the room is not a factor here; it is merely a matter of convenient arrangement. As the function of the kitchen increases to include a place in which meals are served or sewing, reading, or resting is done, one applies the same standards for comfort and appearance as for any other part of the house planned particularly for these activities. But there is always need for a heightened awareness of these standards, so that the influence of living in the kitchen may be as good for the family

Figure 254. (Architect, Kenneth Lind.) *This kitchen is colorful and efficient. The table, on tracks, can be used here or it will slide into the dining room. Cabinets are of natural birch, and counters are stainless steel. The high cupboards with birch doors are painted tomato red, and this red is prominent in the children's paintings.*

Figure 255. (Architect, Lyman Ennis. Photograph by Julius Shulman.) *Work is made easy and pleasant in the compact U-shaped kitchen. Food can be passed to the dining room from the counter at the left or to an eating area in the rear garden from the sliding window above the sink.*

as it would be in the living room. Good standards could be maintained in the kitchen illustrated in figure 58 on page 58. In the area set apart for meals the furnishings may be more rugged and colorful than those in the dining room, but they should be just as attractive.

The modern kitchen is a truly functional room, and because it is so right for its purpose it is often one of the best-looking rooms in the house. Figures 254 and 255 are two kitchens in small homes. In both there are cheerful and pleasant colors along with convenient arrangement and good light and air. The kitchen in figure 254 shows a dining area with a table on tracks. In this position it seats four people, or it can be set here and rolled through the opening into the dining room. Wrought iron legs support the other end of the table.

The bedroom Since the bedroom is distinctly personal, it should express its occupant even more intimately than any other room in the house. The photographs and the special pictures characteristic of the owner and his taste and yet too personal to be placed in the more public rooms of the house have their place in the bedroom.

The function of a bedroom is to promote rest, and so the first requisite is a comfortable bed. Since it is difficult to relax in a room that seems crowded with furnishings or with pattern, the bedroom should be simple; but unless there is a note of vitality in it the room will appear dull and spiritless. Vitality should be expressed in terms of the owner's individuality. It may be obtained through the use of line, color, or pattern, but if it is too forceful the room will become tiring. This is illustrated in figure 256, where there is so much emphasis in the designs on the walls, rugs, and draperies that rest is discouraged rather than promoted. Figure 257 shows how one's fondness for color and pattern may be gratified and still keep a happy balance between pattern and rest space. The colors that seem best in a bedroom will vary with the individual. Some people prefer light colors because they think them more refreshing, while others find dark colors and dull surfaces which do not reflect light to be more restful and conducive to sleep.

The use to which the room will be put is the chief factor in

Figure 256. Such a distracting pattern has been used in the walls and rug in this room that they fail to make a good background for the furniture and curtains.

Figure 257. The handsome pattern of the old blue and white coverlet and the design of the rugs can be fully enjoyed with the sunny yellow walls in this room. Like the rest of the rooms in the house in figure 225, the master bedroom reveals a sense of graceful yet substantial comfort.

determining the type of bedroom furniture to choose. A bedroom may have to serve also as a living room or a study or work room. The rooms shown in figures 258 and 259 are such rooms. Figure 259 was arranged by college students, and much of the furniture in both rooms was designed and made by students. Since the rooms are a part of the equipment of a class room, one wall is missing. In figure 258 the observer is asked to imagine that the study table marks the position of the wall. It was planned to have the closet door on the wall at the left and the door leading to the hall on the open side in

Figure 258. This arrangement was set up in a class room for a combination living and sleeping room or a room in a dormitory. Much of the furniture was designed and made by students and may offer a suggestion to those who like to use tools. Pictures, decorative accessories, and a block-printed hanging give the room individuality in design and color. A room of this type could be made more masculine or more feminine, depending upon the fabrics and colors used.

Figure 259. *Simple sturdy furnishings of this type could be made by al-most any girl. The room would be attractive with white walls and woodwork, white curtains with a red broken stripe, a red and white checked gingham or homespun cover on the cot, and dark blue, red, and light gray in the rugs. The bookcase of prune boxes would be painted white and lined with a blue like the color in the rugs. Any number of equally pleasant color schemes could be substituted for the one described.*

the photograph. This room would take on the more impersonal character of a living room and would give no suggestion of a bed-room if a picture replaced the mirror above the chest of drawers. A mirror and a small shelf for toilet articles could be attached to the back of the closet door, and with the addition of a stool, it would make a comfortable and convenient substitute for a dressing table. There is storage space for extra bedding in the top of the frame built around the slip-covered cot which may be pulled out at night. The cushions are thick enough to leave a comfortable depth for seating space. Inexpensive lamps of a healthful, efficient type are placed to give good light for reading or relaxation. The desk, conveniently planned for typing and studying, can be used as a table for lunches. Above the desk a bulletin board made of cork or fiber-board could

Figure 260. (Photograph by Robert C. Cleveland.) This room suggests
some of the features that a modern young college or professional man might
enjoy. The masculine character has been established by the air of efficiency
in this workroom-bedroom and the use of fabrics with sturdy textures.

be hung to post the latest pictures or programs of current interest.
Two personal photographs are put where they can be enjoyed. The
other pictures in this room were chosen to suggest how pictures of
such different sizes may be hung to balance each other, and they
were intended also to show how much more agreeable a pattern is
created against a wall when small pictures are hung together in this
way with a straight line at the top rather than in steps, as is seen in
figure 305. The basic colors are beige, brown, and green with accenting notes of tangerine.

The bedroom in figure 259 was arranged for a girl. It is easy to see
how the fresh bright colors in the actual room would make it a

cheery place to live. Notice the convenient position of the lamps and the way the units have been completed by the strip of Swedish wall paper hung over the cot, the picture over the desk, and the use of the plant, flowers, and a number of small accessories.

A room that suggests the interests of a young man is seen in figure 260. This room is a setting for a typical young man who likes to work in his room. It is conveniently planned and has a manifestly masculine simplicity and tailored appearance. The attic room in figure 261 was built by a high-school boy. Any young man with interest and

Figure 261. Thoroughly a boy's room, planned and built by the resourceful young man who was given this space in the attic. It is sheathed with pine boards; bunks with seersucker spreads dyed cherry red are on both sides of the dormer, with a matching red in the figured percale curtains at the windows. There is a place for his tennis things; and a collection of guns, games, and bird prints, a fish bowl, books, and personal photographs make this a place of his own in which to work and play and entertain his friends.

Figure 262. (Photograph by Julius Shulman.) Ingenious parents could furnish a room of this character at a fairly low cost. The linoleum floor is practical, and it is quiet. All of the furnishings are sturdy and easy to clean. Colors could be selected to make this room suitable either for girls or boys.

ingenuity and the available space, could create such a room for himself. Wood and composition board are easily cut and handled by an amateur, and they make a good background for the things a boy likes to have in his room. This room serves as a hobby room as well as a bedroom, and the young owner and his friends have good times at games, listening to the radios they make, and pursuing their various hobbies together.

The guest room is the one type of bedroom which should be impersonal, since it is a room in which anyone should feel at home. There should be no personal photographs in the room, and the pictures used should have general appeal. The spirit of hospitality is one of the finest attributes of a home. If it could be analyzed, it would be found to be the result of an aggregate of details, foremost among them a genuine pleasure in the company of other

Figure 263. (Designer, Paul Hoag. Photograph by Robert C. Cleveland.)
Except for the tiny chair, the furniture in this child's room can be used
over the years, while the accessories will change with his age and interests.
The books and toys are easily available, but can be shut away whenever
desirable.

people and consideration for their comfort. The homemaker is
able to show her desire to make her guests comfortable by antici-
pating their wants when she furnishes her guest room. Therefore
the guest room should, if possible, contain the following things in
addition to such necessities as a comfortable bed, a well-lighted
mirror, and sufficient storage space: a desk or a table on which one
may write; a supply of stationery with pen and ink; a well-equipped
work box; a waste basket; a bedside table with a good reading lamp,
books of general interest; and a comfortable chair.

Under the topic of masculine and feminine qualities on page
337, the general characteristics of the man's room, the woman's
room, and the guest room are discussed. There still remains the
child's room. Scientists agree that environment has a strong influ-

ence upon a child's mental and physical well-being and upon the development of his taste. And they say, further, that in the first few years of his life he is highly impressionable and establishes many of his life-long habits. If these ideas are kept in mind children's rooms will be stimulating but not exciting. That is to say there will be a happy medium between drab dullness and over-decoration. So that the child may know and learn to enjoy many good pictures, one or two excellent ones might be hung in his room and changed at intervals. These pictures should be adapted to the age of the child and kept out until they have become familiar, but not so long that he will cease to notice them. Figures 262 and 263 are types of children's rooms that seem to contain a good balance between the suggestions of rest and play. They also show the difference between a well-furnished room for quite a young person and one in which older children live. The furniture will not have to be replaced in either room, but the accessories will change from year to year, and so the effect of the room will keep in step with the child's age level.

In addition to the considerations described as applying to special types of bedroom, there are certain requirements which hold for all types. The furniture should be convenient for use and balanced in arrangement. The bed should be placed where there will be enough fresh air, but where the light will not shine into the eyes of the sleeper. Mirrors should be so placed that a person standing in front of them will be well lighted in the daytime and at night. And, lastly, the room must be thoroughly comfortable.

A special room
in the house

There is one other room that has not been mentioned in this discussion of the homelike house. Nearly every family needs it, but its character would be so different that no one label seems to fit. For one family it would be a room where the parents or children could read or work when some of the family are entertaining or listening to radio or television. It may be a hobby room where work may be left until finished without being disturbed or being in other people's way. Perhaps it is a downstairs dining room where food may be roasted over the coals in the open fire and parties of a very much more informal character can be given than would be possible in a dining room upstairs, where the textures and accessories are very social. An amusement room may be fitted for games and contain a work bench as well. An attic or a basement room may have a stage for puppet shows and amateur theatricals. There could be a photographic darkroom so that the family could have the fun of developing and enlarging its own pictures. Since this special room is not likely to be a serious room, it is just the place to play with plenty of clear, fresh color, and here, too, is the place where home-made and made-over furniture will fit so well.

Most houses could provide some sort of retreat if it is no more than a screened or walled-off corner in the basement which has been made bright and cheerful with fresh paint. With good light, a big table, plenty of shelves, and some comfortable chairs, this may be the most livable of all the rooms in your homelike house.

Chapter Twenty

INTERIOR DESIGN (Continued)

III. MAKING THE BEST OF ONE'S POSSESSIONS

THE PERSON who can build the sort of house he likes and furnish it as he pleases, is fortunate indeed. Most of us are forced to compromise and to make the best of what we have. There are three remedies for the "decorative mishaps" that may have occurred through inheritance or because of unwise purchases. These are: (1) elimination, (2) rearrangement, and (3) concealment.

Elimination   Elimination is the first measure. Each object in a room should be judged practically and impersonally, regardless of its sentimental value. An interest in antiques sometimes leads to the belief that anything old is automatically beautiful. The real test of any design is the quality of its structure and its decoration, and if an object does not add to the beauty or to the comfort of the room, it should be discarded. Even after this has been done there may be still too many objects for the size of the room, and an additional sifting out will be required.

Rearrangement   Rearrangement is the next step. Order is the first requirement for beauty, and what can be accomplished through arrangement is illustrated in figures 39 and 40 and discussed under the topic of orderly arrangement, or "Shape Harmony."

It is pleasant to see an occasional change in the appearance of a room, and very simple rearrangements of the furnishings are often sufficient to arouse interest. Frequently it is only a matter of moving an object from a more obscure position to one of prominence in order to give an impression of having something fresh and new in

Figure 264. (Left.) Although the objects in this group are adequate in size, they have been placed so that they give the impression of a scattered arrangement.

Figure 265. (Right.) The scattered effect of figure 264 has been remedied here. The Chinese horse and rider and the vase with leaves, both of which lead the eye out of the composition, have been reversed, and the small bowl is moved from its isolated position to group with the Chinese figure.

a room. A study of the illustrations in figures 264 and 265 may offer some suggestions for those who know how to choose good things, but are not satisfied with their arrangements. Although the objects in figure 264 are adequate in size and number, the effect is mechanical, and one sees each separate object rather than the group as a whole. Unity is the keynote of successful arangements. In the rearrangement in figure 265, the first step toward unity was to reverse the positions of the Chinese horse and rider and the vase with leaves. It was important to do this because in figure 264, the direction of the horse and rider leads to the left, while the longer line of the leaf arrangement goes to the right—both carrying the eye away from the picture, which is the center of interest. The next step

toward unity was to group the small bowl with the Chinese figure. In
this position, the two objects balance the large arrangement of leaves.

It is not enough that objects be grouped in order to gain the
impression of unity. They must be placed so that their lines will
carry the eye along paths staying well within the boundaries of the
arrangement. So simple a detail as turning a teapot so that its spout
faces toward the center of a shelf, rather than away from it, may
hold an entire arrangement together.

Concealment Concealment is the last measure. After all the unessentials have
been eliminated and the room has been well arranged, some un-
sightly objects, necessary for comfort, may remain. Then the problem of hiding their deficiencies is met. Slip covers frequently furnish the answer to this question in the case of chairs and couches.

Some problems necessitate all three measures. Figure 266 shows
the kind of room too frequently seen in old houses and apartments. The principles of proportion and emphasis are violated
here. There is so much heavy woodwork as compared with the
size of the room that the amount of wood becomes oppressive. This
small dining room has a beamed ceiling, a plate rail with panels below it, and an elaborate built-in buffet. Between the rooms are
built-in bookcases upon which rest heavy, badly proportioned pillars. Lines of wood on the bookcase doors are so emphatic that they
detract from the appearance of the books. The built-in sideboard is
too elaborate in its design. The house in figure 266 is not owned by
the occupants, so the built-in sideboard, the built-in bookcases, and
the pillars must remain, and the occupants must make the best use
they can of them.

There are other mistakes in this room besides the architectural
defects. Good taste demands the elimination of most of the objects
that have been placed on the sideboard, and all that are on the
plate rail. Because there is so much emphasis in the background of
this room there should be fewer decorative objects than can successfully be used in a room where the background is simple. The
vase on the table should be removed because it is too small for the
table, and the white doily because it is too small, too light, and not
a harmonious shape. This room is dark, and the white electric

Figure 266. A type of architectural background commonly found in rented houses. The confusing effect of this background has not been helped by the profusion of objects displayed.

Figure 267. This picture suggests what concealment, rearrangement, and elimination can do for a room. Curtains have been used to cover the bookcases and columns shown in figure 266, and have served to extend the wall space which was too small to accommodate a piece of furniture; the desk and rug have been placed to harmonize with the lines of the room; the window and mirror over the built-in buffet have been covered with the wall paper of the room attached to a rigid compo-board; the fussy and inappropriate decorations have been removed, and a single decorative arrangement has been substituted. These changes have simplified the room and have made it restful.

Figure 268. This room is everything that a dining room should not be. The effect is restless and distracting. It shows that the owner has a mistaken sense of beauty and has had no opportunity to train her taste.

globes stand out too prominently against the dark oak of the sideboard. In figure 267, which shows a rearrangement of this room, the drop lights and chains were removed from the light fixtures and it was placed against the ceiling. White curtains were too light in the dark room, and so corn-colored theatrical gauze was substituted. The small white doily was replaced by a colored cover which is a better size for the table. The mirror and the window of the built-in sideboard were covered with compo-board which was papered with the same grass cloth used in the rest of the room. Then curtains full enough to be drawn across the entire opening when it is desired were hung over the bookcases and pillars. While these curtains are velvet, any inexpensive material harmonizing with the room in color and texture could have been used. The rugs were laid straight to harmonize with the lines of the room. To add color, a pewter and a red lacquered disk, pewter candlesticks, and a seasonal flower arrangement were placed on the buffet and a bowl with fruit on the table.

Figure 269 shows an "after" view of a dining room that once had as many decorative maladies as the room seen in figure 268. Here, too, the background was broken into little patches of dark and light by panels and a plate rail. The owners removed the plate rail and simplified the background by painting the wood like the walls and covering the three too-narrow windows with one wide Venetian blind. One can easily imagine how the room in figure 268 could be made as pleasant as this is merely by removing all of the dishes and the picture from the plate rail and painting the entire room the same color. In the process of elimination it is often necessary to use a saw in order to make ugly furniture presentable. This is a room in which the saw might well be used to remove the top of the sideboard, making it a useful and good-looking chest of drawers. The table legs could be tapered down by cutting away the heavy animal's paws, and a simple light fixture should be substituted for the one shown here. However, if there are no funds to carry out these suggestions and no one in the family who can use tools, an amazing improvement can be made in the appearance of the room by removing the array of objects from the plate rail and the side-

Figure 269. Although figures 268 and 269 do not picture the same room, this shows what was done with a room similar to figure 268. Painting the woodwork the same color as the light walls simplified and enlarged the room. The large Venetian blind was used to gain privacy in the dining room which was very close to the house next door. The blind unified the three windows and, with the curtains, made a handsome pattern on that wall. Colorful objects, plants, and flowers can be enjoyed in this setting.

Figure 270. A number of things in this room that show a lack of taste could be remedied. The room has too much pattern; the lamp base, the stenciled design, and the lines of the furniture are poor; the hanging and the rug are placed at bad angles.

board and keeping the top shelf of the sideboard clear. The white cover on the table is poor in the room for two reasons: it makes too white a spot in the dark room, and it is placed so that its shape contradicts the lines of the room. If it is kept, it should be straightened, but it would be better to substitute a longer, darker cover for this square or to place the bowl of flowers on the bare table, as in figure 269.

Figure 270 illustrates some of the mistakes that can be made by a person who wants to furnish a simple, informal bedroom, but who has given little thought to good design. Bad as it is, even here a decided improvement can be made through the three measures suggested to remedy decorative mishaps: elimination, rearrangement, and concealment. A constructive appraisal will show that some of these furnishings are intrinsically good, while others have a possibility of being salvaged. The good features are the floor covering and the woven hanging over the bed. The curtains and the bed cover can be kept, but with this amount of figured material in the small room, the upholstery fabric on the chair should be plain. The lamp and the

Figure 271.

Figure 271. (Architect, Kenneth Lind. Photograph by Julius Shulman.)
Figure 272. (Photograph by Robert C. Cleveland.) A comparison of these
two bedrooms with the one shown in figure 270 brings out a number of
points: these furnishings are well arranged; the designs of the furniture,
fabrics, and accessories have character; the interests and personalities of the
owners are attractively expressed.

Figure 272.

furniture require drastic measures. The imitative cactus lamp base can be unscrewed and a wooden rolling pin or a simple vase form substituted for it. A plain paper shade would also be an improvement. Some paint remover and a saw are required for the furniture. The removal of the spotty looking stenciled decorations on the furniture and the valance board and sawing off some of the unattractive curves on the furniture can make a great difference in the appearance of the room. If these changes are made and the hanging above the bed and the rug on the floor are straightened to follow the structural lines of the room, a decided transformation shall have been accomplished.

Figure 271 is a young person's room that has some of the same elements as in figure 270, but there is a very different standard of taste. The design of this furniture is excellent. In both bedrooms there is an interest in decorative design, as is seen in the curtains and the bedcover, but the design here is better in organization and in quality. The bulletin board has the typical collection that a schoolboy or schoolgirl likes to have on the wall, and the material is put up in a way that shows a sense of order. The lamps, too, mark a striking difference in taste. The simple lines of this practical adjustable lamp will always be good, while the cactus lamp would be an acute embarrassment as soon as its owner recognized its bad design. Figure 272 was planned as a room that would do service for a living room as well as a bedroom, and it, too, offers a striking contrast to the room shown in figure 270. This furniture is simple, well proportioned, and beautiful in line. A girl who is interested in crafts could make this couch cover, the pillows, and the lamp shades. She could enjoy entertaining her friends in this room.

Besides elimination, rearrangement, and concealment, one can manipulate lines and colors in such a way that remarkable changes may be effected. Rooms and windows which are too square may be made to resemble oblongs through the use of a decided line movement in one direction; oblongs which are too long may be made to appear shorter by using lines that repeat, and thus emphasize the short side. Objects may be emphasized or suppressed at will by the way they are placed in the room, by means of the colors used in the backgrounds against which they are seen, and in the objects around them. When one must make the best of what one has, the ability to use color well, and to apply the principles of art, is of inestimable value.

SOME DO'S AND DON'T'S FOR DECORATIVE ARRANGEMENTS

Good	Poor
Add beauty and homelike quality to your rooms through interesting decorative arrangements.	Do not have your rooms so stiff or barren that they look cheerless and unlivable. Do not forget to change your decorative arrangements occasionally.

Design

Any patterned wall paper or hanging that is to serve as a background for decorative objects should be unobtrusive. (See figures 224, p. 350; and 227, p. 353.) Decorative objects should be placed against backgrounds that will show them to advantage. (See figure 54, p. 53.) Use simple and dramatic decorative objects in functional rooms. (See figures 182 and 183, p. 237; 251, p. 387; 307B, p. 450; and 343, p. 498.)

Do not put decorative objects of intricate design against a strikingly figured background. (See figure 138, p. 150.)

The objects to be used in open cupboards should have decorative quality and should be arranged to create an attractive design. (See figures 1, following p. 2; 139, p. 151; and 308, p. 452.)

Do not use open dining room cupboards as a storage place for piles of dishes.

Use slip covers to conceal unattractive sofas and chairs or to harmonize unrelated furniture. Place ill-shaped furniture against backgrounds that do not create contrast.

Do not put objects that are very small in scale near clumsy or oversized furniture.

Good	Poor
Let your decorative objects supply accents of bright color in rooms in which the colors are quiet. (See figure 3, following p. 2.)	Do not let your rooms be lacking in color or interesting pattern.

Grouping

Arrange the objects in a group so that they will appear to be unified rather than scattered. (See figures 104, p. 103; 265, p. 403; and 299, p. 446.)	Do not have so much space between objects that the arrangement seems to lack an effect of unity. (See figures 264, p. 403, and 301, p. 447.)
Hang a picture, a textile, or a mirror close enough to a shelf or a piece of furniture so that it becomes a part of a group. (See figures 299, p. 446; 303, p. 448; 304, p. 448; 307, p. 450, and 343, p. 498.	Do not hang pictures, textiles, or mirrors so high above a shelf or a piece of furniture that they fail to form a group.
Hang small pictures so that they will become a part of a decorative group. (See figures 106, p. 105; and 224, p. 350.)	Do not hang small pictures so that they will appear to be isolated on the wall space.
Use decorative objects that are large enough for the space they are to occupy. (See figure 123, p. 123.)	Avoid decorative arrangements that appear to be scanty and inadequate. (See figure 300, p. 447.)
Group a number of small objects so that they will appear to be in scale with larger objects, or with a large wall space. (See figure 104, p. 103.)	
Secure rhythmic effects in decorative arrangements by the following means:	
1. By means of the connecting lines of a tray or plate, a plant, flowers, etc. (See figures 54, p. 53; and 265, p. 403.)	

Good | Poor

2. By the use of a horizontal shape between two verticals. (See figure 106, p. 105.)

3. By grouping a horizontal with a vertical shape. (See figure 105, p. 104.)

4. By using varied heights and sizes in the arrangement. (See figure 240, p. 364.)

Place pictures or objects so that the lines of the composition will lead toward a center of interest. (See figure 124A, p. 124.)

Do not place a picture or an object so that its lines carry the eye away from the center of interest. (See figure 124B, p. 124.)

Do not leave a large gap in the center of a decorative arrangement. (See figure 301, p. 447.)

Choose one object or a group of objects to stand out as a principal center of interest. (See figure 56, p. 54; 251, p. 387; and 299, p. 446.)

Do not use two objects so equal in importance that they compete for the center of interest. (See figure 302, p. 447.)

Chapter Twenty-One

INTERIOR DESIGN (Continued)

IV. THE SELECTION AND ARRANGEMENT
OF PICTURES AND WALL HANGINGS

PICTURES SHOULD not only say something, they should do something to an individual. A good picture should stimulate the imagination in such a way that the observer is permitted to share an artist's mood and see the inner meaning of the subject he interpreted. What a picture has to say depends both upon what the artist has put down and the personality and understanding the observer brings to it. There are many laymen whose imaginative insight and sensitiveness are so great that their enjoyment of art takes on a quality akin to re-creation. Appreciating art is to them a form of self expression which gives the same sort of satisfaction another may gain by the actual creation of something beautiful.

The appeal of a picture

Pictures make their appeal in various ways—form, color, pattern, subject matter—each and all have the power to stir the imagination. Subject matter does not make a picture good or poor. It may so determine its appeal that one would say he would or would not care to live with that picture, but the real worth of a work of art lies in the beauty of its color, form, pattern, and character—that is, the way the theme or the design elements have been interpreted. A good artist does not attempt to imitate nature. His picture is an interpretation rather than a literal representation of a subject. The camera can produce more accurate representations of nature than the artist ever can, and a story can be told better through the medium of literature or the drama than by means of line and color. Therefore, painting is put to its best use when the artist so construes

414

his thought in line and color that the person who looks at the picture receives the same impression of the subject that the artist felt. Rembrandt has given this kind of definition to a theme in his "Presentation in the Temple" (figure 132, page 137). One senses a spiritual value in this picture. It conveys the meaning yet is not a literal translation of a subject. Crowds of people are suggested, but Rembrandt has not shown a collection of unimportant portraits. Instead, he has subordinated all but the group that gives the meaning to his subject. Rembrandt has handled his color in such a way as to give an impression of mystery as well as beauty, and in the majesty of the composition there is an indication of his great personality. These qualities are conveyed to the beholder and give him something of the same feeling the artist must have had when he created the picture.

Since pictures should be interpretations, the individuality of the artist is far more important than his technical skill. Pictures are great in the degree of their painter's greatness, spiritually or intellectually. In selecting a picture, one's first concern should be for the individuality it expresses. What was the artist's appreciation of beauty and his capacity for sympathy? Was he sincere? These attributes, in addition to technical skill, are the essential qualifications for the artist if his work is to have character instead of prettiness— sentiment instead of sentimentality.

In every age the thoughts of the people have influenced their artists to such a degree that one who knows how to interpret pictures can go to a gallery of paintings and find an outline history of the modes and manners of the world. An examination of the paintings in this book will show that although each artist was influenced by the period in which he lived, yet the personality of each painter is clearly evident. The ability to recognize this brings an added interest to pictures, and one finds oneself enjoying more types of pictures as understanding grows.

A brief study of the three landscapes shown in figures 273, 274, and 275 will make many of these points clear. Different as they are in appearance, these paintings have several attributes in common. Each is a sincere attempt to present a picture of nature as the

Figure 273. Imaginary landscape—The Arrival at Bethlehem, by Cornelis Massys, Flemish School, 1512–1580(?)

This picture is interesting because of the manner in which the artist has interpreted the design of a landscape. Massys has created a delightful pattern which is so full of quaint and entertaining details that one finds something new to enjoy every time he looks at it. (Courtesy of the Metropolitan Museum of Art.)

artist felt it. All three pictures show that there can be realism without imitation in landscape painting. But how differently each artist has interpreted nature. There is a miniature-like quality in the realism of the Flemish painter, Cornelis Massys (figure 273). With meticulous craftsmanship he has drawn all of the details he knew were in that landscape, but he has done it simply and sincerely. There is an ingenuousness, too, characteristic of the painters of Flanders in the sixteenth century, in the use of a Flemish landscape with its windmills and towers as a setting for "The Arrival in Bethlehem." Massys' color is so rich, and the shapes in the composition are so decorative, that they give the impression of a beautiful pattern when the picture is hung on the wall.

The Impressionists were concerned with manipulating colors so that they would give the effect of temporary light. Monet, one of the leaders in Impressionism, ignored most of what he knew the landscape contained and painted the scene as it appeared to his eyes (figure 274). The Impressionists were not concerned with form. Since they were interested in giving the sensation of the luminous vibrating appearance of colors in nature, they avoided the browns and blacks of earlier painting and used pure colors. In

Figure 274. The Church at Varengeville, by Monet, 1840–1926.
The French Impressionists interpreted atmospheric effects in nature. They were not concerned with the drawing of particular objects, but with the way in which their appearance was affected by the light at different times of the day and year. Their pictures appeal to those who are interested in color. (Courtesy of the University Prints.)

Figure 275. Mt. Ste. Victoire, by Paul Cézanne, 1839–1906. Post-Impressionism.
Cézanne interprets the forms in nature by emphasizing their characteristic features. One feels a sense of reality and solidity in his work, and there are beauty and strength in his simplifications. (Courtesy of The Macmillan Company. From Cézanne, by Roger Fry.)

Monet's work we see his interpretation of the appearance of a landscape at a particular hour of the day. Pictures by these painters of light bring color interest into a room. They may be gay with the brilliant, sparkling colors of sunshine, or they may have the quiet, moody colors of a soft gray day.

The Post-Impressionists emphasized form. To the clear colors of the Impressionists they added rugged strength and solid forms. Cézanne is the most distinguished of this group who sought to interpret the inner meaning of nature rather than its outward appearance. When one studies "Mt. Ste. Victoire" (figure 275), he is conscious of an organized plan, of solid forms, of beautiful, expressive contours, and of such simplification that it seems almost as if one were looking at a powerful symbol of a landscape. This picture has strength and would give character to any room. Moreover it

Figure 276. Gipsy Woman and Child, by Amadeo Modigliani, d. 1920.
Early in the twentieth century some of the artists turned to primitive sculpture for their inspiration, for they wished to break away from the sentimentality of the popular art. A comparison of this portrait by Modigliani with the New Guinea ceremonial mask in Figure 277 discloses a relationship in the two arts—an exaggerated lengthening of the head and the features; small eyes placed close together; and, above all, the organization of all the lines into a rhythmic design. (From the Chester Dale Collection.)

grows upon one, for here Cézanne has penetrated into the fundamental character of nature.

At the beginning of the twentieth century popular art was of the sweet-and-pretty variety, and in reaction a group of French painters searched about for a new art expression. Picasso, Derain, Matisse, and Vlaminck were first to realize that in African sculpture there were strength and character and a rare sense of organic rhythm, and their own work was strongly influenced by their admiration of these

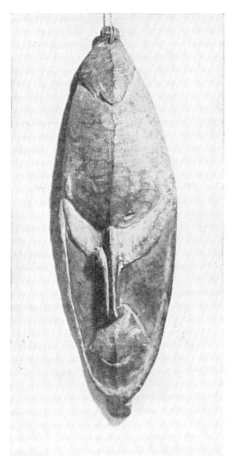

*Figure 277. Oceanic art. From
the Sepik River district in New
Guinea. A ceremonial mask
hewn from wood with a stone
instrument.*

*The sculpture of primitive
peoples reveals an instinctive
feeling for lines repeated rhythmically in relation to each other
and to the design as a whole.*

qualities in primitive art. Since that time the interest has spread,
and now many people have learned to see in these unusual figures
what the group of artists discovered. Examples of primitive sculpture from Oceania (figure 277), Mexico (figure 278), and Africa
(figure 279) have been selected to illustrate a few of the most outstanding characteristics of the art of primitive people. A comparison of these works discloses strong likenesses as well as striking differences. They all have style. In each there is an almost exaggerated
simplification and emphasis on the one significant feature the artist
wanted to stress. Primitive art follows the tradition of its own lo-

Figure 278. Mexico. Transitional between the Archaic and Toltec Periods.

This pre-Toltec head shows beauty and vitality in a design in which the details are reduced to a minimum and the material is handled frankly and freely. That a "way of seeing" runs through the art of a nation is suggested by a comparison of this sculpture with the heads in the painting by the modern Mexican artist, Covarrubias, in figure 135.

cality so closely that one cannot easily be mistaken as to its origin. All of the sculptures are made with primitive tools—for example, the mask in figure 277, a product of a stone age, was hacked out of hard wood with a stone implement. All are spontaneous because the artists are so sure of what they want to do that they work swiftly and directly. These people believe in gods and that while the gods do not look like men there are certain remote resemblances, and they make their masks and images as beautiful and as nearly like the imagined god as they can. The outstanding differences among these sculptures are clear. In Africa there is a degree of realism within the stylization (figure 279), while in the primitive art of the

Figure 279. African Ne-
gro art. A magical statue
holding a magic box. Bel-
gian Congo.

This wood carving illus-
trates the extent to which
the African Negro was free
from any desire to imitate
natural forms. Designed
in three dimensions, their
carvings show a masterly
organization of planes and
a thorough appreciation of
the wood with which they
work. Primitive Negro art
is decorative and full of
imagination.

Pacific ocean there is little realism and more of a flat and decorative
treatment (figure 277). The Mexican sculptured head shows the
same tendency toward rhythmic organization and simplification
as the others. When an artist associates with forms as strong as those
in primitive sculpture and feels them deeply, their influence becomes a part of him and is likely to be reflected in his work. In this

connection, one wonders whether it is through something in the heritage of the Mexican painter, Covarrubias, or mere coincidence that in his painting "The Rice Granary" the heads of the Balinese girls seem to resemble the primitive sculpture of his country. (See figure 135, page 143.)

In Modigliani's paintings (figure 276), it is easy to trace an interest in primitive sculpture and in early Italian painting. There are clear reminders of Botticelli (figure 134, page 141) and of African and Oceanic sculpture. Study the "Gipsy Woman and Child" and observe the grace of the long flowing lines and the exaggeration of length and slenderness of the face, drawn so as to suggest the sensitive wistfulness the artist wished to express. If one studies such

Figure 280. "Folke Filbyter," by Carl Milles.

A commemorative statue of a legendary pagan chieftain of Sweden. Rhythmic line and simplified masses are outstanding in this twentieth century sculpture. The forms are exaggerated to intensify the strong feeling, and they are organized into an inventive, decorative whole. (Courtesy of Pix Publishing, Inc.)

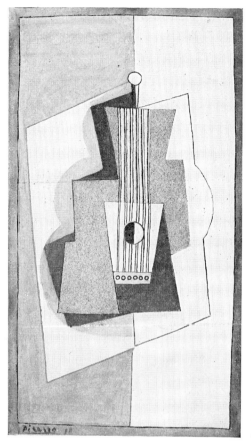

Figure 281. Guitar, by Pablo Picasso. 1881. Synthetic Cubism.

Abstraction is the style farthest removed from representation in painting. Pleasure in pictures of this type will come from an enjoyment of the pattern and color in the design. (Courtesy Museum of Modern Art. Collection of Kroller-Muller Foundation.)

examples as the sculptured mask (figure 277) with the rhythmic repetition of its lines and shapes and its elongated forms, intended to denote the supernatural, it is not difficult to find an analogy and to realize the admiration that Modigliani must have felt for such forms.

Figures 279 and 280 are interesting illustrations of the stylization of a similar theme in two extremely different cultures. In the Negro's wood-carving, the size of the head is exaggerated to indicate his idea of its importance. The simplified, solid forms are repeated rhythmically with slight variations throughout the figure, giving it an impression of unusual strength. The statue of the Swedish folk

Figure 282. Martha Graham and her dance group in "Primitive Rhythms."
(Photograph by Barbara Morgan.)
The separate passages in the modern dance reveal strong abstract patterns
based upon the rhythms of the dance theme.

hero of Carl Milles' native country shows a monumental quality. The artist has dramatized his characterization by a stressed simplicity. There is a flowing rhythm in the pattern and lines of the statue and a decorative treatment of unusual beauty. The African figure has a static balance and does not suggest deep feeling. On the other hand, the dynamic balance in "Folke Filbyter" is a strong factor in the impression of emotion conveyed by the pose of the old man who is searching for a lost grandson.

The influence of Negro sculpture led Picasso in 1906 to paint "The Young Ladies of Avignon," the first painting of the school that was to take the name of Cubism. By 1919 the movement had developed into the abstract style called Synthetic Cubism, illustrated in figure 281. When we look at the "Guitar" we should not expect to find a hidden meaning. In the flat shapes characteristic of this aspect of Cubism, there is little or no consideration of the subject but solely a beautiful relationship of abstract shapes, brilliant colors, and unusual textures on the surface of the canvas. These elements are built into an arrangement to be enjoyed by anyone who can appreciate the power and the beauty to be found in design for its own sake.

The dance is another art form that is influenced by the abstract design of the twentieth century, as may be seen in the arrested movement from a modern dance caught in the photograph of Martha Graham and her group (figure 282). Insofar as it involves line, shape, volume, and weight, the dance is a space art comparable to painting and sculpture. Time and movement are fundamental and actual in the dance, while they may only be implied in clay or paint. But without the two essential factors of time and movement we are able to find analogies in abstract pattern as we look from this photograph to Picasso's "Guitar." Even the costumes have been made into abstract color forms to fit into a formalized design. One feels the weight of the colors just as he does the weight of the bodies of the dancers. In these strong triangular forms, supported by slow curves, there appears to be a three-dimensional design similar to the flat angular designs and organized rhythms found in abstract painting.

It is seen that there is no set approach to the interpretation of beauty. Each artist works according to his own style—that is, his particular way of seeing and feeling. We respond differently to these works. We enjoy some and do not care for others, but we wish to understand them all. For our homes we would choose to live with those we enjoy most.

Even a rather superficial study of the art of the various schools and cultures would make it easy for an amateur to classify them, because they show such strongly similar characteristics. With a little more familiarity one is able to identify the work of particular painters within a group, and very soon one has the satisfaction of being able to appreciate the quality that has given a picture its character.

The composition of a picture

All pictures have a *composition* or design. Sometimes the plan of the composition stands out prominently, like a framework, but oftentimes it is so obscured that the casual glance does not reveal

Figure 283. The Virgin and Child, by Pinturicchio, 1454–1513.
The pattern of this picture is the result of a carefully arranged plan, and its interpretation has the sincerity and the love of beauty seen in so many paintings of the early Renaissance. (Courtesy of Anderson, Rome.)

the outline upon which the picture was built. If the framework is badly designed, the picture appears to lack organization, while if it is so concealed that it cannot be traced easily the picture seems structureless.

In Pinturicchio's "Virgin and Child," figure 283, the plan of the composition is very evident. The framework is a combination of the circle and the triangle. The triangle, formed by the figures of the

Madonna and the Child, has been harmonized with the circle through the curved lines in the figures and draperies. The arrangement is unified still more by the circles of the halo and the rhythmically repeated heads of the cherubs. Within this well-built com-

Figure 284. Japanese print, by Toyokuni, 1769–1825.
The dramatic use of pattern and color has given decorative quality to this picture. It adds to the enjoyment of Japanese prints to remember that the artists conventionalized their forms and their colors. They thought of their figure studies as designs rather than as photographic representations of individuals.

Figure 285. London Bridge, by Whistler, 1834–1903.
The beauty of the drawn line can be enjoyed to a marked degree in a good etching. Such a picture should be hung over a desk or so placed that one can look directly into it. (Courtesy of the Minneapolis Institute of Arts.)

position a pleasing pattern is formed by the spotting of light and dark masses. Pinturicchio has painted his idea unaffectedly and with sincerity.

Pattern is at once evident in a study of the Japanese print in figure 284. In the original print, color contributes to the interest, but the pattern comes first. The photograph shows the distribution of the light and dark masses and of plain and figured surfaces so arranged that a beautiful pattern is formed and decorative effect is achieved. *Pattern, line, and color in pictures*

In many pictures it is seen that the artist is primarily interested in line, as in the Japanese print in figure 112, page 112, and the Whistler etching in figure 285. The quality of the drawn line in these pictures is so beautiful that they would give pleasure, whether or not they were "faithful likenesses" of their subjects. Here one does not feel a need for color.

Color is, perhaps, the quality most universally enjoyed in pictures.

Figure 286. Woman Digging Potatoes, by Vincent van Gogh, French
School, 1853–1890.
   This picture's qualities have given it unusual character. The theme has
been interpreted simply and sincerely and with no trace of sentimentality.
The lines are forceful, and the pattern of dark and light values is beautiful.
(Courtesy of Vogue. Copyright, Condé Nast Publications, Inc.)

Quiet colors and gay, restful and stimulating make their special
appeal to the individual. Just as the great artists interpret forms, so
they interpret colors instead of representing them naturalistically.
It is readily apparent to one who looks thoughtfully at pictures that
each of the art periods as well as the individual artist has a rather
characteristic type of color. As one studies the paintings in a gallery
or turns the pages of a book of colored reproductions of paintings,
he will be aware of the richness of the colors used by the painters
of the Renaissance; of the delicacy of the color in the eighteenth
century; the sparkle of the Impressionist paintings; and of the
starkness of the colors found in the painting after World War I.
A standard for quality in color may be found in the galleries of the
art museums, and if one can visit a museum his own choices of

color in paintings and their reproductions can be measured by comparing them with good original paintings.

When the theme of a picture is interpreted with distinction, it adds character to those other elements—line, color, or pattern—which may have made the picture beautiful. This is true of van Gogh's "Woman Digging Potatoes," illustrated in figure 286, a subject which is expressed with great sincerity. Van Gogh has drawn this peasant woman with dignity and seriousness and sympathetic interpretation. The pattern of the dark shapes is beautiful against the lighter background tones, and such sensitive variation is seen in the lights and darks in the picture that color is suggested even though it is not there. A study of the picture shows that it is full of meaning, for van Gogh, through his skillful use of line, has made every form expressive.

It is well known that excellent reproductions of superior pictures are available. Not so well known is the fact that good original prints and even paintings by living artists are available for not much if any more than the cost of a fine reproduction. In nearly every region artists of merit are painting pictures which are not only suitable for homes but would greatly enrich them. Furthermore, when contemporary art is appreciated to the point of purchase there is a mutual advantage, for families will enjoy living with good pictures of their own time and artists are encouraged to paint. Frequently one hears people say that they would like to buy contemporary prints and paintings but they do not feel competent to choose them. It is not difficult to learn to choose good pictures, and those who wish to can soon gain confidence in their own ability to select pictures which they not only like, but know to be worth liking.

The suitability of the picture to the room

If one is seeking the qualities of line and pattern in a picture, he will find them in etchings, dry points, and lithographs, which may be obtained in original prints and worthwhile reproductions. If color is desired, it is well to choose a picture in which color is an integral part of the technique, as in a painting or a block print, and avoid hand-colored photographs and colored etchings. Since so many types of good pictures are available, one can easily find those which will give pleasure and at the same time are appropriate for

Figure 287. Lily, by Georgia O'Keefe.
This interpretation of a lily is like a sym-bol of the flower. A painting of this type helps one to see the beauty in nature more vividly than ever before. (Courtesy of Mrs. Edward W. Forbes.)

the setting in which they will be used. A worthy picture has one or more of the following characteristics: a well-organized composition, a fine pattern, good color, or a theme well interpreted and having character.

"Lily," by Georgia O'Keefe, is a type of picture which does not need a particular setting (figure 287). It is so universal in its charac-ter and interpretation as to appeal to every taste. To many people, this picture seems to be an essence of the flower world, expressing the nature, not merely the likeness, of a lily.

Another of the many types of picture which seem to be at home in most settings is Adolph Dehn's water-color painting of "A Farm-yard by the Lake" (figure 288). Its appeal is general. Although it has twentieth-century vitality, it is suitable in a house of any type. The picture has the characteristics of a good water-color painting—freshness and a fluid, sweeping quality in the tones. In addition to a beautiful technique, one finds a sensitive, subtle treatment of a landscape. Through his interpretation, Dehn has helped the observer to feel the beauty he saw in nature.

It is not the subject of the picture, but its interpretation, which gives it individuality. The Ackermann fashion print in figure 289 is an example of feminine quality in a picture, a type one might expect to see in the bedroom in figure 209. The characteristics that mark the Ackermann print as feminine and "While the Sun Shines" by Dale Nichols (figure 291) as masculine are due to the way each picture is interpreted and not because of anything in their subject-

Figure 288. Farm by the Lake, by Adolph Dehn.
A painting in which the mood of a landscape is vividly interpreted in water-color. By eliminating all but essentials and arranging those into a beautiful design, the artist makes us see clearly what he felt and enjoyed in this scene. (Courtesy of The Art Digest.)

Figure 289. Engraving from Ackermann's Repository of Arts, 1810.

The feminine quality of this nineteenth century fashion print is due to the interpretation of the subject and to the delicate scale and graceful lines in the composition.

matter. A woman's portrait may be painted in a masculine manner, and a man's may give an impression of a feminine quality. For example, the woman's figure in the print in figure 286 has something of the vigor that characterizes "While the Sun Shines," and one can imagine these pictures used in the same room, in a man's room or in a domestic living room.

In domestic rooms one should avoid pictures that are too distinctly social or formal if he wishes to keep a consistent effect of domesticity. Figure 286 is as domestic as the fashion print is social. One should not hang these two pictures in the same room, because they have nothing in common. Although the extremely social or the very formal picture would be out of place in a domestic room, it is not necessary to go to the extreme of domesticity, as in this subject. For such rooms there is an intermediate type of picture

Figure 290. *Still Life with Music Sheet*, by Georges Braque.
The geometric pattern in this painting by Georges Braque harmonizes
perfectly with the spirit of the simple, functional furniture in this room.
The picture is impersonal and dramatic in type. (Peggy Galloway, Designer.
Photograph by Maynard Parker.)

435

Figure 291. While the Sun Shines, by Dale Nichols.
The subject, the vigorous way in which it is interpreted, the simplified pattern, and the bold, free technique make this picture suited to a man's room or to the living room of a domestic or impersonal type. (Courtesy of The Art Digest.)

Most landscapes, etchings, Japanese prints, and many portraits fall into this group. (See figures 273, 274, 284, 285, 287, 288, 130 on page 135, and 135 on page 143.)

The religious picture that implies worship requires a special setting, for it obviously would be entirely out of place in a gay, social room. Ordinarily, religious pictures are placed in the more personal rooms of the house, but if the atmosphere of the home is such that a religious picture will be a sincere expression of the life of the family, it may be hung in the living room. Usually one enjoys a religious picture over a desk or in a similar place where it will seem to belong particularly to the owner.

In rooms furnished in the twentieth century manner the pictures should have the simplicity of modernism. Some of the pictures in this book suited to a modern room such as the one illustrated in figure 250 are: Cezanne's landscape in figure 275 and figures 276, 287, 265, 135, and 168A, as well as any of the Japanese prints and the Chinese ancestor portrait in figure 56. These pictures have something in common with the modern style because they are simplified, dramatic, and decorative. The reproduction of a Braque painting in figure 290 is seen in a setting of modern furnishings, where it seems especially appropriate. The spirit of the picture is impersonal—fitting well with the mood of the furnishings. In this painting there is a great inventiveness in the treatment of natural objects and they have been made into a design that is more closely related to a geometric pattern than to a photographic likeness. The functional lines of the dining room furniture seem to echo the picture's emphasis on simplified forms, and the arrangement of the fruit in the basket on the table shows the ability to make a dramatic design with the most familiar material. In this group one sees the characteristic qualities of the contemporary manner: simplicity; dramatic expression of ideas; emphasis on craftsmanship rather than on decoration; and above all, appropriateness of the objects to their purpose and setting.

Pictures for children's rooms are of two types: those of lasting interest and some that are good but more or less temporary in their

Figure 292. "Ziemia Kielecka." A Polish poster showing preparations for a wedding feast.
This decorative poster would interest a child because it is entertaining in theme, forceful in treatment, and sparkling in color.

appeal. There should be some pictures that the child will grow to appreciate more and more as he develops. Children enjoy colorful pictures, and when they are very young they do not care much for details. A child should be permitted to choose for himself the pic-

Figure 293. Mary with the Red Ribbon, by Robert Henri, 1865 1929.
A girl would enjoy living with this picture. It portrays a frank, vivid, and unselfconscious character. (Courtesy of The Municipal Art Gallery, Atlantic City.)

tures he finds interesting. However, since pictures must be worthy of being lived with, his selections ought to be made from a varied assortment of good ones.

Many of the illustrations in books and in some magazines are worth a place on the walls of the child's room, as are posters similar to the Swedish print seen on the wall in figure 259 and the Polish

Figure 294. The Three Geese, by John Bauer, 1882–1918.
The pattern created by the geese against the dark background of the hill, the ripples of the water, and the forms of hill and trees give this picture an unusual interest. Because it is so impersonal it would fit into many types of rooms.

poster shown in figure 292. Such pictures may be very good in design and color. Besides being decorative they arouse a child's curiosity about other people and their customs. Decorative maps, too, are intriguing to young people who are interested in stories of travel or adventure. There are so many maps to be found that a particular interest would determine whether the map chosen should show the world, or the stars, or a favorite city.

Robert Henri's "Mary with the Red Ribbon" (figure 293), is a type of picture most girls like because it is a natural and honest interpretation of a real girl. Some pictures are of equal interest to boys and to girls. This is true of the Polish poster or the John Bauer picture of the flying geese (figure 294). The Dürer engraving (figure 295) would interest children of all ages and would appeal particu-

Figure 295. St. Eustace, called also St. Hubert, engraving by Albrecht Dürer, German, 1471–1528.

A boy would respond to this picture through his interest in animals and in medieval tales. An appreciation of its beautiful drawing would be likely to lead him to a better understanding of the great pictures of other periods. (Courtesy of the Minneapolis Institute of Arts.)

larly to boys through their love of animals. It is a type of picture that sets a high standard of quality, and the boy who has grown up with it and has learned to appreciate its beauty, its vitality, and its idealism will bring a finer discrimination to his enjoyment of other pictures. As the child's interest in his world develops, more types of pictures come to be enjoyed.

Young people as well as grown-ups enjoy the spontaneous work of children. When children are permitted to express their ideas in art in their own way guided but not inhibited by adults, they frequently produce pictures remarkable for their freshness and vigor. An example of such work is shown in figure 296—a wood-cut of houses in Taxco, done by a twelve-year-old boy. It is interesting that the forceful, simple way of expressing an idea frequently found in the unconscious work of children is also a characteristic of the paintings of many modern artists, such as Cézanne.

If there is much pattern in the wall paper, it will be better, for *Pictures in re-* the sake of proper emphasis, to have no pictures on the walls. Per- *lation to the background* haps a mirror, or a plain textile that will furnish interesting varia- *of a room* tions in color or shape, will prove to be the desirable wall decoration. If there is a great deal of color in the room or in some part of the room and but little pattern, the most suitable pictures would be

Figure 296. Woodcut, by a Mexican child in the Out-Door School of Taxco.

Children, like primitive people, often have the ability to invent in terms of direct and forcible designs what they see in the life around them.

Figure 297. The Lady in Yellow, by Holbein the Elder.

This picture has been enhanced by a mat of suitable size and shape. The colors of the narrow dull gold frame and the toned mat harmonize with the colors in the picture.

etchings or other prints having interesting line and pattern, yet introducing no more color.

How to frame a picture

Shall a picture have a mat, or be framed close? Oils ordinarily should be framed close. A mat should be used on prints and water colors. A mat will give a pleasant rest space between the picture and the walls if the walls have a slight pattern and will enlarge a picture that might otherwise be too small for the space it is to occupy. Relatively wide mats are desirable for pictures having decided movement, especially when the lines of the picture have a tendency to carry the eye abruptly out of the frame, and likewise when the subject itself seems to fill the space so as to leave very little background. (See figure 124, page 124.)

Ordinarily the most satisfying mat is somewhat darker than the lightest tones in the picture. If the light tones appear in the picture only in very small amounts, then a slightly darker mat might be

Figure 298. This gay, informal stencil is set off to advantage by a simple frame of natural wood and a fabric-covered mat that harmonizes with it in color and texture.

chosen. The "Lady in Yellow" (figure 297) has a mat of agreeable tone and of adequate size. Since the picture is rather delicate in color and in treatment, a light mat was preferred, and it was tinted a pale ivory tone to harmonize with one of the lighter colors in the picture. Another suggestion for a mat for a picture is shown in figure 298. Maize-colored theatrical gauze was stretched over cardboard, providing a good texture for the hand-stenciled print. Sometimes a decorative effect is gained by a mat that contrasts with the coloring in a picture. For example, a grayish blue mat could be attractive on a print in which predominantly warm colors are accented with notes of blue. (For margins, see page 241.)

Since a frame should suit the picture, and there are so many types of picture, it is difficult to make definite recommendations for picture frames. However, it is possible to make some general suggestions. The type of frame chosen should be in harmony with the picture. To illustrate: since the treatment and the color scheme of the "Lady in Yellow" are so delicate, a frame that is fine in scale was selected. It is of a dull gold with a little Van Dyck brown oil paint rubbed into it to make it harmonize with the yellow, orange, and brownish tones in the picture. When choosing frames, it is well to remember that the frame should form a rest space between the picture and the wall and should be less conspicuous than the picture itself. The simple natural gumwood frame in figure 298 is suited to the subject and is the type that can be purchased for a small sum. As a general practice, one is safe in selecting a frame that is not so dark as the darkest tones in the picture. This is not a rule, however, for a narrow black frame is often successfully used—particularly for etchings and prints, which have rich blacks in their pattern. On the simply designed modern paintings, the plainer types of moldings and finishes are used for frames. The most generally useful type of frame is a simple molding of natural wood that may be keyed to the predominant color tones of the picture by having color rubbed into it or by painting the frame a solid color. (See figure 232A.)

How to hang pictures

Light pictures usually are best hung on fairly light walls and dark pictures on dark walls or in dark corners, except when, for balance, one hangs a dark picture over a dark piece of furniture. For the sake of shape harmony, tall pictures should be hung in vertical wall spaces and broad pictures in horizontal spaces (figures 303 and 226). Pictures may be grouped with other objects or so hung that two or more will give a horizontal or a vertical effect to harmonize with a given wall space (figures 343 and 241). One must be very sure, however, that the pictures grouped are in harmony with each other. A painting that shows a broad, bold technique should not be placed next to a fine and delicate one. Scale is the next consideration when hanging pictures. It is easy to see that small pictures are out of scale on large wall spaces, or when hung near large pieces of furniture, unless they are merely a part of a decorative group, as are the small silhouettes near the fireplace in figure 224, page 350, and on the mantel in figure 106, page 105.

Pictures should be so hung that the center of interest comes at about the eye level. One should not first see the furniture in a room, and then look up and see a line of pictures on the wall. Sometimes it is desirable to have them higher than the eye level in order to form a group with a bookcase; or lower, as over a desk or table; but the variation should be slight. (See figures 299, 303 and 304.) Most pictures are hung too high, and the eye is carried up toward the ceiling instead of being kept at the most interesting points in the room, which are at about the level of the eye and below that point.

In successful picture arrangement the principle of emphasis plays an important part. If pictures are to be thoroughly enjoyed there must be plenty of plain space around them. (See figure 299.) Too much space, however, results in meagerness and inadequacy. One is conscious of this defect in figure 300 because the two decorative objects are too small for the picture and for the size of the wall space they occupy. In figure 299 the bowl and the wood-carving are placed so that they group with larger objects and are thus brought into scale with the picture, creating a more unified group. It is well to place something of interest in or near the center of a decorative arrangement. Unless this is done the group seems to fall apart, and two centers of interest are created. In figure 301 this fault could easily be corrected by moving the tray to the center of the mantel, or by hanging a picture there as illustrated in figure 299. In over-mantel arrangements one often sees a picture over a clock, each striving for attention as in figure 302. Note the improvement in figure 299 as a result of removing the clock, lowering the picture to make it group with the mantel, and taking away the photographs and the motto, which so quickly would become trite. Photographs, like religious pictures, are personal; if used in the living room they should be framed and placed on, or over a desk or table.

Pictures should be hung over a single piece or a group of pieces of furniture so as to become an integral part of the furnishing of a room, rather than appear to be isolated spots. When a picture is grouped with a piece of furniture it is desirable to see the two as a unit. This may be accomplished by hanging the picture very near, or by actually resting it upon, the piece with which it is to group. (See figure 299.) Every decorative object near the picture must be considered as a part of the group and should take its proper place in order to secure a balanced scheme. (See figures 299 and 303.)

Rhythm, or consistent movement, must also be considered when

Figure 299. The arrangement of this mantel is simple and unified. The picture makes an attractive center of interest and is hung low enough to group with the mantel. The objects at each end are in scale with the wall space, and, grouped with the picture, they introduce agreeable transitions in height.

arranging pictures and decorative objects. Pictures possessing line movement should be so placed that their lines carry the eye toward a group, and not away from it. (See figures 124A and B, page 124.) They should not be so hung that they carry the eye up toward the ceiling, as in the jagged line in figure 305. If pictures to be grouped are similar in size they may be hung so that their centers will come on the same straight line, as in figure 306. It is also correct to hang them so that their tops are on a straight line, and this is particularly successful in rooms having varied heights in the furniture. Another

Figure 300.

Figure 301.

Figure 300. The arrangement on this mantel is inadequate because the woodcarving and the bowl are too small for the wall space and for the size of the picture. Notice, also, that the Sicilian carving is badly placed because its lines lead the eye away from the arrangement.

Figure 301. The large blank space in the center of this arrangement has divided it into two disconnected parts. Compare this with Figure 299, where the tray might easily have been substituted for the picture.

Figure 302.

Figure 302. This illustration shows that when a clock and a picture are used over a fireplace they create two competing centers of interest. The photographs and the motto, which make too many scattered notes of emphasis here, also are undesirable from a decorative point of view.

option is to create a straight line at the bottoms of the pictures, a plan that may well be chosen when a large object underneath them, such as a sofa or a long table, has a definitely straight line across the top.

Pictures should be flat against the wall, not tipped forward. If the screw eyes that carry the picture wires are placed high in the back of the frame, the picture will not tip forward. When it is possible to avoid it, do not use visible wires, but if the wire must show have two parallel wires rather than one fastened at both sides of the picture, which makes a triangular shape against the wall, de-

Figure 303. (Photographs by Julius Shulman.) Pictures should be hung low enough to group with furniture because they are elements in a design.

Figure 304. (Gordon Drake, Designer.) In this room the picture has been so hung that the center of interest is approximately on the eye level, and it is low enough to group well with the furniture.

stroying shape harmony and violating the principle of rhythm by carrying the eye away from the picture.

The rooms shown in figures 305 and 306 illustrate the violation and application of the art principles to the selection and arrangement of pictures. In figure 305 all of the pictures are of good quality: an old French flower print hangs over the fireplace; a fine Persian miniature and a gaily colored flower painting are above the chair at the left; and a modern Mexican woodblock print hangs above the chair at the right. But the effect in the room is very poor. The picture over the fireplace, which is too small and is hung too high, looks like a small spot floating in space. The two small pictures which are hung in steps that carry the eye toward the ceiling confuse, rather than unify, the room. Even if they were hung in an orderly way on the same line, the effect of these pictures would not be

Figure 305. Even though the pictures are good, their effect in the room can be spoiled when they are so unrelated in size and badly hung.

Figure 306. In this illustration the undesirable pictures seen in figure 305 have been removed and, in order to secure consistent groupings, others have been substituted.

A

B

Figure 307. (B, Courtesy RKO Radio Pictures. C, Robert Cleveland, Photographer. D, Peggy Galloway, Designer. George Szanik, Photographer.) This series was planned to suggest some decorative treatments for a fireplace wall.

C

D

pleasant because the Persian miniature painting is subtle in color and delicate in its details, while the flower painting is so bold in treatment and striking in color that both suffer from the contrast. Because the two chairs are alike and formally balanced, it would seem almost essential that the pictures grouped with them would be the same in size and harmonious in type. In figure 306, the pictures are related to the size and shape of their wall spaces and are hung low enough to group with the fireplace and with the chairs and television set, thus making a pleasant pattern against the wall.

Many ways may be found to treat a fireplace wall. The series of illustrations in figures 307A to D has been included with the thought that these types of arrangement would bring to mind other possibilities. Here, one large picture is centered above the fireplace; a picture is placed at one side; three pictures are hung close enough together to appear as a unit; and a piece of sculpture is used as a center of interest. The plan chosen would depend more upon what one likes and what is available rather than upon the fact that one idea is better than another. In any case the object or group of objects should form a beautiful shape, well related and grouped with the fireplace. Arrangements of the types shown here could be used over a sofa, a low bookcase, or any horizontal structure.

All picture arrangements might well be judged by these three simple tests:
How to judge picture arrangements

1. Is each picture in the room there because it helps beautifully to complete a group?
2. Are the pictures hung low enough to form a unit with the furniture?
3. Are they all hung on about the same level in the room so as to avoid a jagged line upon the walls?

There are several substitutes for pictures on the walls of a room. Mirrors and embroidered, block-printed, or woven textiles may supply the desired color or pattern. Mirrors give an illusion of space and are especially effective in a small room. In the dining room in figure 308, a mirror was used to brighten a wall by reflecting light and color from the opposite side of the room. The choice of a textile
Substitutes for pictures

Figure 308. Two substitutes for pictures are shown in this dining room—an old Spanish wrought-iron utensil rack which makes an engaging pattern on one wall, and a mirror on the other which reflects the light from the window and seems to enlarge the room. (Courtesy of Mr. and Mrs. M. J. Dorsey.)

Figure 309. (At right.) The excellent tapestry over the fireplace was inspired by the best period of tapestry designing. Every shape that was introduced has become a part of a flat, decorative pattern which is consistent for the technique of weaving. (Courtesy of the University of Minnesota. Photograph by Hollis.)

Figure 309.

453

is regulated by the same considerations as is the selection of a picture. The size, shape, color, texture, scale of the pattern, and its
appropriateness for the owner and for the room all need to be considered. The hanging over the fireplace in the room illustrated in
figure 309 was selected with all of these factors in mind. The space
demanded a horizontal oblong, and, since the room is large, it was
desirable to have a pattern that could be enjoyed from a distance.
When it was decided that a tapestry be chosen, a search was made
for one embodying the best tradition in tapestry designing. This
naturally suggested a design of the type made by the weavers of the
Gothic period. For centuries their tapestries have set the standard
for design for wall decorations. They are rich in color, simple in design, and flat in effect, being without perspective. These medieval
weavers did not attempt to imitate a scene or a painting in a realistic
manner, but they adapted their design in a way consistent with the
method of the weaving technique. It was their desire to secure a
beautiful pattern, and to this end they ignored relative sizes and
made a person larger than a house or a tree if they wished to make
that figure an important element in the design. The tapestry in this
room shows a characteristically Gothic treatment of "The Lady, the
Lion, and the Unicorn," with a unifying background pattern into
which such familiar motives are introduced as rabbits, birds, and a
number of decorative plant and flower forms typical of the early
"mille fleur" or thousand-flower designs. The colors are the familiar
deep blues, soft greens, rich tans, and glowing red-orange tones.
Here is a type of decoration that might well be studied when one is
selecting a tapestry. Familiarity with such designs and such craftsmanship as this would make it easy to recognize how poor the ordinary machine-made tapestry is. Unfortunately, the untrained buyer
who is interested in the idea of owning a tapestry finds too many op-
portunities to buy cheap imitations of hand-woven tapestry. Usually
the designs of these tapestries are so pictorial that they look like
imitations of paintings, and they are either weak in color or harsh
and crude. Sometimes they become even more garish because a
shining artificial silk thread is introduced into the fabric. It is often
said that the element of cost is the chief factor in making people

Figure 310. This printed linen, with its richly colored design, is a type of textile that makes an interesting substitute for a picture. The pattern is flat enough in effect to make it suitable for a wall decoration, and it possesses decorative quality to a high degree.

choose these poor machine-made tapestries, and it is true that the hand-woven tapestries are beyond the means of the average person. But if one cannot afford a good tapestry it would be much better to select an inexpensive decorative textile which is an honest and beautiful example of its particular technique than to choose an inferior imitation of something one cannot afford to buy. The block-printed fabric in figure 310 has the decorative quality that a good textile can introduce into a room. Hangings of this type can be purchased by the yard and sometimes in discontinued sample lengths, or they can be made for a small sum.

There is no single way in which a person expresses himself so well as he does through his choice of pictures and decorative objects. For that reason it is not fair to one's self to keep on the walls pictures which have been outgrown intellectually or aesthetically.

Chapter Twenty-Two

INTERIOR DESIGN (Concluded)

V. FLOWER ARRANGEMENT

OF ALL the arts in the home none gives more pleasure and enjoyment than that of flower arrangement. There is no room, however thoughtfully planned and carefully decorated, which will not gain in life and beauty with the addition of a well-placed and well-arranged vase of flowers.

Now flower arrangement, like any other art, may be studied and learned, and in this chapter we shall try to present a few of the principles underlying this particular art.

Flowers, like pictures, may be enjoyed for their line, their mass, *Beauty of line* or their color. Flowers and berries having intrinsic beauty in their *and color* lines should be so arranged as to emphasize this quality. In order fully to enjoy line, a single spray, or a few flowers and leaves may be used as in the arrangements in figures 311 and 330. Some of the flowers having particularly beautiful lines are apple and plum blossoms, forsythia, lilies, and irises. Seed pods, pussy willows, and berries may also have lines of remarkable beauty. Figure 233 shows flowers arranged in a mass. When flowers or berries are massed, the lines of the individual stalks are lost, and the primary interest is in the color of the plant. Such bouquets bring sparkle and richness into a room. Some flowers which are attractive in a mass are peonies, lilacs, chrysanthemums, asters, and zinnias. Many flowers—roses, tulips, marigolds, and calendulas, for example—have both beautiful line and color. Therefore, when only a few are used in a container, they are enjoyed for their line, but when these flowers are massed they will produce fine color. Even when one is working for the

Figure 311. The rhythmic line of the Anthurium blossom, leaf, and stem is seen to advantage in this arrangement. The same impression of rhythm is observed in the colors ranging from ivory through salmon and coral tones, and in the line of the leaf that swings down to make the bowl a part of the composition.

Figure 312. The common garden flowers chosen for this mixed bouquet produce a balanced color effect. There is a strong impression of warmth created by the colors of the red roses and coral bells and the yellow poppies and daisy centers. This is balanced by a smaller amount of blue in the delphinium and cornflowers. The soft celadon green of the container provides a beautiful complement to the red tones in the arrangement.

effect of color in a mass it is desirable to have flowers arranged loosely so that they may not appear crowded.

When one kind of flower is used in a bouquet, importance is given to the character of that flower, inspiring a keener awareness of the grace of the iris and its leaves or, perhaps, the unforgettable color and exotic beauty of a bowl of double tuberous begonias (figure 234). On the other hand, the mixed bouquet has a charm arising

Color combinations

from its variety. When gathering material for a combination of flowers, look for variation in color, size, and line so as to be able to use some of the flowers to give an impression of mass and others to introduce varied heights and transitional lines. A distribution of some of each color throughout the bouquet will give it balance, but, for the sake of agreeable proportion, the amounts should be different (figure 312). Parenthetically, a wise gardener will plan his cutting plot, even if it is small, so that over the season he will have variety in colors and types of flowers.

When selecting flowers for a room, the first consideration is the color scheme of the room. Flowers may supply exhilarating notes of color, and they should be chosen deliberately and placed carefully. Flowers that match the colors in the curtains may create pleasant accents if placed across the room from the windows, where they will repeat the color in the curtains; or contrasting colors might look well near plain curtains, creating a point of emphasis. Since warm colors brighten a room, they harmonize particularly well with a warm color scheme. Almost spontaneously one would choose the warm colors of zinnias or calendulas for a room in which the colors are keyed toward red-orange. Flowers of the cool colors have a subtle beauty, and a bouquet of the varied blue-and-white tones of delphinium in a clear bluish glass bowl would be beautiful in a room keyed to cool colors. Yellow and yellow-orange flowers—the colors of light—are warm colors that will fit into any color scheme, but bright red-orange and bright red-purple need to be handled with care, for rooms containing considerable amounts of orange and scarlet do not successfully receive entire bouquets of the purple and red-purple flowers. Since they destroy each other's beauty, flowers of these colors—bright red-orange and bright red-purple— should not be used together without the skillful admixture of other colors to harmonize them. This should also be remembered when window boxes are being arranged and flowers are being planted in the yard, for too frequently the charming effect of a window box of red-purple petunias, for example, is lost because of the proximity of some salvia, scarlet cannas, or geraniums. If a room seems cheerless or a corner seems too dark, a bouquet of yellowish flowers will

Figure 313. (At left.) Here the flowers are crowded into a vase with no thought of grace or freedom. The container is inappropriate because the decoration competes with the bouquet and the neck is too narrow to admit enough air to keep the flowers fresh.

Figure 314. (At right.) A miniature bouquet adds cheer to a breakfast tray. This combination of flowers is good because the violas and forget-me-nots are similar in character yet varied in size and line. They are loosely arranged in a small green tole container.

supply a glint of sunlight, while blue and purple flowers, which appear lost in the dark corners, will be enjoyed when they are placed in the light.

A collection of good flower containers does not necessitate a large *Selection* expenditure of money. Simple, well-proportioned shapes of good *of vases* color may be obtained without cost, or for very little. Snuff jars, ginger jars, some of the attractive glass bottles, and bean jars often make excellent containers. Colors generally useful for vases are the soft earth colors, wood browns, soft dull blues, grayed greens, white, and black. Clear glass makes a good container for most flowers. However, flowers whose heads seem heavy for their stems present a more balanced appearance when they are placed in an opaque vase. Weeds, seed pods, and berries having a rough texture are out of harmony with the texture of fine glass but look well in pottery or metal containers (figure 337). A vase that has as much emphasis in its design as the one shown in figure 313 does not make a good flower container because it becomes as important as the flowers.

Figure 315. Since tall flowers may be equally attractive in high vases or low bowls, the setting for the bouquet may be the deciding factor in the choice. In this casual arrangement of chrysanthemums, the leaves give a pleasing transition in mass and color between the yellow flowers and the black vase.

The natural growth of the flowers suggests the type of vase in which they should be placed. Short-stemmed flowers seem to require low bowls, and long stems high vases. (See figures 314 and 315.) Although short flowers do not look well in high vases, tall flowers can be used successfully in low bowls if the diameter of the bowl is large enough to give the impression of balance (figure 316). Vases should be selected with reference to the material to be used, for the size of the vase needs to be in scale with the size of the bouquet.

Ordinarily flower arrangements are placed on tables and so are seen below the level of the eye, thus permitting one to look into the bouquet and see the tops of the flowers. Figure 319 was arranged for a low table, and when it was seen in the room one was scarcely conscious of stems, but, rather of the flowers. Contrast this effect with the arrangement in figure 316 where, seen near the level of the eye, the stems are as noticeable as the flowers. This would suggest that one should decide where the flowers are to be placed before beginning to arrange them, for any change in the height of

Placing the bouquet

Figure 316. (*Arrangement by Mrs. Tatsaguchi.*) *In this arrangement the stately calla lilies spring gracefully from the low white bowl. The dark leaves, placed to suggest the way they grow, accent the white flowers and complete the design.*

Figure 317. These quince blossoms are arranged casually in two old glass battery jars which have been fitted into wooden bases and overlapped a few inches to appear as a unit.

its position will alter the appearance of the group. Tall flowers are usually enjoyed below or on the level of the eye. If they are too high, they will carry the eye too quickly to the ceiling. When one wishes to place flowers somewhat above the level of the eye, some drooping lines may be introduced into the bouquet to carry the gaze downward toward the eye level (figure 317).

Flowers can be enjoyed most thoroughly when they are placed against a plain background. Just as pattern in a vase detracts from the effect of the bouquet, so does a figured background. When flowers are used in a room which has figured wall paper, it is well to place them on a table where they will not be seen against the wall; or they may be placed where they will be seen as a silhouette against a window. A plain textile hung on a wall behind a flower arrangement separates it from a figured background, or a tray may be placed behind the group.

It is always well to group flowers or plants with something in the room which makes them an essential part of the decorative scheme

Figure 318. The natural growth of the plant is stressed in the tall, compact arrangement of these three flowers and their supporting leaves.

(figure 337). A decorative box may help to unite a bouquet with neighboring objects; or the flowers may be placed near a picture or mirror, or in front of a tray to secure an interesting group. (See figures 265 and 328.)

After having decided upon the colors, the position in the room, and a suitable container, one is ready to arrange the flowers. The material to be arranged should be studied and one of the most important flowers selected for the center of interest in the bouquet. This may be the lightest or brightest, the largest or tallest, and around it the arrangement will be made. Balance is the first consideration, and the flower with the longest stem is usually placed so that its head comes above the center of the bowl. Then the largest or the most conspicuous flowers should be placed around the center

Figure 319. A few sprays of apple blossoms placed informally in a bowl bring the essence of spring into the house. The deep sapphire blue of the ginger jar makes a beautiful contrast to the delicate pink and white flowers.

Figure 320. A low, open centerpiece of this type that can be enjoyed from all sides is suitable for an informal dining room table. In this arrangement three kinds of flowers are used for variety. The three zinnias and two Shasta daisies form a mass of color and, as a substitute for leaves, five pentstemon blossoms, which have natural curves, give lightness and a varied line to the arrangement.

and balanced by smaller masses of less striking character farther away. The problem of balancing flowers in their vases will be simplified if one remembers that the heavier mass should come toward the center with an impression of equal attractions on each side of the center, although there need not necessarily be equal sizes (figures 319 and 320).

Rhythm is important, for the eye should be carried easily from one part of the bouquet to every other part; it may be gained through the use of rhythmic lines, sizes, or colors. The Anthurium in figure 311 and the lilies in figure 316 have delightfully rhythmic line; rhythmic lines and gradations of height are seen in figure 318; and figure 233 shows a rhythmic gradation of colors.

Beautiful proportions contribute as much to the enjoyment of a flower arrangement as any other factor. One should be mindful of the size of the entire arrangement, for it should be in scale with the space it is to fill in the room. The tall vase with large chrysanthemums in figure 315 would take its place well on a hall table to fit into a composition with a picture or a mirror, or it would be important enough in size and scale to be used alone. Miniature bouquets, such as the two-inch vase with violas and forget-me-nots on the tea tray in figure 314, are scaled to small objects and would appear quite lost if they were placed next to large objects or on a large table. Flowers having very straight stems may appear rhythmic in an arrangement if they are cut so that the blossoms come at beautifully spaced intervals. The effect of too straight stems may be modified if the curved lines of the leaves of the plant can be grouped with them (figure 318). When one is working with straight-stemmed flowers, it is often possible to get a sense of ease in the arrangement by placing a flower into the holder at a slight angle instead of a vertical position. An especially useful type of holder for this purpose is one with sharp needle-like points embedded in lead as used in figure 318. Some of the most charming effects are the result of placing flowers in a bowl in an unstudied manner (figure 319). However, even in such bouquets the relative lengths of the sprays should be varied and balanced. Flowers will take any line desired if some crumpled poultry wire has been placed in the container, for the mesh will hold the stems in place.

Flowers should not be pushed down into a vase, as in figure 313, but should appear amply spaced and free. A vase that widens at the top allows the flowers to assume these graceful, natural lines. If a bouquet looks too tight, it is well to run the fingers down among the stems and gently pull the flowers out beyond the neck of the container (figure 312). The spaces between the flowers and the variations in the lengths of stem should be adjusted to a pleasant relationship. When all the stems are of the same length, there may be either a monotonous line across the top of the bouquet or an unpleasant effect of roundness.

If one wishes to make an attractive arrangement of a few flowers, the proportions of the flowers in relation to the vase should be studied first. In an arrangement of three flowers such as those seen in figure 316, the longest stem is cut so that its length is about once and a half the width of the bowl. If a tall vase had been used, the stem would have measured about one and one-half times the height of the vase. This highest flower is placed so that its head comes above the center of the container. The stem may curve one way or another, but the blossom should be on or near the central axis. The other two stems are cut so that their blossoms will come at attractively proportioned heights, with the leaves grouped to suggest as nearly as possible the way they look when growing. (See also figure 318.) If more than three flowers are to be used, they would be placed between these heights and grouped with the three original blossoms. The height of each flower and leaf would be varied enough to create a rhythmic transition from one to another (figure 332).

One of the best words of advice is to leave a flower arrangement for a few moments when it is nearly completed so as to be able to see it with a fresh vision. It may then be found that some of the flowers should be removed or shortened, or perhaps a change made in the position of a flower or leaf. It is the tendency of the beginner to cut flowers too short; rather keep the stems fairly high at first and cut them down a little at a time. And one more observation: Although flower arrangements are studied as they are being made, they need not look studied. Working with flowers for the sheer enjoyment of handling them and the delight of living with them is, after all, the real goal.

The important part leaves can play in flower arrangement is too frequently overlooked. Usually one would wish to use the leaves of the plant material in the bouquet, but sometimes it is possible to find others which will harmonize with the flowers, or create an interesting contrast in color, size, or texture. People usually prefer not to introduce the leaves of a different plant,—perhaps because they have seen so many arrangements spoiled with the feathery asparagus or the stiff ferns which some florists put into every box of cut flowers. When leaves are grouped with flowers and cut to give varied lengths, they may bring beautiful lines of transition into a

The importance of leaves

Figure 321. *These gladiolus blossoms have been arranged to make a low,*
open centerpiece so that persons sitting across from each other can easily
see over the flowers.

bouquet. (See figures 316, 318, and 321.) Placed close to the long,
slender stems of flowers like tulips and jonquils, their leaves will
unify the base of an arrangement that might otherwise appear to
separate. The leaves of such plants as jonquils and gladiolas may be
shaped into curved lines by dipping them in water and passing them
between the thumb and fingers with a slight pressure.

Flowers and
their substi-
tutes for the
dining room
table

Flower arrangements suitable in type and size for the average
dining room table are seen in figures 320, 321, 322, and 325. If a
flower arrangement appears rather small, it may be enlarged and
brought into scale with the table by grouping it with candlesticks
or some appropriate decorative accessories such as those seen in
figure 227. By remembering that the decoration should never interfere with the use of an object, one will plan table decorations which
make it possible for persons sitting on opposite sides of the table to
see one another (figure 321). If, however, a table is so large that the
people opposite cannot converse with one another anyway, as is
sometimes the case at a banquet, the flower arrangements may be as
large as seems desirable for the size of the table. Low bowls har-

monize best with the shape of the table, and when high bouquets are used they usually need to be brought into harmony with the line of the table by the use of transitional sizes or shapes unless there are drooping lines in the flowers or foliage. Candlesticks may furnish the transitional line, or one may use a lower bowl of flowers on either side of a high bouquet.

Since there are so many interesting substitutes for flowers on the dining room table, one seems to be limited only by his imagination. At almost any time the kitchen will furnish fruit and colorful vegetables, such as red and green peppers, decorative small squash, and eggplant. Gourds may be dried and lacquered as in figure 323. Whether the material chosen will be fine or sturdy will be decided by the occasion and the character of the dishes and linen. The table

Figure 322. Small chrysanthemums and leaves placed in low dishes and set in a circle around one very large blossom offer a change from the conventional centerpiece.

Figure 323. Gourds that are decorative in form and color are attractive on an everyday table. They look well in wooden, pottery, or metal containers.

Figure 324. This colorful centerpiece was planned for an informal Mexican supper. Pottery fruit and a crude glass ball were placed on a straw mat and combined with Mexican clay horses, one of which is shown in color in figure 160.

Figure 325. A ball of bluish-white bubble glass adds interest by its height to the flowers floating in this bowl. Because it is simple in form and texture the ball does not compete with yellow roses and white gardenias in a grayed blue container.

in figure 324 was set for a very informal supper, and the woven mats, the amusingly conventionalized Mexican pottery horses and fruit, with the yellow pottery dishes, made a gaily colored table interrelated both in color and texture. Some leaves and plants, such as a Chinese water plant on a dining room table may supply the everyday table decoration, to be alternated occasionally with whatever flowers or their substitutes may be planned for special occasions.

Flower arrangements floated in shallow bowls or trays may be as beautiful as those of the conventional type. It is said that the art of flower arrangement originated in the desire to preserve blossoms broken by the wind. Broken blossoms, and those having stems too weak to support them, can give a great deal of pleasure when they are floated. Some flowers lend themselves better to floated arrangements than others, for they need to have rather flat heads such as are found in water lilies, roses, and begonias (figure 234). Those that do not float well are jonquils, calla lilies, and flowers of these

Floating arrangements

Figure 326. (Arrangement by Mrs. Tatsaguchi.) A keen pleasure is within the reach of anyone who can see the beauty in such simple materials as roadside grasses and a few flowers. In this arrangement notice that the greatest mass is at the base, the height is at the center, and there is an impression of lightness and openness at the sides.

types. In placing the flowers, one may follow a symmetrical plan with the largest and highest blossom at the center, or informal balance may be used with the largest flower near the center. If one wishes to add an accessory to give more height to the design, it is well to use as simple and natural an accompaniment to the flowers as the glass ball in figure 325. One blossom, such as a dahlia or chry-

Figure 327. *The inherent beauty in a handful of reeds is revealed in this arrangement which might be entitled "A Study in Subtle Proportions and Balance."*

santhemum, may be large enough to be floated by itself (figure 322). If different flowers or colors are used, it is pleasant to see them in odd numbers. If there are as many as seven or nine flowers, arrange them so that there will be masses rather than a spotty distribution of colors. Some gaps should be left allowing the water to be seen, and it is usually agreeable to have some of the leaves along with the flowers.

The beautiful lines and subtle colors of grasses, weeds, and bare *Weeds* branches give a very satisfying arrangement, as a study of figures 326, 327, and 328 will suggest. A vast amount of material is easily available to anyone who has learned to see beauty in line and texture as well as in color and pattern. In figure 326 the tall rhythmic

Figure 328. A grouping of bare branches and seed pods can produce unusual patterns and result in an arrangement that will give pleasure for quite a long time.

grasses combined with the blue bell-shaped flowers show what can be accomplished by the addition of their graceful lines. There is a dramatic simplicity in the strong lines of the reeds in figure 327, and the soft moss covering in the holder in which they are placed makes an interesting contrast in textures. Figure 328 suggests how attractive patterns may result from an arrangement of bare branches.

For winter arrangements pine branches may be used as in figure 240, and they may be combined with sprigs of bright red berries. A few willow twigs may be cut in the late winter to force the pussy willows and the young leaves. These may be arranged alone or combined with narcissus or other flowering bulbs. Apple and plum blossoms can be forced so that they may be enjoyed in the house before they appear out of doors. One is not necessarily dependent upon hothouse flowers in the winter. Flowering bulbs may be easily obtained, and many varieties of seed pods and berries stay beautiful for quite a long time. Seed pods should not be painted or gilded, and artificial flowers and fruit should not be used. Occasionally one finds flowers or fruit of glass, pottery, jade, or metal so conventionalized as to be merely designs and in no sense an imitation of real flowers. (See figures 227 and 324.) In flower arrangement, as in all decoration, sincerity as well as simplicity should be the aim. *Winter bouquets*

Flowers have an important place in the life of the people of Japan. Even in the homes of the poor there is at least one room with a niche in the wall for a picture and a flower arrangement. These groups always have some special significance beyond their beauty, for the picture and the flowers are chosen to symbolize the season or a particular occasion. *Japanese flower arrangement*

Besides using flowers in their homes and shops, the Japanese give them as offerings in their temples. This custom has led to a ceremonial arrangement of flowers, and for many centuries there have been several schools of flower arrangement in Japan. Each of these schools follows slightly different methods, yet most of them achieve similar effects. Figures 329 to 332 show typical Japanese flower arrangements, and figure 329 illustrates the principle they follow and the method. In practically all of their bouquets there are three principles: Heaven, Man, and Earth, which are represented by means of three main sprays. The highest spray symbolizes Heaven, and it ends on the central axis of the vase. In length it usually measures from one and one-half to two and one-half times the height of a tall container. The second height represents Man. It gives the greatest width to the arrangement and is about three-fourths the height of the tallest spray. The lowest spray denotes Earth. This lowest branch is about half as tall as the one signifying Man, and it extends very little, if at all, beyond the diameter of the container. It is placed on the side opposite the branch that signifies Man and serves to balance it.

The Japanese use high vases or low bowls for their flowers. The tall vases may be made of bamboo, pottery, or bronze. Those made of bamboo are sometimes painted with black lacquer, or they may show the light, natural wood. The low bowls are sometimes made of bronze, but are frequently of plain pottery in some subdued color, as brown, tan, gray, dull blue, grayish green, or white. All of these make very successful containers because they are so simple that the interest is centered on the flowers. If the bowl is a low one, the worker uses a metal flower holder similar in type to the metal holders used in America. In the high vases a naturally forked branch is used, or a twig is split to hold the stems in place. For either of these forked holders a branch in which the sap is flowing is selected so that it will bend without breaking. It is cut slightly longer than the width of the vase so that it can be sprung firmly into place. Those twigs to be split at the end are split just far enough to hold the number of stems to be used. A pair of flower shears is used to cut away any flowers, leaves, or stems that detract from the lines of the composition. The shears are used also to make a series of tiny cuts along the under side of a stout stem in order to permit its bending without breaking. It is customary to bend branches in this manner so that they will take the most graceful lines nature might have given to that variety of plant.

One of the striking things about Japanese flower arrangements is that they always give the impression of a natural, growing plant. One way this effect is secured is by bringing the stems together at the base. Japanese flower arrangements always appear simple, for they are never overcrowded. Each stem is adjusted so that its line makes the most beautiful pattern, and every flower is placed where its shape and color will give the best balance. Each flower is seen individually, while, at the same time, taking its place as a part of the whole design.

The Japanese consider odd numbers lucky as well as beautiful, and

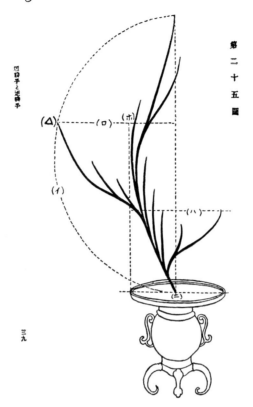

Figure 329. *The Japanese method of arranging flowers. In Japanese flower arrangement three principles—Heaven, Man, and Earth—are represented by means of three main sprays. The highest of these symbolizes Heaven, the next height represents Man, and the lowest signifies Earth. When more than three branches are used they are arranged as illustrated here, so that they give the impression of three stems. Observe that the highest spray ends on the central axis of the vase.*

so in their arrangements they use eleven, nine, seven, five, or three flowers or sprays. But whether there are few flowers or many, the effect is always of the three main branches. Figure 329 shows how eleven flowers or stems are arranged in order to give the impression of the three principles, Heaven, Man, and Earth. In figure 331 five branches are grouped to appear like three, and figure 330

shows one branch which was clipped and bent, giving the effect of
the three principles.

The branches in figure 331 were arranged for a class in flower arrangement. The equipment for the lesson consisted of a mass of

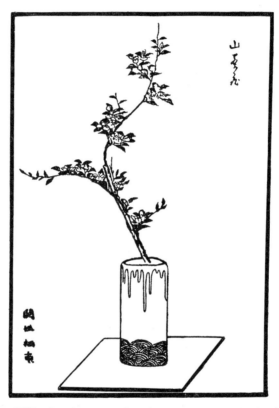

Figure 330. This drawing was taken from a Japanese book of instructions
in the art of flower arrangement. It is typically Japanese in its simplicity and
grace and in the effect secured of a growing plant.

straight, unpromising twigs, a forked branch for a holder, a bamboo
vase, and a pair of shears. First, the forked twig was cut and sprung
into place in the vase. A branch was selected to be the highest one.
It was bent ever so gently to take a graceful curved line. In a few
places where the branch did not bend easily, the shears were used

Figure 331. These budded branches of the plum tree were arranged by a Buddhist priest in Kyoto as a demonstration lesson in the art of flower arrangement. Straight twigs were bent to take these graceful lines symbolizing Heaven, Man, and Earth. Watching flowers open can give as much pleasure as seeing an arrangement in which they are all in bloom.

Figure 332. (Arrangement by Mrs. Tatsaguchi.) This modern Japanese arrangement of gladiolas in a low bowl is less formal than the ceremonial style, but it is based upon the same principles. Seven stalks of flowers and eleven leaves were placed according to the plan of three main heights, with supporting or transitional lines. All seem to come from a common growing point.

to make several tiny cuts along the under side so that it would take a gradual curve. One cut would have made an angle rather than a curve. Next, another straight branch was bent into a graceful line for the second highest spray. Then the lowest branch was put into place. The three branches did not prove to be adequate, and so two bare spaces were filled in with twigs bent to harmonize with the others yet allowed to take slightly varied curves. In the end, however, the three principal lines were dominant. When the arrangement was finished, it was carried away to a niche where it could be enjoyed as the buds opened into blossoms.

The style of flower arrangement that developed in Japan at the beginning of the twentieth century shows a western influence in its approach toward realism. There are many variations of this modern style, and one interpretation of the type is seen in figure 332. As in all Japanese arrangements, the same three major levels are used, with their heights based upon the width of the low container. The tallest item is about twice the diameter of the bowl; the second level is approximately three-fourths the length of the highest; and the third level is about one-half the height of the second. In this arrangement the flowers and leaves have been placed to show their varied aspects, and the blossoms all face toward the center, the stalk signifying Heaven. The leaves form transitional lines at the boundary.

Chapter Twenty-Three

THE HOUSE AS A UNIT

IN THE course of this book, we have seen how utility and beauty may evolve side by side. The chapter on Personality Expressed Through Choices reminds us that there can be as many expressions of beauty as there are individuals, and out of that recognition comes one of the delights of creating a livable home. Furthermore, as we study art, we grow and gain confidence in our own ways of seeing and doing. We find that we express ourselves best when we have the broad understanding of beauty which implies that everything in a design must be related to the whole. Although the problems in home planning and furnishing are complex, the final impression should be one of harmony or unity, and this is achieved when art is merged with the practical considerations involved in buying or building and furnishing a home.

In order to see the house as a unit, with its setting and its furnishings related to a family's pattern of living, and to suggest certain important considerations, two houses have been analyzed and pictured in figures 333 to 347. The ideas interpreted through these two contemporary houses would be applicable whether one is planning a modern or a traditional house and whether the house is to be large or small. Before starting upon the adventure of home ownership, it would be well for people to analyze many types of houses so as to learn the technique of visualizing the activities of a particular family in a plan and to study the arrangement of furniture in relation to their own ideas of comfort, convenience, and hospitality. Such experiences would help the family to choose a home that fits its way of living. Now is the time to make a reminder list, and its importance should not be minimized. It is easy to find good lists for the physical requirements of a house, but because each family has its own personal values, it should have its list of the characteristics that would be considered essential, desirable, and undesirable for the needs and interests of each member. The fact that a wish is on the list gives momentum toward its accomplishment.

As is suggested in the next chapter on City Planning, there are factors that should be checked against when choosing a location for a home. A person who is aware of beauty will look for it as he selects a site. Attractive surroundings and a pleasant view should be given the same consideration as a convenient location; good zoning laws; drainage; convenient utilities; and a well-shaped, adequate lot on firm ground. However, if a lot does not provide a pleasant outlook, it is possible to create an attractive setting through the use of such expedients as high fences and screen-planting. These devices can be so arranged that the family may gain a great deal of privacy for pleasant outdoor living, even if restricted to a small lot.

Some families can live happily in one room or in an open house that has no sound barriers between the living and sleeping areas. Their nerves are not strained by sounds of radio or television, telephone conversation, children at play, and household activities. However, if people are so constituted that they cannot study, rest, or carry on a social conversation under such conditions, privacy should be high on the list of essential requirements because, for them, good family relationships may be closely tied to the choice between an open and a closed plan.

This chapter is written to suggest some of the points to consider if one wishes to build or to buy an already constructed house. It takes critical study to determine whether or not a house is suitable to a family's mode of life and to decide whether to accept the house or the plan, change it to fit its needs, or reject it. Most people must work within some limitations, such as a small budget, land conditions, or unusual family needs, and so one must be prepared to make some compromises when a house is being planned or purchased. However, it is always to be hoped that no features that are essential to good family living have been sacrificed, and that no frills

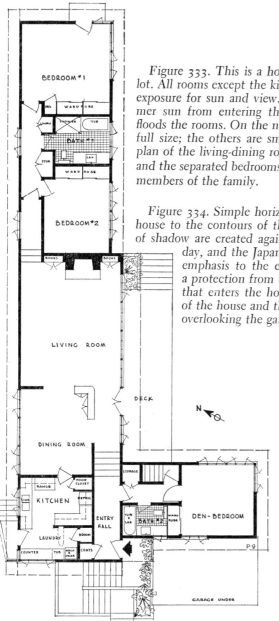

Figure 333. This is a house planned for a long, narrow sloping lot. All rooms except the kitchen face south, which is the desirable exposure for sun and view. A wide roof overhang keeps the summer sun from entering the south windows, but the winter sun floods the rooms. On the north side, only the kitchen windows are full size; the others are small and high. The deck and the open plan of the living-dining room provide for hospitable group living, and the separated bedrooms permit privacy and quiet for individual members of the family.

Figure 334. Simple horizontal lines and varied levels relate this house to the contours of the sloping ground. Interesting patterns of shadow are created against the plain walls at various times of day, and the Japanese pine tree in the planting box gives emphasis to the entrance. The wide roof overhangs are a protection from the rain and control the amount of sun that enters the house. The service areas are at the front of the house and the living areas are away from the street, overlooking the garden and the distant hills.

Figure 335. The house has gained privacy indoors and out because of the planting, high fences, and the sloping ground which permits the living area to be above the roof of the house next door. Along the entire south side of the house the distant view is uninterrupted, thus giving a feeling of added size to the narrow lot and spaciousness to the rooms. The deck, which opens from the living area, becomes an outdoor living-dining room.

Figure 334 (above) and Figure 335 (below).

or fads have been selected to take the place of some substantial comfort.

Simplicity and economy stand high in the requirements for a modern house. The average home is servantless, and the house should therefore be easy to care for so that time and strength may be used for other things. Since it usually is desirable to use every room in a small house for a number of purposes, it is unwise to make them cramped, and a slight increase in the size of a room does not add greatly to the cost. If it is well planned, a house is likely to be usable over the lifetime of a family, and it may be expected to have a good resale value.

The two houses discussed in this chapter were chosen because they show, first of all, the importance of planning a house in relation to its site. The first house, seen in figure 334, had to be planned for a long narrow lot on a hillside, while the other, in figure 342, is planned for a typical level lot. The first house was custom built, and thus could be planned to fit specific needs and interests. The second house was built with factory-fabricated parts, and it would be selected by a family whose requirements could be fulfilled by a ready-made plan. Both houses present characteristic problems and ideas about which decisions must be made when one starts out to select a house.

The house in figure 334 is located on a quiet street with little traffic, good transportation, and nearby shopping, educational, and church centers. A scrutiny of the floor plan in figure 333 will make clear the meaning of the exterior design. Because this house was built on sloping ground, three levels are used, although the same general layout of rooms would be suited to a flat lot. Here, the living, dining, and service areas are on one level, with the den-bedroom slightly below that level and the two bedrooms a few steps above it. The intimate rooms—the living room and bedrooms—are at the side and back, where fences and planting provide privacy. (Figure 335.) The basement contains the furnace area and two rooms that are useful for storage as well as for work and play. This structure took its form from the site and the character of the family activities that determined its plan. The exterior design shows no decoration, but an emphasis has been placed upon the proportions of the mass and the related areas of wall spaces and openings. The shape of the lot called for a long narrow house. On the north side, toward the neighbors, high windows of obscure glass assure privacy and provide cross ventilation. Along the south side, the rooms are opened by large areas of glass to take advantage of the view and the winter sun. The width of the roof overhang was calculated so as to prevent the summer sun from entering the rooms, and wide overhangs protect the garage and other entrances from the rain. A screen-planting of evergreen trees gives privacy to this side of the house and to the garden and serves also to cushion sounds.

The typical family, whose size decreases in later years, may wish to have less room and at the same time supplement its income. In this house, the den-bedroom could be rented if it were not needed by the family. The room lends itself to rental because it is away from the living area and has direct access to the garage and the out-doors. Furthermore, the location makes it unusually quiet and private because two doors and a hall close it against noise.

An entrance hall, which has a roomy closet, gives privacy to the living-dining area. Here, many factors contribute to an impression of size much greater than the actual dimensions. (Figures 333 and 337.) The area is open, except for a wall that extends four feet, and makes a slight separation between the living and dining areas. A low, movable storage cabinet creates another division between the two rooms, although the appearance of one room is maintained. Light colors and close values add to the impression of size, as does the south wall of windows that carries the eye beyond the room to the distant view. The living room is not too large for intimate conversation, and yet it gives a feeling of space. The furniture is arranged so that everybody in the room may feel himself a part of the whole group. Tables, conveniently near chairs and sofas, make it easy for one to pick up a book or magazine or to put down a plate. Flush panel ceiling lights are supplemented by lamps, so placed that members of the family may read or sew in comfort. Light-weight peel cane chairs are used in various rooms in the house and are carried to the living room and deck for added seating space. The tele-

Figure 336 (above) and Figure 337 (below).

Figure 338. When combined with the laundry, the compact working area of this kitchen gains a sense of spaciousness. The drop-leaf serving cart converts the food center to a U-shape when it is desired. This is a strength-saving kitchen where most tasks can be performed while seated, for knee-space is provided by pull-out boards or by opening cupboard doors. Generous counter space is found at each work center. All surfaces in the room are washable.

Figure 336. The room is unified and conversation is made easy by the arrangement of comfortable chairs and sofas grouped with tables and lamps. The backgrounds are subdued so as to emphasize the objects that are used for accents. The south wall of windows gives the living-dining room a view of trees and hills and a pattern of lights at night.

Figure 337. Cupboards that look as if they were built into the room accommodate the materials to be stored in the dining room. While the movable cabinet in the foreground defines the living and dining areas, one can look across it to the entrance hall below and in the other direction along the length of the living room. This gains the impression of one large room.

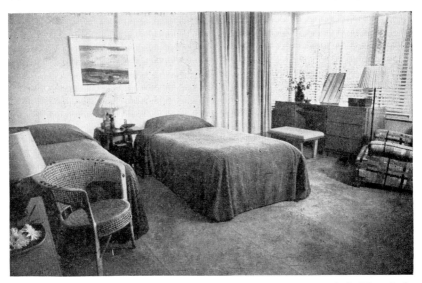

Figure 339. The fabrics in this room are casual and practical. The desk-dressing table is of the same design as the cabinets throughout the house. However, the likeness is not obvious because the accessories that are used are more striking than the furniture, and so it becomes an architectural background.

vision set is behind two easily separated woodweave screens, and it can be turned so as to be seen from the dining room. Plain draw curtains of textured cotton are hung at the living room windows. The curtains are made in sections without traverse fixtures so that they can be pulled across the windows wherever the light is to be controlled. The curtains are heavy enough to give privacy at night, yet they admit a soft, pleasant light in the daytime. On the high windows, curtains of split bamboo are hung over obscure glass.

Both living and dining areas are well provided with storage space in the cupboards and in the movable cabinet. In the dining room, the cupboard tops serve as counters for buffet meals. A desk of the same style as the cupboards is placed against the wall between the dining room and the living room. The comfortable arm chairs harmonize with the living room furniture, and they can be used there when needed. Double doors opening from the living area lead to a

Figure 340. The pattern of sunlight through Venetian blinds which is seen on the bedspread and floor suggests the expanse of the wall of windows. The windows and light walls make this fairly small bedroom seem larger than it is. Simple furniture and quiet backgrounds allow freedom in the use of pictures and decorative groupings which make a room personal.

balcony or deck, which becomes an outdoor living room. The deck, which is a type that can easily be screened, is wide enough for eating and lounging, and it serves as a link between the house and garden.

The kitchen is planned for saving strength, and that consideration has dominated all others. (Figure 338.) Two areas have been combined here—the food center and laundry. The result of this combination is compactness in the work areas, with a sense of space. The laundry center is screened from view by a storage wall, and there is an out-of-traffic area suitable for a playpen or chairs. This is a pleasant arrangement for a woman who does her own work, because it creates a "visitor's gallery" where the family or friends can visit with the homemaker without being in her way. The counter on the end wall gives space for eating as well as a long work surface.

The kitchen has the advantage of the prevailing breezes, which come from the west, and the steady north light. A wide overhang keeps out the early afternoon sun, and later, if the blinds are closed against the sun, the open windows admit the breeze. At this time the north windows above the sink give air and adequate light. Generous counters serve every work space, and since supplies and tools are placed in cupboards near where they are to be used, three people can work at one time. Most tasks can be done while one is seated.

In the bedrooms, there are combination desk-dressing tables, and good light and comfortable chairs are provided so that each person may have a place to read or study if others are entertaining in the living room. (Figures 339 and 340.) A roomy bedside table is used for one bedroom, and shelves in the other bedrooms hold the things one likes to have near the bed. Large deep wardrobes, which allow for miscellaneous storage besides clothes, and ample space to set up folding tables fit the rooms for sewing or other work. The floor plan shows where storage space is provided in bedrooms and in halls.

The living area takes its principal color note from the natural wood and the adobe colored brick of the fireplace. The exterior stucco walls, which are seen from the south windows, are painted a light tone of the adobe color, and the off-white walls of the living area have been keyed to the same color. With slight changes, this wall color has been carried into the bedrooms. It is worth while to remember that the repetition of subtle colors from one part of a house to another will give a feeling of serenity as well as unity. The floor coverings throughout the house are a grayish color, sometimes called "desert sand," that has in it a suggestion of yellow-green. Yellow-green is repeated on the window and door frames of the living room, where the curtains are the color of the wall. The sofas are upholstered in honey-beige, and the two upholstered chairs are yellow-green combined with brown textured yarn. The dining room chairs have a background color like the sofas, with irregular woven lines of brown and terra cotta. The color accents in the living and dining rooms are bright Chinese red and dark blue. Balancing areas of black supply value contrast. Inside the house, the south windows bring an ever-changing landscape, with the color of the distant trees and hills varying with the time of day and the atmosphere, gaining a new interest at night with the pattern of lights in the distance.

Although this house is furnished for adults, the plan recognizes that in the expanding family there are requirements for children in the years before they grow up, and these are provided for. The laundry area in the kitchen could accommodate children of all ages from the playpen to the homework and hobby stages, when the long counter would come into use. Children at play on the deck and in the yard are safe from street traffic, and when they are on the deck they can be watched from the kitchen as well as from the living area. They are content to play there by themselves because they can see into the house and do not feel separated from the adult world. The second bedroom, near the master bedroom, would serve for very young children, and the lavatory counters in the bathroom are convenient for their care.

Because the selection of a house involves the weighing of its advantages against its disadvantages, it may be helpful to analyze this house from the point of view of what had to be given up in order to gain some features that were considered desirable. Locating the house on sloping ground gave it a view, basement storage, and work rooms, but it required the use of a series of steps leading from the street to the entrance, and more than one level inside the house. Most people would agree that it is desirable to be able to go from the kitchen to the bedrooms of a house without passing through the living room. This plan shows a compromise on this point in order to gain other advantages. The building lot is long and narrow (60′ × 178′), and so a plan had to be developed that was only one room wide for most of its length if there was to be a feeling of space between this house and the one below it. The kitchen and service areas were placed across the front of the house in order to give privacy and a view for the living and sleeping areas. This requires many steps between the kitchen and the bedrooms. However, since both bedroom areas have direct access to the outdoors, much traffic is eliminated from the living and service rooms. The separation of the sleeping rooms has given them the advantage of quiet for work and study as well as for rest.

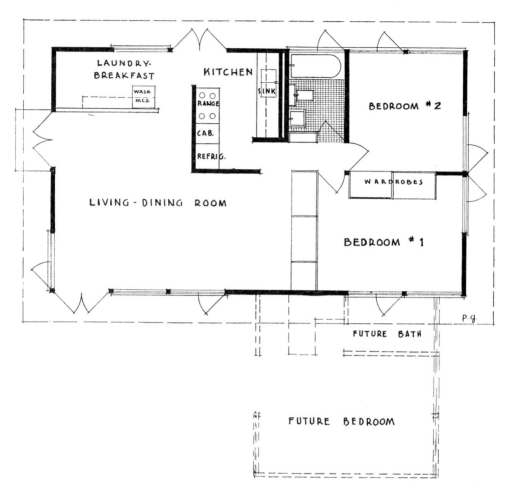

Figure 341. (Designer, Cliff May. Architect, Chris Choate.) The compact, economical house shown in figures 341–347 would fit on a small lot. While the amount of window area and the type of outside doors suggest a warm climate, the house could easily be adapted to a cold climate. The plan shows a good arrangement of rooms, spaciousness in the living area, a compact kitchen-laundry, privacy for the bedrooms, and good storage space. The dotted lines indicate where a third bedroom with a bath could be added to the original plan.

Figure 342. (Designer, Cliff May. Architect, Chris Choate.) Many of the characteristics associated with good exterior design appear in this modest little house. It is simple and well proportioned. The interest is centered upon the massed windows, the decorative effect of the vertical board and batten siding, and the wide overhang of the low-pitched roof.

Turning next to the small house pictured in figures 341 to 346, we find a plan where compactness and economy have been of first concern. It is interesting to see how much convenience and livability have been secured in an area that measures only 815 square feet, without the carport and a storage room which adjoin the house. Although this mill-fabricated house is built for a warm climate, the same plan has been used in a cold one by making some modifications. The dotted lines indicate that the house could be expanded to include a third bedroom without making any change in the basic plan. A partial wall between the living and work areas gives this part of the house an open plan, but the bedroom walls are built to the

Figures 343 and 344. (Interiors by Peggy Galloway. Figure 343 photographed by May-nard Parker.) A sense of beauty is evident in the choice of all the furnishings that have been selected for this house. The furniture is so well scaled for a small house that it makes the interior look large, and it has been so arranged that the dining area, the conversation area, and the work area at the desk are quite distinct. There is interesting variety in the de-sign of the furniture, but a feeling of unity as one looks from one piece to another. Throughout the house one is aware of the skillful blending of textures, furniture designs, and decorative objects.

Figure 344.

ceiling for privacy and quiet. A study of the plan shows these advantages: good circulation from the front door to the kitchen and
breakfast area without going through the living area; the small
kitchen has an attractive place away from the work center for eating
and for children to play; the living-dining area is spacious; a hall
separates the bedrooms and bath from the rest of the house; floors
are quiet and easy to maintain and are of a type that may be left
bare until the time that rugs are desired; fences give privacy both
for the indoors and for outdoor living.

Devices that have been used to make the small rooms look larger
are the high open ceilings, the glass gables, the floor to ceiling windows, and the windows under the eaves. The person who furnished
the house has succeeded further in creating the appearance of spaciousness, for the furniture that was chosen is simple, and it is light
in scale and relatively low, so that the rooms gain an impression of
being larger and higher than they are. In addition to the well-
designed furniture, the use of unusual plants and beautifully chosen
accessories have given the little house an especial charm. The color
scheme has added much to one's enjoyment, for it is stimulating
enough to arouse interest, yet sufficiently quiet to avoid becoming

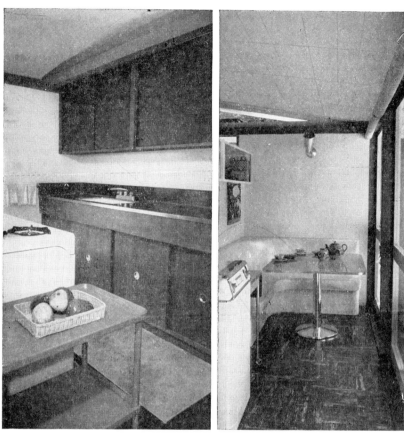

Figures 345 and 346. The two views of this compact kitchen-laundry show equipment conveniently arranged, good storage space, surfaces that are easy to clean, and a pleasant corner for eating. Separated as it is, but within view of the work center, the breakfast area affords a place for children to play.

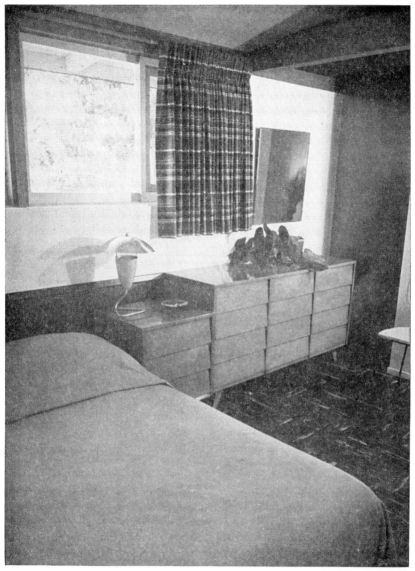

Figure 347. (Designer, Peggy Galloway.) The same air of repose that is seen in the rest of the house is present in the furnishings of the bedrooms. The well-designed chests of drawers supply important storage space and the patterned curtains contrast pleasantly with the plain walls and bedspread.

tiresome. The walls are an off-white that is keyed faintly to the lemon yellow of the painted ceiling and window and door frames; the visible ridge and tie beams of the room are a slightly grayed terra cotta color; and the partial wall that separates the kitchen from the living area is painted black. The floor tiles are black, flecked with white. The curtains and the upholstery fabrics are light gray, and natural wood colors are accented with the black of the desk top and metal supports of the furniture. The cushions supply a contrasting value against the light sofa and repeat some of the wood color.

Here is a little house around which family life can be pleasantly centered. It is individual, easy to keep up, and it is well adapted to entertaining.

We know that beauty may be expressed in very simple terms: it may be merely a matter of using whatever materials are at hand as attractively as we know how, giving them the character that denotes our own individuality. It does not require unusual expenditures to make a home more inviting. It may be achieved as simply as this: introducing a needed accent of color; rearranging the furnishings in a way that will make a room look and feel more hospitable; bringing into the house some flowers or a plant that will give the family the pleasure of watching something that is alive and growing; finding a special place for the latest treasure of rock, driftwood, or a child's newest painting. All such expressions put the mark of the particular family on its home and tell something of the enjoyment it has there. The experience of creating a livable home makes one understand better the philosophy that art should be made to function for our happiness. A person's life will be enriched to the degree that art becomes a part of his habits and his convictions.

Chapter Twenty-Four

CITY PLANNING

THROUGHOUT THE world there is a growing awareness of the need for farsighted city planning which will meet the future as well as the present social and economic requirements of each community.

City planning is an art problem in which one man or a group plans the layout or the groundwork of the design and the public puts in the details of the composition. It is as if an artist had planned the composition of a picture and turned it over to a number of men picked out at random in the city streets, asking each man to select the details to be placed in the picture, within the boundary lines put down by the artist. Some of the people would have better taste than others; some might visualize the picture as a whole, but many would see only their share in it and forget that the composition as a whole is more important than any of its parts. No matter if the details were badly chosen, the picture would still have the merit of a well-organized plan; but if the artist could have supervised the choices the quality of the picture would have been assured.

Artists are not obliged to work in this way, but unfortunately City Planning Boards are. Every person who erects a structure, plants a tree, or puts up a billboard or advertising sign, is taking an active part in an art problem and is either increasing or diminishing the beauty of the entire plan. In city planning, as in all art problems, the structural design is of first importance. This structural design must follow the principles of order if it is to be beautiful. In addition, it must satisfactorily fulfill certain practical considerations if it is to be useful. A successful city plan will adequately meet all the present needs of the community and, so far as it is possible to look

Figure 348. A plan for a satellite town protected by an encircling belt of green in order to prevent the encroachment of industries. The green belt allows opportunity for gardens and small farms, and it furnishes space for recreation. This is a town for the motor age, and for reasons of economy and safety it has been planned in superblocks with a thoughtful grouping of business and community buildings. (Courtesy of Farm Security Administration.)

into the future, will allow for growth. The sociologic, economic, and sanitary conditions must be the first consideration, but the art problem is also important.

To carry out and develop a well-made plan, every city should have an Art Commission, composed of members who have a real art appreciation. This group should pass judgment upon such matters as the designs and colors of buildings to be erected and the design, placement, and limitation of billboards and advertising signs besides

Figure 349. The houses in this block are similar in size and related in color and so they appear to be harmonious neighbors. These houses are good in design and are sufficiently varied to preserve their individuality.

providing for the public parks and recreation grounds. If such a group were planning for the beauty of the city, we should no longer see monotonous rows of ugly houses, nor would there be streets in which there is an incongruous assortment of houses having nothing in common with each other. Such a group could also provide directions for community planting that would help to reconcile any existing rows of ill-assorted houses. Prospective builders could learn from their Art Commission that beautiful designs need not cost more than poor ones and that each person has a responsibility to the whole community to maintain the standards of beauty in his city, just as definitely as he is expected to observe the standards for health, morals, and happiness.

Occasionally one sees a whole city that gives the immediate impression of a people who like their town and are genuinely and unselfishly interested in it. That evidence of this is clear enough for all to see is illustrated in two neighborhoods shown in figures 349 and

350. When each home owner builds so that his house will enhance every other one in the block he has established himself as a good neighbor and a good citizen. These illustrations show the advantage of selecting house designs that seem to belong together. A very large house built in the midst of these small ones would have spoiled the appearance of the entire block, and furthermore, it would tend to lower the economic value of each investment. If a householder has decided that he wishes to build a certain type of house, he should look for a neighborhood in which that type would seem to be consistent with all the others.

More and more, the informed home builder is coming to recognize how important he is in his community, and he is trying to serve it well. He knows that each individual must do his part in setting a good standard for his neighborhood, and if the community does not have a good city plan he realizes that he can add his voice to those demanding desirable regulations for the future. The unexpected lines of development of cities in the past show that to a certain extent the future is unpredictable, but experience has shown that city plans and regulations can have a certain amount of flexibility.

Figure 350. These houses are similar enough in spirit to secure an effect of unity.

It is a matter of good judgment to build or buy a home in a community which is protected by a plan, and whose residents can thus be assured of the kind of environment to be expected. For example, they can know whether there is permanent provision for enough open spaces so that the district will not be congested when it is completely built. Good regulations will help to provide not only for the physical conditions in the community but also those making for health, convenience, comfort, and good morals. If a community does not already possess the agencies for controlling these conditions, it is always possible for interested individuals and groups to work toward securing them.

Some of the factors that should be included in a city or community plan are noted briefly, and they may be used as a reminder to check against when one is seeking a location for a home. As has been said, the first need is for flexibility in the plan in order to take care of growth. There will be regulations against overcrowding and the assurance of pure air and good sanitation. In order that there may be some of the advantages of both town and country, the community will be zoned for homogeneous types of dwellings, shopping centers, and both light and heavy industries. There will be plenty of open spaces for playgrounds and out-of-door recreations for adults as well as children. The shopping districts will be easily accessible, but will not interfere with the homes. In order to avoid noise and danger the arterial highways will be away from the homes, yet near enough to be convenient. Major streets will be well planned for through traffic and, wherever possible, houses will be placed on closed-end streets for the safety of children as well as for quiet. Walks will be shaded and laid out so that children need not cross major roads on their way to school or play.

In some communities, plans have been made with such foresight that all the buildings on a street can get proper sunlight and air, and attractive views. The houses are set back from the street to secure quiet, and some of them are even placed at varying distances in order to obtain light and air at the side and the privacy of windows and porches that are not opposite each other. It is easy to attain these advantages when new communities are being built, but even the old ones are not so hopelessly fixed as to make improvements impossible. In the garden cities, such as Radburn, New Jersey, and in the satellite communities being developed around industrial centers, everyone can see and weigh the advantages being established for the residents. These are towns built for the requirements of today and for tomorrow insofar as tomorrow's needs can be anticipated. The air-view map of the satellite town of Greenbelt, Maryland (figure 348), shows that provisions have been made for the considerations listed above, and in addition one finds that the closed-end blocks are large enough to make for economy in building roads and sidewalks. Each house has a pleasant outlook, and nearby is space where one may have a garden if he wishes. The rural areas surrounding the town will prevent both the possibility of overcrowding and of the encroachment of industries. Such a plan, with adequate community buildings and provision for wholesome types of indoor and outdoor recreation for the adults as well as for children and young people, would do much toward preventing delinquency of all types and would help to build good bodies and healthy minds.

Every American community, no matter how small, should have a plan for its future development. There is great significance in these words of Elihu Root: "I think that the existence of plans known to everybody will give just enough direction to the movement of the multitude of separate impulses to lead the growth of the city along the right lines."

Index